French Émigré Armies of the Revolutionary Wars

Volume 1

The Armée des Princes (1791–1792)

Hughes de Bazouges and Alistair Nichols

Helion & Company

To our children
Aleron, Amélie, Mathilde and Oli

Helion & Company Limited
Unit 8 Amherst Business Centre
Budbrooke Road
Warwick
CV34 5WE
England
Tel. 01926 499619
Email: info@helion.co.uk
Website: www.helion.co.uk
X (formerly Twitter): @Helionbooks
Facebook: @HelionBooks
Visit our blog at http://blog.helion.co.uk/

Published by Helion & Company 2025
Designed and typeset by Mach 3 Solutions (www.mach3solutions.co.uk)
Cover designed by Paul Hewitt, Battlefield Design (www.battlefield-design.co.uk)

ISBN 978-1-804515-38-9

British Library Cataloguing-in-Publication Data.

A catalogue record for this book is available from the British Library.

For details of other military history titles published by Helion & Company Limited, contact the above address, or visit our website: http://www.helion.co.uk

We always welcome receiving book proposals from prospective authors.

Contents

Preface

This work, of two volumes, aims to provide an accessible but comprehensive guide to the armies, rather than individual units in the pay of other nations, formed by French émigrés during the Revolutionary Wars. This first volume covers the creation and subsequent history, as well as the uniforms, of the Armée des Princes from 1791 to 1792. The second will continue with the service and dress of the Armée de Condé, 1793–1801. Both are, above all, a tribute to two men, the Vicomte Robert Grouvel (1900–1965) and our friend Patrice Courcelle.

The former was a descendant of Baron of the Empire François Grouvel and also, through his mother, of Van Coehorn, 'the Dutch Vauban.' He dedicated his life to military history as shown by his astonishing personal archive now held by the Musée Condé, at the Château de Chantilly, north of Paris. His passion was for the Ancien Régime and the émigrés, the royalist combatants to whom he devoted the last 10 years of his life, publishing between 1957 and 1964 the three volumes of *Corps de troupes de l'émigration (1789–1815)*. This veritable encyclopaedia will undoubtedly remain unmatched for the extent of its coverage of the subject. Grouvel's achievement was crowned by the talent of Baron Louis de Beaufort (1914–2004), a fellow Member of La Sabretache and a remarkable illustrator of uniforms of the wars of the French Revolution and Empire. New sources of information, such as memoirs or artwork, have since emerged, and others, such as material held by archives far and wide, have become more accessible through contemporary technology and communications. These have enabled the authors to complete and amend Grouvel's monumental work.

The latter has been relatively difficult to consult outside of a few prestigious, mainly military, libraries and difficult to access for those unable to read French. Interest in the armed emigration may have perhaps waned if it had not been revived some 20 years later by the illustrator Patrice Courcelle. Invited by the magazine *Military Modelling* to choose the theme for the cover of the May 1983 issue, he opted for the novel subject of an émigré regiment in British service, the Uhlans Britanniques. During the following decade, he showed his knowledge and talent in a series of acclaimed articles in the magazine *Uniformes*, featuring various émigré units, including the Chevaliers de la Couronne and Légion de Mirabeau. Furthermore, his collaboration with the late René Chartrand, an internationally renowned

Canadian historian, gave rise to two richly illustrated volumes that included many émigré corps in British pay (*Emigré & Foreign Troops in British Service* (1) 1793–1802 and (2) 1803–1815, Men-at-Arms series, Osprey, 1999–2000).

The final aspect of Patrice's work on this theme are the plates reproduced for articles I wrote in the *Carnet de La Sabretache* over the last 10 years. All convey the same concern for authenticity and historical detail combined with the evocative power of characters in natural poses, often representing the anguish or exaltation of the heat of battle, inspired by the works of Eugène Leliepvre, and Liliane and Fred Funcken.

Nevertheless, this work would probably not have been possible without the passion and friendship shared with Alistair Nichols, a member of the Society for Army Historical Research, as was the artist and historian of uniforms Cecil C.P. Lawson (1880–1967), who collaborated closely with Grouvel. Alistair is now a recognised specialist of foreign service in the British Army – including that of émigrés – during the wars of the Revolution and the Empire. Author of several definitive works on hitherto unexplored subjects, such as the Chasseurs Britanniques, we owe to him in particular the undoubtedly most accomplished work on the Quiberon expedition of 1795, *The Soldiers are Dressed in Red* (Helion, 2022). We have previously worked together on a history of the émigré Légion de Damas, *For God and King* (Helion, 2021). A tireless investigator of British military archives and a critical scrutineer of sources from the Revolutionary Wars, Alistair is the very partner in exploration, discovery, and writing that any researcher would wish for. This is particularly required when one is determined to reconcile the perspectives and analyses of two foreign but complementary cultures on a historical subject that goes beyond the boundaries of a study of uniforms. Indeed, in 1992, Frank Attar, in *La Révolution française déclare la guerre à l'Europe* (The French Revolution Declares War on Europe), denounced the pretended indirect determinism – the inevitability of the chain of events – that has been instrumentalised by Republican or imperial historiography. This has, for so long, justified in the name of *La patrie en danger* (The Fatherland in danger) the exceptional measures taken by the Revolution and then the Republic against its enemies, first and foremost the supporters of the *Ancien Régime* who continued the fight for God and King, as well as for the ancient honour of France.

Hughes de Bazouges
Membre de La Sabretache

Introduction

French military support for the American colonies in their War of Independence (1778–1783) had been the opportunity for the French armed forces, on land and at sea, in India as well as the Americas, to avenge Britain for the cruel defeats and the terrible losses suffered during the Seven Years War (1756–1763). However, little did the officers, returning home across the Atlantic, suspect that some were bringing back the germs that were going to contaminate Europe, propelling it into a succession of deadly conflicts and formidable geopolitical upheavals between 1792 and 1815.

Although France made peace with Britain at the Treaty of Versailles in 1783, the French troops returned to a continent where a series of different strategic tensions threatened to upset the balance of power throughout Europe. One of these was in the Low Countries, where Britain remained at war with the Republic of the United Provinces (now the Netherlands). Politically, the Republic was split between two parties; one was the Francophile and Republican patriots, so named to show support for the American insurgents' cause, who had dragged the country into the war. The other, that of the Stadtholder, Willem V Batavus, Prins van Oranje (William, Prince of Orange) and thus called the Orangists, who were denounced as being anglophile and favouring an aristocratic-monarchical form of government. The patriots' political protest began in 1781 and developed into an underground movement two years later with the creation of the first Vrijcorpsen (free corps) ready to take up arms.

Meanwhile, the Holy Roman Emperor, Joseph II of Austria, sought to profit on behalf of his dominion, the Austrian Netherlands – Luxembourg and present-day Belgium, without the Principality of Liège. In particular he wanted the Barrier Treaty of 1715, which restricted access to the Scheldt from Antwerp to the benefit of the Dutch trading ports, to be reversed. This led to diplomatic relations rupturing on 30 October 1784, and a phoney war called the Kettle or Marmite War. The French court of Versailles feared that a crisis would draw the United Provinces closer to Britain and Prussia, as well as potentially bolstering Austria's strength on its northern frontier.[1] Thus, France proposed mediating while providing military support to the Dutch,

1 Philippe Henri de Grimoard, *Tableau historique de la guerre de la révolution de France depuis son commencement en 1792, jusqu'à la fin de 1794* (Paris: Treuttel et Würtz, 1808), vol.I, pp.

with the aim of convincing Vienna that any armed intervention would lead to a reaction from France. A military mission was dispatched to reorganise the Dutch army, consisting of 150 officers led by the Comte de Maillebois. However, these steps were soon redundant as the crisis was defused and concluded with the Treaty of Fontainebleau on 8 November 1785. This included a payment of 9.5 million livres to compensate the Austrians, to which France contributed 4.5 million, despite its already enormous national debt following its involvement in the American War of Independence. Two days later, France signed a treaty of friendship, mutual assistance and commerce with the Republic of the United Provinces, which was strangely reminiscent of the one it had concluded a few years earlier with the rebellious American colonies.

The patriot party in the United Provinces, determined to exploit the alliance with France, called a congress in Utrecht to which the Vrijcorpsen sent their representatives and demanded a new constitution that reflected their wishes. France hoped to benefit from playing along with both parties; one reason was to prolong Britain's diplomatic isolation since its defeat in America. However, the intervention was chaotic, as a biographer of Louis XVI observed, 'The French ministers and the King … did so individually, as rivals rather than colleagues … each had their agents there and candidates for the command of the Dutch armed forces.'[2] None could have imagined how dangerous the games they played would become.

The patriots had already managed to steadily undermine the Stadtholder's position, and then the Province of Holland withdrew the command of the garrison of The Hague from the Prince of Orange on 8 September 1785. The political situation in the United Provinces had deteriorated into crisis, it being observed:

> … the Stadtholder had the majority in four states, from which it is necessary to detach the city of Utrecht [declared the capital of the new Netherlands Republic], that had delivered itself to the patriotic party. The states of Groningen, Overijssel, and Holland supported this last party, and the city of Amsterdam gave it a great preponderance. Meanwhile the Stadtholder had, in these same patriotic states, the nobility, the old magistracy, a part of the military and people who were attached to him. The patriot party was thus only supported by the democratic bourgeoisie of the cities, and above all by that of Amsterdam.[3]

While the navy remained faithful to the House of Orange, the army was divided; some troops joined the rebels, while others remained in the strongholds to await the outcome of events. Then in May 1787, the patriot vrijcorpen drove the Orangist forces from the cities and William V took

65–72, 'Mémoire sur la nécessité d'empêcher que l'Empereur ne devienne possesseur de Maestricht.' v

2 John Hardman, *The Life of Louis XVI* (New Haven and London: Yale University Press, 2023), p.175.

3 Jean-Baptiste Donatien de Vimeur Comte de Rochambeau, *Mémoires militaires, historiques et politiques de Rochambeau* (Paris: Chez Fain, 1809), vol.II, p.331.

refuge in Gelderland. Emboldened, the States of Holland, which paid for more than half of the troops of the United Provinces, resolved to deprive him of his status as captain-general and to challenge his right to political authority. Finally, on 28 June, it ordered the arrest of Wilhelmina, the Stadtholder's wife, as she attempted to reach The Hague to negotiate with the rebels, keeping her captive for 24 hours. A breach with Prussia was seemingly inevitable, after all, Wilhemina was the sister of the new King of Prussia, Frederick William II, who had succeeded to the throne on the death of his uncle on 17 August 1786.

Soon, the patriots secured the country and looked for a commander for their troops who would be supported by France. The Comte de Maillebois was thought to be too rigid, so they considered the Marquis de La Fayette. A brilliant and wealthy young aristocrat, Gilbert du Motier de La Fayette, had travelled to America in 1777, aged 19, despite the King's ban, to serve the insurgents' cause. He served as an aide-de-camp to Washington before returning home to successfully advocate the American cause and making a decisive contribution to France's commitment (1778–1780). Returning to America, he commanded the Army of Virginia as major general. When he finally returned to France in 1782, his celebrity and success earned him the rank of *maréchal de camp*, equivalent to brigadier general. Nevertheless, on 14 September 1787, Prince Frederick of Salm-Kyrburg was appointed to defend Utrecht and Holland.

The appointment was in response to a Prussian expeditionary force of 13,000 men commanded by Duke Charles William Ferdinand of Brunswick that had entered the United Provinces the day before and, in the rhetoric of the Comte Honoré-Gabriel de Mirabeau, future orator of the French Revolution, was 'thirsty for gold and blood.'[4] It was reinforced by 9,000 to 10,000 of the Stadtholder's own troops and marched on Utrecht. Instead of facing the enemy, the Prince of Salm, purportedly having been bought, abandoned both the city and the patriot cause. Cornered before Amsterdam, the patriots capitulated on 10 October 1787. The city's last garrison commander was the Chevalier Jean-Baptiste de Ternant, who, like La Fayette, had led American troops in the War of Independence. Doubtless a secret agent for one or more of the French cabinet, on his return to France he was made a chevalier de l'Ordre royal et militaire de Saint-Louis.[5]

Although obliged by treaty to have intervened, the French King's council decided on 'the furtive dispatch to Holland of about thirty gunners, and a few engineers, the only help that France had given.'[6]

---

4 Gabriel-Honoré de Riquetti Comte de Mirabeau, *Aux Bataves sur le stathoudérat* (London/Paris: Anonymous, 1788).

5 See Frank Whitney, *Jean Ternant and the Age of Revolutions: A Soldier and Diplomat (1751–1833) in the American, French, Dutch and Belgian Uprisings* (Jefferson: Mc Farland &Company, Inc., 2015).

6 Pierre-Victor Baron de Besenval, *Mémoires du Baron de Besenval* (Paris: Baudouin frères, 1821), vol.II, p.278.

Without any real strategic vision, France flirted with a system of alliances to gain traction internationally.[7] The marriage, in 1770, of the Dauphin (King Louis XVI from 1774) and Marie-Antoinette, the youngest daughter of the Empress Marie-Theresa of Austria, had consecrated the conciliation between Versailles and Vienna that began in 1756. However, Austria was unlikely to intervene militarily in support of the extravagant projects of Louis XVI's disparate cabinet, which was reduced to indirectly destabilising its competitors. One agent of this policy was Charles-François Du Périer du Mourier, or more usually Dumouriez, who, after distinguishing himself during the Seven Years War, began a second career in a series of nefarious missions throughout Europe until he was later reintegrated into the army, being promoted *maréchal de camp* in 1788.

Stadtholder Willem V, restored to his position with increased prerogatives, concluded treaties of alliance with Great Britain and Prussia on 15 April 1788. Then these two powers undertook to jointly guarantee the maintenance of the constitution of the Republic of the United Provinces and of the hereditary stadtholderate of the House of Orange-Nassau on 13 June 1788.

At the same time, since 1787, public disturbances had occurred in the Austrian Netherlands in protest against the reforms of Emperor Leopold II, who wanted to centralise and bring uniformity to the administration of his territories. Despite the aim of improving the lot of the people, they, with the Church, bourgeoisie and nobility, opposed these reforms, which would destroy the traditional constitution of Belgium. The troubles that began in Brabant developed and spread in 1788 following the pattern of the revolt in the United Provinces. However, on 18 June 1789, Austrian troops entered Brussels to put the rebellion down.

After having excited the Dutch patriots against the Stadtholder's regime, France had abandoned them to their fate, contenting itself with accepting them as refugees. In particular, the Dutch patriot leaders found a warm welcome from La Fayette and those of the high aristocracy who prided themselves in their liberal philosophical ideas, as well as their freemasonry.

Patriot officers were even accepted into the French royal army. The Prince-Bishopric of Liège, on the borders of the United Provinces and the Austrian Netherlands, had long been a fertile recruitment area for France. So, the raising of the Régiment Royal-Liégeois, under an ordinance of 18 November 1787, the last regiment of the royal army raised before the Revolution, should not be seen as exceptional. The nomination of its officers was specified, thus:

> The Colonel & the other Senior Officers of the Staff are nominated by the King; the choice will fall, as far as circumstances permit, on officers from Liège. The other posts will be considered upon presentation by the Prince; three-quarters will be given to Liégois Gentlemen, the other quarter to subjects of Liège of good family, or subjects of the King born in Alsace, or in German Lorraine.[8]

7 Gilbert Du Motier de La Fayette, *Mémoires, correspondance et manuscrits du général Lafayette* (Paris: H. Fournier ainé, 1837 & 1838), vol.I, p.481.

8 *Etat militaire de France* 1788, p.290.

However, immediately after the Prussian intervention, on the proposal of the French ambassador to The Hague, the finance minister wrote on 26 October 1787 that, 'The Prince [Bishop of Liège] will be required to compose this regiment of Dutch patriots, at least for the most part. He will be required to make up at least two-thirds or at all events half of the officers from the Dutch patriots'.[9]

Not all of these officers were in fact Dutch, most were foreign officers who had been in the service of the Batavian patriots or had had to leave the Dutch service, among them the Chevalier de Ternant. The new regiment's *colonel*, however, was the Comte Joseph-Clément de La Tour, a Savoyard who had served in the army of Sardinia-Piedmont and then Bavaria, who owed his appointment to having married the widow of the Prince-Bishop's older brother.

The short-sightedness of seeking to conciliate those holding antagonistic principles within the French royal army is symptomatic of the way that the growing storm clouds were apparently ignored, denied or concealed by the main European courts, intent on pursuing their own opaque policies and strategic ambitions. This was to be repeated when the leaders of the Belgian revolt found refuge in the United Provinces as well as northern France.

Louis XVI had set in train the military reforms, from 1776 to 1788, to restore French prestige, ready to avenge itself on Britain and by the time they were finished, the French army was considered the finest in Europe. The 1776 reforms were based on the Prussian model imposing on the infantry stricter discipline, more mechanical training and a tighter-fitting uniform. These were ameliorated by the French spirit that had generated an unprecedented number of reforms and initiatives by 1788. These reconciled the conservatism of the *Anciens*, with the nobility and the Maison militaire (military household) retaining their dominant positions, and the creativity of the *Modernes*. The latter developed light troops, engineers and artillery, a divisional system, as well as regular training camps for the troops. Arms and equipment saw the most significant improvements, including the introduction of the Gribeauval system for artillery and the Model 1777 musket. There was a rapid growth in the number of legions, heirs of the light units that, after the Seven Years War, had emerged during the American War of Independence, such as the Corps des volontaires de la Marine, which was to have eight legions, including the celebrated Légion de Lauzun. The American War of Independence and then the Revolt of the Patriots in the United Provinces provided this new generation of officers, men from a caste for which the profession of arms and service to the King remained its raison d'être, with the chance to gain experience in the art of war and satisfy their thirst for glory. No one objected to the fact that His Most Christian Majesty's army was supporting subjects, Republicans, who were in armed rebellion against their sovereign.

France was the most populous country in Europe with 25 million inhabitants and was sure that its military forces were not only a deterrent but could also be used to intimidate others. Despite successive cuts between 1776

9 Pierre de Witt, 'Les Protestants hollandais en France en 1787', *Bulletin historique et littéraire (Société de l'histoire du protestantisme français)*, vol.34, no.12 (15 décembre 1885), p.573.

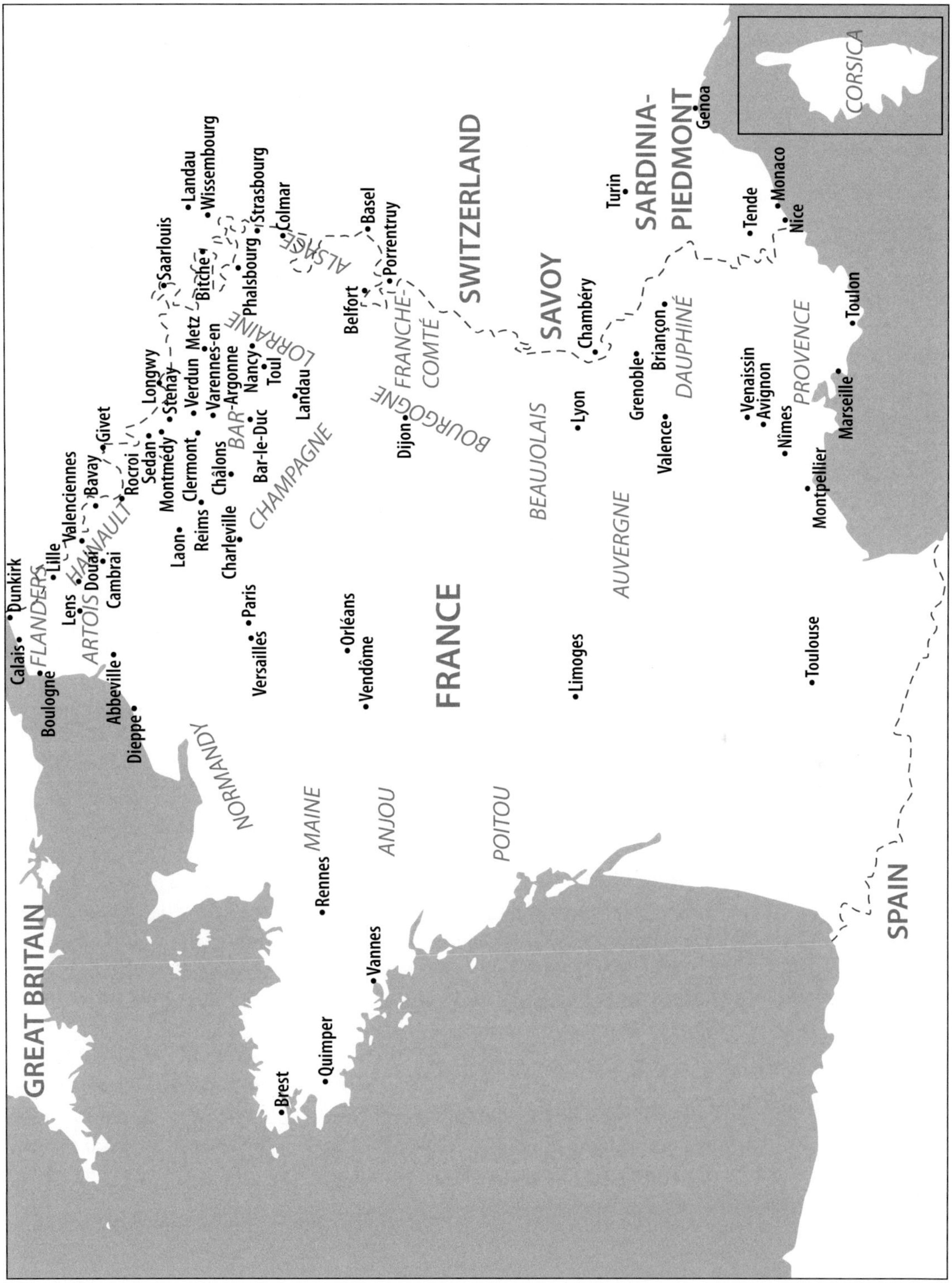
GREAT BRITAIN
Dunkirk
Calais
Boulogne
FLANDERS
Lille
Lens
ARTOIS
HAINAULT
Douai
Cambrai
Valenciennes
Bavay
Givet
Rocroi
Sedan
Montmédy
Longwy
Stenay
Verdun
Metz
Saarlouis
Landau
Wissembourg
Bitche
Phalsbourg
Strasbourg
Colmar
ALSACE
Basel
Porrentruy
Belfort
Abbeville
Dieppe
Paris
Versailles
Laon
Reims
Clermont
Châlons
Charleville
Varennes-en-Argonne
BAR-
Nancy
Toul
Bar-le-Duc
LORRAINE
Landau
CHAMPAGNE
NORMANDY
Rennes
MAINE
ANJOU
POITOU
Orléans
Vendôme
FRANCE
Dijon
BOURGOGNE
FRANCHE-COMTÉ
SWITZERLAND
SAVOY
Chambéry
Turin
SARDINIA-PIEDMONT
Genoa
CORSICA
Monaco
Nice
Tende
Toulon
PROVENCE
Marseille
Venaissin
Avignon
Nîmes
Montpellier
Toulouse
Limoges
Lyon
BEAUJOLAIS
AUVERGNE
Grenoble
Valence
Briançon
DAUPHINÉ
Brest
Quimper
Vannes
SPAIN

France, 1789.

and 1787, the Maison militaire still consisted of 8,000 men, including 10 guard infantry battalions: six French and four Swiss. The militia had 13 regiments of grenadiers royaux, 16 so-called provincial regiments and theoretically, as this force had fallen into disuse, 78 garrison battalions: 55,240 men increasing to 76,000 in the event of war. The royal army consisted of 102 line infantry regiments: 79 French and 23 foreign, these last being 11 Swiss, eight German, three (nominally) Irish and one Liégeois.[10] In addition, there were 12 battalions of light infantry (chasseurs à pied). The cavalry consisted of 62 regiments: 24 simply called cavalry, two of carabiniers, six of hussars, 18 of dragoons and 12 of chasseurs à cheval. There were also seven artillery regiments, a corps of coastguard gunners and a corps of engineers (limited to 329 officers). The infantry and cavalry of the line, alone, were supposed to have 162,000 men, although it was already short of 10,000 men at the eve of the Revolution. Furthermore, the colonial forces consisted of six infantry regiments, one of artillery, and the depot on the Île de Ré – a little less than 7,000 men.

The French Royal Navy was transformed, as a naval officer wrote later, 'Certainly the navy took a giant step from 1774 to 1778. Peace was made in 1783 and from that time until the time when the Revolution began, it equalled the English [sic] navy and surpassed all the navies of Europe.'[11] The number of French prizes brought into the British navy, as well as its use of French designs for the construction of new ships, bears testament to the improvements made.

However, the improvements to its armed forces came at a cost, when the kingdom's finances were already weak. For example, the rearmament of the navy and then its involvement in the war with Britain, added to the ever-growing debt. From the usual peacetime budget of 30 million, 'Naval expenditure in 1776 was some 47 million livres and 59 million in 1777, the last year of peace, by which time France had some sixty capital ships. Naval expenditure in 1778 and 1779, however, reached 150 million and 155 million livres, respectively.'[12] The ruinous state of the royal treasury meant that the King's ministry was loath to use its military forces and, at least in part, led it to undertake underhand policies with regard to its friends as well as its enemies.

France's debt needed to be controlled, and fiscal reform was required. However, reform threatened the nobility's privileges and so was thwarted by the parlements. These were appellate courts, that of Paris being the most significant, but they had also gained legislative authority through their role in registering new laws and were occupied by leading members of the *noblesse de robe*. It was argued that the required fiscal reforms altered the constitution so significantly that they needed to be approved by the Estates General. This was constituted by representatives of the three tiers, or estates, of French society: the first being the clergy, the second the nobility, and the third comprising the rest of the population. The parlements gambled that the convocation of such an assembly would be a step too far for King Louis XVI,

10 *Etat militaire de la France*, 1788, p.121.

11 G. de Colbert Turgis (ed.), *Souvenirs maritimes de Scipion de Castries* (Paris: Mercure de France, 1997) p.57.

12 Hardman, *Louis XVI*, p.121.

as it would imperil the existing power structure of the *ancien regime* that had lasted since 1614, the last time the Estates General had been convened.

In 1787, Louis tried to circumvent the parlements by using an Assembly of Notables to build a consensus for reform, but this failed even after the full scale of the financial crisis was revealed. After this, he resorted to trying to intimidate the parlements, even exiling the members of that of Paris to Troyes. This caused outbreaks of public disorder throughout France, significantly at Grenoble and Rennes, homes of provincial parlements. The parlements' opposition, although it could be regarded as vested self-interest, became the focal point for wider dissatisfaction over the way royal power was being exercised. In 1788, after an attempt to replace the parlements had failed, Louis finally decided to call their bluff and convoke an Estates General for the following year. Although he provided that the Third Estate would have double the number of representatives of the other two, he went no further in challenging tradition, so alienating potential allies from that Estate. They began to doubt Louis's sincerity when it came to reform; his conduct of foreign policy had been regarded as duplicitous, and now, whatever his aims, this was suspected in his handling of domestic politics. Thus, on 20 June 1789, two days after Austrian troops entered Brussels to suppress the Belgian revolt, 576 deputies, mainly from the Third Estate but joined by some from the clergy and nobility, gathered in the Salle du Jeu de Paume at Versailles. There, they refused to disperse until the kingdom had a constitution and so launched the French Revolution.

The nobility's opposition to Louis may seem an anachronism given that, as previously stated, service to the King was its raison d'être. However, this, and indeed other conduct, may be understood by the, perhaps simplistic, analogy of a family business. In this, the royalty and nobility were the family, all of whom had shares in the business. The shares were distributed unevenly, those at the top of the hierarchy, the royalty and higher aristocracy, having the most, and those at the bottom, generally the least wealthy, the fewest. Every share was to be safeguarded and passed on to the next generation. Following this analogy, the King was the head of the enterprise, but he could not expect blind obedience if the shareholders, especially the more powerful ones, considered that the business was taking the wrong course.

There was no register of nobility in France, as historian William Doyle observed, 'Nobody knew, or knows, for certain how many nobles there were. Credible estimates vary between 120,000 and 350,000'.[13] The French nobility had its roots in the societal structure of the Roman Empire, adapted by France's subsequent rulers, in which they dedicated their swords, and so their lives, to the service of the King.[14] Thus, even as the eighteenth century drew to a close, they were virtually exempt from paying the principal and heaviest direct tax, the *taille*. The development of a hierarchical church also provided its members with positions and power. Noble status allowed the possession of a fief, land with seigneurial rights, and the class owned between a quarter

13 William Doyle, *The Oxford History of the French Revolution* (Oxford: Oxford University Press, 1990), p.28.

14 See Karl Ferdinand Werber, *Naissance de la noblesse* (Paris Librairie Fayard, 1998).

to a third of France. Nevertheless, their ranks were not closed, 'access to the nobility still remained open to wealthy commoners ... by the purchase of hereditary offices. Thus, since the seventeenth century, a new and wealthy administrative nobility, the *noblesse de robe*, had grown up to challenge the social status and pretensions of the old-established *noblesse d'épée* (nobility of the sword)'.[15] The burgeoning middle class sought such places, and using wealth earned through commerce, they pushed up the prices for such offices. In addition, without a register, some individuals, such as Ternant, adopted the status without, strictly speaking, having the lineage to do so. In France, unlike Britain, the term *gentilhomme* (gentleman) was restricted to nobles and was generally used by those without a title.

Nobility offered many advantages, including trial by their peers, but the chief was access to privilege and power, principally through royal service. The higher offices in the Church were held by nobles and the King was surrounded by nobles, indeed the appointment of Jacques Necker to the council in 1776 was sensational because he was a commoner, as well as a foreign-born Protestant. Although noble status meant that they could not take part in commerce, they were encouraged by the sovereign to invest in key industries in order to guarantee France's economic independence. Nobles directly or indirectly controlled most of the country's heavy industry in France, for example, as a *maître des forges*. They were able to do so as such activities were considered to be land-based as opposed to commerce. The *maître* was originally a military term, and in that context, by this time, meant a noble serving in the ranks.

At the court of Versailles and in Paris, there were very wealthy nobles,

> But away from such centres of conspicuous consumption, the nobility often consisted of threadbare gentry with impeccable lineages but no resources. These were the only nobles most peasants, and therefore most Frenchmen, ever came across. They found them haughty, keen to exact their feudal dues and exercise their seigneurial prerogatives, and ferociously attached to their ancestry and privileges as noblemen.[16]

Their status was underlined by all non-nobles being termed *roturiers*, or commoners. The country nobles formed the majority of the army's officers but, in general, most would not reach the rank of *major*, the higher grades being the domain of wealthy young men of the court nobility. Over time, they found it increasingly difficult to raise the money required to purchase junior positions due to competition from the scions of less-established but richer families, which inflated prices. The Ségur Ordinance of 1781, requiring candidates for commissions to have four degrees of nobility, was an attempt to mitigate this as well as being part of a wider programme to professionalise the officer cadre.

There was, however, a minority of officers, about 1,700 or 14 per cent in 1789, who were *roturiers*. They had risen from the ranks and so were

15 George Rudé, *Revolutionary Europe 1783–1815* (Glasgow: Fontana/Collins, 1964), p.15.
16 Doyle, *French Revolution*, p.29.

called officiers de fortune, distinguishing them from their comrades from the nobility. They generally went no further than *capitaine* and in this were in a similar position to the country noblemen. However, with long service, they would be made a chevalier of the Ordre militaire de Saint-Louis and so have the opportunity of their families taking the first steps into the nobility.

The author's own family illustrates a path to noble status. The Aumonts were a Parisian bourgeoisie family, a member of which became a cloth merchant in Sillé-le-Guillaume, in Maine. In 1743, his son, François Julien, married Marie Hubert from one of the province's oldest noble families. Her father was an officer in the company of the Garde de la Prévôté de l'Hôtel du Roi (Guards of the Provost of the King's Mansion) and was also steward to the Marquis de Sourches, the company's *capitaine* who, as such, was Grand Provost of France. A year later, in 1744, François Julien joined his father-in-law in the same company, and in 1755 he purchased the position of *capitaine exempt*, which brought with it ennoblement as *écuyer* (squire). This, in turn, allowed him to buy the fief, lordship and castle of Bazouges-sur-Loir, in Anjou, the following year. In 1760 he was created chevalier de Saint-Louis but died four years later, with his wife, Marie, inheriting his seigneurial rights.

In 1748 they had had a son, François, known as the Chevalier de Bazouges, who entered the Régiment d'Orléans-cavalerie as a *cadet* aged 20 and then served as a *maître*, *brigadier* and *maréchal des logis* before purchasing a post as *sous-lieutenant* on 1 June 1772. Steadily rising through the ranks, he was *capitaine en second* of the second squadron in 1789, but during the Revolution he emigrated and so was dismissed by the constitutional decree of 1 March 1792.

What effect did service in the American War of Independence have on the officers and men of the French royal army? Scipio de Castries, a naval officer, was rare in criticising it:

> M. La Fayette brought with him to America many young men who were to attach their fortunes to his own ... Officers of a more advanced age brought their experience and knowledge to the rebels ... all asked to go to war and support this perverse cause. France was struck with such blindness that no one questioned or considered what was odious in this pretended generosity supporting subjects against their legitimate sovereign.[17]

Some have sought to place the responsibility for the French Revolution solely on the shoulders of the *Américains*, La Fayette and those young officers. One was Dumouriez, who would opportunely join the Jacobins, who wrote, 'The American war had not formed great generals; but the young Frenchmen ... brought back ill-digested ideas, and, wishing to adapt them to their national spirit, they embraced this spirit, and had ignited a volcano which covered this land of happiness with rubble and ruins.'[18]

---

17 Colbert Turgis (ed.), *Souvenirs maritimes*, pp.72–73.

18 Charles-Antoine Du Périer Dumouriez, *La vie et les mémoires du général Dumouriez* (Paris: Baudouin frères, 1822), vol.II, p.10.

However, the great majority of the officers crossed the Atlantic simply to serve the interests of their sovereign. Indeed, after research of the regular officers and men who served in the French regiments sent to America under the command of *lieutenant general* Comte de Rochambeau, the historian Samuel F. Scott has concluded that, 'The impact of the American experience of Rochambeau's veterans on their response to the French Revolution was largely negligible', indeed the regiments, 'generally remained among the best disciplined in the French army until 1792.'[19]

The nobility and the Church were the main bulwarks of the throne. Those who wished to undermine and isolate the monarchy needed to destroy the nobility and clergy as well as the ancient feudal structures of the French state, among which the royal army occupied a privileged place. Menaced and attacked, sometimes killed, noble army officers were to be gradually forced from the service, to retire to their provinces, even to self-exile, to save their lives before taking up arms to try to save those of the royal family. Approximately 150,000 people emigrated from France, the majority between 1789 and 1792, and perhaps 15,000 or so would serve their God and King in the various armies of royalist émigrés between 1791 and 1801. The greatest number were noble officers, but there were also other gentlemen, at least one noblewoman serving under an assumed name, former soldiers, craftsmen, peasants or bourgeois, and sometimes children along with old men. Foreign volunteers joined the ranks of these émigrés who, until the Treaty of Lunéville in 1801, considered themselves to be the guardians of the traditions of the former royal army.

This current volume is devoted to the history as well as the organisation, emblems and uniforms of the Armée des Princes (Armies of the Princes), the first armed émigré units in the Revolutionary Wars, in 1791 and 1792. A second volume will cover those who continued the struggle under the Prince of Condé, 1793–1801.

19 Samuel F. Scott, *From Yorktown to Valmy: The Transformation of the French Army in an Age of Revolution* (Niwor: University Press of Colorado, 1998), p.215.

1

From Emigration to Counter-revolution

The deputies of the Estates-General who refused to disperse from the Salle du Jeu de Paume on 20 June 1789 formed themselves into a National Assembly, that subsequently took the name National Constituent Assembly, or simply Constituent Assembly, which was retained until the end of its self-declared term on 30 September 1791. This Assembly, in the name of the Nation, seized legislative power and henceforth would propose decrees which, once agreed by a simple majority and ratified by the King, were promulgated as letters patent (1790) or laws (1791). Three authorities now governed France concurrently: the King, the Nation and the Law. Louis XVI, however, was 'a monarch as weak and indecisive as he was good and well-intentioned.'[1] He became a 'captive, dominated by the Assembly, menaced by riot, reduced to impotence.'[2] Having been crowned an absolute monarch, ruling by divine right, he was to be a figurehead, his power limited to the right of a suspensive veto, gaining him the nickname Monsieur Veto. He had no other means to show his will, or 'nolonté' as Mirabeau termed it, making a play on the French word for will, 'volonté'.[3] His only independence was influence over the time it took for him to sign the Assembly's decrees.

Emigration began with the flight of individuals, fearing imminent physical danger or simply those who wanted to leave until the crisis blew over, publicly demonstrating a refusal to endorse a political situation which they deemed intolerable. As early as June 1789 a plan was afoot for the King's immediate family to escape Paris, instigated by the Duchesse de Polignac, a confidante of Queen Marie-Antoinette fearing for the Queen's safety. She, 'began to form the plan, not to leave the kingdom, but to advise the royal family to leave the centre of sedition to go and live temporarily in Lille or

1 Archives départementales de l'Eure, Evreux (ADE): I J 240: *Mémoires de Jacques de Chambray.*

2 François Dominique de Reynaud comte de Montlosier, *Souvenirs d'un émigré (1791–1798)* (Paris: Hachette, 1951), p.7.

3 Louis Barthou, *Mirabeau* (Paris: Librairie Hachette, 1920), p.204.

The storming of La Bastille 14 July 1789. (Collection Musées Ville de Paris, licence CCØ)

Strasbourg, or another frontier stronghold.'[4] Lille was suggested due to its proximity to the border with the Austrian Netherlands, which was governed by the Archduchess Maria Christina, Marie-Antoinette's older sister, and her husband, Duke Albert of Saxe-Teschen. The project was almost enacted on the night of 15/16 July, immediately after the storming of the Bastille, but it was opposed by the Comte de Provence, the King's eldest brother and, as heir, titled Monsieur. Whether due to Monsieur's arguments or his own volition, Louis rejected it for fear of precipitating the country into civil war or leaving his throne vacant for their cousin, the Duc d'Orléans.

It was decided not to stand in the way of others who wished to leave. Indeed, those whose hostility to the so-called new ideas might have inflamed the situation were encouraged to go. It was later observed:

> Louis XVI ordered his youngest brother, the Comte d'Artois, 'to withdraw from the kingdom' in order to save him from the dangers from which he thought he was threatened. Thus he [the King] himself gave the signal for emigration, this emigration the consequences of which were to be so harmful to royalty, to the nobility, to France that it would cut in two.[5]

4 Le Duc de D**** (ed.), *Mémoires de Louis XVIII* (Brussels: Louis Hauman et Cie., 1832), vol.IV, p.166.

5 Montlosier, *Souvenirs*, p.7, introduction written by his great grandson the Comte de Larouzière-Montlosier and Ernest d'Hauterive.

The Comte d'Artois, 'left in numerous company … there were, among the first emigrants of 16 July 1789, the duc, duchesse, and all the Polignacs, the Comte and Comtesse de Polastron, the Prince de Lambesc, the Maréchaux de Broglie and de Castries'.[6]

Among them was the King's cousin, and prince of the blood, Louis-Joseph de Bourbon-Condé, generally regarded as the only soldier in the royal family, who was created *Colonel général de l'Infanterie* in 1780. This gave him supreme command of all the French and foreign infantry regiments, except for the Swiss and Grisons units and the Gardes Françaises of which the Comte d'Artois and the Duc de Châtelet were, respectively, *Colonel général*. As such, Condé could not condone the disorders that the Revolution instigated within the army and the crimes that went unpunished. However, as the King refused to use force to suppress the revolt, and thus his services, the Prince preferred to leave the kingdom, taking his son, the Duc de Bourbon, and grandson, the Duc d'Enghien, with him. Once Artois had reached Brussels, he was joined by his sons, the Ducs d'Angoulême and de Berry, who had travelled separately.

Others followed these leaders of the conservative party, Hyppolite d'Espinchal recalled, 'My father, the Comte d'Espinchal, maréchal de camp, emigrated in July 1789, a few days after the storming of the Bastille, charged by the Prince de Condé to bring his daughter, Princesse Louise de Bourbon-Condé, to Brussels where, a few days later, the prince's entire family was reunited.'[7] It was not just senior aristocrats, Condé noted in his journal, 'Tuesday 28 [July] … every day French people arrived, many officers of the guards.'[8]

The Régiment des Gardes Françaises had participated in the revolutionary unrest in Paris from the start. The regiment, part of the household troops, was 3,500 strong in 1789, more than double that of a normal regiment, and was traditionally based in the capital where it participated in policing. However, by 20 June 1789, some of the regiment had joined the rioters. Three days later, two companies of grenadiers refused to open fire, and on 30 June, the soldiers who had been imprisoned in the Abbey Prison for disobedience were freed by the mob. On 12 July, when the Régiment de Royal-Allemand-cavalerie, under the Prince de Lambesc, went to clear the Tuileries garden and the Place Louis XV (now the Place de la Concorde), in the heart of Paris, a detachment of the Gardes Françaises intervened. The following day, another detachment took part in the looting of Les Invalides when 40,000 muskets were removed and distributed to the rioters, who the guards quickly instructed in their use.

Antoine de Tardieu de Maleyssie, had served in the Gardes Françaises since he was 15 years old in 1779, and was then *premier lieutenant* of the regiment's artillery company. He recalled the riots fomented since 27 April by the Duc d'Orléans, who, 'had avowed an implacable hatred for the King,

6 D**** (ed.), *Louis XVIII*, vol.IV, p.229.

7 Hyppolite d'Espinchal, *Souvenirs militaires du comte Hyppolite d'Espinchal 1792–1814* (Paris: Librairie Paul Ollendorff, 1901), p.1.

8 Louis-Joseph de Bourbon-Condé, *Journal d'émigration du Prince de Condé 1789–1795* (Paris: Georges Servant, 1924), p.14.

worked surreptitiously to raise the people, and his emissaries distributed money profusely; but, as long as the troops were faithful, this agitation could produce no effect; to achieve his aim, above all he had to make himself master of Paris and to corrupt the regiment of French guards.'[9]

Finally, two companies of the Gardes Françaises marched to the Bastille on the afternoon of 14 July, to assist the Parisians who had been trying to seize the fortress since the morning. Despite promises of safe conduct, the governor and three officers were murdered and decapitated, while two *invalides* (veteran soldiers) and a Swiss soldier were hanged; but the guards managed to save the rest of the garrison, which included a detachment of an officer and 31 soldiers from the Swiss Régiment de Salis-Samade. By that evening, the six battalions of the Régiment des Gardes Françaises, with the exception of eight men, had rallied to the insurgents. With the rioters and mutinous soldiers going unpunished, on 15 July the Duc de Châtelet, the regiment's commander, presented his resignation to the King, which was followed by those of other officers, 220 in all.

Meanwhile, on 13 July, a Bourgeois Guard had been raised in Paris, and two days later, the National Assembly decided it would be renamed. From 16 July, this new public force officially adopted the name Garde Nationale, and similar units soon appeared throughout the country, to replace the former militias. Their stated aim was to ensure order and the security of persons and property, in particular that of the grain supply. The Assembly also ratified the decision of Paris to entrust the Marquis de La Fayette, the so-called Hero of the Two Worlds, with its command. Instigator of the destruction of the Bastille and then the adoption by the Parisian electors of a tricolour cockade on 26 July, he established himself as the strong man of the moment. He was leader of the Monarchiens who favoured a constitutional monarchy with, inspired from across the Channel, a bi-cameral legislature, one chamber being dominated by the high aristocracy and the other entrusted to the provincial nobility.

The Garde Nationale was initially to be formed of electors of the Estates General's Third Estate, lawyers, magistrates, bourgeois, farmers, artisans and others who had sufficient means to dress and equip themselves. Its composition thus matched that of the earlier Dutch patriot Vrijcorpsen. No one envisaged entrusting weapons to the ordinary people whose ferocity, once excited, was difficult to control, as the aftermath of the storming of the Bastille had shown. It was not to be simply for ceremonial or policing duties, but was formed as a functional military force. Notably, the same symbols and rank insignia as the royal army were worn, but over time, revolutionary symbols began to appear, replacing those of the monarchy, most conspicuously the tricolour cockade, but also Masonic ornaments embroidered with the slogans *CONSTITUTION* or *LIBERTÉ*.

---

9 Antoine de Tardieu de Maleyssie, *Mémoires d'un officier aux gardes françaises (1789–1793)* (Paris: Librairie Plon, 1897), p.15. Written at the end of 1792, his memoirs were discovered at the end of the nineteenth century by Roberti, professor at the Turin military academy. They constitute one of the best testimonies of the events that ran from 14 July 1789 to the disbanding of the émigrés at the end of November 1792.

From its creation, the mutinous soldiers of the Gardes Françaises were admitted into the Parisian Garde Nationale and they were soon joined by deserters from the line regiments that were gathered about the city. The King had given his agreement to the formation, so this exodus was not denounced. Soon, the former soldiers of the Gardes Françaises formed 60 permanent paid companies, one per battalion, in the Parisian Garde Nationale, leading to the guards regiment being formally disbanded on 30 August. The Paris Garde Nationale was, from its inception, a formidable military force of 48,000 men forming, 'six superb divisions composed of sixty battalions, [each] with six volunteer companies and one paid. The former grenadiers of the guards, the chasseurs of the barriers, artillery of one hundred and forty cannons, a mounted gendarmerie.' La Fayette saw it as, 'both a civic and military institution, which is to triumph over the old tactics of Europe, and which will reduce arbitrary governments to the alternative of being beaten, if they do not imitate it, and reverses, if they dare to imitate it'.[10]

Comte Valentin Esterhazy, a privileged observer of the actors and events, considered that the monarchy's cause was lost as early as Friday, 17 July, when the King went to Paris.

> The whole of an armed populace without his orders forms a hedge wherever he must pass. He goes to the City Hall, climbs the steps that were still stained with the blood of M. de Flesselles [provost of merchants who had been shot, decapitated and his head paraded on a pike on 14 July], and goes to receive from the hands of the factious Bailly, elected Mayor of Paris, the cockade symbol of the rebellion.[11]

Despite there still being enough faithful regiments which would undoubtedly have supported him, instead of taking energetic measures, Louis resigned himself into the hands of the National Assembly. It was then that the factions resorted to a stratagem that Esterhazy attributes to the Duc d'Orléans, called by future historians the Great Fear, to spread armed insurrection across the kingdom.

> At the same time, the same day, messengers are sent out on all roads; they have the tocsin sound, announce the arrival of brigands to whom they give different names ... and who come, they claim, to cut the wheat which is not yet ripe, to slit the throats of children and women. Fear spreads in the countryside the inhabitants of which take refuge in the towns, and the emissaries of the faction urge the new municipalities to ask for weapons. Sanctioned by the example of Paris, and by the authority that the constitutional plan gives to the new officers, the magazines open up everywhere. In three days, all of France is armed; the arsenals and arms factories are empty, and the new laws giving precedence to the national guards over the regular troops, who continue to be diverted from their duty, royal authority no longer has defenders.[12]

---

10 La Fayette, *Mémoires*, p.20.

11 Ernest Daudet (ed.), *Mémoires du comte Valentin-Ladislas Esterhazy* (Paris: Plon, 1903), p.227.

12 Daudet (ed.), *Esterhazy*, p.228.

As a result of the widespread disorder, the troops who had been massed around the capital were recalled to the provinces.

Indiscipline was fomented among the troops, as described by the Chevalier de Mautort, who then commanded a company of the Régiment d'Austrasie:

> We found ourselves in garrison at Briançon at the start of the Revolution, and it is to this isolation from the revolutionary centre, that vulcanised everything, that we were indebted for the good order that we maintained in the regiment. Daily many others gave examples of the disorders that an unbridled soldiery that has broken all the bonds of discipline can indulge in. The post brought us, every day, packets of tracts, each more incendiary than the last. This printed garbage was sent to non-commissioned officers and soldiers. They preached revolt and impunity.[13]

The wealthy bourgeoisie retained power among the Third Estate; however, the changing political environment saw the spread of revolutionary clubs throughout the country. These Sans-Culottes, a name reflecting their lack of fashionable clothing, were fervent supporters of the Revolution, and although kept to the fringes of the political process, they sustained a climate of hatred and violence, fuelled by propaganda from Paris.

Meanwhile, on the night of 4 August 1789, liberal elements of the nobility and clergy in the National Assembly proposed that feudal privileges, not only those of the nobility and the upper clergy but also the rights and customs peculiar to each province, cease. Enacted on 6 August, 'the entire organic constitution of the kingdom was destroyed in a moment.'[14] Among others, the tithes and other rights of German princes with possessions in Alsace and Lorraine, which had been safeguarded by the Peace of Westphalia of 1648, disappeared.

Little by little, indiscipline was fostered in both the army and navy to break the bonds between the noble officers and the soldiers so the latter would find common cause with the rioters. Those soldiers who remained loyal were also threatened. An officer reported on disturbances at Valenciennes between 19 and 21 August:

> The Régiment de Schomberg [dragoons], or rather a very small part of this regiment … had arrived on 16 August in Valenciennes whose garrison was made up of the Régiments d'Orléans, Royal Suédois, a battalion of Xaintonge [Saintonge] infantry, and the cavalry Régiment d'Orléans. On the 19th, there was a great ferment in the Régiment d'Orléans Cavalerie. The greater part of the troopers left the city after forcing the guard at the gates. They were soon followed by a great number of soldiers from the garrison, to whom the cavalrymen had sent invitations to go drinking in the suburb of Anzin. The Régiment de Schomberg remained in its quarters and no dragoon left the city or even appeared in the towns,

13 Louis-François de Paule Tillette de Mautort, *Mémoires du chevalier de Mautort, capitaine au régiment d'Austrasie, chevalier de l'ordre royal et militaire de Saint-Louis (1752–1802)* (Paris: Librairie Plon, 1895), p.389.

14 ADE: I J 240: *Mémoires de Jacques de Chambray* (1812).

> to mix with the soldiers and cavalrymen who were scattered there. This wise and truly rare conduct in a time of general insurrection, attracted particular insult to the dragoons from both the soldiers and the people, who insulted the regiment and spouted horrors against several officers. The officers retired without deigning to respond. The dragoons conducted themselves with the same prudence. Not a single man was missing at the roll-call.[15]

Civilian authorities would often actively support the process, so in December 1789 the naval commander at Toulon was arrested with five *capitaines de vaisseau* (equivalent in rank to a *colonel*) for having punished two sailors.

The royal forces were being gradually ripped apart. Already, as early as 13 August 1789, allies of La Fayette proposed that the National Assembly establish a Military Committee, 'to do everything that would be necessary to prepare a prompt reorganisation of the entire army corps.'[16] It was finally adopted, and on 2 October 1789, the 12 members of the first Military Committee met to consider all aspects involving the armed forces. Membership changed over time, reflecting the general radicalisation of the political process and, more particularly, the subversion of the royal army by the Garde Nationale and other popular forces. At the same time, committees made up of subaltern officers, non-commissioned officers, and soldiers' representatives began appearing in the regiments, demanding above all improvements in pay, advancement and even control of regimental funds. While the Military Committee reported its conclusions for the overhaul of the army and navy to the National Assembly, these regimental committees also addressed the Assembly, reporting difficulties they encountered, justifying themselves or even requesting arbitration, in liaison with the municipalities and the Garde Nationale.

The royal Household troops had been substantially reduced between 1776 and 1787, and then, in May 1789, the Gardes de la Prévôté de l'Hôtel du Roi were removed to provide security for the National Assembly. After the disappearance of the Gardes Françaises, there only remained the four battalions of the Régiment des Gardes Suisses, four companies of the Gardes du Corps du Roi (King's Body Guards) and the Household troops of the Comtes de Provence and Artois, each of two companies of Gardes du Corps and one of Suisses de la garde ordinaire. Then, on 5 October 1789, a mob marched on Versailles, the very day that Louis XVI had definitively renounced the sacred nature of his power, as well as its legitimacy, writing, 'I accept purely and simply the articles of the Constitution and the Declaration of the Rights of Man that the National Assembly presented to me.'[17] He and the Queen had also made a brief appearance at a meal laid on by the Gardes du Corps for the officers of the Régiment de Flandre on the occasion of that regiment's departure from Versailles. It was alleged that during the

15 Archives municipales de Valenciennes (AMV): EE404 report signed by Chollet, *major en second*, commanding the Régiment de Schomberg; also see Daudet (ed.), *Esterhazy*, pp.239–242.

16 Pierre Caron 'Les comités militaires des assemblées révolutionnaires (1789 -an VIII)', *Revue d'Histoire Moderne & Contemporaine*, 1904, p.690.

17 Archives Nationales, Paris (AN): AE II 2983, cote d'origine C 31, pl.263.

event, tricolour cockades were removed from hats, trampled underfoot and replaced by white ones. These acts were supposed to have somehow triggered the spontaneous fury of the Parisians. However, witnesses accuse the Duc d'Orléans of having organised, or even, disguised as a woman, of taking part in the march on Versailles that conveniently coincided with the departure of the Régiment de Flandre.

The conventional, revolutionary, account of the march on Versailles runs that it only resulted in two Gardes du Corps being killed, victims of the crowd's justifiable anger, who had their heads cut off and attached to pikes to serve as trophies for the procession which brought the royal family back to Paris to be placed under house arrest at the Tuileries Palace. The last-minute intervention by La Fayette and the Paris Garde Nationale preventing a tragedy. However, Madame Elisabeth, the King's sister, writing only a week later, on 13 October, gives a different account. Informed that 15,000 men were approaching from Paris, she returned to Versailles:

> Meanwhile I learn, before leaving, that there were two thousand women, armed with ropes, hunting knives, etc., who were arriving at Versailles. They were there at five o'clock. It was to ask for bread, of which Paris was absolutely lacking, so they said. They came to the King to ask him for some. His answer seemed to satisfy them. They went to establish themselves in the chamber of the Estates[-General]. We were still uncertain of knowing if troops were arriving from Paris or not. During this time, the people of Versailles, already very animated against the Gardes du Corps, mingled with the bandits who were arriving from all quarters, to destroy them. The King having forbidden shooting, no one thought of it. There was only one officer who, attacked by a sabre blow, sought to defend himself. This was considered such a grave crime that a man shot him at point-blank range and broke his arm. But, as they wanted to find fault in these gentlemen, they accused a Gardes du Corps, whose horse was killed under him, and who himself was pierced by blows, of having fired his pistols. These are the means used by the people of Versailles, to be able to say that these gentlemen had attacked, while they only showed moderation and courage. They were fired upon much of the rest of the evening. Those who were in the hôtels [their accommodation] were injured with blows with timber. Both that day and Tuesday night, there were eleven killed and many wounded. At eleven o'clock in the evening, M. de La Fayette, who had been forced to come at the head of thirty thousand men, entered the King's accommodation after having made these troops renew the oath of loyalty. They said that they came to demand the dismissal of the Régiment de Flandre, and that the Gardes Françaises were taking back the guard of the King. They all took their posts, and everyone returned to their quarters quietly … I slept without waking until half-past seven, when I was told that the King requested for me; that I was going to find a detachment of twelve grenadiers to take me there; that the Gardes du Corps had been pursued again. Their rooms, in fact, had been forced. Two guards had their heads cut off; others, wounded by the women in a dreadful way. The Queen, obliged to flee to the King in her chemise, because someone was entering her quarters [with the intent to assassinate her]; all the courtyards filled with women, bandits, and national guardsmen who were trying to bring some order. Without the grenadiers, all the Gardes du Corps would have

> been massacred. They saved many of them, took them under their protection to bring them to Paris … Finally, at one o'clock, we got into a carriage; Versailles was marked by signs of joy. We marched surrounded by all the national guard, several Gardes du Corps on foot, who had exchanged their hats for grenadier caps. I forgot that after the King, they [the gardes] had appeared on the balcony, thrown down their bandoliers and their hats as a sign of peace …[18]

The events at Versailles led more to leave the country, particularly the aristocratic nobility of the court, but also military officers. It is estimated that 2,000 (or 17 percent) of the latter had left their post, most having resigned or retired, by the end of 1789.

Meanwhile, the long-running discontent in the Austrian Netherlands became a general insurrection that spread across the territories, with the exception of Luxembourg. On 17 November 1789, Archduchess Maria Christina and her husband were forced to leave Brussels and retired to Bonn. Finally, on 11 January 1790, the citadel of Antwerp fell to the insurgents. Two weeks earlier, the Confederation of the United Belgian States, or United Belgian Provinces, had been declared. It was in such circumstances that Emperor Joseph II died on 20 February 1790, in Vienna.

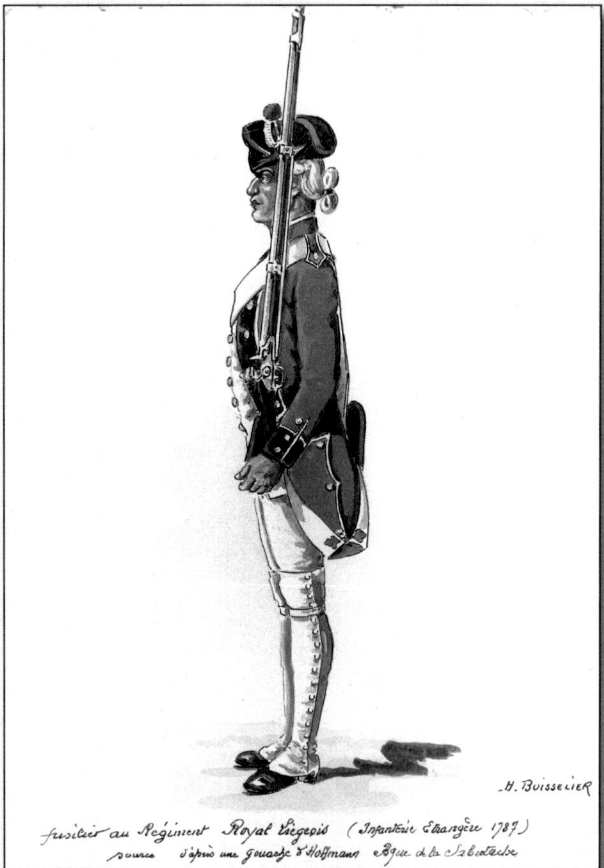

Fusilier Régiment Royal-Liégeois 1789-1791, by Henri Boisselier. (Courtesy of La Sabretache)

The conflict soon developed into another proxy war but France was unable to respond militarily as its army was teetering on disintegration. On 28 February 1790 the National Assembly revoked the Ségur Ordinance of 1781, so any citizen could be employed as an officer. While most of the officiers de fortune who had risen from the rank and file favoured the Revolution, the authority of noble officers in the royal army was increasingly contested. No effective measures were taken to restore discipline, to prevent the poaching of soldiers by the Garde Nationale, or to stop desertion. On 7 March 1790, the chasseur company of the Royal-Liégeois mutinied at Avesnes. This coincided with the Régiment d'Auvergne marching through the town, having quit Le Quesnoy, where it had also mutinied a few weeks earlier. A large number of the Royal-Liégeois, as well as other Belgians serving in the French army, deserted and crossed the frontier into Belgium.[19] The Royal-Liégeois

18 Joseph-Adrien Le Roi, *Récit des journées des 5 et 6 octobre 1789 à Versailles* (Versailles: E. Aubert, 1867), pp.90–92.

19 Louis Prosper Gachard, *Documents politiques et diplomatiques sur la Révolution belge de 1790* (Brussels: H.Rémy, 1834), p.89.

was simply moved to Saarlouis without any other disciplinary measure being taken, the minister dared not punish the guilty for fear of displeasing the Assembly. Little by little, it was the municipalities, even the revolutionary clubs, which decided if a particular regiment was removed from a garrison for having displeased the local Garde Nationale or these radicals. The political fermentation sowed chaos:

> In April 1790 at Lille, there are veritable fights that took place between the 'patriot' infantrymen of the Royal-Vaisseaux and Couronne and the chasseurs of the Normandie supported by the 'aristocrats' of the Colonel-Général cavalry. In the same April, at Valence, the colonel of the Régiment de Besançon (artillery), M. de Voisins, who had punished a 'patriot' gunner, was dragged by the crowd into the Saint Jean church and assassinated there. At Bastia, it will be Colonel de Rully, commanding the Régiment du Maine (infantry) who will suffer the same fate. The previous November, the Régiment du Maine had already been bested by the mob and the national guards. It had lost two soldiers killed and several wounded including a captain, without the Assembly reacting … The Régiment [Royal la Marine] had already had to quit Marseille at the end of April following incidents provoked by the blundering of its colonel with regard to the national guards. After its departure, the city demanded the departure of all regular troops, occupied the Saint Nicolas and Saint Jean Forts and assassinated the major of the Vexin infantry who claimed to be engaged in its occupation.[20]

On 2 May, when *Major* Beausset of the Régiment de Vexin and commander of Fort Saint Jean, was going to the municipality to hand over the keys, escorted by three national guardsmen, he was killed by the mob, decapitated and his head paraded through the streets, apparently followed by grenadiers of his own regiment, singing and dancing. Afterwards, the Minister of War, La Tour du Pin, and the Constituent Assembly demanded that the Garde Nationale and Vexin leave the forts guarding the port to be replaced by the Swiss Régiment d'Ernest.

Another aspect of the systematic undermining of the royal army was denounced by *Colonel* de Puységur, of the Régiment de Strasbourg artillery, to the National Assembly,

> … the enemies of the public good go so far as to lavish money in the garrisons to divert French soldiers from their duty. As proof of this fact, he offered as a patriotic donation a sum of 240 livres that was sent to M. Mangin, Caporal of his regiment, & which this brave Soldier did not want to profit from.[21]

Once again, no investigation was made into the source of such bribes; acts of insubordination, including the assassination of officers, went unpunished. Rather than deal with them, the Assembly, complicitly silent or cowardly, was soon to choose new 'ennemis du bien public' (enemies of the public good) as targets for popular vengeance.

20 Bernard Deschard, *L'armée et la révolution* (Paris: Librairie Desjonquières, 1989), pp.193–194.
21 *Journal des débats et des décrets*, 10 June 1790 sitting.

Those who followed events closely saw a deliberate plan developing to strip the King of the protection of the royal army. Indeed, in May 1790, he, in the spirit of fraternity, recommended that his troops adopt, like the entire Nation, the tricolour cockade. In the meantime, he was being isolated from the support of the nobility, which was itself increasingly divided politically. The divorce was finalised on 19 June 1790 when the National Assembly abolished the nobility (letters patent of 23 June):

> ... in consequence the titles of marquis, chevalier, écuyer [esquire], comte, vicomte, messire, prince, baron, vidame, noble, duc, and all other similar titles, will not be taken by whoever, nor given to anyone; that any French citizen will be able to take only the real name of his family; that he will no longer be able to wear, nor cause to be worn, a livery, nor have a coat of arms ...[22]

A year after the storming of the Bastille, the deconstruction of the Ancien Régime continued without too much difficulty. Indeed, in January 1790, on the pretext of rationalising the administrative and judicial organisation in the kingdom, 83 départements had replaced the former provinces (National Assembly decree of 22 December 1789). Thus, the Jacobin project of centralising political power in Paris began as the emotional and cultural attachment to existing structures was considered to be both archaic and an obstacle to the progress of the new ideas. Each département was to bring together all functions that had previously been carried out by different traditional structures in the hands of the prefect, the representative of the Parisian executive.

All the while, only the Gardes Nationaux, with some of the old maréchaussée faced the looters and arsonists. The royal armed forces could not be relied on to provide assistance due to the risk of the men deserting or rallying to the revolutionaries. This situation above all benefited the Jacobins, or Société des Amis de la Constitution, in the Assembly who systematically defended Sans-Culottes.

As order broke down, long-standing tensions broke into conflict. Protestants had faced legal persecution in France since the Revocation of the Edict of Nantes in 1685, and despite some toleration with the Edict of Versailles in 1787, they welcomed the weakening of royal power. On 13 and 14 June fighting between Catholics and Protestants at Nîmes left 300 dead. The Chevalier de Forton was a naval officer who, being sick, had left Paris to join his family in Montpellier:

> I arrived at Beaucaire on the 13th, very tired from the journey and very unwell. I had barely had a few hours rest when I heard [drums] beating the general alarm. A messenger from Nîmes announced that the Catholics and Protestants had come to blows. The Beaucaire National Guard immediately took up arms, it was joined by 100 dragoons from the Régiment de Lorraine and 200 from the Tarascon National Guard. According to the orders of our municipality, based on the decrees

22 Anon., *Archives parlementaires de 1787 à 1860, Volume XXVI, du 31 mai 1790 au 8 juillet 1790* (Paris: Société d'Imprimerie et Librairie administratives et des Chemins de fer, 1883), p.378.

> of the National Assembly, we could not enter the territory of Nîmes without having received express permission from the administrators. We therefore halted near the Pont du Gard, and we dispatched a trumpeter to request the necessary authorisation. In this interval, the National Guards from the towns and villages of the Côte du Rhône and surrounding areas came to join us. A large number of peasants, armed with scythes, further augmented this little army, that could grow to 3,000 men. If the same spirit had animated it, one could have undertaken to change the face of things in the département or at least to stop the floods of blood that were shed at Nîmes. But it was composed of heterogeneous elements, which it was impossible to make serve the same purpose. The Lorraine dragoons and the Tarascon National Guard entirely approved of the new system and would have joined the Nîmes Protestants; the National Guard from Beaucaire, split between its hatred for the Calvinists and its attachment to the Revolution, would not have known which side to take; the rest of the small army declared itself for the Catholics with a fury which did not suffer the least contradiction. Our entry into Nîmes, far from calming the troubles, would only have increased them.[23]

The events gave rise to one of the sporadic attempts by the nobility at the regional level to reconcile with the bourgeoisie and the Garde Nationale still loyal to the King, and even to sway still undecided regiments. This was a project to gather several Garde Nationale units at a camp at Jalès in the Ardèche to renew their loyalty to the King as an act of Catholic solidarity; however, it was judged to be unconstitutional by the Assembly. Another was:

> A royalist and clandestine organisation, called the 'Coalition de Poitou,' seems to have formed around 1790, in that province, to support the enterprises of the Comte d'Artois and the Prince de Condé in France. It has for its principal leaders the Comte François des Cars [d'Escars], capitaine of the Comte d'Artois's guards and deputy of the nobility of Châtellerault, and the Baron de Lézardière, former procureur général syndic of Poitou. The members of the coalition first try to win over to their cause the Régiments de la Sarre and du Roi-cavalerie, and the greatest number of municipalities.[24]

The Roman Catholic Church, another pillar of the Ancien Régime, was a target of the Revolution. It was the kingdom's leading landowner and was to make the greatest financial contribution to deal with France's enormous debt. As early as 2 November 1789, the Constituent Assembly had decreed that both the movable property and estates of the Church would be 'put at the disposal of the nation.'[25] In other words they were put up for sale, along with part of the Crown domain (decrees of 19 and 21 December 1789). On 19 December, bonds guaranteed by the national assets called assignats were

---

23 Gaston Vidal (ed.), *Mémoires historiques (1781-1815) du chevalier de Forton, officier de Marine* (Montpellier: Éditions de l'Entente bibliophile, 1961), pp.48–49. Soon Forton and his family had to flee Montpellier and take refuge at Nice in the face of violence due their nobility.

24 Vicomte Robert Grouvel, *Les corps de troupes de l'émigration française* (Paris: Les Éditions de La Sabretache, 1957–1964), vol.III, p.113.

25 Anon., *Collection complète des Lois, Décrets, Ordonnances, Règlements, Avis du Conseil d'Etat* (Paris: Librairie Guyot, 1834), vol.I, pp.54–55.

created to repay the national debt. Assets were to be sold at local public auctions (decree of 14 May 1790), divided into lots which could be paid for in 12 annual instalments. The project was an immediate success, and on 25 June 1790, the Assembly accordingly decreed that the sale of national assets would continue beyond the initial amount set at 400 million livres, the estimated extent of the debt. Furthermore, the Assembly adopted a decree on 12 July 1790 for the creation of a new national church, independent of the papacy and subject to the French government alone, steps that some considered as the dechristianisation of the country. Above all, the decree provided that parish priests, like bishops and archbishops, would be elected by municipalities or authorities after having taken an oath of obedience to the Nation, the Law and the King.

In recognition of its achievements, on 9 June the National Assembly decided to hold a Fête de la Fédération in Paris on 14 July 1790, marking the anniversary of the storming of the Bastille. At the event, Louis XVI was to reaffirm his loyalty to the Nation as well as his determination to protect the Constitution and the laws that he was forced to sanction. This coincided with the military having to take a civic oath of their own before the municipal officers and Gardes Nationaux of each garrison. Those at Lille did so on 6 July:

> … the National Militia of three Departments, & four Regiments garrisoned at Lille. Here is the oath: We Citizen Soldiers & Soldier Citizens, swear on the Altar of the Fatherland, in the presence of the God of Armies & on our arms, to be true to the Nation, the Law & the King, to maintain in all our power the Constitution decreed by the National Assembly, & accepted by the King, as well as all the decrees of the National Assembly, sanctioned by His Majesty. We also swear to remain forever united and to lend each other all the assistance that fraternity requires, as well as to all our brothers of the French Empire, immediately we are legally required to do so.[26]

It was hoped that the patriotic display at the Fête de la Fédération, testifying to the position La Fayette and the Monarchiens had established, would dissuade those who sought to achieve their political ends by violence in Paris and elsewhere, and to some extent it had a positive influence. At Laon, for example, 'For a long time frightening insubordination reigned in this regiment [the Régiment de la Reine cavalerie]. The Federation of this regiment with the National Militia of this City, which finally took place, has returned the Regiment to the most perfect order.'[27]

The spirit was not universal, and the indiscipline of the royal troops at Nancy in Lorraine degenerated to breaking point by the middle of June 1790. The continuous disorder in the Régiment du Roi spread to other corps, causing mutinous conduct among the Swiss of the Régiment de Châteauvieux on 20 July. Three weeks later, troopers from the Mestre-de-Camp cavalry broke into the Swiss barracks to free the prisoners and then forced the Swiss

26 *Journal des débats et des décrets*, 2 June 1790 sitting.
27 *Journal des débats et des décrets*, 10 June 1790 sitting.

officers to reinstate them before they paraded in triumph through the city. The following day, 12 August, 'at four o'clock in the morning, the general alarm beats everywhere; the garrison goes to the Place Royale where a proclamation from the National Assembly and the King against gatherings and seditions, and to restore military discipline is read out.'[28] It had the contrary effect and triggered a general uprising.

The city was part of the governorship of the Marquis de Bouillé, who, a week earlier, had been ordered to suppress the insurrection by the National Assembly. The significance of the order was stated in a letter to him from La Fayette, dated 8 August, 'here, my dear cousin, is the moment when we can begin the establishment of institutional order, which must replace revolutionary anarchy … we must strike an imposing blow for the whole army and stop, by this example, the general disbandment which is impending.'[29] It was not to be easy as the mutinous soldiers, and those of the city's population who had joined them, outnumbered the troops Bouillé could rely on by four or five to one, and failure would undoubtedly trigger a much larger civil conflict. As he approached Nancy, the Garde Nationale and the Régiment du Roi submitted to the Assembly's decree and the latter left the city. However, the other mutineers opened fire on Bouillé's troops, who stormed the city on 31 August 1790. The mutineers were dealt with immediately, those of the Régiment de Châteauvieux were tried by their comrades in the Régiments de Castella and Vigier under the traditional and public judicial system of the Swiss service, 'out of 113 Châteauvieux prisoners taken, one of them was sentenced to be broken, 22 to be hung, and 44 to be sent to the galleys.'[30] The three mutinous regiments were then transferred to new garrisons.

Initially, Bouillé received universal praise, but the 'Affaire de Nancy' soon became a political battle between the constitutionalists, the established order, and the revolutionary radicals, the Sans-Culottes, who regarded the mutinous soldiers as having legitimately revolted against the tyranny of royal authority. The events at Nancy were not unique and disorder meant that more and more army units were sent to reinforce overwhelmed Gardes Nationaux, to guard grain convoys, depots and arsenals in towns, ports and the countryside. However, the interaction between the Gardes Nationaux, accountable for internal security, and the royal troops, now only responsible for the frontiers and war beyond them, resulted in a number of clashes.

Esterhazy had that spring renounced his command at Valenciennes, where his authority was no longer respected and his life was threatened. He joined the royal family but despaired at what he considered to be weakness on the part of Louis XVI. The King's lack of resolution had allowed several opportunities to escape to be missed, and after having got his wife and daughter to England, Esterhazy left France but not before the Queen

28 National Archief, The Hague (NAN): 2.21.008.01/IN – 19: *Journal de Constant Rebecque*, Volume 1.

29 La Fayette, *Mémoires*, vol.III, p.135.

30 NAN: 2.21.008.01/IN – 19: *Journal de Constant Rebecque*, Volume 1. The last sentence was in fact one of hard labour.

informed him, 'that this hope [of escape] destroyed, others remained; that the Netherlands were going to return to the obedience of the Emperor, and that it would be in this direction that the King thought of leaving.'[31] As a result, Esterhazy placed himself near the frontier to await new orders. In October, the Comte d'Artois asked him to join him in Chambéry, but the King dissuaded him, refusing to allow his agents to have any contact with the princes, distancing himself from and even condemning their projects and declarations that undermined his sovereignty.

After having served at Nancy the Royal-Liégeois was posted to Belfort, undoubtedly to keep it from the Belgian frontier and the temptation of further desertion. On 21 October, as was tradition with regiments in the same garrison, the officers of the Hussards de Lauzun provided a meal to those of the Royal-Liégeois. At the end of the meal, nine of the Royal-Liégeois officers, clearly drunk, took to the streets, as Bouillé reported, 'After dinner and before coffee, the major of the Royal-Liégeois said: We are the masters, we must chop down the bourgeoisie. Then, most of the officers poured into the streets shouting: Long live the King! long live joy! Colonel La Tour joins them and adds: To hell with the nation!'[32] As a result, *Colonel* de La Tour and *Major* Baron de Grünstein were punished along with two other officers, and all four fled across the Rhine. La Tour's replacement was the regiment's *lieutenant-colonel*, Chevalier de Ternant, and the regiment was moved to Phalsbourg while the National Assembly decided if it should be disbanded.

In the summer of 1790 the Prince de Condé published a 16-page manifesto in which he denounced the upheavals of the Revolution as well as the illegitimacy of the National Assembly, the establishment of chaos and the abasement of the monarchy. He vowed to restore the throne and, in doing so, the place of the nobility and the Church in a counter-revolutionary crusade in which the ruling dynasties of the rest of Europe should take an interest.

> A year ago I left my homeland; I must expose to the eyes of Europe the reasons which forced me to leave it, & the means which I must use & which I will employ to return there in a manner worthy of me. My misfortunes have not made me forget what I owe to my birth, they have perhaps strengthened this courage which I owe to my ancestors, & which I here swear never to deny: my cause is that of princes & kings; it is important for them to favour it, if they still hold power, & if they do not want to see their sceptre slip from their hands ...
>
> 14 July arrives, the era when the murders begin ... from this moment, more bridles, more laws; the army is corrupted; the soldier knows neither chiefs nor discipline; on one side the people massacre, slit throats in Paris, Marseille, Lyon, Valence; on the other, the so-called National Assembly invades, destroys property; it does not blush to lay sacrilegious hands on the altar; the Church's assets, the patrimony of the poor, falls prey to the rapacity of these so-called legislators; religion is trampled underfoot ... châteaux delivered to the flames, after having been pillaged; lords slain in their homes; ministers of justice blamed,

31 Daudet (ed.), *Esterhazy*, p.289.

32 Louis Susane, *Histoire de l'ancienne infanterie française* (Paris: Librairie militaire, maritime et polytechnique, 1853), vol.VII, p.369.

> condemned, for having opposed the disorders; all is at its peak, anarchy cannot go any further.[33]

Condé's manifesto was also intended for the French people, but he had little illusion about the difficulties that would be faced in 'returning to duty a generous but fickle people, always ready the next day to break the idol that they praised the day before.'[34] He wished to be at the head of the crusade, 'I will go, iron and flame in hand ... I will go, followed by all subjects loyal to their King, who will rally under my flags, to try to deliver this unfortunate monarch ...'[35]

In response, Mirabeau proposed that the National Assembly decree:

> That Louis-Joseph de Bourbon, formerly Prince de Condé, will be required to make, within three weeks, the authentic and legal disavowal of this text; failing which, his silence will be deemed to be a confession, and as a consequence, Louis-Joseph de Bourbon, known as Condé, will be declared a traitor to the fatherland, and his assets will be administered by the directories of the districts and départements in the territory in which they are to be found ...[36]

This motion was incidental to a debate about Austrian troops preparing to cross French territory on the march from the Rhineland to the Austrian Netherlands, something to which the Minister of War had already consented. Thus, Mirabeau sought to place the threat from the Prince de Condé alongside the fallacious fear of an Austrian invasion. Illustrating how such actors put the elements in place to lead to the declaration of war against Austria in April 1792, which was to finally set Europe aflame.

The Minister for Foreign Affairs, who had considered it unhelpful to inform the Assembly, had instructed the Minister of War, La Tour du Pin, to agree to the passage of Austrian troops in accordance with agreements made in the entente between France and Austria of 1770. The Assembly immediately denounced this lack of notification and, from then on, the King was excluded from matters involving the armies and diplomacy despite his supposed authority in these areas. The ministry was to be supervised by the Assembly, and 60,000 men were deployed to the Ardennes.

On 25 July 1790, following a report from the Military Committee, the Assembly was presented with a recommendation to increase the size of the army. The draft decree proposed that the effective force for 1791 would be 190,000 men, of which 144,000 were to be active soldiers and 46,000 auxiliaries. The most significant recommendation was that the infantry was to be formed of 46 so-called French regiments of four battalions, with the reintegration of the chasseurs á pied, and the existing 11 Swiss regiments of two battalions. Each battalion was to be commanded by a *lieutenant-colonel,*

33 Anon., *Copie du Manifeste attribué à Louis-Joseph de Bourbon, dit Condé* (1790, no further details), pp.3–9.

34 Anon., *Manifeste*, p.14.

35 Anon., *Manifeste*, pp.14–15.

36 *Journal des débats et des décrets*, 28 July 1790 sitting.

and the companies increased from 50 to 54 men: 43 *soldats*, one *tambour* (drummer), six *caporaux* (corporals), one *fourrier* (a company quartermaster/clerk) and three *sergents* (sergeants), commanded by a *capitaine*, with a *lieutenant* and a *sous-lieutenant*. The cavalry was to have 12 heavy cavalry, eight dragoon and 12 chasseurs à cheval regiments, so the hussar regiments were apparently to be abolished.

The primary objective, both militarily and politically, from now until the outbreak of war, was to gain time for the Revolution to be completed. The enemy was to be kept at the frontier long enough for the forces to be increased, drawing upon France's population, the largest in Europe, and then the war could be taken into the enemy's territory. To do so, the army was to form three corps, one facing the Austrian Netherlands, which could be penetrated quickly, another to defend the Rhine and Alsace, and a third to guard the frontier from the Alps to the Mediterranean. However, these plans did not recognise the advanced disintegration of the royal army and its progressive abandonment by officers encouraged by Condé's manifesto to emigrate and join the armed counter-revolution.

The first counter-revolutionary plot had been hatched in December 1789, and at its centre was the Comte de Maillebois. After the royal family had taken refuge in a French stronghold on the frontiers, such as Valenciennes or Montmédy, three armies were to converge on Paris. One was to march via Lyon from Savoy, and the others from Lorraine and Brabant. This was with the financial and military support of the realms of the other branches of the Bourbon family: Sardinia-Piedmont (25,000 men and 6 to 7 million livres), Naples and Spain (8 million livres), as well as German princes who had had lands in Alsace-Lorraine: the Duke of Zweibrücken (Deux-Ponts in French), Margrave of Baden and Prince of Hesse, who would provide 10,000 men.

It seems that Louis XVI sanctioned the project, and although it did not originate from the Comte d'Artois and the Prince de Condé, they were associated with it. Until the summer of 1791, both considered it viable with the support of the regiments that remained faithful and gentlemen who were expected to rally en masse to the King. In addition to securing Lyon as a base for the march on Paris, it relied on an invasion by foreign troops which the Comte de Vaudreuil, an intimate friend of the Comte d'Artois, had already warned against as early as September 1789; 'Foreign troops would frighten the kingdom instead of rallying it to the good cause; and all good Frenchmen would have a well-founded repugnance of rallying to foreigners.'[37] Thus a manifesto would have to be published in France to coincide with the start of the campaign. This was to be based on the declaration read at the royal session of 23 June 1789, so recognising concessions made by Louis XVI. However, the planning, or rather the scheming, became unstuck as the Kingdoms of Spain and Sardinia-Piedmont would not engage with the project. In the end, all that was achieved was some correspondence and activity of an emissary,

37 Jospeh-Hyacinthe-François de Paule de Rigaud comte de Vaudreuil, *Correspondance intime du comte d Vaudreuil et du comte d'Artois pendant l'émigration (1789–1815)* (Paris: Librairie Plon, 1889), vol.I, p.16; also see p.28 and 38.

the Chevalier de Bonne-Savardin, formerly a *lieutenant-colonel* in the Légion de Maillebois.

As early as 28 July 1789, the National Assembly had created a reporting committee, which was later renamed the comité des recherches, responsible for investigating and preventing disturbances in the provinces. On 25 August, the Paris Commune followed suit and created a police committee, also known as the comité des recherches, to monitor mail and carry out investigations, the results of which were sent to the National Assembly's committee. Soon, these committees concentrated on activities that were detrimental to the security of the nation, namely those of the nobility. Crimes committed by the people were ignored, being considered politically expedient or justifiable. Bonne-Savardin was denounced to the Parisian comité des recherches in March 1790, and his correspondence revealed the names of those implicated in the plot. These included the Interior Minister, the Comte de Saint-Priest, and the Comte de La Châtre, first gentleman of the Comte de Provence, *maréchal de camp* and a deputy of the nobility in the Estates-General. However, the authorities considered the plan so contemptible and improbable that Bonne-Savardin was finally released in March 1791.

In September 1789 the Comte d'Artois had sought asylum at Turin with Victor Amadeus III, King of Sardinia-Piedmont, who was not only his father-in-law but also that of his brother, Provence, and their sister, Marie-Adélaïde-Clotilde-Xavière de France, known as Madame Clotilde. He was immediately joined by the Prince de Condé who was included in an advisory cabinet formed by Artois.[38] Soon, there was a colony of French émigrés in Turin and the surrounding area, numbering about 150 gentlemen with their families by the end of January 1791. Their activities, and those of Artois's entourage, were reported to Louis XVI and his ministers by the Duc de Choiseul, the French ambassador.

The presence of Artois and Condé at Turin meant that, for the time being, all invasion or counter-revolutionary projects were centred on the east or south-east of France and, to a lesser extent, the Spanish frontier. Furthermore, in the spring of 1790, the first initiatives to organise royalist, counter-revolutionary military resources appeared. As the Comte d'Espinchal noted:

> It was some weeks ago [in May 1790] that four gentlemen from Auvergne, included were the Comte de Fargues and the Comte de Bosredon, came here to assure the Princes of the good dispositions of all the nobility and give them their word, that at the slightest notice on their part, all the Auvergne gentlemen would render themselves under their orders and at the place indicated to them.[39]

The Comte de Bussy, a native of Beaujolais and formerly a *major* attached to the Lorraine-dragons, had organised a mounted body called the Volontaires de Bourbon in the Mâcon region to protect the nobles' properties. When he

38 Louis-Antoine-Henri de Bourbon Duc d'Enghien, *Mémoires et Voyage de Monseigneur le duc d'Enghien* (Moulins: P-A. Desrosiers, 1841), p.247.

39 Jean Martial Champflour (ed.), *La Coalition d'Auvergne, Avril 1791. Carnet du Comte d'Espinchal* (Riom: Imprimerie U. Jouvet, 1899), p.45.

went to Turin to pay his respects to Artois, the latter had ordered him, 'to augment his unit, intended for an enterprise that the Princes were to attempt on Lyon.'[40] The city was to be taken as envisaged in the Maillebois plot and this was considered viable as the commander at Lyon, the Comte de La Chapelle, felt he could rely upon the troops in garrison. In addition, a significant part of the city's population was considered to be royalist.[41] However, Bussy was arrested:

> On 12 October, the municipal officers of Valence learned that two young men had had uniforms made different from those of the National Guards. They asked M. Dupuis, tailor, who declared to have made green coats with green piping, and to which they had reserved to put on the buttons themselves. The municipality then learned that MM. Blin and Borry, former gendarmes, who had had these coats made, had left at night to go to the Château de Villers, the home of M. de Bussi [sic], to arm themselves from head to toe, to join other persons, and march, two hundred in number, towards Besançon, where M. d'Autichamp commands. It was also said that three armies from neighbouring powers were to enter France at the same time, go to Paris, and kidnap the King and dissolve the National Assembly …[42]

When arrested at his château, 'Weapons, balls and eighty pounds of powder were found. Part of the troops, stationed outside and at the rear, seized a trunk that the servants had thrown out of the window, and in which were six new uniform coats, absolutely similar to those the Valence tailor had made.'[43] When questioned, Bussy admitted planning, 'to form a company of fifteen men to defend his château which, like several others in the neighbourhood, was threatened with being set on fire.'[44] A letter from Borrie was also found, in which he stated that, after having been accused of being a counter-revolutionary in Lyon, he was preparing to flee France to take refuge at Chambéry and he invited Bussy to join him. Bussy was transferred to Paris for questioning. However, the authorities did not recognise the links between the different actors and so were unable to believe the veracity of such a plot. After all the only evidence found revealed a planned invasion by Bussy with eight uniforms, of which only two owners were known, a few weapons and some powder. The Assembly had to avoid ridicule to protect the position of the Monarchiens.

Nevertheless, the princes were on the verge of embarking on their venture, even without the support of foreign powers, but then:

> … a formal order came from the King, brought by M. de Bourcet, to undertake nothing and, on the same day, the report that everything had been discovered at Lyon by the imprudence and levity of overly young emissaries sent into the city;

40 Grouvel, *Troupes de l'émigration*, vol.II, p.171.

41 Théodore César Muret, *Histoire de l'Armée de Condé* (Paris: Bureau de la Mode, 1844), vol.I, p.3.

42 Armand Sigismond Comte de Sérent, 'Discussion sur l'arrestation de M. de Bussy, lors de la séance du 26 octobre 1790', *Archives Parlementaires de la Révolution Français*, 1885, No.20, pp.45–46.

43 Sérent, 'Discussion sur l'arrestation de M. de Bussy', pp.45–46.

44 Sérent, 'Discussion sur l'arrestation de M. de Bussy', pp.45–46.

> a large number of persons were arrested … About 200 gentlemen from Auvergne had come to Lyon, on the day indicated. Several were imprisoned, then, soon released, but after this outbreak, they could not return to their province and had to emigrate.[45]

The Queen wrote to her brother, Leopold:

> Louis XVI, frightened of the danger of such a sudden impulse, sent M. de Jarjayes to Turin, bearer of letters for the King of Sardinia and the Comte d'Artois, in which he formally informed them that if they persisted in their designs, he would be obliged to openly disavow them and to call all his still faithful subjects to tranquillity and obedience.[46]

The volunteers who had to leave France were mainly from Auvergne and Dauphiné and went, 'to different towns, to Chambéry, Geneva, Fribourg, Bern, etc.'[47] Once in Savoy and Switzerland, they formed what can be considered the first unit of the military emigration.

That the plan for the King and royal family to flee to a frontier stronghold was not dead is confirmed by Monsieur, the Comte de Provence, who was still in Paris:

> The rumours, that spread in November 1790, of the King's imminent escape, had made me consider my own … the rumours dissipated, and as one might expect, we postponed the execution of the plan until a more favourable moment; I spoke about it to the Queen, who assured me that neither the King nor her had given any basis to this news; but she added that sooner or later it would surely come, promised to warn me in time, and advised me to be always ready.[48]

Queen Marie-Antoinette was hostile to Provence as well as Artois and Condé. They had hoped that after an uprising at Lyon and a march on the capital to dissolve the Assembly, Louis would have no other choice than to join them and lead the still loyal troops to reconquer his kingdom. The King's pusillanimity led to the first measures being made against the émigrés when it was demanded that the Sardinia-Piedmont court expel Artois and Condé. Furthermore, on 22 December, the National Assembly adopted a decree, ratified by the King the day after Christmas, obliging émigrés to return to the nation's territory in order to take the civic oath; failure to do so would see them deprived of their employment, rank, pensions and other emoluments. However, the unpunished murders of officers and other nobles that year foretold the fate of any who returned to France.

---

45 Champflour (ed.), *Coalition d'Auvergne*, pp.29–30.

46 Maxime de La Rocheterie, *Marie-Antoinette et l'émigration d'après documents inédits* (Paris: Charles Douniol et cie., 1875), p.24, Marie-Antoinette to Leopold II, 19 December 1790.

47 Champflour (ed.), *Coalition d'Auvergne*, p.45.

48 Louis XVIII, *Relation d'un voyage à Bruxelles et à Coblentz (1791)* (Paris: Baudouin Frères, 1823), p.1.

It was at this time that Artois was joined by his former protégé, Charles-Alexandre de Calonne, who had been controller-general of finances from 1783 to 1787, after which he had lived in England. As well as his talents, he brought his wife's immense fortune to the Prince, so immediately improving his financial position. From then on, Calonne was to be at the centre of Artois's private council. On 1 January 1791, before quitting Turin to go to Venice, Artois wrote to Emperor Leopold II, hoping for his support and to be received at Vienna. However, the latter rejected the requests and even refused to see Calonne as an emissary. Leopold considered the émigrés' projects extravagant and dangerous, and they undermined the sovereignty of both Louis XVI, his brother-in-law, and his sister, Marie-Antoinette. Artois was to be hindered from repeating the Lyon adventure, as nothing should be done without the King. Feigning acceptance, Artois agreed to distance himself from Condé, seen by some as his evil, warmongering, genius.

Condé left Turin on 6 January 1791, travelling northwards through Savoy and Switzerland to the Rhine. On his way, the Prince encountered French émigré gentlemen who sought his leadership and offered their services.

> Thursday 13th, I was very surprised to learn that twenty-five gentlemen not trusting the inhabitants of Carouge [a Sardinia-Piedmont city near Geneva] very much, had spent the night in my anteroom to guard me …
>
> Monday 17th … arrived at noon a league from Fribourg where we found around twenty gentlemen who came by horse before us … I arrived there a little before one o'clock, I got off at an inn, where I found about sixty gentlemen waiting for me …
>
> Sunday 23rd, I did not leave my house until two o'clock, I gave dinner to the Auvergne gentlemen, an excellent race, full of honour, courage, and disinterestedness, never reasoning, knowing how to abandon themselves to their leaders, and devoted to the blood of the Bourbons …[49]

At the end of the month, Condé reached Stuttgart, where he received a lukewarm reception from the Duke of Württemberg, who was threatened by the French National Assembly and feared a popular uprising as revolutionary ideas seeped from France. Nevertheless, the French princes could now switch the focus of their counter-revolutionary activities from northern Italy to the banks of the Rhine. On 10 December 1790, the Treaty of The Hague put an end to the adventure of the Republic of the United Belgian States. On 19 December, the Austrians were back in Brussels, and, on 12 January 1791, they entered the Principality of Liège, allowing the Prince-Bishop to return to power.

Meanwhile, due to the lack of evidence of the Comte de Bussy participating in the Lyon affair, he was released on 5 January 1791 and joined his wife in Chambéry. There he wrote to the Comte d'Artois to announce his resolution to raise a corps of cavalry, to be named the Chevaliers de la Couronne, for the service of the princes. Artois replied to him from Venice on 1 February,

49 Condé, *Journal*, pp.175–176, 178.

assuring him of his support. Baron de Vitrolles, aged 15, joined the corps at its formation as a standard-bearer, with the rank of officer.

> The corps of Chevaliers de la Couronne, in which I served, had been formed in Savoy by the attention of Comte de Bussy. He had collected around 400 young men [150 to 160 at that time, 400 being the strength at the end of 1793 when Vitrolles began his memoirs], mainly from the provinces of Dauphiné, Provence, Auvergne, Velay, Lyon and the surrounding lands. He had obtained authorisation from the King of Sardinia to form this corps at Le Bourget, near Chambéry. M. de Bussy had made some expenditure for general expenses, but each of us had purchased our horses, our equipment, and, at the beginning, we received no pay. In M. de Bussy's mind, we were intended to furnish a corps of the King's household. The simple chevaliers had the rank of second lieutenant, which gave the officers of the corps superior ranks.[50]

In February, the Prince de Condé moved to Worms, as was reported to Mirabeau, 'The Elector of Mainz has lent the episcopal palace of Worms to the Prince de Condé for six weeks; it is M. de La Tour, former colonel of the Régiment de Royal-Liégeois, who performed the negotiation.'[51] It was there, on 1 March, that he was joined by two gentlemen from Poitou, one of whom was Louis Marquis Aymer de la Chevalerie.[52] The Prince authorised them to stay with him, 'The Marquis d'Avisart, capitaine in the Régiment de Condé [dragoons], had them admitted to the table of the gentlemen who responded, like them, to the prince's appeal; and Louis Aymer is the 24th who registered.'[53] From 17 March 1791, a guard was established for Condé and his family.

> A rumour had spread that the National Guard from Landau wanted to come to remove us (I believe that this rumour had no basis); some unknown persons were seen lurking around the castle, one of them was seen in the castle itself, well known as a revolutionary and friend of the Duc d'Orléans: it did not take more for the decision of all the gentlemen who surrounded us to want to guard us: they determined between themselves that there would be ten on guard day and night, that they would post sentries and make patrols ... and from that day this guard was established.[54]

The émigrés movement northwards to the banks of the Rhine was given further impetus as revolutionary propaganda gained traction in Savoy. The Marquis de Marcillac, a young *capitaine* in the cavalry Régiment de Royal-Picardie who had emigrated the month before, remembered:

---

50 Eugène-François-Auguste-Arnaud Baron de Vitrolles, *Souvenirs autobiographiques d'un émigré* (Paris: Emile-Paul Frères, 1924), p.44.

51 Ad. de Bacourt (ed.), *Correspondance entre le comte de Mirabeau et le comte de La Marck pendant les années 1789, 1790 et 1791* (Paris: Librairie Ve Le Normant, 1851), vol.III, p.66.

52 Henri Carré (ed.), *Journal d'émigration de Louis, marquis Aymer de la Chevalerie (1791-1797)* (Poitiers: Société française d'imprimerie et de librairie, 1933), p.787.

53 Carré (ed.), *Journal d'émigration*, p.789

54 Condé, *Journal*, p.191.

> The people of Chambéry insulted the French who wore the white cockade: they had resolved to have it removed; and, to achieve this, threats against all those who wore it were posted up on every street corner. Far from being intimidated by this provocation, the French émigrés affected to show this sign of loyalty. On Sunday, the day designated for the insurrection against the royalists, the rebels gathered in the main square, three hundred in number, around eight o'clock in the evening.[55]

The same month saw the birth of another armed body of the emigration. On 10 April 1791, at Fribourg in Switzerland, the Comte d'Espinchal (senior) opened 'the Estates General of the coalition of Gentlemen composing the companies of Auvergne and of the Gentlemen adhering to the Coalition.'[56]

All the while, the situation in France deteriorated and, on 14 April, Condé learned of the insurrection of the infantry Régiment de Beauvoisis at Wissembourg, in which the officers fought for more than four hours against 700 mutinous soldiers. Five days later, the Prince was joined by the regiment's *colonel*, Comte Alexandre de Damas, and 27 of its officers; in recognition of his conduct, the Prince appointed Damas as his first equerry.[57]

On 13 April, the Pope condemned the Civil Constitution of the Clergy as schismatic and heretical and five days later, the Garde Nationale prevented Louis XVI from leaving the Tuileries to attend Easter mass celebrated by so-called refractory priests at Saint-Cloud. This illustrated how weak the King's position now was, as, although decreed on 12 July 1790, he had still not ratified the Civil Constitution. On 4 May, the National Assembly decreed the assimilation of the papal enclaves of Avignon and the Comtat Venaissin into the Kingdom of France.

Marcillac and two companions were attacked during the disorder at Chambéry, and, although the insurrection was soon quelled, he, like many others among the émigrés, left Savoy for Germany, arriving at Worms around 10 May.

> My first care was to have myself presented to my lord the Prince de Condé, to the Ducs de Bourbon and d'Enghien. I was inscribed on the list of honour: I was the sixtieth. This list was soon increased to a hundred, and such was the exaltation of the moment of reaching this number of a hundred, the list was closed, and we declared unanimously, as dishonoured and unworthy to serve the King, anyone who was not inscribed on this sacred register of which we all took a copy in legal form … The hundred valorous men organised themselves; and the Emperor of Austria having forbidden armed gatherings, we were content to practice cavalry manoeuvres, as we were all mounted. Only a guard was established for security at the castle that the princes occupied, but for weapons we only had our sabres and pistols.[58]

55 Pierre-Louis-Auguste de Crusy de Marcillac, *Mémoires de l'émigration (1791–1800)* (Paris: Librairie de Firmin-Didot et Cie., 1897), p.90.

56 Champflour (ed.), *La Coalition d'Auvergne*, p.47.

57 Grouvel, *Troupes de l'émigration*, vol.II, p.247.

58 Marcillac, *Mémoires*, pp.93–94.

This was an example of a nobility that was ever jealous of their honour, to the extent that they would exclude those who arrived later to serve the same cause. The refusal to reopen the list, undoubtedly inspired by the example of the Coalition d'Auvergne, meant, for example, that the *colonel* of the Régiment de la Reine cavalry was turned away, having arrived shortly after some of his own officers.

There was soon a desire for the gentlemen to be organised more formally, as Condé found on 17 April:

> … in the evening, I received a deputation to ask me to form them into a corps, and to allow the guard to be increased. With regard to the first request, I thought it necessary to avoid it, to await the arrival or at least certain news of the progress of the Comte d'Artois, and so to grant something, I agreed to allow an increase in the guard by two or three more gentlemen.[59]

When, on 18 May, the Elector of Mainz dined with the Prince, he found 150 gentlemen around the Prince de Condé.

Meanwhile, the Comte d'Artois had finally obtained an interview with Emperor Leopold II at Mantua on 17 May. The following day, the latter announced, in the Declaration of Pavia, his intention to act in concert with other European powers to oppose the policies of the French Revolution, which amounted to a thinly veiled threat of war. Having obtained a promise from Artois that he would not try anything unilaterally, Leopold agreed that he could establish himself at Koblenz, with his maternal uncle, the Elector of Trier, Clément Wenceslas, Duc de Saxe. Despite the rhetoric, none of the protagonists were ready for war. However, diplomatic manoeuvring may have been effective in the past, between sovereign states subject to the system established by the Peace of Westphalia, but it was unknown how the new French regime would react. New political forces wished to wipe clean the slate of the past and to make the revolutionary process irreversible by exporting it to neighbouring states by force of arms, knowing that support would be found among sections of their populations.

Artois established himself at Koblenz in the Schönbornslust, a palace that the Prince-Bishop had put at his disposal, and then on 12 June, joined by the three Condés, he went to Mainz where he was greeted in a manner worthy of the brother of the King of France, '… the troops under arms, the noise of the cannons, a great throng of people, the Elector on the bank with all his Court, the three of us at the head of four hundred gentlemen, all this formed the most magnificent and touching sight.'[60]

On 17 June, the Prince of Condé was informed of the 'Law relating to the oath to be taken by officers of all ranks, & Soldiers of the French army, & containing in addition provisions specific to the former Prince of Condé. Given at Paris, on 15 June 1791.'[61] Then four days later, he received

59 Condé, *Journal*, p.196.
60 Condé, *Journal*, p.206.
61 Anon., *Loi relative au serment à prêter par les officiers de tous grades, & Soldats de l'Armée Françoise, & contenant en outre des dispositions particulières au ci-devant Prince de Condé* (Rouen; L. Oursel, 1791).

a messenger on behalf of the King bearing two letters, one private and the other official. The first conveyed the King's request that he either return to France or move away from its frontiers. The second contained details of the decree, the relevant articles being:

> XVI
>
> The National Assembly decrees that its president will withdraw during the day to the King, to ask him to with the briefest delay notify Louis-Joseph de Bourbon-Condé, that his residence near the frontiers, surrounded by persons whose the intentions are notoriously suspect, affirms guilty projects.
>
> XVII
>
> That calculating from this declaration having been notified to him, Louis-Joseph de Bourbon-Condé will be required to return to the kingdom, within fifteen days, or to distance himself from the frontiers while declaring, in the latter case, that he will never undertake anything against the Constitution decreed by the National Assembly & accepted by the King, nor against the tranquillity of the State.
>
> XVIII
>
> And with the failure of Louis-Joseph de Bourbon-Condé to return to the Kingdom, or distancing himself from it, to make the declaration expressed above, within the fortnight of the notification, the National Assembly declares him a rebel, deprived of all rights to the Crown, renders him responsible for all hostile actions that could be directed against France on the frontier; decrees that his assets will be sequestered, and that all correspondence & communication with him or with his accomplices & adherents will remain prohibited to all French citizens without distinction, on pain of being prosecuted & punished as traitors to the country; & in the event that he presents himself armed on the territory of France, orders any citizen to chase him down, & to seize his person as well as that of his accomplices & adherents.[62]

Then on 24 June, Condé was with Artois at Schönbornslust when they received the unexpected news that the King, Queen and the royal family had left Paris. Both had been kept in the dark about the plans as the Queen did not trust them, as she had told her brother, 'The Princes, the Comte d'Artois and all those who surround him, absolutely want to act, they have no real means at all, and will lose us. Their indiscretion and the men who lead them mean that, until the last moment, they will not have our secret.'[63]

A few hours later, a messenger from Monsieur, the Comte de Provence, informed them that he, having left an hour after the King, was safe and well at Mons. However, in compliance with orders he would not specify, he would not be joining his brother. The King took the route through Champagne seeking to reach Montmédy, a stronghold on the frontier, in compliance with his determination not to leave his kingdom, even briefly. Soon, however, it

62 Anon., *Loi relative au serment 1791*.

63 Louis-Philippe, *Mémoires* (Paris: Editions Librairie Plon, 1973), vol.I, p.221, letter from Marie-Antoinette to Emperor Leopold, 22 May 1791.

was learned that the royal family had been arrested at Varennes-en-Argonne, which was confirmed the following day, 25 June, by an aide-de-camp of the Marquis de Bouillé who, after the failure of the King's escape, had retired to Luxembourg. The King, along with the royal family, was being escorted by the Garde Nationale back to Paris, where he would henceforth be kept under ever closer surveillance.

The King's escape from Paris had failed. However, that of Provence marks the end of the first phase of the emigration, which had, at first, been carefree and frivolous before becoming more political and militant, even conspiratorial. The second phase was to be strictly military, an expression of the outbreak of a civil war aimed at expurgating or eliminating the supporters of the old order.

For all, it had become increasingly difficult to leave France. The National Assembly, itself, preferred to see those who might resist disorder and violence, something that was increasingly dangerous as the Jacobin party grew in strength, quit France. However, municipalities on the major roads to the frontiers assumed the right to control these routes, even contesting the validity of passports granted by the King and the city of Paris. This ranged from simple administrative harassment to complicity with Sans-Culottes who, in the name of the Nation, robbed or terrorised the unfortunate travellers one last time. This forced emigration to be clandestine with subterfuge to conceal identities and nationalities. Indeed, Provence, the future King Louis XVIII, travelled abroad with his friend, the Comte d'Avaray, posing as English merchants.

He had to leave on 20 June as there would be no opportunity to do so once the King and Queen had fled. Louis informed him that the royal family was leaving for Montmédy and ordered him to go to Longwy to wait to be called to his side. After some adventures, Provence arrived at Mons at dawn on 22 June, where he was reunited with his mistress, Madame de Balbi, along with his first gentleman, the Comte de La Châtre. Considering that Longwy may not be safe, he decided to go to Luxembourg to await news from Montmédy, and it was on the way that he was told that the King's flight had failed. Once he had further information about what had happened, he requested his younger brother, Artois, to meet him in Brussels.

News of the failure of the King's flight, his arrest and detention in Paris, effectively a prisoner at the Tuileries, caused consternation in the army.

> The officers of the regiments garrisoned in Flanders rendered themselves with their flags to the Netherlands, those of the Colonel Général [from Dunkirk] to Bruges, those of Auxerrois to Tournai, those of the Chasseurs de Gévaudan to Mons. They brought with them a large number of soldiers; but they did not want to receive these at the frontier, and it was with great difficulty that the government received the officers. They were given Ath as their assembly quarters and M. de La Châtre was sent to command them.[64]

64 Daudet (ed.), *Esterhazy*, p.302.

In Brussels, Artois and Provence could now act as princes of France, holding an audience for the French community who came to present their respects. The two brothers then left on 3 July for Aachen, where the Swedish King Gustav III was waiting for them. Gustav had known, apparently in confidence, of the King's flight and had come to offer his help. From there, the princes travelled to Koblenz, where they arrived on 7 July, establishing themselves at the palace of Schönbornslust that became the heart of the counter-revolution. The day before, Leopold II had released a new threatening declaration from Padua, inviting other sovereigns to join him in regarding the King's cause as their own and demanding his release, refusing to recognise as legitimate any law to which Louis XVI had not voluntarily consented. He, as well as Gustav and Catherine of Russia, were convinced that the French Revolution now posed a threat to the rest of Europe. The arrest of the King, the insults he and the royal family were subjected to, including their detention, the collapse of the royal army and the measures taken against the Church, now made the recourse to arms inevitable.

2

Inevitable or Planned Chaos?

July 1791–August 1792

The Beginnings of the Counter-revolutionary Crusade

When Emperor Leopold met Artois at Mantua on 10 May 1791, the latter had unveiled an extravagant project devised by Calonne to form a coalition to march on Paris. This was to be accompanied by a declaration holding the citizens responsible for the royal family's safety, threatening terrible reprisals should they be subjected to violence. Austria was asked for 35,000 men, plus 4 million francs and the Swiss Cantons, Sardinia-Piedmont and Spain were to each provide 15,000 men. In addition, Britain and Prussia were to be persuaded to support the coalition, which was to be ready to march on 15 July precisely. So, to be rid of Artois, the Emperor granted him a million and a half livres to establish himself at Koblenz. When the news of this meeting reached Paris on 2 June, Marie-Antoinette was fearful of some madness on the part of the émigrés. She warned her brother that the situation was forcing Louis to rush their escape, which had been postponed several times since the beginning of the year.

The royal couple's plan was to get to Montmédy, where Bouillé's troops, faithful subjects, still loyal regiments and the noble volunteers who were with the King's brothers would assemble. With this support, Louis XVI would retake the throne but above all demonstrate his regained freedom and therefore his ability to act on his own initiative. With this in mind, Marie-Antoinette had asked her brother to provide 8,000 to 10,000 Austrian troops, 'for the first moment' and to guarantee the security of Montmédy.[1] In the worst-case scenario, the royal family could seek sanctuary at nearby Luxembourg thanks to the presence of such troops.

Until now Leopold had other geopolitical tensions and competitions among the European powers to be concerned with, particularly the Polish

1 La Rocheterie, *Marie-Antoinette*, p.39.

question that had already seen Prussia, Russia and Austria strip the Polish-Lithuanian Commonwealth of approximately a third of its territory and its population in the First Partition of 1772. On 11 June Leopold met the King of Prussia, to discuss these issues as well as events in France and, the following day, he sought to reassure his sister not only about his own actions, but also those to restrain the émigrés:

> I agreed firstly that, in the event that you with the King were at liberty, we would all act immediately, but that otherwise we would not act and that we would dispose Spain to prepare a helping hand and to concert itself with the King of Sardinia and the Swiss, and with the Empire, to be able, if the case required, and you and the King agree and approve it, to publish, in due time, the manifesto, not in July, as the Comte d'Artois says, but when everything would be anticipated and prepared in concert, if the case required it. In the meantime, I answer you that nothing will be done, no demonstration, no manifesto, no troops to march, neither on my side nor that of the Comte d'Artois; because, for the Prince de Condé, I cannot answer.[2]

The Queen particularly distrusted Condé, who, for his part, suspected her of having a role in the failure of the Lyon affair the previous year. Fear of a unilateral initiative from the latter had pushed Marie-Antoinette to decide that her husband should wait no longer; indeed, only a succession of contrary events had postponed the project of fleeing Paris until 20 June. When he finally departed, Louis XVI left a document, addressed to the Assembly, protesting about the attacks on his sovereignty. He also reminded them of the concessions that he had already declared himself ready to negotiate on 23 June 1789 in response to the grievances expressed by the Third Estate, agreeing to renounce, in return for the Assembly's submission, any form of despotism, and therefore the French model of absolute monarchy by divine right. News of the flight of the royal family was confused:

> One was for some time in the dark before knowing the true result of the attempt of 21 June. The happy arrival of Monsieur and Madame [the wife of the Comte de Provence] in Mons had initially led people to believe in a similar success for the King and his family. Then the rumour of the arrest in Varennes spread; but it was added that M. de Bouillé had arrived at the head of his troops, rescued the King and led him to Metz in the midst of his army; as for the Queen, she had withdrawn to Luxembourg.[3]

On 5 July, Leopold wrote to his sister to congratulate her on the happy outcome, 'Everything that is mine is yours; money, troops, everything. My sister [Archduchess Maria Christina] and Mercy have all the necessary orders to make any manifesto, declaration, movement and march of troops that you may order'.[4] Then came the news that the royal family had been arrested at

2 La Rocheterie, *Marie-Antoinette*, letter of 12 June, p.37.
3 La Rocheterie, *Marie-Antoinette*, p 43.
4 La Rocheterie, *Marie-Antoinette*, p.43.

Varennes and returned to Paris, the Emperor resolved to approach the main powers – Spain, Russia, Britain, Prussia, Sardinia-Piedmont and Naples – and ask them to join him in addressing a common manifesto against the Assembly. The same day, he also informed Maria Christina of his resolution to oppose revolutionary excesses, 'I flatter myself of preventing them. If I do not succeed, I will avenge them exemplarily.'[5]

Leopold's change of heart was due to Gustav III of Sweden proposing to take the lead in the counter-revolutionary crusade, alongside the Empress of Russia and the German princes, as well as the King's brothers. In addition, on 5 July, Gustav proposed that Monsieur take the title of Regent and constitute a government to deal with the other powers, in the name of his brother, who was no longer able to act; 'The name of regent, said he, will save Monsieur and all French people attached to their duty, from the imputation of revolt with which the Assembly will not fail to wish to sully them. It will not be Frenchmen who will fight Frenchmen, but loyal subjects who will attack rebels to rescue their oppressed sovereign.'[6]

In a letter of 9 July, Gustav revealed his project to Catherine the Great, from whom he sought a contingent of 6,000 to 8,000 men. He, with 16,000 men and, 'the imperial troops 35,000 men strong, were to enter France through Flanders, while 12,000 Swiss would invade through Franche-Comté, 15,000 men under the orders of the King of Sardinia-Piedmont, by Dauphiné; the princes of the empire, through Alsace and Breisgau, and that 20,000 Spaniards would cross the Pyrenees.'[7] As for Britain, its neutrality would be secured by giving it free rein to help itself to the French colonies in the West Indies, but also to authorise Hanoverian troops to join those of the Empire. In addition, Leopold was to negotiate for Prussian troops from Westphalia to join those of the other sovereigns. Furthermore, it has been alleged that, while at Aachen in July, Gustav and Condé consulted on a similar plan that respected King Louis's wish to secure a French stronghold as the springboard to reconquer his throne. In this case, the place was to be Dieppe, secured by a 'maritime expedition led by Gustav IIII on the coasts of Normandy, while the émigrés and their allies would make forced marches on Paris to deliver the King, such was this plan which then offered every chance of success.'[8] However, Leopold showed that he considered Louis's plan to regain his throne alone, without leaving French soil, dead and buried, finished by the King himself in his botched attempt to escape.

Royalists received the news of the arrest of the royal family at Varennes in a variety of ways. Some, like Bouillé, were in despair but the majority of émigrés considered that it vindicated their views. Now was the time for those who had refused to recognise or support them to join them in taking energetic steps to stem the revolutionary flood that was going to submerge Europe. Whether these were to be by diplomacy or war, the émigrés convinced

---

5 La Rocheterie, *Marie-Antoinette*, Letter of 12 June, p.59.

6 La Rocheterie, *Marie-Antoinette*, Letter of 6 July, p.49.

7 La Rocheterie, *Marie-Antoinette*, p.49.

8 Jacques Crétineau-Joly, *Histoire des trois derniers Princes de la Maison de Condé* (Paris: Imprimerie Lahure, 1867), vol.I, p.62.

The royal family returns from Varennes, print 1791. (Public Domain)

themselves that they would be a party to them. Thus, incorporating the influx of officers and other royalists leaving the kingdom, they continued to form their first units, even if such forces may seem symbolic or contemptible.

On 26 June 1791, Bouillé sent a letter to the National Assembly explaining his position.

> I wanted to save my fatherland; I wanted to save my King, his family: that is my only crime. You will answer for their days, I do not tell myself but all the kings, and I announce to you that, if one hair is taken from their heads, before long no stone will remain on top of another in Paris. I know the roads, I will guide foreign armies to them, and on your own heads you yourselves will be responsible for it.[9]

Nevertheless, he was fully aware of the real state of France and its troops, rather than the deluded ideas of those at Koblenz. In particular he recognised the spirit of revolt shared by the soldiers and people, those who had no vote, who would refuse to give up the first achievements of the Revolution. So, on 9 July, he warned the princes.

9 La Rocheterie, *Marie-Antoinette*, p.68.

> If one believes one can reestablish the former order of things, if the nobility thinks to regain all its privileges, the parlements to recover their authority, the clergy its wealth in full and its prerogatives, the government its independence, one deludes oneself. Sacrifices have become necessary, if they want to recover and preserve, not only their own existence, but that of the kingdom.[10]

However, the failure of the King's flight and its consequences, such as the final suppression of the Gardes du Corps on 25 June,[11] soon drove officers and gentlemen, by the hundreds, then thousands, over the frontiers of the Kingdom of France. In the eyes of such men, from this point on, to refuse to follow the path of honour amounted to condoning the excesses of the Revolution and even to becoming an accomplice to the revolutionary chaos which aimed to create a new order.

While Leopold began to establish an armed coalition, he feared unilateral action by the émigrés. On 30 July, he warned his sister, Archduchess Maria Christina, in the Austrian Netherlands:

> Believe nothing, do not let yourself be drawn into anything, and do not do anything that the French and the princes ask you, other than courtesies and dinners; yet neither troops, nor money, nor security for them. I really pity their situation and that of all the French who have had to emigrate; but they only think of their romantic ideas and their revenge and personal interests, believing that everyone must sacrifice themselves for them …[12]

Leopold recognised that his former enemy, Prussia, would henceforth have to be a close ally, like Sweden and Russia. So, a meeting of various powers was proposed to discuss Poland and France at Pillnitz, near Dresden in Saxony, and the parties arrived there on 25 August. Present were the King of Prussia and his ministers, and the Prince of Nassau-Siegen, representative of the Empress of Russia, as well as Bouillé, charged with full powers by Monsieur, and Artois, who had conferred beforehand with Condé. Calonne accompanied Bouillé. The conference took place the following day in the presence of the Emperor. The discussion about France centred around two areas: the first was the pursuit of Leopold's initiative by issuing a cautionary manifesto aimed above all at ensuring the freedom of the royal family, and the second was the curbing of the émigrés' aspirations. Thus, Monsieur was not to be recognised as regent, as it would have acknowledged, even sanctioned, the political impotence of the French King. Furthermore, the émigrés were not to take any form of political initiative or raise troops until sanctioned by the Emperor. The Pillnitz Manifesto was published on 27 August:

---

10 La Rocheterie, *Marie-Antoinette*, p.55.

11 Anon., *Table générale par ordre alphabétique des matières des lois, sénatus-consultes, décrets, arrêtés, avis du Conseil d'Etat, etc. publiés publiés dans le Bulletin des Lois* (…) (Paris: Imprimerie royale, 1816), vol.I, p.178.

12 La Rocheterie, *Marie-Antoinette*, p.60.

> His Majesty the Emperor and His Majesty the King of Prussia, having heard the desires and representations of Monsieur and the Comte d'Artois, jointly declare that they regard the situation in which His Majesty the King of France currently finds himself as an object of interest to all the sovereigns of Europe. They hope that this interest cannot fail to be recognised by the powers from whom assistance is called for; that as a consequence, they will not refuse to use, with their aforementioned Majesties, the most relatively effective means, to put the King of France in a position to strengthen, in the most perfect freedom, the foundations of monarchical government, equally suitable to the rights of sovereigns and the well-being of the French nation. Then, and in this case, their aforementioned Majesties the Emperor and the King of Prussia are resolved to act promptly by mutual accord, with the forces necessary to obtain the proper and common good. In the meantime, they will give their troops the appropriate orders so that they will be ready to mobilise.[13]

If many of their demands had been thwarted, the émigrés had every reason to be satisfied. On the other hand, they knew it would provide the extremist party in France with an opportunity. With France at war, exceptional internal measures could be driven through in order to save the Revolution and justify the total mobilisation of the nation in arms to oppose the coalition led by Austria and Prussia.

The Constitutional Monarchy and the Triumph of the Jacobins

The flight and forcible return of the King to Paris in June 1791 set the monarchy on an irreversible process of decline, leading both to a new wave of emigration but also, at the same time, to the adoption of the first constitution intended to save the King, along with the Revolution. However, the extremist party henceforth had the objective of attacking the monarchy and removing the supporters of a constitutional monarchy in order to establish a republic.

On the morning of 21 June, as soon as the King's flight had been known, Parisians flocked to the Tuileries Palace. They turned their anger on anything related to the King, Queen, the King's brothers or royalty, as related by Nicolas Ruault, a supporter of the Revolution.

> … wherever one saw the name of King or royal, lampblack, soaked in oil, was spread. In a few hours these words had been removed from all public and private establishments. In the evening, in the garden of the Tuileries, in that of the Palais Royal, people made the most abusive motions at the King and the royalty with a calm and reassured air.[14]

---

13 Pierre Granié, *Histoire de l'Assemblée Constituante de France* (Paris: Chez Desenme, An VI), pp.257–258.

14 Nicolas Ruault, *Gazette d'un parisien sous la Révolution* (Paris: Edition du club France Loisirs, Librairie Académique Perrin, 1976), pp.246–247, letter of 22 June 1791 to his brother. The 400 letters written by Nicolas Ruault, editor and admirer of Voltaire (who had died in 1778), to his brother, a parish priest in Evreux, Normandy, between 1783 and 1796, provide one of the richest testimonies from this period.

The royal family's return, on 24 June, was an opportunity for a formalised demonstration of challenge, even contempt. Everyone kept their hats on, and the Garde Nationale, lining the route to the Tuileries, did not present arms. The procession, with nearly 10,000 troops, halted from time to time to clear the crowd, which was screaming: 'Long live the Law, long live the Nation!'[15]

In the days that followed, commissioners appointed by the Assembly discussed the future of the King as the head of the monarchy and executive. His replacement by the former Duc d'Orléans was ruled out from the outset, as Ruault noted, 'What a fine opportunity for the Duc d'Orléans, if he were loved and esteemed! This is what one gains from having neither talent, courage, nor virtue! He will not be considered to fill the void left by Louis XVI. Mr. d'Orléans is not worthy of it.'[16] Some advocated replacing the King with his son, the Dauphin, surrounded by a regency council. The least-worst solution was to force Louis XVI to accept a constitution as quickly as possible, both in his interests and that of the Revolution, since the free consent of the King would draw the teeth of any coalition as well as the émigrés.

It was expedient to ignore the King's attempted flight, so the story of a trip to Montmédy was adopted. However, the declaration he had left behind on 20 June or Bouillé's letter to the Assembly were not forgotten. Furthermore, Artois had overstepped, as Ruault reported:

> They [the émigrés] were so certain at Worms to have the King in their power, in the last days of June, that the Comte d'Artois, wrote a little too soon and very thoughtlessly on 22 June in the name of his brother the King, an order for the enrolment of soldiers … A circular … dated 23 June invites the soldiers remaining in France to leave the kingdom, to come soonest to join the Princes and serve His Majesty; and to encourage the soldiers' prompt desertion, they are promised rewards of advancement by virtue of the full powers of the King given to Monseigneur, Comte d'Artois.[17]

The King repudiated these circulars on 6 and 7 July, and the Assembly was content to let matters rest and so, as they put it, restore the King to his full powers. The trip became the accepted version, despite the Assembly, at the instigation of La Fayette, having declared on the morning of 21 June that the royal family had been kidnapped by the émigrés.

The political situation in the Assembly, and more widely, was evolving. Until now the supporters of a constitutional monarchy, a moderate revolution, the so-called Monarchiens, including La Fayette, Barnave, Lameth and Bailly, the Mayor of Paris, had dominated the Société des Amis de la Constitution, better known as the club des Jacobins. However, on 16 July 1791, it split into two factions, the former being the Feuillants who were opposed by the increasingly extremist Jacobins, such as Robespierre, Brissot, who would soon become the leading advocates for war, and Danton. The Feuillants wanted a constitution to be adopted as quickly as possible to retain power in

15 Ruault, *Gazette*, p.247.

16 Ruault, *Gazette*, p.246.

17 Ruault, *Gazette*, pp.250–251, letter of 15 July 1791.

the Assembly, where they could look for support from the moribund royalist party. The Jacobins grew closer to the Cordeliers, who were always the most violent, and other groups increasingly hostile to the monarchy, gaining influence across the country through incendiary newspapers, such as Marat's *Ami du Peuple*. Although there were only about 30 Republican deputies, they could mobilise large parts of the disenfranchised population. Therefore, the Jacobins opened a petition on 15 July demanding that the King be deposed. Two days later, it was moved to the Champ de Mars, where the Eiffel Tower now stands, to be signed on the Altar of the Nation that had been used three days earlier for the celebration of the Fête de la Fédération. Thus, the Champ de Mars became the focus for agitation. Faced with the threat of riot, the Assembly ordered Bailly to declare martial law and La Fayette to march on the rioters with several battalions of the Garde Nationale. Bailly was stoned as he tried to parley with the crowd, and La Fayette gave the order to open fire. The exact number killed or wounded is unknown; the official line was that there were 50 deaths, while contemporaries described the violence of the repression, with Ruault writing of 1,200 to 1,500 casualties. This event marked a definitive fissure between the moderates and the so-called democrats.

It was at this time that the main impetus of military emigration occurred. Until 1789, the bond linking every officer to the King was implicit and associated with the brevet he received from the monarch, building upon those already linking gentlemen to the King through the ties of nobility. This tradition had been modified, as has been described, with the Fête de la Fédération of 1790, when the oath was made on the 'Altar of the Fatherland … to be true to the Nation, the Law & the King'.[18] Given the significant level of emigration at the end of spring 1791, the Assembly had decreed that a more explicit oath would be required, by the aforementioned 'Law relating to the oath to be taken by officers of all ranks, & Soldiers of the French army, & containing in addition provisions specific to the former Prince of Condé. Given at Paris, on 15 June 1791'.[19] All active officers were to undertake an oath, 'in their capacity as public officials.'[20] It was worded thus:

> I promise on my honour to be faithful to the Nation, the Law & the King; to not take part either directly or indirectly but on the contrary to oppose with all my strength, any conspiracy, scheme or plot which comes to my knowledge, & which could be directed either against the Nation & the King, or against the Constitution decreed by the National Assembly & accepted by the King; to employ all the means that are confided in me by the Decrees of the National Assembly, accepted or sanctioned by the King, to have them observed by those who are subordinate to me by these same Decrees; consenting, if I fail in this engagement, to be regarded as an infamous man, unworthy to bear arms and to be considered among the number of French citizens. [Article 3][21]

18 *Journal des débats et des décrets*, 2 June 1790 sitting.
19 Anon., *Loi relative au serment 1791.*
20 Anon., *Loi relative au serment 1791*, Article II.
21 *Gazette nationale ou le Moniteur universel*, 12 June 1791.

Punishment for failure to take the oath was prescribed in Article 4:

> On failure on the part of an officer, of whatever rank he be, to comply with the provisions of the preceding articles, within the time limit set for him by the King, he will be deemed discharged by the very fact of his refusal; & as a consequence he will be attributed for a salary on discharge, a quarter of the salary he currently enjoys, unless, in accordance with the Decree of 3 August 1790, he is entitled, by his seniority, to a more considerable salary, in which case this will be granted to him.[22]

Article 5 contained further conciliation:

> The National Assembly, taking into consideration the misfortunes of free men given over to prejudices or guilty suggestions, forbids that any insult or ill-treatment be offered to those who may refuse to comply with the provisions of articles 2 and 3 of this decree, enjoining the guardians of the law and the public force to grant them the protection due to any citizen who does not disturb the order of society.[23]

In effect, to conceal the true number of officers who might refuse to take the oath, the oldest officers were encouraged to retire, and the others would be discharged and replaced. Only after the lists of the officers who refused to take the oath, and of those who would replace them, had been compiled and sent to the ministry, and they had fulfilled the obligation themselves, would the commanders have their units take the oath. Each officer would then receive a letter confirming his rank in the name of the King.

However, the recent events caused, on 22 June, the oath to be replaced by a new one:

> I swear to employ the arms placed in my arms in the defence of the Fatherland, and to maintain, against all its enemies within and without, the Constitution decreed by the National Assembly, to death rather than suffer the invasion of French territory by foreign troops and to only obey the orders that are given in consequence of the decrees of the National Assembly.[24]

This time, there was no mention of the law or the King. For ardent royalists, anyone taking such an oath forsook the very name of gentleman. In the dragoon Régiment de Chartres, known as the 14e Dragoons by the decree of 1 January 1791 (see below), it was implemented by Louis-Philippe, the former Duc de Chartres and eldest son of the Duc d'Orléans, who had been appointed colonel of the regiment in November 1785 at the age of 12 and had taken command of it at Vendôme on 16 June 1791. The new decree arrived in the first days of July, and Chartres made it known to his officers immediately. Only he and seven officiers de fortune took the oath; the other 20 gentlemen officers refused and left the corps, either to emigrate or to retire

22 *Le Moniteur*, 12 June 1791.

23 *Le Moniteur*, 12 June 1791.

24 Louis-Philippe, *Mémoires*, vol.I, p.196.

to the provinces. This reaction was general, as observed by an officer, 'it was the moment of the oath which, in almost all the regiments, had been refused; the emigration had really just begun.'[25] The refusal to take the oath even extended to Swiss regiments that had been otherwise unaffected by the new regulations, in the Régiment de Reinach, for example, two *capitaines* and a *sous-lieutenant* resigned rather than take the oath.

The draft of the constitution was completed on 30 July, and the threat from Austria and Prussia was used as a reason to hurry its adoption:

> ... one has taken great trouble to trumpet in our ears that we will be attacked, invaded next week; this fear is in the Assembly itself which hastens to review the constitution and to ameliorate the fate of the King, his brothers, the princes, to disarm the anger of the Emperor and the King of Prussia who threaten us. No matter how hard the deputies try, they will only disarm these Majesties by restoring ours to what he was before the Revolution ... I have in mind that it is better to expose ourselves to the anger of the kings, to the hazards of war, than to weaken and distort our monarchical constitution.[26]

It was adopted by the Assembly on 3 September 1791, and the King subscribed to it 10 days later. The few reservations he had about the distribution of powers were purely formal; care had been taken, above all, to exclude any reference to the Civil Constitution for the clergy. The Nation was the source of all power, which it delegated on the one hand to the Assembly and on the other hand to the King, both sharing the right to make peace and war. The new Assembly was to take the name Legislative, and Louis XVI was to be the King of the French, losing his title of King of France. To sit for two years and be indissoluble, this new assembly would have 745 deputies, shared among the 83 départements and elected by indirect census suffrage. France was thus to have four million active citizens with the vote and three million who were not wealthy enough to vote and so were passive citizens. Furthermore, following a proposal by Robespierre, previous deputies could not be re-elected to this legislature, which saw the exclusion of royalist, monarchien and other moderate deputies for new, more radical and pro-war representatives.

The King was now the hereditary delegate of the Nation, who was free to choose his successor. He was to govern with the assistance of six ministers, and, powerless to prevent the adoption of legislation, he could only express his opposition by veto. The Assembly held the real power and initiative, passing laws, fixing contributions and monitoring the use of public funds. This power was also such that, on La Fayette's proposal, it 'decreed by acclamation the immediate release of all those detained for reasons relating to the Revolution, and the abolition of all procedures on these events. It then added a general amnesty for both soldiers and the émigrés, permitting all French people to travel freely within the kingdom and to leave without a passport.'[27]

---

25 Marquis de La Maisonfort, *Mémoires d'un agent royaliste sous la Révolution, l'Empire et la Restauration*, (Paris: Mercure de France, 1998), p.108.

26 Ruault, *Gazette*, p.259, letter of 12 August 1791.

27 Louis-Philippe, *Mémoires*, vol.I, p.267.

This absolved not only, for example, royalists implicated in the Lyon affair but also those condemned for events at Nancy.

When Louis XVI went to swear the new oath and deliver a speech at the Assembly to mark the beginning of a new era, he found he had only been provided with a simple armchair and when he stood to take his oath, after a few moments, all the deputies sat down and put on their hats in a concerted gesture. Despite this humiliation, both Louis and Marie-Antoinette benefited from a temporary surge in popularity, but this ended with the publication of the 'Letter from Monsieur, & the Comte d'Artois, to the King their Brother, with the Declaration signed at Pillnitz, 27 August 1791, by the Emperor & the King of Prussia.'[28] This sought to justify the émigrés' projects as a reaction to the recognition of the Constitution. Louis XVI, by sanctioning it, had placed himself in opposition to the sovereigns of Europe. His legitimacy was ruined because:

> As usufructuary trustee of the Throne that you inherited from your ancestors, you can neither alienate its primordial rights nor destroy the constitutive basis on which it is set.
>
> Born defender of the Religion of your Estates, you cannot consent to what leads to its ruin, and abandon its Ministers to opprobrium.
>
> Arbiter of Justice to your subjects, you cannot renounce the essentially royal function of having it rendered to them by legally constituted Courts, and of overseeing its administration yourself.
>
> Protector of the rights of all Orders, and of the possessions of all individuals, you cannot allow them to be violated and destroyed by the most arbitrary of oppressions.
>
> Finally, Father of your People, you cannot deliver them to disorder and anarchy.[29]

The Legislative Assembly began its work on 4 October 1791, and far from being extinguished, the Revolution would continue; indeed, it was immediately proposed that the titles of Sire and Majesty be suppressed, along with the term sovereign. The Jacobins in particular were to become the advocates for those determined to continue the Revolution, at whatever cost. The election of a Jacobin, Jérôme Pétion de Villeneuve, as Bailly's replacement as Mayor of Paris, in preference to La Fayette, would soon have dramatic consequences.

The clemency approved by the Assembly should have seen the return of the émigrés. However, religious persecution, the position of the King and constant threats against those labelled as aristocrats, and thus enemies of the Nation, the opposite was seen during October 1791:

> What confirms the most troubling predictions, is the emigration of what remains of the great lords in Paris since the acceptance. Around thirty among them who

28 Monsieur et le Comte d'Artois, *Lettre de Monsieur, & de M. le Comte d'Artois, au Roi leur Frere, avec la Déclaration signée a Pilnitz, le 27 août 1791, par l'Empereur & le Roi de Prusse* (Worms: Kranzbühler, 1791), p.2, in letter from the Comte de Provence dated 10 September 1791.

29 Monsieur et le Comte d'Artois, *Lettre au Roi*, pp.5–6.

> had not yet set foot outside France since 1789 left last week to go to Koblenz which is the general meeting place for these gentlemen. They are taking advantage of the unlimited freedom to travel granted at the same time as the general amnesty to swell the party of discontents in Germany … It appears certain that more than 80,000 people left Paris this month.[30]

This led the Assembly to make a U-turn, first signalled by a decree on 30 October, ordering Louis-Stanislas-Xavier, formerly Monsieur, to return within two months of 6 November or risk losing his rights to the regency. The King, determined to preserve the rights of his son, the Dauphin, subscribed to it. Then, on 9 November, it was decreed that the émigrés had to return by 1 January 1792 or face being convicted of conspiracy, 'pursued as such and punished by death.'[31] A further article specified that if the Princes and public officials, civil and military, had not returned by that date, they would also be guilty of conspiracy and subject to the same sanction.[32] Other articles detailed all the measures to be taken, ignoring the general amnesty of 15 September, in terms of suspension of income and sequestration. A high national court was to be established as soon as possible at Orléans to adjudicate these matters. Furthermore, courts martial in each military division would deal with military offences committed since the amnesty, specifically, 'Any military officer, of whatever rank, who abandons his duties, without leave or accepted resignation, will be deemed guilty of desertion, and punished as a deserting soldier.'[33]

The actions of émigrés abroad were also sanctioned: 'Any French person who, outside of the kingdom, engages and enrols individuals to go to the assemblies set out in articles 1 and 2 of the present decree, will be punished by death, in accordance with the law of 6 October 1790. The same sentence will be imposed against any person who commits the same crime in France.'[34]

Finally, the diplomatic temperature was cranked up to another level: 'The National Assembly charges its diplomatic committee to propose measures that the King will be asked to take, in the name of the nation, with regard to the neighbouring foreign powers who suffer on their territory gatherings of French fugitives.'[35]

Louis did not veto this decree, as he did for one which targeted refractory priests, so on 2 January 1792, Monsieur, Artois and Condé, among others, were accused by decree and on 18 January, Monsieur was deprived by the Assembly of his rights to the regency.

Furthermore, another decree, of 29 November, drew the country towards war by directing that the King announce measures against 'the combinations of perfidious Frenchmen armed and gathered outside the kingdom, and

---

30 Ruault, *Gazette*, p.262.

31 Anon., *Recueil général des lois, décrets, ordonnances, etc. Depuis le mois de juin 1789 jusqu'au mois d'août 1830* (Paris: Journal des Notaires et des Avocats, 1839), vol.III, pp.10–12, 9 novembre 1791. Décret relatif aux émigrans Article 2.

32 Anon., *Recueil général*, vol.III, Décret relatif aux émigrans Article 3.

33 Anon., *Recueil général*, vol.III, Décret relatif aux émigrans Article 11.

34 Anon., *Recueil général*, vol.III, Décret relatif aux émigrans Article 13.

35 Anon., *Recueil général*, vol.III, Décret relatif aux émigrans Article 14.

from those who hatch plots within, or incite the citizens to revolt against the law'. In particular, he was to demand that 'the Electors of Trier, Mainz and other princes of the Empire who welcome the French fugitives, put an end to the gatherings and the enlistments that they tolerate on the frontier.'[36] The Assembly was confident of being able to mobilise 'the forces necessary to compel by means of arms these princes to respect the rights of the people, in the event that they persist in protecting these assemblies and to assure the justice that one demands.'[37] To remove any ambiguity, the following paragraph was added: 'And finally that the National Assembly believed it necessary to make this solemn declaration, so that the King would be in a position to prove, both to the imperial court and the Diet of Regensburg, and to all the courts of Europe, that his intentions and those of the French nation are one.'[38]

While Louis had no other choice but to comply, both he and his wife sent secret messages to the principal sovereigns, assuring them that he did so to buy time for them to come to his aid. He still favoured foreign intervention over a civil war, but he recommended maintaining the armed assemblies that attracted a growing number of émigrés to keep the pressure on the Assembly. So, preserving his public face, on 14 December he announced in the Assembly that he was prepared to demand that the German electors expel the émigré assemblies from their soil, specifying that he would declare war if they had not complied by 15 January 1792.

Encouraged, the Assembly addressed an ultimatum to the Emperor on 25 January, demanding that he disavow the Pillnitz Declaration before 1 March 1792.[39] Silence, or any evasive or dilatory response, from him would be regarded as a declaration of war. The Girondins, who now dominated the Assembly, favoured war, but the more radical factions, the Jacobins and Cordeliers, wanted to delay it, Robespierre commenting:

> I also wish for war, but as the interest of the nation requires: let us subdue our internal enemies, and then march against our foreign enemies, if any still exist … What is the war we can foresee? … It is the war of the enemies of the French Revolution against the French Revolution. The most numerous, the most dangerous of these enemies are they not at Koblenz? No, they are among us.[40]

On 1 February 1792, the radicals appear to have got their way when it was decreed that anyone who wished to travel within and outside national territory required a passport. After having encouraged royalists to leave the country, then suddenly closing the borders behind them, the Assembly decreed the

---

36 Anon, *Recueil général*, vol.III, p.17, 9 novembre 1791. Décret relatif aux rassemblemens des émigrés.

37 Anon, *Recueil général*, vol.III, p.17, 29 novembre 1791. Décret relatif aux rassemblemens des émigrés.

38 Anon, *Recueil général*, vol.III, p.17.

39 Philippe Joseph Benjamin Buchez, *Histoire parlementaire de la Révolution – Histoire de l'Assemblée Législative* (Paris: Edition Hetzel, 1846), vol.II, p.262.

40 Anon., *Discours de Maximilien Robespierre, sur le parti que l'Assemblée nationale doit prendre relatviement à la proposition de guerre, annoncée par le pouvoir exécutif : prononcé à la société, le 18 décembre 1791* (Paris: Société des Amis de la Constitution, 1791), p.3.

seizure of émigrés' property.[41] The confiscation of the property of all nobles who had emigrated since 1 July 1789 was decreed by the Assembly on 30 March; it was to be registered as national property and then sold. Finance was needed for the imminent conflict that became increasingly certain. This last point was underlined as early as 29 February in a lesser-known decree urgently raising the pay of the army, to support the expenses and fatigues of war.[42]

Then on 1 March, Emperor Leopold II died of pleurisy, and his eldest son succeeded him as King of Hungary and Bohemia and, after election, Holy Roman Emperor as Francis II. Two days later, Archduchess Maria Christina was confirmed as head of the Austrian Netherlands, alongside her husband, Duke Albert of Saxe-Teschen. Unlike his father, Francis did not seek to avoid war, and, indeed, events were to leave him with little other choice.

The very same day, 1 March, the Assembly was read a note from the Prussian Minister in Paris, reminding it that it had already been made clear 'that an invasion by French troops into the territory of the Empire, would be regarded as a declaration of war, by the Germanic Corps and that in consequence His Prussian Majesty could not avoid, jointly with His Imperial Majesty, from opposing it with all his forces.'[43]

In the prevailing political circumstances, Louis brought Jacobins into his cabinet on 10 March. It was observed:

> The entire ministry will be incessantly renewed and, what is no less essential, all the ministers' offices. We already have Mr de Grave to that of War and Dumouriez to Foreign Affairs: both Jacobins; and to that of the navy Mr de Lacoste; a 3rd Jacobin. It only remains to know if these very Jacobins are honest. The ministries of the interior, justice and direct contributions still need to be Jacobinised. If that happens as is probable, the King will have to become a Jacobin himself, and that would perhaps be his salvation…[44]

An explanation may be that Louis considered the appointment of bellicose ministers might precipitate France into war. Both the King and Queen now considered that only an invasion by a foreign coalition would save the throne. In the case of a French victory, the constitutional monarchy would be strengthened, and, if defeated, it had to be hoped that the coalition army could push on to Paris in time to prevent them from being killed.

The Dismantling of the Royal Army

The upheavals in the kingdom's armed forces from 1789, especially the undermining of discipline, were reactionary, often inspired by external agencies. However, the reforms that appeared from 1791 were part of a political programme, led by a Military Committee that was subordinate

41 Anon., *Collection complètei*, vol.IV, p.78, Décret relatif au séquestre des émigrés (9–12 février 1792).
42 Anon., *Collection complete*, vol.IV, pp.,75–76.
43 Louis-Philippe, *Mémoires*, vol.I, p.298.
44 Ruault, *Gazette*, pp.281–282, letter of 20 March 1792.

to the Assembly. The aim was to erase the army's identification with the monarchy and replace it with the secular institution of the Nation. But the more immediate objective was to rid it of noble officers; the destruction of the cadre of both army and naval officers, like that of the units of the royal household, reconciled these two objectives.

On 16 November 1790, Louis-Antoine Jean Le Bègue de Presle du Portail, or simply Duportail, was placed as Minister of War with a mission to accelerate the reform of the army. An engineer officer, he had been among those sent on a secret mission by Louis XVI to Washington in 1777 to develop the engineer branch in the Continental Army.[45] A legacy of his ministry was the creation of the Gendarmerie Nationale, still present today as a police force with its constituent corps, the Garde Républicaine, dedicated to the security of the political institutions of the Republic, such as the Elysée Palace, National Assembly and Senate, as well as official ceremonies.

Article 1, Paragraph 1 of the decree of 22 December 1790/16 February 1791, stipulated that the Maréchaussée would henceforth take the name Gendarmerie Nationale and would continue to be part of the army.[46] It was to be 7,455 strong and retain the previous uniform, without the aiguilette, but with white piping on the facings, the tricolour cockade, and buttons bearing the motto Force à la Loi (Strength to the Law, see plate commentary).[47] As well as the Maréchaussée, the Gendarmerie Nationale incorporated various other units that had fulfilled similar functions and, by a decree of 15 May 1791, the former company of Gardes de la Prévôté de l'Hôtel du Roi, which since 1789 had been responsible for the security of the National Assembly and its archives. Thus, to this day, the Gendarmerie Nationale displays symbolic links to the former Maison militaire, preserving the élite white braid, the insignia of the helm of chivalry and the grenade.

Duportail's ministry also saw the first measure, decreed in December 1790, to adopt the new national colours on all the army's standards. Tricolour cravats, attached to the staves immediately above the flags, replaced the former ones which were white, the colour of the monarchy. The new cravats were often presented by local municipalities, and the regiments, in return, handed the old ones over to them. This was followed by a 'Decree relative to the flags, standards and guidons of the regiments' of 30 June 1791, published on 10 July, which applied to all but the Swiss units. Articles 1 and 2 stipulated that first flag (for the infantry), guidon (dragoons) and standard (other cavalry) 'will henceforth bear the three national colours' (Article 1) and the other such symbols 'will henceforth bear the colours assigned to the uniform of each regiment' (Article 2) each 'following the arrangements and forms which will be presented to the Assembly by its Military Committee.'[48] Each was to 'bear on one side the following inscription: Discipline et obéissance à

45 See Serge Le Pottier, *Duportail ou le Génie de Georges Washington* (Paris: Economica, 2011).

46 *Journal militaire,* Samedi 8 janvier 1791, pp.13–23, Décret relatif à l'organisation de la Gendarmerie nationale, Section première and *Journal militaire,* Samedi 15 janvier 1791, pp.25–28, Section seconde.

47 Anon., *Collection générale des décrets rendus par l'Assemblée nationale … Mois de Janvier 1791* (Paris: Baudouin, Imprimeur de l'Assemblée nationale, 1791), p.160, Décret du 16 janvier 1791.

48 Anon., *Collection complete*, vol.III, p.69.

la Loi [Discipline and obedience to the Law]; on the other side, the regimental number.'[49] Article 5 dealt with the symbolic links with the past: 'Those of the regiments which bore on their flags, standards and guidons honourable proofs of some brilliant action in war, will retain these marks of their good conduct and their valour; but all coats of arms or other distinctions which could have any relation to feudalism, will be entirely removed from the flags, standards and guidons.'[50]

This complied with the decree of June 1790 that abolished titles and marks of nobility as well as the 1 January 1791 regulation that replaced the traditional names of the regiments with a simple number according to precedence.[51] In addition, the regulation had stipulated that the flag would be carried by a *sergent-major*, rather than an officer as before.[52]

The adoption of national colours on the cockade, from May 1790, and the regimental cravats had been generally well received by all, including the troops. Indeed, when André-Benoît-Boniface-Louis de Riqueti, Vicomte de Mirabeau, an ardent royalist, unlike his older politician brother, attempted to flee with the cravats of both flags of the Régiment de Touraine infanterie, which he commanded, it was an isolated and desperate act. However, the loss of not only the white *colonel*'s flag but also the traditional regimental flags, the drapeaux d'ordonnance, was strongly resented.

A further decree of 29 September 1791 proposed a variation:

> … the first flag of each regiment will be white, surrounded by a tricolour band; at the top will be a small frame of tricolour bands, in the middle the regimental number with this motto: '*Discipline et obéissance à la Loi*.' The flags of the other battalions will vary according to the rank of the battalion; the cravats will be in the national colours.[53]

Thus the second battalion of each infantry regiment would receive flags in the regiment's facing colour which, in the case of the French regiments, depended on the series to which the regiment belonged, there being six series of 12 regiments and a seventh of six.[54] Notably the flags still bore the fleurs-de-lys, as did the turnbacks of the fusiliers' coats and the officers' gorgets. In addition, all the drummers and trumpeters would have a blue coat bearing the King's livery.

The overturning of military traditions faced some challenges:

---

49 Anon., *Collection complete*, vol.III, p.69.

50 Anon., *Collection complete*, vol.III, p.69.

51 Anon., *Règlement arrêté par le Roi pour l'Habillement & l'Equipement des Troupes – Du premier octobre 1786* (Metz: Imprimerie Collignon, 1786).

52 *Journal militaire*, dimanche 20 février 1791, p.63.

53 Charles d'Héricault, *La Révolution, 1789-1882* (Paris: Librairie Dumoulin, 1883), p.436, citing a contemporary journal, *le Patriote françois*. The decree is also mentioned in M.J. Mavidal and M.E. Laurent, *Archives parlementaires françaises de 1787 à 1860* (Paris: Société d'Imprimerie et Librairie administrative et de chemin de fer, 1884), vol.XXXI, p.594.

54 Liliane and Fred Funcken, *The Lace Wars* (London: Ward Lock, 1977), Part 1, pp.81–83.

> … at Rennes, in February 1792, the soldiers of the 1st battalion of the 48e (ci-devant Artois) refused to give up the flags with white crosses of the monarchy [in times of peace, both flags were kept in the *colonel*'s lodgings] in exchange for the national colours which had just arrived from Paris. Instead of handing them over to the authorities, they wanted to hang them in the vaults of one of the city's churches. The lieutenant-colonel and four of his officers protested against this act of disobedience to the decrees of the Legislative Assembly … and submitted their resignations. They were arrested by the Garde Nationale![55]

The former Duc de Chartres, went to Paris at the beginning of March 1792 in order to obtain the deployment of his regiment, the 14e Dragons, nearer the theatre of operations. He attested to the difficulties he encountered in his memoirs:

> I went to Laon as soon as I knew that my regiment was established there, taking with me the new tricolour guidons whose delivery had been delayed until then under different pretexts by the War Office. I presented them to the regiment in the presence of the Administration of the Aisne département and all the authorities, and I then returned the old guidons bearing my arms to the Ministry of War to comply with the military regulation decreed by the National Assembly and sanctioned by the King, an article of which forbade the colonels from keeping the abolished flags, standards or guidons, in order to prevent them from reappearing in the event of a counter-revolution, or from being taken to Koblenz, as some colonels had tried in vain.[56]

Indeed, the Military Committee considered this sufficiently important to announce, two days before the declaration of war, the 'Decree relating to burning of old flags, standards and guidons.'

> Art. 1. The Minister of War will give orders that the old flags, standards and guidons, as soon as they have been replaced, are burned in front of the unit under arms, and in the presence of the municipal officers, who will draw up a statement of it to be sent to the legislative body and deposited in its archives.
>
> Art. 2. Those of the flags, standards and guidons which may have been sent to the Minister of War, and which have not yet been burned, will be in the presence of the municipality of Paris, [which will report it a copy of which would also be sent] … to the commanders of the respective regiments.[57]

Thus, at the beginning of the conflict, the four standards of the 3e Hussards (formerly Esterhazy) were 'delivered into the hands of the executioner' to be burned at Cambrai on 20 May and, two days later, two from the 1er Hussards (formerly Bercheny) 'still bearing the "the depiction of the arms of Monsieur

55 Deschard, *L'Armée et la Révolution*, p.211.

56 Louis-Philippe, *Mémoires*, vol.I, p.54.

57 Anon., *Collection complète*, vol.III, p.117.

Bercheny", [were] taken from deserting officers and burned at Metz at the foot of the Tree of Liberty.'[58]

The aforementioned 1 January 1791 regulation allocated numbers to the 101 line infantry regiments. Of these only the 11 Swiss regiments officially retained their names, as well their own formations; this nation still provided the Gardes Suisses.[59] There were also 12 battalions of light infantry clothed like the chasseurs à cheval in dark green. The cavalry had two regiments of carabiniers, 23 of (heavy) cavalry, six of hussars, 18 of dragoons, and finally 12 of chasseurs à cheval. The (non-Swiss) line infantry regiments were to have two battalions each of nine companies; one of grenadiers and eight of fusiliers. This provided for 1,029 men, which at full war establishment would rise to about 1,500. The non-commissioned officers were no longer referred to as *bas-officiers* but *sous-officiers*, a term then applied to the *tambour-major*, *sergents-majors*, *sergents*, *caporaux fourriers* and *caporaux*.

A decree of 4 March 1791 abolished the old militia (the 13 regiments of Grenadiers Royaux, 16 so-called provincial regiments and 78 garrison battalions), it being replaced by the Garde Nationale.

A directive of 4 April 1791 brought in alterations to the uniforms of various arms.[60] However, it is particularly noteworthy for other reasons. It is the last time that Louis XVI is mentioned as monarch. All drummers, trumpeters and musicians were still to wear a blue coat of the King's livery. Another related to the introduction in the infantry of the patent leather helmet with a fur chenille (caterpillar) running centrally front to back, the last paragraphs of the directive stipulated that 'The regiments of the different arms which have received the order to bring themselves to war strength … The brevity of time not allowing helmets to be provided to the Infantry regiments, for their augmentation, the administrative council of these regiments, as well as those of the cavalry, are authorised to provide themselves with hats.'[61]

Some regiments were already to be on a war footing, and the conflict was so imminent that emergency measures were authorised.

However, matters of dress were the least of the former royal army's issues, its numbers had dwindled. So, on 28 January 1791 a degree, promulgated on 4 February, followed the recommendation of the previous year for the raising of 100,000 auxiliary soldiers, to complete the line regiments in the event of conflict. The men were to be recruited across the 83 départements, with Paris contributing 1,800 men.

On 26 March 1791, the Assembly was informed of the measures that had been taken to make the land forces ready for war:

> The state of the army consisted on 1 March, not including officers, of 130,728 men; thus, the shortfall was only 10,000 men. We have almost as many cannons

58 Pierre Charrié, 'Les étendards des régiments de hussards', *Carnet spécial de La Sabretache*, 1971, p.119.

59 *Etat militaire* 1791, table de matieres and p.121.

60 Anon., *Instruction provisoire sur l'Habillement des Troupes. Du 1er avril 1791* (Paris: Imprimerie Royale, 1792), p.1.

61 Anon., *Instruction l'Habillement*, pp.16–17.

Garde Nationale 1789–1792, by Rousselot. (*Le Passepoil* 1935/3, courtesy of La Sabretache)

> as are needed for the garrisons; but as the distribution of them had been badly done, transports were made, which obliged the number of artillery horses to be increased to 1,000 instead of 300. The contractors will provide these horses on 1st April next; the expense will not be considerable. Orders have long been given to put the artillery trains into service. They will be before the season. The foundries received the order to make 300 cannons; as there are currently only 195 in the magazines; a number which would be insufficient, in the event that we arm the auxiliaries … The situation of camp effects is not as satisfactory; the distribution made to the regiments in 1790, and the pillaging which was done in different places, emptied the stores. Moreover, the unrest prevented the soldiers from having all the necessary care of them. It is therefore essential to renew them; the expense would be approximately 5 million. I have already taken the King's orders to have the tents made.[62]

The Assembly continued to issue decrees relating to the armed forces. One, of 16/27 April, related to the levy of the 100,000 auxiliaries, a quarter of whom, by a decision of 4 June, were to be allocated to the navy, with the rest going to the army.[63] However, this national recruitment campaign was a failure and was soon cancelled, so other measures were required. On 21 July, it was decreed that the foreign regiments, except for the Swiss, were to be considered national and so wear the white coats of the French infantry.[64] Then, following the disbanding of the paid element of the Paris Garde Nationale, three new infantry regiments (102–104), two light infantry battalions (13 and 14) and two gendarmerie divisions were created by the law of 28 August 1791.[65] Furthermore, the Régiments du Roi infantry and Mestre-de-Camp cavalry, having been disbanded following their mutiny at Nancy in the summer of 1790, were subsequently reformed, at least nominally, after a law of 5 January 1791. They took the numbers 105 in the infantry and 24 in the cavalry.[66] By the law of 16 October 1791, the colonial infantry, the Régiments de Port-au-Prince, du Cap (both in Saint-Domingue), de la Martinique, de la Guadeloupe, de l'Île de France, de Bourbon, de Pondichéry, the Bataillons d'Afrique and de la Guyane, and the Compagnie de Saint-Pierre et Miquelon, were disbanded. They then formed six new regiments, numbered 106 to 111, on the same footing as the other line infantry.[67] The colonial units had, as of the previous 20 July, been transferred to the Ministry of War, a change which was also to see the colonial artillery form an eighth artillery regiment.

On 21 June 1791, when the King's flight had just been discovered, extraordinary measures were proposed in the Assembly to 'provide, in the

62 Mavidal and Laurent, *Archives parlementaires*, vol.XXIV, pp.398–399.

63 Anon., *Collection complète*, vol.II, p.307.

64 Anon., *Collection générale des décrets rendus par l'Assemblée nationale … Mois de Juillet 1791* (Paris: Imprimerie de l'Assemblée nationale, 1791), p.244, Décret portant que le quatre-vingt seizième régiment d'infanterie, ci-devant Nassau, & tous ceux-ci-devant désignés sous le nom de régiments d'infanterie Allemande, Irlandoise & Liégeoise, font partie de l'Infanterie françoise et porteront l'uniforme.

65 *Etat militaire*, 1793, p.166 and Anon., *Collection complète*, vol.III, pp.343–344.

66 *Etat militaire*, 1793, pp.171, 248.

67 *Etat militaire*, 1793, p.173.

current circumstances, for the external and internal security of the State and the maintenance of the Constitution.'[68] Adopted the following day, the Garde Nationale was to enrol volunteers throughout the country, the commune of Paris advocating, 'all good citizens to enlist voluntarily for service on the frontiers.'[69] This national levy of 101,000 men was intended to provide 169 battalions of Volontaires Nationaux, and a month later, on 20 July, the uniform of the Garde Nationale, and therefore the Volontaires Nationaux was defined.

> Royal blue coat [soon renamed national blue], white lining, scarlet piping, scarlet cuff and collar and white piping; white lapel and scarlet piping, sleeve opening with three small buttons, outside pockets with three points and three buttons with red piping; the button as it is [that is to say in accordance with the decree of the previous 5 January]; the fleuron [fleur de lys] of the turnbacks scarlet, white waistcoats and breeches.[70]

The establishment of the new type of unit was finalised by the decree of 28 December 1791/3 February 1792 defining 'the training, organisation and pay of the gardes nationaux volontaires,' the number of battalions of which was increased to 200 on 15 March 1792.[71]

The oaths that the new, constitutional, troops were to take, prescribed by the decree of 17 September 1791, not only differed between ranks but also from those required earlier from the army.

> Oath of the officers and non-commissioned officers.
> I swear to be faithful to the nation, the Law and the King, to maintain with all my power the constitution, to execute and have executed the military regulations.
>
> Oath of the soldiers.
> I swear to be faithful to the nation, the Law and the King, to defend the constitution, to never abandon my flags, and to wholly conform to the rules of military discipline.[72]

As can be seen, the oath again included being faithful to the King. Thus, it is valid to ask if its removal from the previous version, which is often presented

---

68 Anon., *Collection générale des décrets rendus par l'Assemblée nationale … Mois de juin 1791* (Paris: Imprimerie de l'Assemblée nationale, 1791), p.317, 21 juin 1791. Décret pour mettre la Garde Nationale en activité, & qui règle la formation des Compagnies & des Bataillons, ainsi que la solde des Officiers & Volontaires.

69 Charles-Louis Chassin and Léon Hennet, *Les Volontaires nationaux pendant la Révolution* (Paris: Librairie Léopold Cerf, 1899), vol.I, p.11, Arrêté du conseil général de la Commune de Paris, du 22 juin 1791.

70 Anon., *Collection complète*, vol.III, p.127, 13–20 juillet 1791. Décret qui règle définitivement l'uniforme des Gardes Nationales, see also p.458, 27 juillet 1791. Décret sur l'organisation des gardes nationales.

71 Anon., *Collection complète*, vol.IV, pp.33–38.

72 Anon., *Collection générale des décrets rendus par l'Assemblée Nationale … Mois de Septembre 1791* (Paris: Imprimerie de l'Assemblée nationale, 1791), p.364, Décret concernant la formule du serment à prêter par les Officiers & soldats de l'Armée.

as the main cause for the majority of royalist officers to emigrate from July 1791, had not been one of the political tricks taken at the time to provoke such a reaction.

Whilst many of the reforms were designed to create a national, rather than royal, army, the foundations were also laid for its future organisational strength and tactical superiority. For example, a new Regulation of 1 August 1791 for infantry exercise and manoeuvres was to be retained for the wars of the Revolution and the Empire. Nevertheless, from the end of 1791, the Ministry of War was to become a major prize in the internal political struggles in which the Jacobins would ultimately benefit; after Duportail was dismissed on 7 December 1791, he was followed by a succession of ministers.

With the exception of the Régiment des Gardes Suisses, there was now nothing left of the old Maison militaire du Roi. The King's Gardes du Corps were to be replaced by a new Garde Constitutionnelle du Roi composed of 1,800 men: 600 cavalry and 1,200 infantry. Although envisaged by the Assembly in 1790, the decision was only enacted on 16 October 1791, and it began to be formed from 1 January 1792. Its commander-in-chief was Louis Hercule Timoléon de Cossé-Brissac, peer of France, *lieutenant-general*, royal governor of Paris and commander of the Cent Suisses, who was a personal friend of Louis XVI. The infantry and cavalry were led by *maréchaux de camp* Jean-Georges-Claude Baude, (Baron) de Pont-l'Abbé and (Comte) Louis Charles d'Hervilly, respectively. A third of its men were transferred from the line, and the rest were young men from the Garde Nationale drawn from across all the départements of France.

This broad composition was an anathema to the Jacobins, with their power base in Paris, who suspected the corps to be a nest of aristocrats sympathetic to the émigrés who would encourage a new flight by the King, so they resisted and delayed the unit's creation. However, it finally commenced duty on 16 March 1792, 'jointly with the Parisian Garde Nationale.'[73] Very soon, the Jacobins would succeed in having its commander arrested and the unit dismissed.[74]

One of the officers of the new Garde was Jean Edme Xavier de La Chapelle who had previously served in the Régiment du Maine and then as *lieutenant-colonel* of the Bataillon de Guyenne before returning to civilian life when the provincial troops were disbanded (20 March 1791). He had hesitated to join, having decided to emigrate:

> … he opened up to his former colonel in the Régiment du Maine, the maréchal de camp Comte de Clarac, who replied to him from Koblenz that 'the Princes wanted the King to remain surrounded by people on whom he could count.' Silencing his repugnance, he accepted out of duty a company in the foot guard, and his brevet is dated 30 November 1791.[75]

73 Ruault, *Gazette*, p.281.

74 Marthe Robinet and Isabelle Chave, *Fichier de la garde constitutionelle de Louis XVI (1791–1792)* (Pierrefitte-sur-Seine: Archives nationales, 2016), pp.3–4.

75 Jean Edme Xavier de La Chapelle, *Souvenirs d'Edme de La Chapelle de Bernarès, de Bergerac à Quiberon* (Paris: Librairie Plon, 1913), p.46.

The guard were targeted by radical Parisians and were soon instructed to wear uniform only on duty at the Tuileries.[76] There they and the royal family faced increasing hostility, 'there was not a week that the château was not threatened, there was not a day that the grossest insults, the most disgusting remarks came to strike the ears of Their Majesties.'[77]

When a large threatening crowd approached the palace on Wednesday, 4 April, the Gardes Constitutionnelles could rely on the Gardes Nationaux serving alongside them. However, the following Sunday when a crowd at the Place du Carrousel tried to prohibit access to the Tuileries and confronted the relieving guard, trying to grab its commander, the Garde Nationale took the rioters' part and hurled insults at the Garde Constitutionnelle. On the afternoon of Sunday, 26 May, a hostile crowd returned to the Tuileries, and the following Wednesday, the officer of the day was almost lynched by the mob. La Chapelle, serving inside the palace that day, noted that the Queen did not leave her apartment, 'She did not appear by her windows as the people overwhelmed her with insults and the most outrageous remarks.'[78]

The same night, 29 May, the Girondins and Jacobins in the Assembly sought to have the Garde Constitutionnelle dismissed. Knowing that they would succeed, Hervilly planned a desperate gambit:

> It was nothing less than to prevent the decree of dismissal by the slaughter of all those who were to render it. Everything was arranged. At ten o'clock in the evening, the cavalry ready to mount, the infantry armed was to move, in small platoons and a combined march, some on the National Assembly, others on the Jacobins; those who were at the château were to be under arms, ready to repel the first movements of the people, in whose souls an enterprise of this nature, carried out in the middle of the night, would probably have brought only terror and fear.[79]

Once again, however, those who were ready to sacrifice their lives to save the King and the monarchy came up against Louis's lack of resolution. He refused to run such a risk and betray his oath to the constitution, even though he had already forgotten that he had taken at his coronation.

The decree was passed at midnight and, at 8:00 a.m. on 30 May, Brissac, indicted by the Assembly, was taken away in a carriage to Orléans. At the same time, the crowd once again invaded the Place du Carrousel and the relief guard was unable to reach the palace. Finally, the Garde Nationale took over all the posts at the Tuileries and marched the Garde Constitutionnelle to the Ecole militaire, with detachments of cavalry at the front and back of the column. There, a municipal officer tried to deny them access, but gaining their quarters, the Gardes Constitutionnelles waited there for the order from the King to hand over their weapons, which they did on 5 June. At the end of

76 La Chapelle, *Souvenirs*, p.45.

77 La Chapelle, *Souvenirs*, p.46.

78 La Chapelle, *Souvenirs*, pp.48, 50. In his journal, La Chapelle, places this event on a Sunday while 29 May was a Wednesday, thus it appears he reversed the two days.

79 La Chapelle, *Souvenirs*, pp.51–52.

this ceremony, it was necessary to escort the disarmed guards once again as the populace wanted to massacre them.

The crowds that continued to go to the palace became more threatening and were reinforced by the presence of Fédérés, Volontaires Nationaux, notably from Marseille, who had been diverted on their way to the northern or eastern frontiers on the pretext of attending the forthcoming Fête de la Fédération, hence their name. Despite this, the King refused a new guard in which all the officers would have been Jacobins. The latter illustrates the manner in which the army's cadre had become politicised; officers could be revolutionaries, even Republicans, but not monarchists, despite the constitutional regime still being overtly a monarchy. He only had for his protection the unshakeable Garde Suisse and the Garde Nationale, the loyalty and even impartiality of which was at best questionable.

The erosion of the military institutions continued, and plans were made to dissolve the line regiments to replace them with a new national army. However, these had to be suspended, paradoxically, due to war with Austria, declared in premature haste. Due to the shortfall in numbers, the formation of legions of foreign volunteers, at first one for each of the three armies, was decreed on 27 April 1792. One was to be commanded by John Money, a Briton who had had a varied military career, finally serving as a general in the Brabant forces during the Belgian Revolution.[80] He accepted the role, with the rank of *maréchal de camp*, in May 'and returned to England, to prepare for the campaign.'[81] Back in Paris, he found the new minister knew nothing of the arrangements, but in the end his brevet in that rank was signed by Louis XVI on 19 July.[82]

France Attacks the Austrian Netherlands

On the day Emperor Leopold died, 1 March 1792, a letter from his chancellor, Kaunitz, was read in the Assembly:

> The Emperor believes he owes the well-being of France and all of Europe, as he is authorised to do by the provocations and the dangerous actions of the Jacobin party, to publicly unmask and denounce this pernicious sect as the enemies of the Most Christian King, and of the fundamental principles of the current Constitution, and as the disturbers of public peace. Will the illegal ascendancy of this sect prevail in France, over justice, truth, the health of the Nation? This is the question to which all others are reduced. Whatever the result, the cause of the Emperor is that of all the Powers.[83]

80 James Money, *The History of the Campaign of 1792, between the Armies of France under Generals Dumourier, Valence, &c. and the Allies under the Duke of Brunswick; with an account of what passed in the Thuilleries on the 10th of August* (London: Harlow, 1794), pp.ix–x.

81 Money, *Campaign of 1792*, pp.1–3.

82 Money *Campaign of 1792*, pp.4–7.

83 Louis-Philippe, *Mémoires*, vol.I, p.301.

Despite the overt strength of the message, the new sovereign, Francis, needed time to secure his thrones, as well as mobilise troops. He was crowned King of Hungary on 6 June 1792, but, although elected Holy Roman Emperor on 5 July, he had to wait until his coronation on 14 July to fully express imperial power. Nevertheless, after having rejected France's ultimatum demanding the dissolution of the émigré gatherings and their expulsion from the Rhineland on 25 March, Francis found himself the head of the counter-revolutionary crusade; Gustav of Sweden, having been mortally wounded on 16 March in an assassination attempt, was to die 13 days later.

On 5 April, Francis proclaimed that he did not want war, but only intended that the King of France be guaranteed his freedoms and authority and that his brothers, Provence and Artois, as well as the German princes, who had possessions in Alsace, have their rights and properties guaranteed. Furthermore, the French clergy and nobility were to be restored to their property and former status. Faced with these demands, on 14 April the Assembly announced a decree, 'containing the declaration of the motives that determine the resolutions of France, and the exposition of the principles which will direct its conduct in the exercise of the right of war.'[84] Thus, on 20 April 1792, the King of the French declared war on his wife's nephew, the King of Bohemia and Hungary.

The declaration at this time may be seen as a ploy to keep the German Empire out of the conflict. Indeed, there were attempts to isolate Austria, exploiting latent hostility in Europe. A leading proponent of what may be termed 'austrophobia' was Dumouriez, who, as stated above, had been appointed Minister of Foreign Affairs on 15 March 1792. Austrian territory was to be the subject of offensives launched the day after the declaration of war.

The French army was organised into three principal corps: the Armée du Nord, commanded by *maréchal* de Rochambeau, was responsible for the frontier from the English Channel to the Ardennes. The Armée du Rhin was commanded by *maréchal* Luckner; both men having been raised to the dignity of *maréchal* on 28 December 1791. The Armée du Centre was placed under the orders of *lieutenant-general* La Fayette, his promotion having had no other purpose than to keep him from Paris and so weaken his political position. It also meant he had to relinquish his command of the Garde Nationale.

They faced about 80,000 Austrian troops, 30,000 having been sent from Bohemia to reinforce those already present in Breisgau, Luxembourg and the Netherlands. In time, there was the prospect of many more as Austria and Prussia had signed a convention on 18 February 1792. Narbonne, the Minister of War, had promised the previous December that France would have 150,000 men on its frontiers by 15 January 1792. However, when the minister visited the frontiers that very month, he, according to Rochambeau, acknowledged, 'the lack of means that remained to him for such a reckless enterprise.'[85]

84 Anon., *Collection complète*, vol.IV, pp.106–107.

85 Rochambeau, *Mémoires*, vol.I, p.393.

> It was not long before he realised how much indiscipline, insubordination, then openly protected by popular societies, and as a result the legislative body [the Assembly], had disorganised our troops. The emigration of the officers, which increased every day, was for this minister the work of Penelope; the next day she undid all the work of the day before.[86]

Rochambeau considered that the state of the troops meant they should avoid attacking the Austrian Netherlands but could only undertake a limited operation such as 'an incursion to the small States of the princes of the Empire, and especially in what the late King of Prussia called the street of the priests [the ecclesiastical electorates of Trier, Mainz and Koblenz].'[87]

Soon Narbonne was replaced as minister by Grave who was, in reality, a puppet in the hands of Dumouriez. The latter had already decided, publishing it in newspapers and broadsheets, that widespread desertion from the Austrian army and unconditional support in Brabant would bring 30,000 men to the French invaders. Rochambeau, however, knew that such desertion was minimal, 'and the spirit of Brabant, without being favourable to the Austrian government, was even more hostile to our revolution, since the agitations of this people were always led by the priests and nobles.'[88] He managed to convince the King and ministers that the army's disorganisation had to be rectified as a priority, asking for hostilities to be delayed until 15 May. This would give him time to train the troops who would assemble in large, entrenched camps protected by strongholds along the defensive system of northern France: 20,000 at Valenciennes, and about 5,000 at both Maubeuge and Dunkirk. In addition, Rochambeau would give the forces in the Ardennes and the Marne département to La Fayette so he could threaten Namur and Liège from the entrenched camp of Givet.

Nevertheless, on 24 April, he received new orders to immediately prepare three columns so that, on 29 April, they would be, 'before Mons, Tournai and Veurne [given in French as Furnes], and promote a general insurrection, on which we counted in Brabant.'[89] For his part, La Fayette was to be at the gates of Namur the following day, 30 April, while Rochambeau, himself, was to assemble all available troops at Valenciennes to break through between Liège and Roermond into Germany and so drive between the coalition forces. No heed was given to the 50,000 men that Francis could assemble in Brabant. Things began very badly when the column marching from Lille, under Théobald Dillon, was routed by the Tournai garrison and driven back into Lille, where, on 29 April, already wounded, Dillon was murdered by a mob of his own soldiers. The force under the orders of Biron, formerly the Duc de Lauzun, marching on Mons, was also worsted at Quiévrain, 29 and 30 April, and it fell back to Valenciennes in the greatest disorder. In doing so, the retreating troops murdered officers who tried to rally them. The column from Dunkirk succeeded in reaching Veurne but, learning of the rout of the

86 Rochambeau, *Mémoires*, vol.I, p.394.
87 Rochambeau, *Mémoires*, vol.I, p.395.
88 Rochambeau, *Mémoires*, vol.I, p.401.
89 Rochambeau, *Mémoires*, vol.I, p.405.

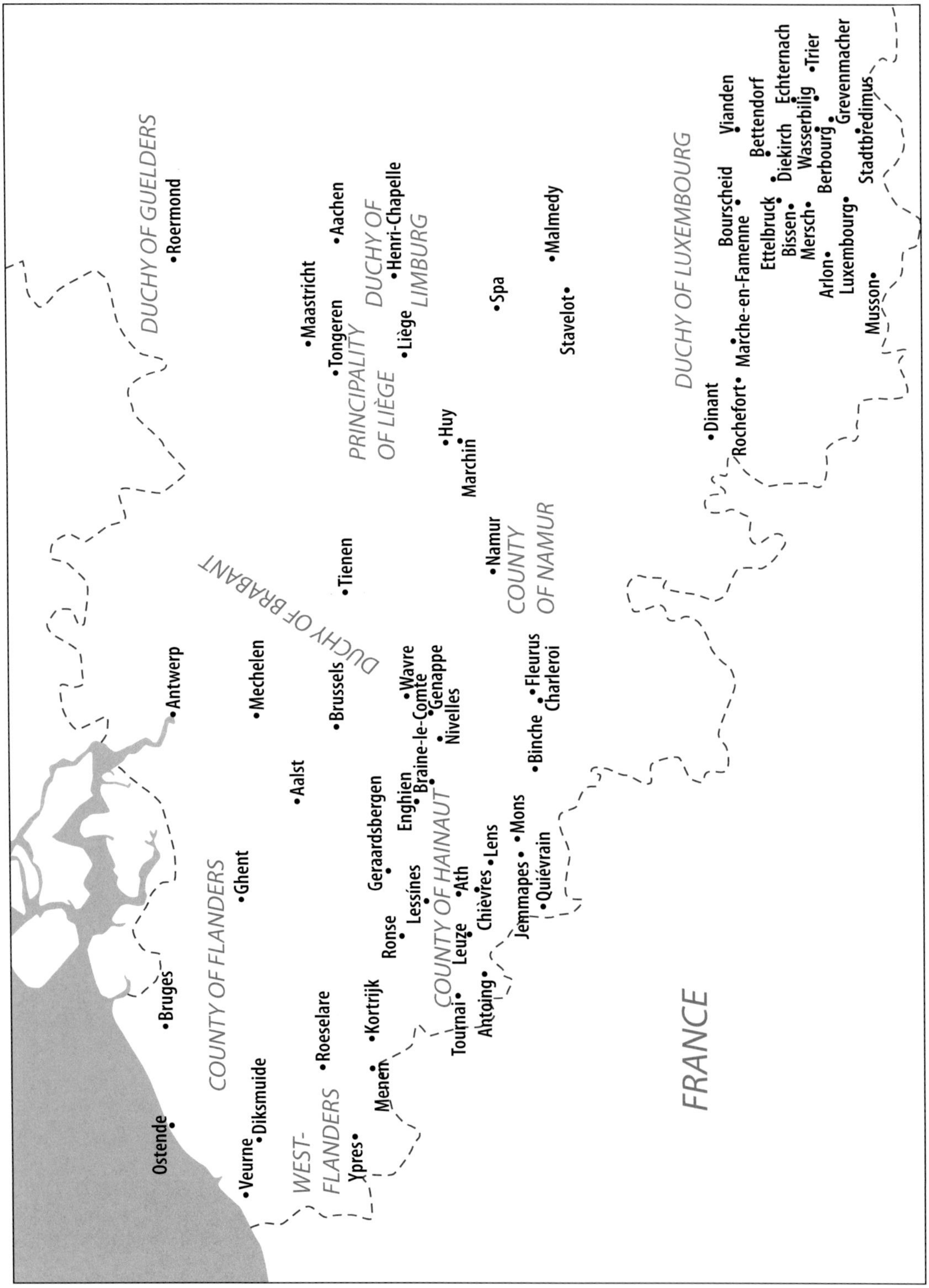

The Austrian Netherlands and Principality of Liège, 1789.

other columns, had to fall back, doing so in good order. La Fayette's command was in such disorder that he had reported that he would be unable to march before 2 May, so he was saved from a similar disaster; hearing of the debacles at Tournai and Mons, he retreated to the stronghold of Sedan.

The plan was Dumouriez's and Rochambeau resigned in disgust, giving the state of his health as a pretext; he was immediately followed by Grave and about 20 general and staff officers of the Armée du Nord. Paradoxically, Dumouriez was to be appointed Minister of War on 13 June 1792 in recognition of the role he played in the dismissal of the Garde Constitutionnelle. Reluctantly, Luckner agreed to replace Rochambeau as commander-in-chief, but before the handover took place, on 11 May, the Austrians seized Bavay and attacked the Maubeuge camp. Rochambeau resolved to retake it, but the confidence in the troops was such that it required both *maréchaux* to command the comparatively small expedition that, on reaching Bavay on 20 May, found that the enemy had already withdrawn.

Luckner formally assumed command on 9 June, and he decided to attack on two fronts, in Flanders and towards Mons. The latter was entrusted to La Fayette, who advanced from Maubeuge and Valenciennes on 11 June. However, two days later, his vanguard, commanded by *lieutenant-general* Gouvion, was routed. In Flanders, Luckner captured Kortrijk on 18 June and then Menen and Ypres the following day, but this victory could not be exploited, and on 1 July, the Austrian commander, Clerfayt, retook the three Flemish cities. In Paris, the defeats were not attributed to the indiscipline and inexperience of the troops but to an Austrian ploy to aid the royalists:

> We were warned yesterday that the Austrian generals received orders from their court to spare the French line troops and to direct all the force of their fire against the volunteer and paid gardes nationales. The line troops are said to belong to the King of France with whom there is a bond of friendship, and in whose fate the greatest interest is taken; war is only waged against the National Assembly and the people who support it. This is the obvious reason for the loss suffered by the Garde volontaire de la Côte d'Or in the last affair. The line troops suffered almost nothing in this fight where the brave Gouvion was killed.[90]

The Agony of the Monarchy

Nicolas Ruault was a lucid and insightful observer of events in Paris, but he was also an actor. An active citizen, an elector, he was a member of the Garde Nationale, although he admitted that he would be incapable of firing a shot, and had been a Jacobin from the start. Thus, he was well informed about the events that incrementally heralded the fall of the monarchy and led to the last wave of military emigration as men who had remained steadfastly loyal finally abandoned all hope of the King regaining his freedom.

90 Ruault, *Gazette*, p.293, letter of 26 June.

Cavalry *maréchal-des-logis chef*, by Rousselot, 1791–1792. (Courtesy of La Sabretache)

On 25 April 1792, a celebration was held in Paris to honour the 40 soldiers of the Régiment de Châteauvieux who, following the Affaire de Nancy in 1790, had been sentenced to the galleys (hard labour) at Brest but had been released on the orders of the Assembly. They were adorned, by whom is not clear, with red Phrygian caps as worn by former freed slaves during the Roman Empire. After the celebration in Paris, the crowd took themselves to the Tuileries to hurl insults at the Garde Constitutionnelle. Ruault noted the seemingly orchestrated way in which this headgear was adopted widely as a revolutionary symbol of Liberty, its use by the French Republic continuing to this day:

> On Wednesday the 15th of this month, we had a bizarre spectacle at the Jacobins; a few members entered wearing a red cap and were warmly applauded. In the following session … more than 300 members presented themselves wearing the red woollen caps; the next day, this red cap was to be seen in the streets, in

> the squares, in the gardens and even in the theatres. This novelty appears very strange: for me I have not worn it and will not wear it … It is to be feared, if this lasts, that the cap will create a schism, between those who wear it and those who do not want to wear it … Finally, the red cap was to become the headdress of all the French patriots, the compulsory headgear of three-quarters of the men of the nation…[91]

From mid-May, the threat to the King and Queen increased, 'It was decreed yesterday and the day before yesterday that forthwith there would be a camp of twenty-five thousand men around Paris. The approach of the Germans and the Austrians is feared'.[92] This was a manufactured fantasy and Louis opposed the decree authorising the establishment of this camp. After submitting his resignation as Minister of the Interior on 13 June, Roland wrote: 'There is no longer time to go back, there is no longer even means of delaying; the Revolution is made in the minds; it will reach a conclusion at the price of blood and will be cemented by blood, if wisdom does not prevent the misfortunes that there is still time to avoid.'[93]

On 20 June, an armed crowd, estimated to be of 25,000 men and women, marched on the Assembly, then, via the Place du Carrousel, to the Tuileries. There, the Gardes Nationaux and gendarmes let them pass and, having hoisted a cannon to the top of the grand staircase, they gained access to the King's cabinet where he was found alone. There, a man in the crowd declared to him, 'All your heart, all your affections are for the émigrés of Koblenz.'[94] To this, he responded by shouting, 'I love the constitution, I will support it with all my heart!'[95] Then, climbing onto a chair, with a Phrygian cap that a Garde Nationale had placed on his head, he drank to the health of the Nation from a bottle. Ruault observed, in the days that followed, the contempt with which the King was held in the Assembly.[96]

That same month, June 1792, Louis planned to have the Dauphin taken to safety in the Netherlands. He chose the Marquis de La Queuille, representative of the King's brothers at Brussels, a *maréchal de camp* and one of the first signatories to the Coalition d'Auvergne, for the task. La Queuille asked his nephew, the Marquis de Marcillac, to join him in this secret mission. They were to travel from Mons and, having collected the Dauphin, return to the Austrian Netherlands immediately. Only once there was La Queuille to announce the heir to the throne's escape and then go to join his uncles at Koblenz.[97] However, once again, the King decided to take no risks and

91 Ruault, *Gazette*, p.280, letter of 20 March 1792.

92 Ruault, *Gazette*, p.287, letter of 8 June 1792.

93 Mortimer Ternaux, *Le peuple aux Tuileries. Le 20 juin 1792* (Paris: Lévy-Frères, Imprimeurs-éditeurs, 1864), p.68.

94 Ternaux, *Le peuple aux Tuileries*, p.290.

95 Ternaux, *Le peuple aux Tuileries*, p.290.

96 Ruault, *Gazette*, p.293.

97 Pierre-Louis-Auguste de Crusy de Marcillac, *Souvenirs de l'émigration ou Mémoires du Marquis de Marcillac* (Paris: Baudouin Frères, 1825), pp.39–40. Copies of the coded correspondence relating to the plan are included in the book.

renounced the plan; it was only then that La Queuille informed Monsieur and Artois of the plan.

Following the dismissal of the three Girondin ministers, Servan, Roland and Clavière, on 16 June, La Fayette sent a letter to the Assembly denouncing the Jacobins and calling on the King to resist all pressure for the sake of constitutional principles and the Law. In response, the Jacobins denounced La Fayette as a dictator, a new Cromwell, and enemy of the people. Robespierre led the attack from the platform of the Assembly, 'Strike La Fayette and the nation is saved … The salvation of France is attached to the fate of La Fayette; if we give him time to achieve his plots, liberty is done, but if he is overthrown immediately, the cause of the people triumphs, and liberty with it.'[98]

Learning of this speech, La Fayette addressed a proclamation to his army and then, with leave from Luckner, went to Paris to complete his political suicide. On 28 June, he appeared at the bar of the Assembly to denounce the attack on the Tuileries on 20 June and, acting as spokesperson for the army, asked the Assembly to guarantee that the Constitution would not be threatened from within while its soldiers shed their blood to protect it. Although applauded by many, he was received coldly by the King and Queen, who did not want to owe their security or throne in any way to the man who, according to them, had already done so much harm to them. Attacked by the Jacobins from all sides and soon threatened with assassination, La Fayette left two days later, realising what was to be the outcome of this crisis.

As events evolved, the Assembly proclaimed 'la patrie en danger' (the homeland in danger) on 11 July and a new levy of volunteers took place with the men being placed in the existing Volontaires Nationaux battalions regardless, this time, of whether they were active citizens or not. When hostilities had begun the line regiments were still short of 51,000 men, including nearly 10,000 officers. The old army had barely 120,000 men, including 40,000 to garrison the strongholds, and, on 1 June 1792, 27,000 men were still needed to complete the infantry alone. In addition, noble officers who still remained with their regiments were systematically denounced, even suspected of treason. In turn, the Garde Nationale was considered too conservative by the Jacobins and Girondins who dominated the Assembly; politically, the battalions of Volontaires Nationaux were preferred. Little by little, the battalions of the Garde Nationale were merged into those of the Volontaires Nationaux, nicknamed les Bleus because of the colour of their uniforms, in contrast to the white of the royal infantry. With the Fête de la Fédération of 14 July drawing close, volunteers, Fédérés, converged on the capital on the pretext that they would then go on to the various theatres of operations. Despite his Jacobin sympathies, the arrival of the Fédérés worried as much as intrigued Ruault who also noted Louis's apparently failing mental health:

> The King … has become a fanatic or fatalist: he is resigned to die, to perish. He said this in his last proclamation on the events of Wednesday. The Pope consoles him from time to time through secret letters. The Brestois are on the march to

98 Etienne Chavaray, *Le général La Fayette (1757-1834) – Notice biographique* (Paris: Société de l'Histoire de la Révolution française, 1898), p.305.

> Paris on 14 July. The Marseillais do the same: they come, it is said, to support the Parisians, as much as for the annual fête. However, they are neither called nor invited publicly. This meeting seems very illegal; there is something beneath it that I do not understand but I will not be ignorant for long, I know where to get information…[99]

After making his enquiries, he wrote on 17 July, as the Prussian invasion of France began:

> They will force the patriots to do what has never been done in the Revolution, to carry out ruthless acts. The leaders of these patriots, of the Jacobins, frequently gather … projects are fashioned against the executive power that itself forms them against the patriots. Frightening resolutions are taken for vulgar souls or friends of peace. It is nothing less than a question of seizing the Tuileries by storm as was done for the Bastille. The project is done; I know it, it is a secret that I confide to you…[100]

The Jacobins considered that the only means to save the Revolution and their own positions was a republic and the elimination of any political opponent. Nevertheless, everything had to be ready, after all, there were suspicions about the Garde Nationale that only a year earlier had opened fire on the people assembled at the Champ-de-Mars. Another force was needed, 'A number of Fédérés arrived these recent days after the fête; and you must suspect why they came; they are men with moustaches [so lower class] for the most part'.[101] The fate of the royal family was discussed openly:

> The National Assembly, which sees the storm advancing is in the greatest confusion; it does not know which side to take. Will it decree, to prevent horrible misfortunes, that the King is deposed from the throne? But it is necessary the following day to organise a new executive; who would assume it? What would be done with the deposed King, his wife, his son? Would he be reduced to the status of a simple individual or would we send them abroad to get rid of them altogether? Or better to keep the young prince in minority?[102]

Then on 4 August, Pétion, the Mayor of Paris, informed the Assembly, in the name of the 48 sections of the Paris Commune, that Louis XVI should be stripped of his position and the royal family expelled from the national territory. Ruault described the denouement:

> Finally the blow was struck. The 10th of this month [August 1792] will be the match, if it does not surpass it further, of 14 July 1789. The victory remained with the people after a cannonade and the play of musketry of around an hour. The affair began at half past nine, before eleven the battle was won … The

99 Ruault, *Gazette*, p.294, letter of 26 June 1792.
100 Ruault, *Gazette*, pp.296–297, letter of 17 July 1792.
101 Ruault, *Gazette*, p.297.
102 Ruault, *Gazette*, p.298.

> Marseillais, Brestois and many other Fédérés from different départements mixed with Parisians gained the victory over around two thousand Swiss and others who defended the château. It must be admitted that without these Fédérés, strangers to Paris, the battle was lost … without the help of the Fédérés from Marseille, Brest, etc. those who ordered the attack would have done nothing that day or would have postponed it. Those who did not fight, who only had the sabre or pike as a weapon, were the most determined to cover the victory with blood, to kill, to slaughter the rest of the Swiss and the other defenders of the château. It is an execrable horror … It must have been yesterday that the King was informed of the day and the hour of the attack on the château as the apartments, the galleries were found full of former nobles, officers, servants armed to defend themselves and who perished for the most part during and after the action. Yesterday, the 13th, around four o'clock in the afternoon, the King was led to the Temple [prison], with his family, amidst the curses, the insults of a crowd of common people. He is locked in one of the towers…[103]

The ancient and constitutional monarchy perished together. In the days that followed, it became clear that this new Revolution would erase that of 1789 and herald a republic. Profiting from the political vacuum, the Jacobins and their most extreme supporters declared the creation of a new insurrectionary Commune which would dictate to the Assembly the wishes of the people, that is to say, the Sans-Culottes. They, with a thirst for blood and fury, would be the instrument of tyranny.

103 Ruault, *Gazette*, pp.301–303, letter of 14 August 1792.

3

Formation and Organisation of the Armée des Princes

From the Lyon Conspiracy to the Creation of the Armée des Princes

The first two units of the emigration, Coalition d'Auvergne and Chevaliers de la Couronne, had been formed, at least on paper, around the end of 1790 to support the projected invasion of France through Lyon and Savoy. Then, from May 1791, royalist troops were to be raised to participate in the invasion plan Artois proposed to Emperor Leopold. The émigrés would require a safe place of assembly, a military organisation, and finally arms for the conflict that was considered by all parties to be inevitable.

The installation of the princes in Koblenz and Worms had given rise quite early to the creation of guards for their protection. How that around Condé was formed has been described above, and Artois certainly had some of his former guards with him. Then, when his brother joined him at Schönbornslust in Koblenz, a unit was set up for their security, probably at the beginning of July. The Marquis de La Maisonfort, formerly an officer in the Dragons de Monsieur commanded by the Comte de La Châtre, had emigrated in May 1791 and gone to Worms where he joined Condé's guards. He then went to Koblenz:

> Monsieur ... had just arrived in Koblenz [on 7 July]; I paid court to him as well as to the Comte d'Artois, and I was inscribed as one of the first to form a sort of guard of honour that was called 'the dragons [dragoons] des princes.' To serve in it, it was necessary to have been a dragoon officer.[1]

The events of the summer of 1791 that provoked the increased emigration of officers, gentlemen and those of the Third Estate, as well as several army units, added impetus to the formation of military units. The departure of 38 officers of the 1er (ci-devant Colonel-général) Infanterie from the Dunkirk garrison for Veurne in the Austrian Netherlands, taking the regiment's two flags with them, has been mentioned. Then, a few days later, those of the

1 La Maisonfort, *Mémoires*, p.184.

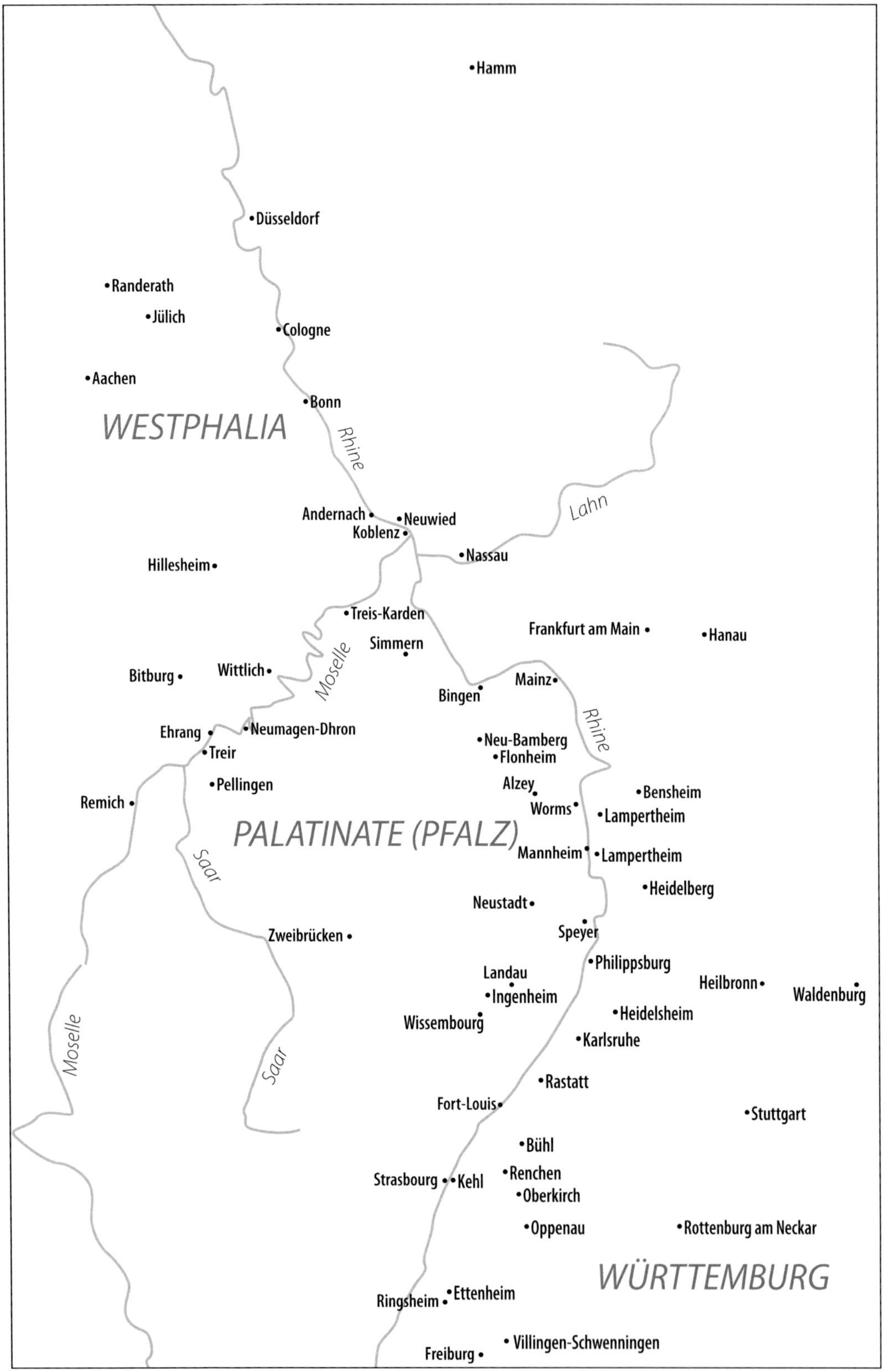

Western Germany.

1er (Colonel-général) Cavalerie also left with their standards. In Phalsbourg, the non-commissioned officers of the 17e (ci-devant Auvergne) Infanterie assembled the regiment upon hearing of recent events and took the initiative to drive out the officers, 'It was to be done on the 29th: for the first time, non-commissioned officers took charge of the insurrection.'[2] From the battalion of the ci-devant Orléans-infanterie stationed at Maubeuge, the *colonel*, the Comte de Vauban, and 34 officers deserted; only five remained.

Officers, on their own volition or by force, emigrated alone, in small groups or even in larger numbers from the same regiment, sometimes bringing with them a small number of non-commissioned officers and soldiers. At the beginning of July 1791, the Prince de Condé noted: 'On Monday 4, there arrived to me that day, like the following ones, many officers who preferred the loss of their position and the service of the good cause, to that of the National Assembly which demanded an oath which they rightly found contrary to their honour.'[3]

The new arrivals needed to be accommodated while they waited to be organised into military units. The first units, Coalition d'Auvergne, Chevaliers de la Couronne and Légion de Mirabeau, being individual initiatives. Condé recorded in his journal: 'Friday 8, after having made all the arrangements to accommodate all the officers who arrived with me having not wanted to take the oath, I left … Saturday 16, … I went to see the officers of the mounted troops in the quarters that I had assigned to them, in Horchheim [just southwest of Worms].'[4]

Thus, new strictly military cantonments were being established. However, the German princes were, at best, reluctant hosts, as was seen when part of the 88e Régiment, formerly the nominally Irish Berwick, emigrated:

> Monday 18, I learned that more than two hundred soldiers from Berwick [in fact three hundred] on route from Landau to Wissembourg, where this regiment was being sent, had left the column with their arms, torn a scrap from their shirt to put on their hats, shouted 'Long live the King and the Princes,' and had come to join me without the rest of the regiment having opposed it; I sent officers on all the roads by which they could reach me, to direct them to Ettenheim, the only place in Germany where they still wanted to give asylum to French soldiers loyal to their King and their honour.[5]

Cardinal de Rohan, Bishop of Strasbourg, not only a Frenchman but also related by marriage to Condé, was the Prince-Bishop of Ettenheim. Since 14 March, the Cardinal had permitted his lands to be used for the initial assembly of volunteers for the Légion de Mirabeau.

The still spontaneous exodus grew, and the princes, Monsieur, Artois and Condé, were joined by an ever-increasing number of the nobility, active or retired officers, as well as gentlemen who had never served, refractory clergy

2 Deschard, *L'Armée et la Révolution*, p.203.
3 Condé, *Journal*, p.212.
4 Condé, *Journal*, pp.213–215.
5 Condé, *Journal*, p.215.

and some of the general population – peasants, artisans, bourgeois and magistrates. The Rhineland, where they were now installed, was strategically advantageous, being a rich and dynamic area with established banking networks and potential sources of clothing, equipment, armament, remounts and recruits. The tapestry of territories in the wider region, with enclaves, exclaves and overlapping sovereignties and allegiances, made it difficult for revolutionary France to isolate or target the princes, diplomatically or even militarily. Furthermore, as well as individual entrepreneurs, small German sovereign states had the motivation to raise regiments in the context of a counter-revolutionary crusade, to demonstrate their attachment to the Bourbon dynasty, protect their lands within Alsace, or even to protect themselves from the contamination of revolutionary ideas.

Commissioners were key to the princes' project, as one of their number wrote:

> The functions that Général Baron de Pouilly exercised at Luxembourg, in his capacity of commissioner of the Princes for the French nobility (functions with which he had been entrusted, since 1791, by their Royal Highnesses Monsieur and Monseigneur d'Artois), consisted above all of receiving gentlemen, officers and soldiers, as they emigrated from the kingdom to join the flag of honour raised on the banks of the Rhine by the hands of royalism and loyalty. It was from the hands of the commissioner of the Princes that each of the emigrants received the necessary instructions, either to go to Koblenz in order to take orders directly from the princes, or to learn where were the places of assembly of the different corps of the army or of the various coalitions of the provincial nobility, according to the views, projects, or convenience of each of the arrivals. For this purpose, their Royal Highnesses had established commissioners of the nobility in each of the foreign principal cities within reach of the country where the loyal army had been forming for several months. Luxembourg, Brussels, Tournai, Mons, Trier, Liège, Frankfurt, Aachen, Maastricht, Cologne, Antwerp had these commissioners almost all general or senior officers. Those of Brussels [where the largest community of émigrés was gathered] were four in number …[6]

A key function of the commissioners was to examine the service records and proofs of seniority of the active and retired officers. Without military experience but determined to fight for the King, the Chevalier Blondin d'Abancourt left his home in Abbeville for the nearest Belgian city:

> I left the paternal roof on 12 September 1791, with that enthusiasm that still inflames a twenty-seven-year-old head, and I went to Tournai, where I knew that the King's brothers had organised a commission to receive émigrés who wanted to enrol. It was M. Comte de Conchy who presided over this commission; he received me very well and had me enrol in a company of gentlemen, where I remained for six months, occupied learning the military profession … Meanwhile, the émigrés

6 Jean-Antoine de Brons, *Journal d'émigration* (Saint-Quentin-de-Baron: Chez Entre-deux-mers, 2014), p.36. On 9 September 1792 Brons was designated commissioner at Luxembourg, to replace Pouilly, by the Princes.

> were gathering on all the points of the frontier. The Comte de La Châtre had also established a cantonment of gentlemen in the town of Ath, and he had divided them into companies of different arms.[7]

In this part of the Austrian Netherlands, the infantry cantonment was at Ath and that of the cavalry at Aalst, both west of Brussels, but the émigrés had to be lodged more widely; 'the émigrés of the Ath cantonment were distributed in the cities of Ath, Tournai, Braine-le-Comte, Geraardsbergen, Lessines and in the large villages in the surrounding area.'[8] In the province of Luxembourg, the émigrés were distributed in Mersch, Ettelbruck, Diekirch, Echternach, Bettendorf, Vianden (belonging to the Prince of Orange), Berbourg, Bourscheid, Grevenmacher and Wasserbilig. Each month a *capitaine* was detached by an infantry company to reside with the commissioner and be responsible for the distribution of correspondence and orders to the different cantonments. In Luxembourg, three times a week, an orderly officer came from Mersch to collect the packages from Luxembourg city; on his return, those for onward distribution were collected by another orderly officer from Ettelbruck, they then continued on to the other cantonments, starting with Diekirch.

At Worms, Condé had similar issues to deal with, the officers of the Régiment de Beauvoisis, who had joined him on 19 April 1791, decided to remain together.[9] They were lodged, 'in one of the rooms of the Worms hospital, after the Elector of Worms, taken with pity, had had windows installed there. We sleep on wooden frames, the hard way'.[10] Their example was followed by all the officers of the Régiment de Vivarais who, on 28 June, emigrated en bloc, led by their *colonel* and *lieutenant-colonel*, from the garrison at Rocroi, to first reach Koblenz, then Worms. The influx of new arrivals was distributed in the surrounding villages, so by the beginning of July, there were cavalry officers at Horchheim, while others found quarters in the city, the officers of the Condé-infanterie being housed at the city gate. By 10 August there were 500 gentlemen gathered in Worms and Mannheim, looking to the Condé for organisation. He noted in his journal the steps he took:

> On Wednesday, 3 [August], I received from Koblenz a letter from Monsieur, which I expected, according to what we had agreed: the Nobility pressed for a formation; we found, according to our news, that this was too soon; on the other hand, we realised that all the delays (which did not depend on us) discouraged them and we wanted to avoid that: to make them have patience, we had arranged that the Princes would ask for a statement of the names, age, and services of all the gentlemen who wished to enter the formation of the Corps of the Nobility, and the Princes charged me directly with all the part on the Rhine up river from Mainz; I shared this news, which did not fail to have its effect and raise spirits;

---

7 Gabriel-Isidore Blondin d'Abancourt, *Onze ans d'émigration : mémoires du chevalier Blondin d'Abancourt* (Paris: Alphonse Picard et fils, 1897), pp.5–6.

8 Anon (ed.), *Mémoires d'Olivier d'Argens et Correspondances des Généraux* (Paris: Baudouin Frères, 1826), p.13.

9 Grouvel, *Troupes de l'émigration*, vol.II, p.247.

10 Marcel Chapron, *Mirabeau-Tonneau* (Paris: Les Editions Haussmann, 1956), p.214.

> this gave us a month to have the time to receive what we asked from Ostende to Nice … On Thursday the 4th, the Nobility who were at Worms began to write to the Comte de Choiseul, my capitaine of the Guards; I had written the day before to M. de Vaubecourt, lieutenant-général, so that he would take charge of those at Mannheim; I wrote all morning, for the same task to Rastatt, Horchheim, and to Fribourg in Switzerland; I had charged M. de Turpin, lieutenant-général, with the part at Heidelberg.[11]

Particular attention was paid to the arrival of significant numbers of soldiers as described by the Duc de Fitz-James, proprietary *colonel* of the Régiment de Berwick, when he wrote a week after its emigration:

> They took neither the chest nor the flags; I regret the first, it would have provided subsistence for 4 or 5 months; as for the flags, I cannot regret them since they have been soiled by the so-called patriotic cravats. I am having them made anew at Mannheim, I will have them consecrated in Salsbach, where M. de Turenne was killed; it is there that the regiment is gathered, it is there that it reassembles.[12]

On 28 July Monsieur, on behalf of his brother Louis XVI, wrote to the officers and men of the Régiment de Berwick thanking them for their devotion to the royal cause: 'I respond to you in advance that it will soothe his sorrows, and that he will receive with pleasure from you the same marks of fidelity that James II received, 100 years ago, from your ancestors. This double era should forever form the motto of the Régiment de Berwick, that will be seen on your flags'.[13] This motto, written in Latin, was, '1691. Semper et ubique fidelis [Always and everywhere faithful]. 1791.'[14]

The 72e Régiment d'infanterie (ci-devant Vexin), or at least the majority of its officers, stationed at Monaco, were to follow the example of Berwick. On 13 August 1791 some officers, non-commissioned officers and soldiers, in concert with others in the garrison, were to open the gates at night to admit émigrés who had gathered at Nice and the nearby towns of l'Escarène and Sospel. However, the plan being betrayed, the conspirators had to escape to Nice. There, the following day, the French consul informed the Assembly that 26 officers and NCOs of the Régiment de Vexin had arrived; in addition, 200 to 300 soldiers were arrested, suspected of having participated in this plot. Two weeks later Condé noted:

> 27 August – During supper someone came to ask for me: it was an officer from the Régiment de Vexin who came as a courier on behalf of his comrades to inform me that almost all the officers of this regiment, and some soldiers, had left Monaco to avoid taking the oath, and had gone to Nice, where they awaited my orders as colonel-general of the infantry.[15]

11 Chapron, *Mirabeau-Tonneau*, p.218.
12 *Le Moniteur*, 14 August 1791, letter dated Koblenz, 25 July, published after its interception.
13 *Le Moniteur*, 14 August 1791.
14 Anon., *Correspondance et écrits de Sa Majesté Louis XVIII* (Paris: Rapilly, 1824), p.2.
15 Condé, *Journal*, p.222.

Flag of the Régiment de Vexin-infanterie. (Author's collection)

Artois was also informed at the same time.[16] In recognition of its conduct, the King's brothers decided that the regiment should be reconstituted under its *colonel*, the Chevalier de Damas-Crux. On 1 September 1791:

> … the Princes issued a special regulation for the Régiment de Vexin of which the principal provisions were as follows: recognition of the émigré part of the regiment as the sole and true Régiment de Vexin – maintenance of the mess, administration and composition as in France – suppression of the grenadiers who conducted themselves badly at Fort Saint Nicolas in Marseille – preservation of the ranks and appointments among the émigré officers and non-commissioned officers, upon presentation from the colonel – additional pay of 15 sols per day granted to the caporaux, appointés, chasseurs, fusiliers and tambours.[17]

The officers had brought the regiment's *colonel*'s flag with them, and it was decided to mark the emigration by adding, to the vertical branch of the central cross, the device: PRO DEO ET REGE – DIE 14 MENSIS AUGUSTI 1791.[18]

16 Muret, *Armée de Condé*, vol.I, p.237, citing a letter from the Duc de Berry to his father.
17 Grouvel, *Troupes de l'émigration*, vol.II, pp.129–132.
18 The flag was discovered around 1975, at the Musée Barrois, Bar-le-Duc; according to Professeur Charrié, a leading expert on flags of the Ancien Régime, it would have been from the collection of Maréchal Oudinot who found it at Maastricht in 1810.

As for the individual émigrés, who generally gathered among friends, relatives or those from the same region, or otherwise with fellow officers of their former regiment or arm, they needed to be organised within a military structure that would serve as the nucleus of a future army – the Armée des Princes. On 18 August 1791, Monsieur, Artois and Condé met to finalise a set of regulations drafted by *maréchal* de Broglie, and these were published the following day as the 'Definitive Regulation, For the formation in different Companies, of the Nobility gathered with Monsieur & Monseigneur the Comte d' Artois.'[19] It contained 25 articles that were mainly concerned with organising military units:

> ... composed of officers of the troops of the line troops who left France, either because of the insurrection of the soldiers, or for not having wanted to take the oath; of a fairly large number of other officers, who, after having served, were in the case of taking their retirement, or of undergoing a reform, & finally of gentlemen who had not served at all.[20]

Each company of officers or gentlemen, both infantry and cavalry, would be composed of 54 gentlemen, including a *commandant en premier*, a *commandant en second*, four *chefs de section* and eight *chefs d'escoude* (squad leaders). This conformed with the ordinances of 1788 for cavalry and infantry, except for the use of the ranks of *chef de section* and *chef d'escouade* (another one used during the emigration was *chef de peloton*). They denoted those performing the roles of non-commissioned officers, *bas-officiers* in the former royal army, so different titles were used to avoid upsetting the sensibilities of gentlemen, all members of such a unit being considered to be officers. The drummer or trumpeter of each company, wearing the King's livery on the coat collar, cuffs and pockets, would be maintained by the prince brothers of the King, as well as a farrier for two mounted companies, which formed a squadron.

Officers from a particular regiment would be assembled in a company that would bear the name of the regiment from which the greatest number of officers came. This was with a view of rallying men from the regiment to the cadre. Article 5 specified that, 'the *colonel* will command the company, that the *lieutenant-colonel* will be the second in command, & that the *major* & the first three *capitaines* will each command a section, the other officers will be placed in the ranks, according to the seniority of their grade.' So, the remaining *capitaines* along with the *lieutenants* ranked as volunteers, unless they were promoted or took a place in another corps, such as provincial coalitions (Article IX), that offered better positions. They could also transfer in order to join relatives (Article X). The 'officers of the regiment of guards, those of the royal corps of artillery, & that of engineers' were not expected to serve in such companies (Article VI). Units of Gardes du Corps du Roi and

---

19 Anon., *Règlement définitif, Pour la formation en différentes Compagnies, de la Noblesse rassemblée auprès de Monsieur & de Monseigneur le Comte d'Artois* (Paris: Senneville, Libraire au Palais-royal, 1791).

20 Anon., *Règlement définitif,* Article I.

those for Monsieur and Artois were to be formed, in addition to units based upon the former Compagnies Rouges (Red Companies) of the old Maison Militaire (see Chapter 4).

In each cantonment where retired officers, discharged officers and gentlemen who had not served before were gathered, a list was to be drawn up indicating for each their seniority, rank, services and age – in fact, there would be two lists, one for the cavalry and another for the infantry companies. Officers of the Marine royale (the navy), while waiting for enough comrades to arrive to form one or more companies, would be authorised to join the companies of the gentlemen from their province or any other of their choice, in a function that equated to their rank in relation to the line (Article XI).

The company commanded by the most senior *colonel* would take precedence, with the seniority of the others established according to that of their commanders. However, in the event of an incumbent's death or transfer, the company would retain its rank as fixed. Condé would have:

> … the task of assembling into companies all the gentlemen who find themselves placed in the towns and countryside, on the right and left of the Rhine, from Mainz to Switzerland. He will indicate the points he has chosen to effect the formation & assembly of the companies. The princes wished to reserve to themselves the details for the companies which will be formed from Mainz to Cologne, on the right and left banks of the Rhine, & in the lands of Luxembourg, Flanders and Hainaut.[21]

The regulation also fixed the uniform, armament and equipment for the noble volunteers:

> Article XX Clothing
> The uniform of all the companies is to be a blue coat, red waistcoat, yellow breeches; gilded brass buttons, with a fleur-de-lys in the middle.
>
> White plume on the hat, white cockade & black [inner] collar.
>
> However, in those that will be composed of officers who were active, it will be permitted to them to retain the uniform of the regiments in which they served before their departure from France [thus to the regulation of October 1786 modified by that of 1 April 1791].
>
> And in the case where some companies have already adopted a uniform different from that prescribed by the regulation, the princes allow them to keep it provisionally.
>
> Article XXI Equipment
> In the mounted companies of gentlemen, [any] saddles that can be obtained will be made use of indiscriminately; but they will be adapted with holsters, & they will be covered with a shabraque of red wool, or of such other colour that will be adopted by the company, the said shabraque simple & without lace.

21 Anon., *Règlement définitif*, Article XVIII.

> The horses will have a bit in the French style; they will have the snaffle, bridle and halter on the head.
>
> Article XXII Armament
> Each mounted gentleman will have two pistols & a sabre.
>
> The gentlemen on foot will be armed with a musket with its bayonet, which will be furnished to them, as well as the pouch, as soon as possible; they will have in addition a sabre or a sword.[22]

The Comte de La Châtre organised those at Ath, while Condé arranged matters at Worms, sharing the regulation with the senior officers he had with him on 24 August. The following day the first registration office was established at Worms, and the first companies were organised on Friday, 9 September, in the courtyard of the Elector's castle, and were soon followed by others. Among these earliest companies were those of Colonel-général, Royal-Auvergne, Vivarais, Neustrie and Beauvoisis, followed by Beaujolais and Brie. In October, there were 19 companies in training, both at Worms and in the Netherlands, and the following month there were 24, nearly 1,200 men. The number of émigrés would continue to grow, 'There would be 3,000 émigrés in Koblenz in December 1791 according to the Comte d'Espinchal, 5,000 in January 1792 according to the Minister of France, Sainte-Croix.'[23]

Among other caricatures, the revolutionary press portrayed the émigré troops as wooden soldiers with which Condé could play *Kriegsspiele* (wargames). However, they were far from being paper tigers. If the troops were mainly noble volunteers, former officers or gentlemen, they would now be organised on a strictly military footing. Although Monsieur's and Artois's military experience was effectively limited to being honorary or proprietary *colonels*, they had two experienced *maréchaux*, Castries and Broglie, as well as Condé to turn to, all three were to show that they were as good tacticians as they were organisers. From August 1791 to July 1792 a dozen regulations were issued in the name of the princes, devoted to the troops' organisation, equipment, clothing, quartering and training (see Appendix 1).

However precise they were, it must be recognised that the first regulations would be adapted to both circumstance and means, just as much to the susceptibility or pretensions of the French nobility as well as to the particularities of the different corps. At this stage, the main difference between the corps was the means that their personnel could devote to the crusade; some continued to live in style, mounting and equipping themselves at their own expense, like the Coalition d'Auvergne and Chevaliers de la Couronne. Others had hardly enough to house themselves, their property having been seized and their pensions cancelled. The 'Regulation for the Cantonments, with Letter sent from the Princes, brothers of the King, and declaration of their sentiments. Schönbornslust, 30 October 1791' fortunately announced

22 Anon., *Règlement définitif*, Articles XX–XXII.

23 Karine Rance, 'Le rassemblement de Coblence: le mythe fondateur', in Alain Cabantous (ed.), *Mythologies urbaines, les villes entre histoire et imaginaire* (Rennes: Presses universitaires de France, 2004), p.186.

that, from 1 November, volunteers would be paid, 45 livres for the infantry and 75 livres for cavalry. The news was well received, but the gentlemen of the Coalition d'Auvergne decided that they would continue to serve at their own expense, so the princes could use the amount saved in other ways.

In November, the Armée des Princes remained embryonic; in the cantonments around Worms there were only eight companies of cavalry, as many of infantry and a single artillery company, lodged in the city itself.

There was equality and even fairness among the different gatherings, the uniformity with which the companies of gentlemen were treated being extended to the free companies. However, the restoration at Koblenz of the Maison Militaire and prestigious corps such as the old Gendarmerie, to which higher pay would be granted, was to create another divide between the rich aristocracy and penniless provincial or military nobility. The meagre means available to the Armée des Princes would be tested to maintain the brilliance of the troops gathered around the King's brothers, even leading to the ruin of grands seigneurs (great lords) who had taken on debt or stood surety for the loans raised for this purpose. La Maisonfort, who had returned to France in the late summer of 1791 to try to save part of his property, rejoined his squadron at the turn of the year 1791/1792 and found, 'Koblenz had increased tenfold since my absence. Blues, reds, greys, greens, whites, one only saw uniforms, all that was heard was the dragging of sabres on the pavement. Everything was plumes, epaulettes, hope and madness.'[24]

Pierre Augustin Tercier, was already an experienced officer before he served in the Gardes du corps de Monsieur between 1 January 1782 and 12 September 1791, when the guards of both Monsieur and Artois were disbanded. Having emigrated, he joined the latter's reconstituted Gardes du Corps squadron at Koblenz. He gives a damning portrayal of the aristocratic courtly society that had been reconstituted there:

> All the vices and pretensions of the court have rushed to Koblenz. One sees people with no other talents than those of intrigue and arrogance, getting themselves appointed to employment and ranks that they are unfit to fill. The most unbridled ambition, abstract of feelings, brazenly takes the place of true royalism. There is not an émigré who does not count on a higher rank when royal authority is reestablished. The most revolting luxury, the most dissolute morals are put on display to the Germans, astonished by our conduct and our habits. We have none of the virtues of self-denial that should be the virtue of military men in the difficult circumstances in which we find ourselves. The great, instead of making themselves popular and cherished by the provincial gentlemen, make themselves despised. Incapable of any privation, they possess none of those austere virtues that one must know to face down adversity. If they had consulted and studied history, they would have learned from it how those struggling with misfortune ought to conduct themselves. It is not in slippers and dressing gowns that one should hope to make an armed counter-revolution. It requires austere virtues that we do not have. There are among us more modern philosophers than one thinks,

24 La Maisonfort, *Mémoires*, p.108.

> that self-esteem has brought here, and on whom one cannot count. At the first setback, one will see them change livery.[25]

The contrast between the aristocratic Court of Koblenz and the military camp at Worms is often cited, but it ignores the cantonments in the Austrian Netherlands, where, despite dispersion and sometimes confusion, an army had to be organised. One officer who arrived there was the Comte Jean-Antoine de Brons, of the corps d'état-major (staff corps), most of whom favoured the new French regime. He described himself as, 'one of the very small number of colonels of the staff who remained attached to the good cause.'[26] He recalled:

> My son and I were accepted as volunteers [on 6 May 1792], in the company of the régiment d'infanterie de Picardie, then in cantonment at Diekirch, a small town in the province and duchy of Luxembourg, where the said company was provisionally brigaded with that of the régiment d'infanterie d'Armagnac and that of the chasseurs à pied des Cévennes. Under the command of Messieurs the Chevalier de Braquemont (Picardie), de Blau (Armagnac) and de Tourtoulon (Cévennes). The officers of these three corps and the gentlemen volunteers who had gathered at this cantonment formed a total of about one hundred maîtres, not including a small number of soldiers of Picardie and Armagnac who had followed their officers as well as a few workers (such as tailors, shoemakers, wigmakers) and the servants of the officers who had emigrated with their masters. The total of this small colony, including women and children, amounted to nearly 150 people and significantly increased the population of the small town of Diekirch whose inhabitants, not very wealthy but humane and compassionate, had in general only good dealings with us.[27]

For God, the King and the Ancient Honour of France

As has been seen, the first significant wave of military emigration took place in the aftermath of Varennes and in October 1791, 1,900 officers were reported to be missing from the colours. The exodus continued sporadically in reaction to the events of the Revolution and then the death throes of the monarchy in the successive crises of 20 June and 10 August 1792. At the outbreak of the war, 3,720 officers had abandoned the army, and they had been joined by other aristocrats and simple gentlemen who had enrolled in the ranks of the counter-revolution. While some émigrés slipped from France without too much difficulty, others faced danger.

---

25 Charles de La Chanonie (ed.), *Mémoires historiques et politiques du général Tercier (1770-1816)* (Paris: Librairie Plon, 1891), p.54. For Tercier's later service in the emigration see Hughes de Bazouges and Alistair Nichols, *For God and King. A history of the Légion de Damas (1793-1798)* (Warwick: Helion, 2021).

26 Brons, *Journal*, p.40.

27 Brons, *Journal*, pp.29–30.

One such was Louise-Françoise de Bennes (née de Haussay), who, before the Revolution, had been living with her husband and two children in a modest manor in what is now the Orne département. Her husband, with no military experience, had declined the post of *colonel* of the local Garde Nationale, and so he was denounced and arrested, with his wife, on 11 December 1791. Facing death, the couple escaped, and together they decided to join the émigrés. Facing many dangers, they succeeded in reaching Tournai, where they were given a letter of recommendation for a fellow Norman, the Marquis Jacques-Etienne du Mesniel, Marquis de Sommery, an infantry *colonel* and former *lieutenant* of the Gardes Françaises. With little money left, they continued on foot for Koblenz.[28]

Each person's experience of emigration was individual to them. The Chevalier de Pradel de Lamase, a young artillery *capitaine* in the Régiment de Strasbourg, remembers that in mid-November 1791 he decided to emigrate. He confided this to his *colonel*, M. de Puységur, who admitted that he was thinking about it himself, no longer having any authority over his rebellious soldiers. On the evening of 11 December, Puységur gathered his officers to inform them that he had decided to emigrate (in fact, he would resign in March 1792 and retire to his lands near Soissons). Everyone who decided to do likewise had to settle their affairs before making an irreversible decision. There was always the threat of being denounced, Pradel de Lamase noting in his journal on 24 December 1791:

> … my comrades left one by one, without fuss, avoiding any untimely publicity … None of the former officers of my fine regiment remain. Many of our first opponents, whether they realised that they had been duped by the Revolution or they had returned to good sentiments of their own accord, drew nearer to us in these last months and wished to share our fortune … none of the defaulters, even those I distrust the most, betrayed us at the last hour. We had not concealed our intentions from them and it was up to them to thwart them, or at least to put obstacles in the way of their realisation. They did not do so. A final surge of the sentiment of confraternity of arms doubtless stopped them.[29]

Many of those who wished to emigrate from the west of France sailed to England or the Channel Islands, from where they could continue to Belgium.[30] Pierre Olivier d'Argens left Quimper, in Brittany, on 8 January 1792, reached Jersey, and very soon embarked with 55 émigrés for Ostende, where he landed on 28 January. There, he and his companions were detained until their identities were established by Austrian officers, after which their weapons were returned, and they were lodged in some inns. The following day, they continued to Bruges before the group, now numbering about

28 See Louise-Françoise de Houssay de Bennes, *A narrative of the sufferings of Louise Françoise de Houssay, de Bennes, who served in the army as a volunteer, from 1792 to July 21, 1795, when she was made a prisoner at Quiberon* (London: Author, 1796).

29 Paul et Martial de Pradel de Lamase, *Nouvelles notes intimes d'un émigré (Le chevalier de Pradel de Lamase, officier à l'armée de Condé)* (Paris: Emile-Paul Frères, 1920), pp.119–120.

30 See Comte Régis de l'Estourbeillon, *Les familles françaises à Jersey pendant la Révolution* (Nantes: Imprimerie Vincent Forest et Emile Grimaud, 1886).

a hundred volunteers, continued to Ath, where the Comte de La Châtre received them. On 4 February 1792, Argens was registered at the cantonment of Lens where there were 24 or 25 young men of the bourgeoisie.[31]

Brons, cited above, at first intended to join émigrés in Spain when he left with his son to emigrate on 29 October 1791 as he was at Libourne, near Bordeaux. His brother had already left with a large number of gentlemen from Sarlat, and another group of about 30, waited for news of how the first got on. However, learning that no armament was imminent in Spain and, by contrast, 'the Princes assembled on the banks of the Rhine a faithful army to which French gentlemen from all the provinces were flocking'.[32] So they changed plans and reached Luxembourg, via Paris, in May 1792.

The arrival of those who emigrated during the Revolution was to be the cause of friction among the émigrés. After all the later an officer or other gentleman had remained in France, the greater the chance they had acquiesced or even co-operated with the Revolution. No one wished to see the reputation of his unit, and by association himself, tarnished by such an individual. This was inevitable given that, from the start, the émigrés placed such importance on personal honour. Indeed, the members of the Coalition d'Auvergne made the following undertaking, literally the act of coalition:

> The undersigned members of the province of Auvergne and those accepted by it, united and bound by the same sentiments, engage among themselves on their word of honour:
>
> To employ all their strength and their efforts to maintain the Catholic, Apostolic and Roman religion, and to reestablish it in its entire exercise and its ancient splendour;
>
> To march together, and always united, to render to King Louis XVI his crown and his power, of which a criminal, perjured and powerless Assembly has seized, and, in a word, to reestablish the monarchy;
>
> Willingly consenting to renounce all their pecuniary advantages, but wishing to sustain their nobility and transmit it to their children as they received it from their ancestors, without any right to tarnish it or undermine it;
>
> Swearing on their honour and faith as gentlemen never to disunite, to obey Mgr. the Comte d'Artois and the princes of the house of Condé;
>
> … If any other gentlemen from the other provinces, imbued with the same sentiments, desire to unite with those of the province of Auvergne, they will be obliged to sign the act of Coalition; but can only be received by a plurality of votes and proposed by a gentleman from the province of Auvergne …[33]

The gentlemen who left the kingdom to take part in the counter-revolutionary crusade came to serve Pro Deo et Rege (For God and King). This was essentially a battle cry that drew on the motto of French chivalry: My soul is

31 See Anon. (ed.), *Olivier d'Argens.*

32 Brons, *Journal*, pp.28–29.

33 Francisque Mège, 'Notes biographiques sur les députés de Basse-Auvergne – Le marquis de La Queuille', *Mémoires de l'Académie des Arts, Belles Lettres et Sciences* (Clermont-Ferrand; Ferdinand Thibaud, Imprimeur-libraire, 1868), vol.X, p.104.

God's, my life is the King's, my heart is my Lady's, and my Honour is mine. If honour required them to fight to restore the crown of one who had betrayed them, their allegiance was transferred to his brothers. In doing so, they had given up so much that honour was the most precious possession they had left, and on this point, any gentleman who was rejected by his peers, whatever his status, would become an outcast. As Brons noted:

> The émigré nobility believed that pure royalism, incorruptible loyalty, conduct always beyond reproach during the early periods of the Revolution, were the only titles that could give the right to serve with them, and their estimable and illustrious general (maréchal de Broglie) shared this opinion with them. All these valiant chevaliers, these brave gentlemen, these officers full of talent and courage thought and proclaimed loudly that their numbers, however inconsiderable they were, were enough to bring about a counter-revolution in France.[34]

In practice, a new arrival had to find two gentlemen from his region or officers from his regiment to vouch for him; that his ideas or behaviour were free from any revolutionary stain. Only then could he be presented to the Princes of the House of Bourbon, not only Monsieur and his brother the Comte d'Artois, but also the Prince de Condé, his son the Duc de Bourbon, and grandson the Duc d'Enghien, and so be definitively admitted into the ranks of the nobility gathered around them. This process was clearly valid to prevent the intrusion of a Jacobin or a spy, but the attitude and confidence described by Brons was extended towards those considered as being somehow tainted by having co-operated or acquiesced with the Constitution.

A case in point is that of the Comte François de La Rochefoucauld. A courtier and soldier, in 1789 he was a *major en second* of the Régiment des Chasseurs à Cheval de Champagne. He was wounded in the operations against brigands in Alsace. After a brief stay in Switzerland, he returned to France in October 1790 to help ensure the safety of the King and Queen, remaining with them almost continually after their return from Varennes and was at their side on 10 August 1792.[35] After that day, he escaped to England, where he equipped himself and bought horses before travelling to the Austrian Netherlands, reaching Marche-en-Famenne and the headquarters of the Armée de Bourbon on 17 September 1792.

There he found his cousin who, although a *major en second*, served as a *maître* in the ranks of the 1ère compagnie des Gentilhommes de Champagne, and La Rochefoucauld wished to join the company. With four gentlemen to vouch for him, rather than the two required, he requested to be admitted.[36] He was received immediately by both the Ducs de Bourbon and Enghien, but was made far from welcome by the gentlemen of the company, despite support from the Comte d'Allonville, who commanded the squadron, as well as the Comte d'Egmont, who had effective command of the Armée de

34 Brons, *Journal*, p.87.

35 François, duc de La Rochefoucauld, *Souvenirs du 10 août et de l'Armée de Bourbon* (Paris: Calman-Lévy, 1929), p.123.

36 La Rochefoucauld, *Souvenirs*, p.106.

Bourbon. Finally, after eight days, La Rochefoucauld wrote an open letter that summarised his actions during the Revolution and cited all those within the company itself who could attest that he had never professed any revolutionary idea nor associated with anyone who did. The letter began:

> The Comte François de La Rochefoucauld arrived at the Marche camp with the most ardent desire to be admitted to the company of the Gentlemen of Champagne, and fearing that reasons that are not known personally to him, or his emigration was too late, give rise to prejudices that are unfavourable to him, he has the honour of presenting before the Gentlemen the summary of his conduct since the beginning of the Revolution ...[37]

Only then was he finally admitted to the company.

The Émigrés, Troublesome Allies of Austria and the German Empire

After the Austrians had regained control in Belgium, it might have been considered that the émigrés would have been welcomed. However, largely due to their conduct, this was not the case. As early as April 1791, due to agitation caused by the numerous French ecclesiastics present, the Comte de Mercy-Argenteau, the Emperor's representative in Brussels, recommended that they be sent as far away from the border as possible. Then, ordinances were published on 16 and 24 May concerning the stay of foreigners; these were primarily targeted at arrogant aristocrats residing in Brussels who behaved as if in a conquered country. The authorities reminded the French exiles not to abuse the asylum they had been granted so that the government there was not, 'suspected of favouring in any way their intrigues or to espouse their anti-revolutionary hatreds.'[38]

It should be recognised that the governors-general, Archduchess Maria Christina and her husband, the Duc de Saxe-Teschen, only returned to Brussels on 15 June 1791, after almost two years in Bonn. This was only a week before the arrival of Provence, so it is reasonable to think that this directly influenced the date for the attempted flight of the royal family from Paris. As seen above, it was the catalogue of events that followed the failed attempt that triggered the first mass emigration of officers to the Netherlands, where they gathered in the region of Tournai and Mons in particular, then Ath and Aalst. If it was not possible to remove them, the archduchess, who shared the suspicions of the French émigrés of her sister Marie-Antoinette and brother Leopold, had Monsieur and Artois leave Brussels. Before doing so, they designated the Marquis de La Queuille as their minister to the governess, and ensured the reception and organisation of newly arrived refugees with their commissioners and commanders of the different cantonments.

37 La Rochefoucauld, *Souvenirs*, p.119.

38 Félix Maignette, 'Les émigrés français aux Pays-Bas (1789-1794)', *Mémoires de l'Académie royale de Belgique – Classe des Lettres et des Sciences morales et politiques* (Bruxelles: Hayez, Imprimeur des Académies, 1908), vol.IV, p.37.

The authorities in the Austrian Netherlands were particularly concerned to prevent French soldiers from arriving in their territory, so when it was learned that some of the garrisons in the north of France, estimated at 8,000 men, wished to join the Princes, Mercy opposed it. He refused some squadrons refuge in Austrian territory, 'and he gave orders for a cordon to be established at the frontiers intended to allow only unarmed men to pass.'[39] Furthermore, on 30 July, *Feldmarschall* von Bender, commander-in-chief of the 30,000 troops in the Austrian Netherlands, was warned that, 'the French refugees in the Netherlands and above all those who have taken asylum at Ath make arrangements to establish themselves as an armed body in the territory of His Majesty, that they negotiate for arms and ammunition underhand, and that they are on the verge of giving themselves the same uniform coat.'[40]

Nevertheless, La Queuille, knowing of the negotiations which were taking place that would lead to the Convention of Pillnitz (27 August), continued his activities. Indeed, on 18 August he solicited, 'suitable accommodation for the refugee officers at Ath, whose number, he said, grew daily, and requests for them an old barracks or empty rooms located above the city gates, and beds … he then asked, after having disarmed it, that a "transit" be given to the Régiment de Penthièvre so that it could go to Mons.'[41]

Nevertheless, the day after this request, the Emperor informed Artois that: 'Although His Majesty accepts that the French officers and soldiers who have come to take refuge in his States continue their stay there peacefully, he cannot however agree that entire regiments come to place themselves in them, before agreement with the different courts is fixed and he has made his military arrangements accordingly.'[42]

While Austria negotiated the formation of an armed coalition, its diplomatic position was, 'Everything will be done to not compromise the government in its political relations with France.'[43] The King's brothers, while recognising this dichotomy, continued on their own path and, on 23 August, Artois instructed La Queuille to present a new note to the archduchess, requesting in his name, 'permission to establish a recruitment depot at Henri-Chapelle, in Limburg, to be able to transport units of fifteen men across the country, to make Charleroi a second refuge, and to devote to the emigrants the old abandoned barracks there.'[44]

The Convention of Pillnitz strengthened the Princes' position as increasing numbers of émigrés joined them. In mid-September, the number of officers stationed in Ath and its surrounding area was estimated at between 600 and 700, growing to nearly 1,200 in October.[45] By now, 'fugitives also filled Tournai. They were reported at Chièvres, Leuze, Antoing, Lens, Enghien,

39 Maignette, 'Les émigrés français', p.38.
40 Maignette, 'Les émigrés français', p.38, note Baron von Feltz, Secretary of State for War.
41 Maignette, 'Les émigrés français', p.45.
42 Maignette, 'Les émigrés français', pp.46–47.
43 Maignette, 'Les émigrés français', p.47.
44 Maignette, 'Les émigrés français', p.47.
45 Charles-Georges Cacqueray de Valmenier, *Mémoires inédits* (Cholet: Editions Pays et Terroirs, 2006), vol.II, p.16.

Binche, Nivelles, not to mention the border towns of Flanders, the Pays de Namur and Luxembourg.'[46]

In June 1791, Prince von Metternich-Winneburg (whose son would be a famous Austrian diplomat) replaced Mercy, but the policy regarding the émigrés remained the same. So after two officers of the Régiment de Berwick recruiting for the Princes were arrested at Ostende, on 2 November Metternich reminded La Queuille, that, 'the government can neither permit nor conceal the fact that the Emperor's territory in the Netherlands does not serve as a rallying point for any invasion or for hostile acts against any neighbouring state.'[47] He concluded, 'The generals of His Majesty will be forced to act against any attempt or conspiracy of this kind.'[48] A copy of this note was then sent to France's representative in Brussels to provide fresh assurances to the Assembly.

The overt position taken by the Austrians in the Netherlands was not unique, as an émigré illustrates when describing events in December 1791:

> 20 companies of gentlemen cantoned at Mons and the area surrounding Ath received orders to be ready to leave, to go, one part into the Electorate of Trier and the rest to the army of the Prince de Condé, near Worms. Some companies had already set out when a maréchal de camp from the maréchal de Broglie came bringing a counter-order. The cause of this change was known a few days later. The regency of Trier and the magistrates of Worms had given orders for the dispersal of the cantonments in these parts. This news caused great concern, but they were soon calmed by the certainty that this measure had become necessary to avoid an invasion that one was not for the moment in a position to repel. This incident had no influence on the cantonment of the Netherlands. The government limited itself to reiterating the order to cease any exercise.[49]

The façade was maintained into the following year by the Austrian authorities taking various measures, including those focused on military preparations such as the ban on émigrés buying horses in the Ardennes for what was now called the Armée des Princes and the 'condemnation of one named Gordon de Sinclair who had engaged a surgeon from Ghent to join a regiment that this royalist agent was charged with raising for these same Princes.'[50]

This did not mean, however, that no military preparations took place, as is shown by a report of 28 January 1792 from Brussels:

> A great number of French of all ranks continue to arrive here in our Provinces, almost all of whom go to Germany. Enlistments also continue for the French Princes, especially in the region of Liège. A M. Renoz … formerly an officer [*sous-lieutenant*] in the Régiment Royal Liégeois, occupies himself with much activity with these enlistments. Some time ago he went to Koblenz and had himself presented to M. d'Artois.[51]

46 Maignette, 'Les émigrés français', pp.48–49.
47 Maignette, 'Les émigrés français', pp.48–49.
48 Maignette, 'Les émigrés français', pp.48–49.
49 Cacqueray, *Mémoires inédits*, p.20.
50 Maignette, 'Les émigrés français', p.61.
51 *Rédaction du journal de Paris*, Numéro 41, 4 February 1792, report from Brussels, p.237.

Having considered its future, on 20 January 1791, the Assembly decided to retain Renoz's former regiment, numbered 101. By the summer of 1791 it was at Strasbourg where it was soon reported as displaying royalist sympathies.[52] Eight officers apparently emigrated, noted as having 'deserted' at the review of 14 January 1792.[53] Nevertheless, it had 1,495 men, just 20 short of its wartime footing, which was exceptional at a time when many French regiments were at half-strength.[54]

The regiment was then sent to Grenoble, where, on 26 June 1792, at the planting of the Tree of Liberty, the regiment's officers were insulted. This led to a violent confrontation between the regiment's soldiers and a battalion of volunteers. As a result the Assembly was informed on 6 August, that 'The Royal-Liégeois regiment was ordered to leave Grenoble; but the soldiers deserted in great numbers, & the administrators [of the département] demand the disbanding of this corps, which is threatened with absolute disintegration'.[55] Three days later, its disbanding was decreed although it, in effect, no longer existed, only 60 men being incorporated into other units. It seems likely that many of the soldiers returned home, and at least some returned to arms, but in the service of the King's brothers.

Whatever threat Monsieur and Artois faced, it was not as immediate as that faced by Condé and, on 1 October 1791, he reconnoitred defensive positions around Worms, 'in my position, it was necessary to provide for anything; I had already equipped myself with muskets and cartridges.'[56] Despite an incursion by French troops appearing crazy, as such a violation of its territory would amount to a declaration of war on the German Empire, Condé sent officers to the frontier to gather information from the spies he kept there:

> On Saturday the 5th [of November] in the evening, one of these officers returned who informed me that indeed there was an order for troops at Landau to be ready to march, that it was said that more of them were still arriving, and that the corps which should undertake [the mission] would be of seven thousand men with twelve pieces of cannon; I had none of them and in view of those on leave and the gentlemen who had not joined although registered, I only had six hundred effective men; I could therefore only consider my retreat in the event of an attack.[57]

Condé soon received a copy of the French orders and confirmation of troop movements in Alsace, but, on 12 November, the Elector's minister at Mannheim informed him that he had received assurances that French *général*

---

52 François Alphonse Aulard, *La société des Jacobins*, (Paris: Librairie Jouaust, 1889), vol.III, p.195, séance du 19 octobre 1791.

53 Anon, *Etat des Officiers généraux & de leurs Aides-de-camp déserteurs ou émigrés ...* (Paris: Imprimerie Nationale Exécutif du Louvre, 1793), pp.122–123.

54 Anon, *Journal militaire contenant tout ce qui est relatif à l'Organisation et à l'Administration de la force publique, 1ère Partie,* (Paris: unknown, 1792), without pagination. The regiment is given under its former name.

55 *Le Moniteur*, 7 August 1792.

56 Condé, *Journal*, pp.226–227.

57 Condé, *Journal*, pp.231–232.

Kellerman had only been ordered to defend against an attack by the émigrés and was forbidden from violating the Palatinate (Pfalz) territory. Rumours of war gradually faded, but Condé had reason to maintain the highest degree of vigilance. On 14 December, Prince Louis de Rohan and some chasseurs encountered eight men in the woods near Ettenheim who fled after a brief fight. Then, two days later, an attempt to assassinate Condé was discovered. A former officer of the Régiment de Hesse-Darmstadt who had served in the Garde Nationale admitted to having been paid a significant sum to kill the Prince.

On 25 December, Austrian and German troops arrived in the area.[58] However, the threats made by the Assembly against German states that gave asylum to the émigrés had been effective, and Condé had already received a request from the city magistrates of Worms to leave the territory. The Elector of Mainz showed no inclination to defend himself:

> Thursday & yesterday, most of the bourgeois [of Worms] packed & sent off their belongings; & there are many boats prepared to embark all hands, if the news continues to be frightening … The caissons, waggons & artillery horses, which were in Rheindürckeim, were transported to the opposite bank of the Rhine, to the episcopal villages & a large number of emigrants have already gone there. All the baggage of the princes is packed at the castle of Worms, & must leave there today or tomorrow.[59]

Two days later, Condé received a message from Koblenz to move to the estates of Cardinal de Rohan. After this was confirmed, he had little time to organise the movement of between 1,000 and 1,200 officers and gentlemen with him:

> On the 29th, I assembled all my generals, I announced to them the departure, and I attached them to the brigades that I formed of two companies; I made all the preparations, I gave all the orders, among others that of only marching in small units, and with weapons in the chests, being very sure that the German princes would not let me pass in columns, nor even in assembled companies. On Friday the 30th, a cavalry brigade left, that of the Comtois and the Dragoons, which was in front on the road to Mannheim; I ordered the officers I had on the frontier to remain until the departure of the last companies, so that they would be warned in case of invasion. On Saturday the 31st, two more left, and was to continue thus, until the last evacuation.[60]

The Duc d'Enghien noted in his memoirs that:

> The journey for the gentlemen was not easy to make. It was in the most severe season of the year, and the persecutions they experienced were infinite. In the Palatinate, in the Bishopric of Speyer, even on the Imperial lands, the innkeepers

58 *Courrier Français,* 4 January 1792, report of 25 December 1791.

59 *Courrier Français*, 1 January 1792.

60 Condé, *Journal*, p.242.

> were ordered not to receive them. If they were granted lodging for one night only, it was to make them pay for everything in gold. They could not travel more than three together, without weapons, without any military distinction, otherwise everything was closed to them.[61]

Condé, with some of his immediate entourage, was the last to quit Worms and the lands of the Elector of Mainz. At Ettenheim, he would find the Légion de Mirabeau (1,200 men), the Régiment de Berwick (a little more than 300), as well as the Chevaliers de la Couronne (about 200) cantoned nearby. On 5 January, he was met by a detachment of Mirabeau's uhlans and, upon arriving at Renchen, he found the entire legion under arms.

The respite was short-lived as the Cardinal was informed by the Regency of Freiburg and the Emperor that he would not be rescued in the event of an attack by the French. Then, on 31 January, a new note from the Regency of Freiburg intimated that the Légion de Mirabeau and the Régiment de Berwick should be disbanded and Condé and the nobles should go to the region of Konstanz, on the Swiss frontier. However, recognising the ill disposition of the Duke of Württemberg, Condé decided he would go to Koblenz with his noble detachments after dispersing the Chevaliers de la Couronne, the Régiment de Berwick and the Légion de Mirabeau. Then, on 6 February, he learned that the Duke had placed his troops to prevent Condé's men crossing Württemberg territory. Then a first glimmer of hope was provided on the evening of 8 February, when the Prince learned of the signing of the simulated treaty between the King's brothers and the princes of Hohenlohe. This provided asylum for the Légion de Mirabeau, while it was arranged that the Régiment de Berwick would go to Neuwied, north-west of Koblenz and on the right bank of the Rhine.

Condé, along with his companies of officers and gentlemen, were to go to the County of Sayn, a dependency of the neighbouring Margraviate of Anspach, to the northeast of the Hohenlohe lands, where the King of Prussia was willing to receive them. To this end, the Chevaliers de la Couronne set off on their march on 16 February, 'in small units of five or six, without cockades, and without uniforms.'[62] It was then that Condé learned that his units' final destination was to be the Duchy of Cleves, another Prussian territory, a march of more than 400 kilometres. The following day, his infantry and cavalry took separate routes to Oberkirch; from there, the march continued, skirting Württemberg. Then, on 20 February, when the Prince had just crossed the Rhine at Mannheim and was heading towards Koblenz, he received good news. The Elector of Mainz had abstracted a guarantee from the Emperor that he would intervene in the event the electorate was invaded. This allowed the elector to authorise the émigrés to establish themselves at Bensheim, about 25 kilometres from Worms and 30 kilometres from Mannheim, before permanently installing them at Bingen and surrounding villages where there were already some cantonments of the Armée des Princes. Bingen, on the

61 Enghien, *Mémoires*, pp.283–284.
62 Condé, *Journal*, p.261.

right bank of the Rhine, between Koblenz and Mainz, became the centre of the cantonments that extended to the far bank of the river.

The alliance with Prussia, on 7 February 1792, strengthened Leopold's role at the head of the counter-revolutionary crusade. The émigrés may have considered that they would be treated as allies who needed to be organised, armed and equipped as quickly as possible. However, the Emperor pursued the policy agreed with Louis and Marie-Antoinette that they should be restored to their thrones by foreign intervention, an invasion led by the émigrés would create civil war, so they should only return to France in the wake of the coalition troops. The practical result of this was that the émigrés were to move from their cantonments in the Netherlands, to make way for coalition troops who were arriving in the wider region. At the beginning of February, it was announced that troops from Bohemia would soon be arriving, and Austrian military hospitals would be installed at Ath and Enghien. On 11 February, the Comte d'Hector, commanding the Corps royal de la Marine that was forming at Enghien, was told his unit was to leave and days later, 'the officers cantoned at Ath had received the order to be all assembled there by the 5 March and ready to march.'[63] Their final destination was not known, but there were rumours that all the émigrés were to form a single army corps in the Duchy of Cleves. Leopold's death did not alter the course taken by the Austrian authorities, and, in a note of 3 March, Metternich pressed La Queuille to clear the émigré cantonments to make way for Austrian troops.[64] The émigrés dragged their feet claiming, for example, a lack of money for the move, while seeking alternative locations to stay, 'the government was advised, at the beginning of March, that a Marquis Brinilpont [sic, Marquis de Breuilpont], a French officer, had presented himself at Courtrai [Kortrijk], Ypres, Diksmuide, Roulers [Roeselare] and other places on the extreme border of maritime Flanders to solicit from the magistrates for accommodation described as "cantonments", for companies of men on foot and horse.'[65]

The final order to leave the cantonments of Ath and Enghien arrived on 17 March, and the émigrés began to march the following day. On 24 March, Olivier d'Argens and the other men in his Breton company learned that they were to travel individually, by stages given to them, to their destination. Going via Nivelles, where the Norman gentlemen were cantoned, he arrived at Namur on 26 March.[66] The following day, he embarked on a boat with a hundred émigrés, and travelled down the Meuse to Liège and, after crossing the city, spent the 29th and 30th in a village on the road to Spa: 'During my stay, I saw many émigrés from the cantonment of Ath and Enghien pass by for Stavelot and Malmedy, two small towns three leagues [12 kilometres] from Spa. The volunteers from Enghien were in the latter.'[67] On 31 March, Argens reached Stavelot where there were three companies of infantry officers from

63 Cacqueray, *Mémoires inédits*, p.23.
64 Maignette, 'Les émigrés français', p.65.
65 Maignette, 'Les émigrés français', p.65.
66 Anon. (ed.), *Olivier d'Argens*, p.16.
67 Anon. (ed.), *Olivier d'Argens*, p.17.

the Ath cantonment. He stayed there until 16 April before moving onto a new cantonment at Hillesheim where his company was finally reunited two days later.[68]

From 21 March the removal of the émigré assemblies within reach of the northern frontiers of France was prominently reported to reduce tensions between France and Austria.

Diplomatic U-turn in Favour of the Émigrés

The French princes had found few friends among the German princes, however France's declaration of war on 20 April 1792 changed this, and six days later Condé wrote to his son informing him that, after negotiations, the Elector of Trier had promised, 'he would send two thousand muskets to arm the French in Trier, in the event of an invasion.'[69] In addition, Maximilian of Zweibrücken had asked for émigré assistance against the threat of attack from Metz by Kellermann. The fears of an attack on Imperial territory were not far-fetched as, on 26 April, French troops seized Porrentruy, part of the Prince-Bishopric of Basel.

In the meantime, the émigré units gathered around Koblenz moved closer to the Rhine and the river's right bank to be in contact with those with Condé. La Maisonfort remembered the movement that occurred after the declaration of war, 'we were sent to canton in all the small towns of the Electorate of Trier, the squadron of the dragons des princes was at Oberwesel, a small town on the banks of the Rhine … We spent May and June there.'[70]

As the French forces attacked the Austrian Netherlands, only the royalist units that were still there could have countered their offensives. Those still at Ath offered to join *Feldmarschalleutnant* Beaulieu's troops, 'The four companies of émigré cavalry that were stationed at Ath went to Brussels after having had their services accepted by General Beaulieu.'[71] However, they saw no action.[72] In the region of Liège, émigrés were deployed near Huy, a strategic crossing point on the Meuse halfway between Namur and Liège, to monitor the frontier, particularly French troops at Givet. Nevertheless, at least one émigré is reported to have taken part in the fighting in April 1792; the Marquis de Breuilpont, attached to Beaulieu's staff, was, 'At the battles of Quiévrain and Mons, he was the first to fall upon the enemy guns, with his chasseurs, and was the first to penetrate the camp. This action earned him the cross of Saint-Louis at the age of 27.'[73]

68 Anon. (ed.), *Olivier d'Argens*, p.18.
69 Crétineau-Joly, *princes de Condé*, vol.I, p.18.
70 La Maisonfort, *Mémoires*, p.111.
71 Cacqueray, *Mémoires inédits*, p.39.
72 Crétineau-Joly, *princes de Condé*, vol.I, p.23.
73 Joseph Valynseele, *Les enfants naturels de Louis XV, étude critique, biographie, descendance et nombreux documents inédits* (Paris: Centre d'Etudes et de Recherches historiques, 1953), p.221. Valynseele used a certified statement of service dated 20 November 1815 and the archives of the Breuilpont family as his source.

In reality, very few émigré units were in a condition, in terms of arms and equipment, to fight in April 1792. Furthermore, it should be remembered that, until the beginning of May, hardly any troops, as opposed to officers, had defected from the old royal army to the Armée des Princes. Indeed, when they began to arrive, it was necessary to find money to keep them together, which was to the detriment of the rest of the army, in particular of the volunteers or former officers who, for the most part, continued to meet their own expenses. The future of the émigré forces remained uncertain, funds were short, and, at least for the Austrians, arming and equipping them was not then a priority. Nevertheless, things were beginning to change. On 4 May, Condé was able to share the news that he had secured a loan from Parisian financiers, but there was also less welcome news, 'Russia has cooled considerably; it will neither send us men nor money.'[74] Catherine had been disappointed by the émigrés' inaction as well as the failure to use the four million roubles she had previously offered them. On the other hand, Prussia prepared for the future deployment of its troops in Trier and then, on 1 June, King Frederick William II arrived at Koblenz and met the princes the next day:

> The King of Prussia is charming to us; he promises us a place in the front line, and he explained clearly in the official note that his troops will be behind us to support us. He charges the Duke of Brunswick to furnish us with artillery; he gives four hundred thousand francs per month for the maintenance of the French troops who have passed over or will pass and who will always be under our orders … In addition, he gives us four million to maintain the Emigrés …[75]

Condé was frustrated with the Austrians, 'always this eternal recommendation to keep tranquil, and not to arm unless requisitioned by the German princes. It is absurd to make us leave for war, without us being exercised.'[76] He also feared that his men may have to vacate the territory of the Elector of Trier to make way for Prussian troops. However, by 22 June, he felt confident that his headquarters would remain at Bingen despite objections from some of the neighbouring rulers.

The situation in the Austrian Netherlands was complex due to the nature of its frontier with France and the recently crushed Brabant revolution. On the declaration of war, the French generals openly called for the Belgian population to revolt and their soldiers to desert. This was followed by uprisings at Wavre, Nivelles and Tienen, which were suppressed by force of arms, and clearly coordinated with the advance of French troops into Belgium.[77] Nevertheless, Vienna wished to maintain its previous position, getting Metternich to inform Calonne that they did not want, 'to attract into our provinces émigrés who might embarrass us.'[78] Any premature action,

74 Crétineau-Joly, *princes de Condé*, vol.II, pp.25–26, Koblenz 4 May.

75 Crétineau-Joly, *princes de Condé*, vol.II, p.34, Prince de Condé to his son on 2 June.

76 Crétineau-Joly, *princes de Condé*, vol.II, p.34, Prince de Condé to his son on 2 June.

77 *Leyden Gazette*, 17 May 1792.

78 Maignette, 'Les émigrés français', p.74.

before a coalition army had been formed, had to be prevented. However, those responsible for the security of the Netherlands had to be more pragmatic regarding the émigrés. From January 1792, the government had introduced measures to police the French who were present but, on 28 April, it issued an order that identified its enemies and allies:

> His Majesty being unable, given the state of war in which he finds himself with France, to tolerate in his states the stay of other subjects of this kingdom [France] than those who are in the situation of fleeing the persecutions of the party which has usurped all powers there, He has declared, as He declares, that all the French who find themselves in the provinces of the Netherlands under his dominion and who have not been recognised by a formal act of the Commissioners of the French Emigrés established for this purpose in the city of Brussels, namely those who are currently in this city within two times 24 hours from the publication of this, and those who can find themselves in the other cities or places of these Provinces, in the term of 8 days, will have to leave the States under the dominion of His Majesty on pain that those who are found there after the said terms have elapsed respectively will be made prisoners of war.[79]

After the failure of the French attacks, the authorities in the Austrian Netherlands had more to fear from a new uprising in Brabant than a new offensive, while they waited for reinforcements from the coalition. Following the edict of 28 April, other than registered émigrés, only the French legation at Brussels and the consul at Ostende were permitted to remain. To assist in the enforcement of this, the lists of the émigrés prepared by the commissioners were distributed among the civil authorities. The number of commissioners was increased in Brussels, and soon the commanders of the cantonments, such as the Comtes de La Châtre and du Luc, were so designated.[80] The commissioners were asked to help in identifying Frenchmen in their area of responsibility who may be suspect. Such steps were shown to be necessary when, in May, a message from Dumouriez to the secretary of the French legation in Brussels was intercepted.[81] A spy who had been added to the legation's staff prior to the declaration of war to foment a new uprising by the Belgians was arrested on 26 May and expelled.

The change in attitude by the authorities encouraged the King's brothers to request that the émigré companies in the Electorate of Trier move to villages between Namur, Liège and Luxembourg. The archduchess agreed on condition that such arrangements did not in any way hinder the arrival of Austrian troops, thus the émigrés would be in the interior of the country. Encouragement was also given to the emigration of defecting troops who were no longer turned away, in May 1792 an émigré reported:

---

79 Maignette, 'Les émigrés français', pp.78–79.

80 Maignette, 'Les émigrés français', pp.79–80.

81 See Henri Boulanger, 'L'Affaire des Belges et Liégeois unis, 1792-1793', *Revue du Nord,* 1e année, n°1, 1910, pp.3–40.

> There arrive with us here many deserters from the French army; the government gave orders that they be given money on arriving on the frontiers to go to the various cantonments, where when they are gathered to the number of three hundred, they are given arms, and the means to go to join the Princes. The camp of Tournai is reinforced every day by new troops.[82]

Early that month the Régiment de Bercheny (numbered the 1er Hussards) arrived and asked the Prince of Stavelot for permission to halt on his lands.[83] Soon afterwards, the Royal-Allemand (15e Cavalerie) passed through Bitburg, then to the Duchy of Luxembourg.

Elsewhere, the reception of defecting troops was not straightforward, as many German rulers continued to raise difficulties. This occurred with the first such unit, the Régiment de Saxe (4e Hussards) that emigrated in its entirety, except for its fourth squadron, on 4 May. Having joined Condé, the regiment was ordered to leave the region of Bingen, so the Prince had to rely on the new attitude of the Elector of Mainz towards the émigrés, but difficulties still arose, as is seen in a letter he wrote to Bouillé:

> As soon as I received your letter, I sent for MM. de Vioménil and de Fumel, to whom I imparted the proposal of the five villages of the county of Ingenheim for placing the regiment there, pending the success of your negotiation at Worms. This arrangement appeared to us to suffer the greatest difficulties: firstly, because yesterday we sent an officer to Neu-Bamberg to make lodgings, not doubting, according to the assurances we had, that the regiment would be placed in any place in the country of Worms. Secondly, how to announce to this regiment already dissatisfied with the outrages it has weathered on its journey again a sudden change in its march, without making it foresee new inconveniences. Thirdly, the displacement of the companies which are established in these villages would be an occasion of expense for the gentlemen and would give infinite embarrassment. After these considerations, we agreed that the regiment would still leave today to go to Neu-Bamberg. M. de Vioménil has just left at the moment to go to Soremburg where the regiment slept; he will tell Mr. de Gottsheim [Baron von Gottesheim, the regiment's *colonel*] on my behalf that you have sent me word that you were going to try to get them the town of Worms, or a cantonment in the Bergstrass [sic], or in the country of Darmstadt. It is certain that they absolutely must be placed in one of these three places, or else expect to lose this regiment; how much this would be terrible and humiliating for us. The first regiment that devotes itself to our cause, to the cause of the King, to see it disband, perhaps return to France, saying that it has been chased from everywhere. This would be the greatest misfortune that could happen.[84]

---

82 Xavier Maeght, 'Un Journal d'émigré en 1792', *Revue du Nord*, vol.XLIX, no.93, p.315, citing *Journal général*, no.40, of 18 May 1792. The *Journal* was edited by the royalist Madame Veuve Marchand who had been a printer since 3 August 1790 at Arras and took refuge in January 1792 at Tournai.

83 Cacqueray, *Mémoires inédits*, p.40.

84 Crétineau-Joly, *princes de Condé*, vol.II, pp.30–31, letter from Bingen, 16 May.

Impetus for a successful outcome was given when it was learned that the battalion of the Régiment de Walsh that was being sent to Longwy wanted to defect.[85]

Chancellor Kaunitz in Vienna was concerned that official recognition of the Armée des Princes within the coalition would mark the end of the illusion that had been hitherto maintained, that Louis XVI still had a political role rather than simply being reduced to endorsing the excesses of the Revolution. Nevertheless, Metternich, concerned with defending the Netherlands and supported by the local Austrian commanders, managed to convince the governors that the time had come to help the émigrés prepare for a role within the armed coalition. Steps began to be taken to distribute arms among the émigrés, a volunteer in the Corps royal de la Marine noting between 9 and 11 May 1792, 'The arms having arrived from Liège, they were distributed to the companies [at Malmedy]. Although there were not yet enough to complete the armament of mine, there was a guard of 8 men and a picket of 10 men always ready to mount on horses.'[86] Furthermore, on 31 May, the government agreed that weapons that could not be placed in Antwerp's citadel, due to the lack of space, would be sold to the émigrés.

On 16 June, *Generalmajor* von Diesbach, military commander of Brussels, responding to La Queuille, agreed to provide subsistence for 200 émigré soldiers at Ath, Brussels and Enghien as well as 400 at Tienen. The émigrés were authorised to have an armed guard, 30 men at Ath and Enghien and 60 men at Tienen, 'to maintain good order'.[87] Diesbach, having been instructed to provide all assistance to the émigrés, the Comte de Carneville was authorised 'to form a depot of a hundred men in the towns of Mons and Tournai.'[88] While the émigrés in the Austrian Netherlands, commanded by the Duc de Bourbon, benefited from these changes, those elsewhere experienced mixed fortunes. The Condéens (*Condeischen* in German) were dispersed, with units stationed in the lands of Hohenlohe-Waldenburg-Schillingsfürst and others on either side of the Rhine. Those with Monsieur and Artois were in cantonments stretching from the Principality of Stavelot, in the Ardennes, to the territories belonging to the King of Prussia or the family of Orange-Nassau, beyond the Principality of Liège and the Dutch stronghold of Maastricht.

The Armed Emigration's Last Rallies

Newly arrived émigrés generally joined units that had been gradually created from August 1791. The Armée des Princes was formed from November 1791 but was only fully established from the beginning of May 1792, as the obstacles imposed by the Austrian authorities were removed and the Princes received financial support. The Comte de Romain described the activity as the émigrés prepared for the forthcoming campaign.

85 Crétineau-Joly, *princes de Condé*, vol.II, p.28, letter from Koblenz, 14 May 1792.

86 Cacqueray, *Mémoires inédits*, p.40.

87 Maignette, 'Les émigrés français', p.83.

88 Maignette, 'Les émigrés français', p.83.

> The Princes are authorised to organise a royal army; one is no longer occupied, among us, with anything other than making purchases of arms, horses and military effects of all kinds. The Empress of Russia is having a lot of money passed to our Princes to cover all these expenses, which are immense: this is understandable, since it involves levying, equipping and maintaining several paid corps which are of soldiers or individuals who do not have the means to mount and equip themselves at their own expense … there are even gentlemen fortunate enough to have left France with considerable sums, who have offered and given them up to our Princes, in order to provide them with some additional means to undertake enterprises useful to the good cause …[89]

Among the latter was the Marquis de Breuilpont, who gave 400,000 livres and covered the costs of raising a legion.

As for the organisation of the force, Romain reported that:

> … it appears decided that the army of the émigrés will be divided into several corps, which will act on different points. This is without doubt with the design of offering more means of rallying the royalists scattered throughout the interior, because on seeing regimented Frenchmen, commanded by Bourbons, within their close reach, they will not hesitate to come to rally to them.[90]

The staff of the Armée des Princes was organised in June 1792.[91] The Armée itself was divided into three divisions, which were to be named armies under the final organisation of 23 July 1792: the Armée du Centre was commanded by Monsieur and Artois; the Armée de Condé by the prince of that name and the Armée de Bourbon, in the Austrian Netherlands, by the Duc de Bourbon.

The Armée des Princes doubled in size between January and July 1792; however, between June and August, the new authorities in France made it almost impossible to leave the country, while strengthening the measures taken against the émigrés. New local revolutionary committees made lists of émigrés that were then combined at the national level, and their families were subject to close surveillance. For those in France still loyal to the King, the alternatives were starkly clear. They could leave the kingdom, now via England or the south of France, to join the counter-revolution being organised on the banks of the Rhine, stay to try to form a last bulwark to protect the royal family in the event of an invasion by the coalition, or take part in armed uprisings in the provinces. The second alternative came to an end with the massacre at the Tuileries, 10 August 1792.

The foundations for the third alternative had, however, already been laid as early as 13 February 1791 when Breton peasants, inspired by their clergy, had marched on Vannes, but they, the first of the royalist uprisings in the west, were dispersed by 150 men of the Régiment de Walsh. However, independently, Armand-Charles Tuffin Marquis de La Rouërie, who had been a dissolute young officer in the Gardes Françaises before being banished

89 Félix de Romain, *Souvenirs d'un officier royaliste* (Paris: Egron, 1824), vol.II, pp.227–228.

90 Romain, *Souvenirs*, vol.II, p.229.

91 Brons, *Journal*, p.40.

following a duel and then distinguishing himself while serving in America, gathered a group of nobles around him, who eventually were to become the Association bretonne. His aim was to resurrect the ancient rights of his native Brittany through the full restoration of the monarchy. On 5 June 1791, Artois provided La Rouërie with, 'a declaration by this prince to the citizens of Brittany to keep them in counter-revolutionary sentiments.'[92] Then, on 2 March 1792, he was sent, by the princes, 'a commission … to command the military in the province of Brittany and to form an association useful to the service of the King.'[93] At the first coalition victory, he was to have rallied Brittany and the neighbouring provinces to march as quickly as possible on Paris to help restore Louis XVI to his throne. The signal never came, and La Rouërie, having been betrayed, died on 30 January 1793, but his project was a precursor for the subsequent wars in the west, the Chouannerie and the Vendée.

In the south, specifically in the region of Nice and, more broadly, Provence, another source of émigré combatants was provided by the little-known Légion de Colbert. As early as January 1791, *lieutenant de vaisseau* Etienne-Edouard-Louis Marquis de Colbert-Cannet had assembled a group of officers for a future legion. Active at Tende, in the mountains north-east of Nice and on the road to Turin, 'It would also open the way for the emigration of 2 companies of Maine-infantry, to one of la Marine, former soldiers of the Royal-Corse, 40 gendarmes, 9 brigades of employees of the [customs] farms and 250 various individuals.'[94] Condé wrote on 14 May 1792, 'I have just seen a letter from Marseille, which says that the Nation has placed twelve thousand men on the Var, that the next day the Régiment de Maine passed to Nice, and that it was followed by all the officers of the Régiment de la Marine and Barrois.'[95] The news was suppressed, it being forbidden to report the desertion of entire units in gazettes, to make people believe that emigration was limited to that of so-called aristocrats, and therefore only the nobility.

It is likely that the volunteers of the Compagnie des Méridionaux of the Légion de Mirabeau took the same route. The company was not present at the review of 1 January 1792, but, as Toustain recalled, 'It was in March 1792 that the legion was truly formed and trained; we received a large number of volunteers coming from Spain.'[96] Grouvel noted that, 'in June, a quite considerable number of émigrés coming from Spain, had disembarked at Genoa and went to the Armée des Princes.'[97] Diplomatic pressure on Sardinia-Piedmont resulted in Colbert being ordered to cease his recruiting, nevertheless, while reporting this on 28 August 1792, the French consul at Nice noted, 'the desertion of 4 or 5 officers of the Vieille Marine [the 11e Régiment d'infanterie], with 15 soldiers of this regiment, who had been,

92 Anon., *Le Tribunal criminel extraordinaire* (Paris: undated), Livre I, p.46. This tribunal searched through the documents seized after La Rouërie's death.

93 Anon., *Le Tribunal criminel extraordinaire*, Livre I, p.46.

94 Grouvel, *Troupes de l'émigration*, vol.II, p.136.

95 Crétineau-Joly, *princes de Condé*, vol.II, p.28.

96 Marquise de Perry de Nieüil (ed.), *Mémoires du Marquis de Toustain 1790–1823* (Paris: Plon, 1933), p.11.

97 Grouvel, *Troupes de l'émigration*, vol.II, p.136.

without doubt, debauched to enter the Légion de Colbert.'[98] Then, on 29 September 1792, French troops invaded Nice and 800 émigrés took up arms to oppose it, but the King of Sardinia-Piedmont refused to support the resistance or to take the Légion de Colbert into his service. The legion, with 60 or so men and at least 20 officers remaining, would join Condé on 30 October 1792, who attached it to the Légion de Mirabeau.

On 8 August 1792, the Princes issued a declaration justifying their counter-revolutionary crusade and calling all true Frenchmen to rally to their standards:

> We address to the troops of the King the most pressing invitations and even orders that the state of captivity in which His Majesty finds himself authorises us to give in his name, so that, in accordance with the summons contained in Article 3 of the declaration of His Serene Highness the reigning Duke of Brunswick [see Chapter 5], and without believing themselves bound by an illusory oath that they were unable to validly take, to the prejudice of the first of their engagements, they hasten to return to their former loyalty towards their legitimate sovereign; that, following the example of most of their officers, they join the troops that we, the brothers of the King, command for His Majesty, that they open all passages for us to march to his aid, and that with us they give him proofs of an inviolable attachment to his service.[99]

The Princes may have stated their wish, but the reception of these last-minute émigrés, some of whom arrived directly from the patriotic armies, was, in fact, in the hands of the gentlemen who were supposed to become their comrades-in-arms, as seen by the example of François de La Rochefoucauld.

On 19 August 1792, La Fayette quit his army with almost his entire staff, at least 50 men.[100] Their intention was to sail for America, but they were arrested near Rochefort in the Ardennes and brought to Luxembourg, where Brons was Commissioner of the Princes. It was then that Brons also learned of the arrival of *général de brigade* Joseph Theodore Gabriel Lallemand, a former comte, 'accompanied by two aides-de-camp and some officers of the light troops among whom was the young Malseigne, nephew of the brave general officer of that name, so celebrated for his incredible acts of composure and courage during the famous mutiny of the Nancy garrison in the first moments of the Revolution.'[101] Considered a brave and experienced officer, Lallemand had been appointed *colonel* commanding the 11e Chasseurs à Cheval (ci-devant de la Normandie) on 23 November 1791 and promoted a general officer on 10 June 1792. Placed in command of La Fayette's vanguard on 16 August, the latter had left him a single line, 'I am leaving in the very

98 Grouvel, *Troupes de l'émigration*, vol.II, p.136. The Régiment de La Marine was so named due to historical reasons and had no other connection with the Navy, now being numbered the consul refers to the 11e Régiment as the 'old Marine.' The regiment was in garrison at Toulon at this time.

99 Félix-Martin Doisy, *Manuscrit inédit de Louis XVIII* (Paris: I.G. Michaud, 1839), pp.423–424, the full text of this long document runs from page 407 to 436.

100 Brons, *Journal*, p.75.

101 Brons, *Journal*, p.84.

instant and advise you to do the same.'[102] Believing that La Fayette intended to join the princes, Lallemand headed for Luxembourg. Instead of the welcome declared by the Princes, while he and the other constitutional officers waited for Brons to arrive, they were berated by émigrés. Brons was able to help the young Malseigne, enabling him to go to his uncle, now commanding the squadron of carabiniers, however Lallemand was ignored by Monsieur and Artois. So, after a few days the *général* left for Switzerland, but by December 1792 he was commanding the 3e division de cavalerie noble in the Armée de Condé.

Brons noted the number of new arrivals:

> Every day, every hour, every moment saw the arrival of the gentlemen from all the provinces, officers as well as soldiers from all the conventional armies and all the line regiments. The Gardes Nationaux themselves emigrated in very great numbers and many of them asked to take up service in the Imperial army. The general officer who commanded at Luxembourg (Baron Wilhelm Schröder) had ordered that all who arrived from France be brought to me. It was only after my questioning and on my signature that they were issued with passes to go to the destination that I had indicated to them. I sent the non-military gentlemen to the coalitions of the nobility of their respective provinces, the active officers to their different corps, the soldiers of the line to the regiments raised for the service of the King and the Gardes Nationaux to the corps in which they only asked to serve.[103]

Despite the decisions taken by such commissioners, the great majority of gentlemen and all officers upon their arrival with the various corps were met with intolerance and were contemptuously rejected. So, they continued their journeys, mainly to Holland, Germany, Switzerland or Italy. Brons deplored it, recalling to his son:

> I saw at this time, with a well-known and very distinguished general officer, an Etat militaire of France for the year 1792 in which all the officers of the French army had their name annotated with one of three letters: B [for bon, good], M [mauvais, bad] or D [douteux, doubtful]. This singular work had been made by a committee of very zealous royalists but on unfaithful memories in many regards. Nevertheless this ... was regarded by some very considerable personages as the infallible register of the sentiments or actions of all the individuals of this army. You will note however that among those chosen marked with the letter 'B', were found people not only doubtful but assuredly bad and who have since given irresistible proof of this, and among those designated either as bad or equivocal, there were some who were excellent in all respects. There even existed some who rendered to the cause of honour and the monarchy the most signal services.[104]

102 Brons, *Journal*, p.81.
103 Brons, *Journal*, pp.84–85.
104 Brons, *Journal*, p.86.

In 1792, Swiss units in French service were posted in strongholds along the border with the Austrian Netherlands – the Régiments de Châteauvieux, Diesbach and Courten respectively at Bitche, Lille and Douai and the second battalion of Salis-Samade at Calais.[105] To enlist soldiers who left these regiments, La Châtre established a company at Ath under the command of the Baron de Reinach, the brother of the proprietary *colonel* of the regiment of that name raised by the Bishopric of Basel. The company was joined in mid-April by three officers and 18 former guards of the Cent-Suisses, a month after their unit had been disbanded. However, by 25 May, they were at Koblenz, providing the guard at the palace of Schönbornslust. On 26 April, after war was declared, the *colonels* and *capitaines* of the regiments wrote to Rochambeau to remind him that in accordance with the capitulations between France and the Cantons, Swiss troops could not be engaged in offensive operations against the House of Austria. Furthermore, the Canton of Bern was already demanding the return of the Régiment d'Ernest due to the manner in which it had been treated by the revolutionary authorities in Provence (it returned to Switzerland in May). Then, on 28 April, French forces invaded Swiss territory and seized Porrentruy, in the Bishopric of Basel, causing several officers of Reinach to resign and make their way to Ath along with some of the regiment's soldiers.

Finally, there was the massacre at the Tuileries on 10 August and 10 days later the Assembly decreed the disbanding of all the Swiss regiments. On 3 September, Artois wrote to the Prince-Bishop of Basel asking that the Régiment de Reinach be directed to join the Armée du Centre near Thionville. He begged:

> His Highness to give orders to the commander of the said regiment, that he has to go with MM. the officers who have not manifested an open opinion in favour of the Constitution, to the said army, and to bring there the disbanded subjects of the said Highness, in groups of 15 to 20 men, one day to another, directing their march by Trier and Luxembourg, if they had already left from Dunkirk.[106]

However, the Swiss Diet had to continue its neutrality, in particular so as not to hazard the repatriation of its soldiers. This was far from being guaranteed, as Gardes Suisses who had been taken prisoner on 10 August were murdered on 2 and 3 September, and, furthermore, *major* Karl Josef von Bachmann was guillotined in his uniform.

The Régiment de Reinach was finally disbanded on the morning of 25 September. The men were assembled in a square, in the centre of which the officers cut the flags into pieces to be distributed among them. Then, for reasons of safety, the soldiers who did not want to remain in France were given an allowance of 3 sous per day to return to Switzerland in civilian clothes in groups of 10. Before and after the disbanding, efforts were made to enrol the soldiers of the Swiss regiments into what was very soon to be the army of the

105 *Etat militaire*, 1792.

106 C. Folletête, *Le régiment de l'Evêché de Bâle au service de la France, 1758-1792* (Fribourg: Imprimerie Catholique Suisse, 1882), p.80.

French Republic. About a hundred or so men from Reinach so engaged but, 'The greatest number declared the wish to return to Switzerland. Among the latter, many intended to go to join the Armée des Princes at Thionville.'[107]

Other Swiss joined the Prince de Condé, 'When the Régiment de Châteauvieux left France to return to Switzerland, twenty soldiers came in 1792 to the Armée de Condé.'[108] These formed the basis of the Compagnie suisse de garde du quartier-général (the guard company of the headquarters) that was organised from this period, September 1792.

It should be noted that, unlike French and Irish units, Swiss units in the Armée des Princes were not linked to former units of the royal army because they were not raised under capitulations with the Swiss Cantons. They formed guard units within each of the constituent armies: the company mentioned above in the Armée de Condé, the Compagnie franche (free company) des Suisses, or de Porrentruy, a headquarters guard in the Armée de Bourbon and a company formed of former members of the Cent-Suisses and the equivalent units in the households of Monsieur and Artois within the reconstituted Maison militaire in the Armée du Centre.

107 Folletête, *Le régiment de l'Evêché de Bâle*, p.85.

108 Champflour (ed.), *La coalition d'Auvergne*, p.291.

4

The Composition of the Armée des Princes

The Armée des Princes, as has been mentioned, was divided into three battle corps, which were later to be called armies, on 23 July 1792. By August of that year, its units fell into 10 categories, which are described in turn, reflecting the chronological order in which they were formed. However, it should be noted that some units within these categories underwent changes, even being dissolved or transferred between the three émigré armies, from June to September.

The first categories were:

1. The Chevaliers-dragons de la Couronne
2. The former royal troops that left France
3. The Légion de Mirabeau

Then units were organised according to the regulation of 19 August 1791:

4. The companies of officers and gentlemen
5. The Coalitions de province (Provincial Coalitions)
6. The Corps de la Marine Royale
7. The reconstituted Maison militaire

Finally, there were newly raised units:

8. The German corps in the service of the Princes and King
9. Light troops
10. The staff, administration and services.

The process of the formation of each unit, from June 1791 to August 1792, follows a similar pattern, namely:

a) The assembly of men to form a structured military unit, of whatever size, at cantonments in the Austrian Netherlands or Germany, under its own chief or a general officer designated by the King's brothers.

b) The unit moves due to pressure exerted by France, the arrival of coalition troops, or to join one of the three émigré divisions/armies.
c) Moving with one of these armies in a theatre of operations attached or even subordinate to a coalition force.

Compagnies Franches

The Compagnies Franches (free, or independent, companies) were not a separate category of émigré unit, as they did not have a single model. They fall into different categories depending on their individual characteristics. These could be their personnel, role, organisation or uniforms. For example, the Compagnie franche du Tiers (free company of the Third Estate) within the provincial Coalition de Bretagne was distinctive as its personnel were specifically not nobles, unlike the coalition's seven other companies, and wore a uniform of a different colour from them. On the other hand, the Compagnie de Chasseurs de Rouault, despite its light infantry role in the vanguard, was otherwise considered as a company of gentlemen.

Companies took the name of their *capitaine* and often operated autonomously; frequently ephemeral and not regimented, they were distinguished by a particular uniform or weaponry and were generally between 30 and 100 men strong. Such units are shown within the Armée de Bourbon, but it is certain that, at one stage or another, there were also half a dozen in the Armées du Centre and Condé. However, they are not listed as they had disappeared or changed status by the time the lists and orders of battle for each of the armies were compiled, and used by future historians, notably Pinasseau or Grouvel.[1]

Proportion of Troops in Each Category

It is estimated that the Armée des Princes, at the start of the campaign, had between 22,000 and 24,000 men.

Table 1: Approximate numbers of men in the different categories of units of the Armée des Princes, circa August 1792, and the proportion they contributed to the whole, on the basis that there was a total of 23,285 men.

Category of unit	Proportion (%)	Strength (men)
1. Chevaliers de la Couronne	1.3	300
2. Former royal troops	12.6	2,900
3. Légion de Mirabeau	6.5	1,500
4. Companies of officers and gentlemen	26.9	6,190
5. Coalitions de province	12.6	2,900
6. Corps de la Marine Royale	3.0	700
7. Maison militaire	21.7	5,000
8. German regiments	6.8	1,575
9. Light troops	6.5	1,500
10. Staff, etc.	3.3	770

1 Jean Pinasseau, *L'Émigration Militaire: Campagne de 1792* (Paris: Éditions A. et J. Picard et Cie., 1957), Part 1, pp.49–72 and Grouvel, *Troupes de l'émigration*, vol.II (Armée de Condé) and vol. III, (Armée des Princes, Armée de Bourbon etc.).

1. The Chevaliers-dragons de la Couronne (Plate 1)

Following the release of the Comte de Bussy from prison in Paris and his emigration to Chambéry in Savoy, on 1 June 1791, the Comte d'Artois wrote to him there, asking him to raise a corps for the defence of religion and the throne. Founded on the Volontaires de Bourbon that Bussy had already organised in France, it was to attract gentlemen from regions near Savoy such as Dauphiné, Provence, Auvergne, Velay, Lyonnais and Bourgogne. However, it was only in September, when he had gathered 150 to 160 volunteers, that the Princes granted him a capitulation for a corps to be called the Chevaliers-dragons de la Couronne.

The regulation of 1 June stated that, 'none will be admitted to the corps unless presented by a member of the corps; each chevalier will swear on his honour to never abandon its guidons without having obtained permission from his chiefs.'[2] The initial organisation was modified on 15 November by an establishing ordinance.[3] This not only stipulated the unit's uniform and definitive organisation but also the privilege granted to the Chevaliers de la Couronne that each trooper had the rank of *sous-lieutenant* of dragoons, and *brigadiers* that of *lieutenant*, which was confirmed on 5 January 1792. Bussy was granted the rank of *colonel* of cavalry while his younger brother, the Vicomte de Bussy, was named *colonel en second*, second in command. The volunteers were all young men, many from the upper echelons of society, and the corps was soon considered remarkable both for its military qualities and its brotherhood of arms, soon serving as a model for other volunteers who assembled about the Prince de Condé.

The Chevaliers de la Couronne left their first depot at Le Bourget on 24 November 1791, in groups of six, to reach the territory of the Cardinal de Rohan at the end of the month, where they were cantoned at Renchen with a strength of about 200, organised in four divisions. At this time, the unit was sometimes referred to as the Légion de Bussy, as it also had a hundred or so infantry. The latter, commanded by the Vicomte de Bussy, were still present on the return for February 1792 in eight squads, each with a *chef de section* and a *chef de peloton* (platoon leader).[4] Due to their small number, on 1 May 1792, they were reformed to create a free company that took the name of its *capitaine*, the Comte de Corsac.[5]

Meanwhile, the organisational structure of the Chevaliers de la Couronne, adopted in 1792, envisaged that it would consist of 400 men, although it only had 300. They were divided into two squadrons, each commanded by a *lieutenant-colonel*. Each squadron had two divisions subdivided into two platoons, which, in turn, had two sections of two squads. Considered to be

2 Grouvel, *Troupes de l'émigration*, vol.II, p.171.

3 Grouvel, *Troupes de l'émigration*, vol.II, p.172.

4 State Archive of the Russian Federation, Moscow (GARF): Collection 728, Inventory 2, Dossier 18, *Armée de Condé/Chevaliers de la Couronne*.

5 Grouvel, *Troupes de l'émigration*, vol.II, p.173 and confirmed in the nomination of the Comte de Corsac in the Order of the Phoenix on 12 August 1793 (Joseph Albrecht, *Archiv für Hohenlische Geschichte* (Dehringen: Ph. Haumann, 1857–1860), p.254). His brother, the Baron de Corsac, served in the Légion de Mirabeau.

dragoons, each squadron had a *porte-guidon* rather than a *porte-étendard* (standard-bearer).

Table 2: Organisational structure of the Chevaliers de la Couronne, 1792.

Staff
1 *Colonel commandant*
1 *Colonel en second*
1 *Lieutenant-colonel en premier*
1 *Lieutenant-colonel en second*
2 *Adjudants-majors*
2 *Adjudants d'escadron*
2 *Porte-guidons*
1 *Quartier-maître trésorier* (quartermaster treasurer)
1 *Aumônier* (chaplain)
1 *Chirurgien major* (surgeon major)
1 *Maréchal expert* (master farrier)
1 *Maître sellier* (master saddler)
1 *Armurier* (armourer)
Each of the four divisions had:
1 *chef de division*
1 *chef de peloton*
2 *chefs de section*
8 *brigadiers* (corporals)
56 *chevaliers*
1 *trompette* (trumpeter)
1 *maréchal-ferrant* (farrier)

The return for February 1792 shows that it was incomplete.[6] None of the divisions had either a trumpeter or a farrier, sometimes only one *chef de peloton*, and five *brigadiers* instead of eight. The staff had a trumpeter and two farriers, instead of a master farrier, who served for the whole corps.

Having moved to the Ettenheim area in January 1792, the Chevaliers occupied several cantonments there until 16 February 1792, when they moved north towards Bingen. After spending some time at Lampertheim, the corps was sent to Alzey, south-east of Bad Kreuznach. In June 1792, still 300 strong, the Chevaliers de la Couronne formed part of the cavalry of the left wing of the Armée de Condé.

2. The Former Royal Troops That Left France (Plates 1–8)

The royal troops who left France to join the émigrés posed a thorny issue. The officers were tolerated abroad, as any gentleman could travel at that time with his weapons, although they had to obtain permission from the local authorities to appear in uniform. However, soldiers could not be on Austrian territory, and only a few German principalities linked through dynastic

6 GARF: 728/2/18, *Armée de Condé/Chevaliers de la Couronne.*

French Infantry 1786–1790, by Rousselot. (*Le Passepoil* 1934/3, courtesy of La Sabretache)

or personal ties to the kingdom of France, and thus to the Princes, would receive them. Furthermore, once they had arrived, they had to be paid, steps taken to increase their number and, above all, kept in the ranks. Desertion and poaching of men were dreaded by any unit that remained static and unemployed, especially as coalition forces flowed into the region wishing to fill their ranks by whatever means.

Initially the princes sought to keep the few loyal troops under arms in France for as long as possible. This was to save costs and have them ready, for example, to hand over a frontier stronghold to the royalists. However, the Assembly took measures to prevent such projects, and the emigration of different corps took place between June 1791 and May 1792 and even, to a lesser extent, beyond. It was only on 15 May 1792 that the Princes authorised, 'the commanders and officers of all regiments to bring off and remove from France the corps to which they are attached, with arms, baggage, and the military chest, and this, as soon as they can.'[7] Officers of the old royal army had been leaving as individuals between June 1791 and February/March 1792, but, with the exception of the Régiments de Berwick and Vexin, it was only in April/May 1792, after the war had begun, that a second wave occurred with units, or soldiers and non-commissioned officers, individually or in small numbers, deserting to join the Armée des Princes.

The Irish Brigade

A report to the Assembly shows that by 27 December 1791 elements of the Irish Brigade had already emigrated.

> The Régiment de Berwick, Irish, occupies the village of Oberkirch, situated in the dependency of Cardinal de Rohan. It is only of 300 or at most 350 men; & meanwhile the roll of recruits rises to 1,100. Desertion is prodigious there. Two causes contribute to this desertion; first, the total lack of discipline; secondly, the trickery & bad faith that is used to obtain recruits. Most of these recruits are furnished by recruiters who, in agreement with the Liège regiment, engage in that country under the name of the Régiment de Royal-Liégeois, in the service of France, & then forcibly lead these men to this Régiment de Berwick … Some officers & deserters from Dillon, claim to form, at Oppenau, the nucleus of the regiment to which they have given this name. They flatter themselves that they will soon see their comrades & flags arrive. Fifteen officers & 18 to 20 soldiers currently form this pretended regiment.[8]

The Régiment de Berwick had had a recruitment depot at Liège, and it is conceivable that some of the soldiers who deserted from the Royal-Liégeois at the end of 1791 and through to the summer of 1792 may have joined its ranks. As for the Régiment de Dillon, or 87e Régiment d'Infanterie, 31 of its officers, along with about 30 cadets and no more than 140 men, had emigrated on 18 October 1791 when it was stationed at Bergues, south of Dunkirk. After crossing the frontier to Tournai, the

---

7 Quoted in Grouvel, *Troupes de l'émigration*, vol.III, p.13.

8 *Courrier Français,* 7 January 1792.

group crossed the Austrian Netherlands to reach Oppenau, on the right bank of the Rhine, a journey of at least 450 kilometres. Last to join this reconstituted Irish Brigade in the Armée des Princes were approximately 25 officers and 100 men of the 1st battalion of the 92e Régiment d'Infanterie (ci-devant Walsh). This battalion, the other having just been sent to Saint-Domingue, was on the march from Vannes in Brittany for Longwy when, on 22 March 1792, they crossed into Luxembourg from where they were then sent to Oppenau.

Other than the Régiment de Vexin, which may be considered as somewhat symbolic, there were only three infantry companies of loyal French soldiers dressed in the royal army's uniform. Furthermore, one of these was a failure and was therefore disbanded. This was the Compagnie de grenadiers, an initiative of La Châtre's at Ath, which was replaced by a Compagnie de bas-officiers that went with him when he took command of the vanguard of the Armée de Bourbon.

The Compagnie Franche de Maillard and the Provost

As early as 4 July 1791, Jacques Maillard, former *lieutenant prévôt* in the maréchaussée at Valenciennes, had taken the initiative of creating a 2e Compagnie de Chasseurs à Cheval, 'composed of troopers from the Maréchaussée and loyal bourgeois.'[9] These were joined by men from a variety of units. It was later renamed the 3e Compagnie de Volontaires à Cheval, Compagnie de Chasseurs à Cheval de Maillard or Compagnie du Tiers de Maillard, and finally the Compagnie Franche de Maillard. This last name was borne on its oval belt plate, probably after the dissolution of the other companies of chasseurs à cheval alluded to, of which there is no other trace. It has been categorised among the former royal troops because of its personnel when initially raised. First formed at Ath, it was considered as a cavalry company of about 100 men and it would also follow La Châtre to the vanguard of the Armée de Bourbon, at Huy.

When, in June 1792, it was intended to provide a Prévôté, provost corps, for the émigré forces, the Princes asked Maillard, 'lieutenant prévôt commanding the company formed of the cavalrymen of the Maréchaussée, cuirassiers, dragoons and bourgeois' to detach 10 men – a *lieutenant prévôt*, two *sous-lieutenants*, a *sergent*, five troopers and a volunteer. These were to be the basis for the formation of a provost of about 20 men for the Armée du Centre at Koblenz. That of the Armée de Condé, created in July, included a *prévôt général* (provost marshal), a *lieutenant prévôt* and about 20 troopers, mostly from the Royal-cavalerie, La Reine-cavalerie and Condé-dragons, formed in brigades of one *brigadier* and three troopers. Thus, Maillard's men not only formed a free company of cavalry but also the cadre and instructors for the provosts of the three armies.

9 Frédéric Masson, *Autour de Sainte-Hélène*, 2e série, (Paris: Société d'Editions Littéraires et Artistiques, 1909), p.8; the first section of this book, pp.1–120, is entitled 'Un émigré à Sainte-Hélène. Le comte de Montchenu, Commissaire de Sa Majesté Très Chrétienne.'

Artillery

The Comte de Romain, a young artillery *capitaine*, described the state of the artillery of the Armée de Condé when he joined it at Worms after emigrating in November 1791:

> We are unfortunately not yet in very large numbers from the royal corps: about twenty officers and as many élèves [students]. There are more at Koblenz. Moreover, a few arrive daily … The artillery officers form a separate company which remains at Worms, waiting for better days, and above all cannons; it is occupied during the day in rooms handling weapons, and in the evening making ball cartridges of which a small depot is formed at the castle.[10]

Furthermore, when Romain served in the Prince's guard, in May 1792, the situation was unchanged:

> The royal artillery, until now, suffer the most, for lack of cannons: it is heartbreaking for the Prince, almost as much as for us. We resign ourselves to making war as infantrymen, while waiting to seize some French pieces … He wanted to have us at his side: it is doubtless to console us, and probably also because our corps not being considerable, it was easier to establish us at the headquarters; it is for this reason that we are often charged with mounting guard near the person of the prince.[11]

When the Armée des Princes was formerly divided into three, *lieutenant-général* Marquis de Thiboulot proposed to the King's brothers to bring together all the artillery officers before distributing them in proportion to the size of each army. Condé immediately went to Koblenz to ensure that he would keep those who had joined him, which was granted. However, the artillery of the Armée du Centre, with Monsieur and Artois at its head, was the priority in the allocation of the meagre resources. Even then, at the start of the campaign, this army, 'lacked artillery; they had only been authorised to obtain pieces of the smallest calibre. Twelve cannons of 3 pound balls formed the park. These pieces were served by the artillery officers who had emigrated, doing service as simple gunners.'[12]

The artillery not only had few guns, but there were also almost no non-commissioned officers or gunners. This was also true of the companies of miners and *pontonniers* (bridging specialists), which were attached to the artillery. The Corps Royal du Génie (engineers) had always consisted of officers only. It was estimated that the Armée des Princes needed ten 12-pounder, ten 8-pounder, and fifty 4-pounder cannons (on the ratio of an artillery company with two 4-pounders per infantry regiment), as well as four 5-pounder howitzers. Six cannons were bought from the Prince of Hesse-Darmstadt, however, another consignment of 24 small-calibre guns ordered from the Count of Schaumburg-Lippe, although of good quality,

10 Romain, *Souvenirs*, vol.II, p.191.
11 Romain, *Souvenirs*, vol.II, p.228.
12 Marcillac, *Souvenirs*, p.47.

were considered unsatisfactory after they had been delivered to Bingen on 18 July 1792. It was only when hostilities began that captured French pieces became available to the émigrés after the first Prussian or Austrian successes.

Cavalry

On 9 April 1792, 15 officers and 40 men of the Dauphin-cavalerie crossed the Rhine as a body to join the émigrés.[13] However, it is the mass emigration of the hussar regiments and the Royal-Allemand-cavalerie that is better known, indeed the Saxe-hussards and Royal-Allemand are often described as having emigrated in their entirety. This is not accurate as, in both cases, their fourth squadrons refused to emigrate and went on to form the cavalry of the Légion patriote de Kellermann, raised in the summer of 1792.

Having emigrated, both regiments were completed to full strength, with four squadrons, as described by Brons:

> The corps that had passed [emigrated] in their entirety such as Royal-Allemand, Saxe and Bercheny-Hussards, were also completely mounted, and to these corps were added many volunteers, gentlemen or from the high Third Estate, mounted, armed, dressed and equipped at their own expense. Royal-Allemand alone then had more than forty and there were about as many in Saxe and Bercheny. It was to this last regiment that the officers of the other hussar regiments incorporated themsleves: Colonel-général, Chamborant, Lauzun and Esterazÿ who had passed as details and individually. Their current cantonment was at Biedbourg [Bitburg] and depended, like ours, on the headquarters of Ettelbruck and the commissariat of Luxembourg.[14]

It should be noted that this source was not available to both Pinasseau and Grouvel, who thus show in their works a squadron formed of officers from the Chamborant and Lauzun-hussards and the loyal hussars who followed them, serving in the vanguard of the Armée du Centre. Grouvel states that as early as May, at Bissen, in Luxembourg, this squadron consisted of, 'a hundred or so officers, non-commissioned officers and hussars.'[15] The most likely scenario was that the independent squadron from the Chamborant, Lauzun and Esterhazy only lasted until August 1792.

Table 3: Former royal units that joined the émigrés, the dates they did so, their strength and destination.

Corps	Date	Strength	Destination
Rgt de Berwick	June 1791	600	Armée du Centre
Rgt de Dillon	October 1791/January 1792	190	Armée du Centre
Rgt de Walsh	May-June 1792	80	Armée du Centre
Rgt de Vexin	August 1791/June 1792	100	Armée du Centre
Infanterie suisse	September–October 1792	25	Cie suisse du QG (HQ) Armée de Condé

13 Grouvel, *Troupes de l'émigration*, vol.II, p.185.
14 Brons, *Journal*, p.39.
15 Grouvel, *Troupes de l'émigration*, vol.III, p.82

Corps	Date	Strength	Destination
Infanterie suisse Compagnie franche de Porrentruy	August 1791–October 1792	50	Cie suisse du QG Armée de Bourbon
Infanterie française	March/October 1792	50-60	Cie française du QG Armée de Condé
Compagnie de Grenadiers	April/ August 1792	25 approx.	disbanded
Compagnie de bas officiers	April 1791/June 1792	45 approx.	Armée de Bourbon – replacement for above
Rgt de Saxe	May/July 1792	360–400 in 4 sqns.	Armée du Centre
Rgt de Bercheny	May/ August 1792	195–210 in 2 sqns.	Armée du Centre
Rgt de Chamborant, Lauzun et Etserhazy	July/August 1792	100 in 1 sqn.	Armée du Centre
Rgt Royal-Allemand	April 1792	450	Armée du Centre
Rgt de Dauphin cavalerie	April/August 1792	100	Armée du Centre
Prévôté	June /August 1792	50	Armée du Centre Armée de Condé Armée de Bourbon
Corps royal de l'Artillerie	From 1791 only a few gunners and soldiers of the attached corps, such as miners etc., to add to the officers	430, of which 25 were officers of the artillerie des colonies	Armée du Centre Armée de Condé Armée de Bourbon
Officiers du Génie	From 1791	45 approx.	As above

In total, the elements coming from the old royal army and kept in the various reconstituted corps, so excluding the companies of cavalry or infantry officers, amounted to approximately 2,900 men: 1,150 infantry; 1,300 cavalry, including the provost, and 470 artillery and engineers; or 13 percent of the strength in the summer of 1792.

This number does not include the former soldiers, in particular Alsatians and Lorrainers, who found employment in different corps, such as the Légion de Mirabeau and other light units, as well as in the new German corps.

Other Ranks

It was not uncommon for some French non-commissioned officers and soldiers to follow their officers when they emigrated, remaining with them in the first gatherings in the hope that a company or battalion of their regiment could be reconstituted. According to Bittard des Portes, when the officers of the Colonel-général-infanterie emigrated from Dunkirk:

> There a large group of non-commissioned officers and soldiers, belonging in the most to the grenadiers and chasseurs of the regiment, wished to follow their flags and emigrate with the officers. The same thing happens at Sedan in the Colonel-général-cavalerie, when the standards leave with a guard of honour, composed of the officers of the regiment and around fifty troopers.[16]

16 René Bittard des Portes, *Histoire de l'Armée de Condé (1791–1801) pendant la Révolution française* (Paris: E. Dentu-Editeur, 1896), pp.5–6.

On 14 December 1791, the Prince de Condé noted in his journal, 'There arrived with me in the afternoon, six cavalrymen and a trumpeter mounted from the Régiment de la Reine.'[17] Then four days later, 'there also arrived this day more French deserters than have arrived in three months; care was taken to have them pass immediately.'[18] But when it was apparent that, due to their large numbers, companies composed exclusively of officers would be formed, these soldiers were either placed in the few regular units of royal troops or in the newly raised corps, where, given their rarity, they were sure to find employment and be well paid.

This form of emigration continued into early 1792. In February, for example, the *Courrier français* reported that 18 officers and 11 soldiers of the 7e Bataillon de Chasseurs à Pied (ci-devant Chasseurs Bretons), stationed north of Strasbourg, at Bischwiller, Bas-Rhin, 'deserted their flags & crossed over the Rhine.'[19] Then, in May or June, Brons noted that at Mersen in the canton of Mersch, Luxembourg, where were gathered the officers of Rouergue-infanterie, 'Émigrés in totality with some non-commissioned officers and soldiers of their regiment; in all numbering 90 or 100 combatants, under the name of Rouergue and under the provisional command of Général de Klingling, maréchal de camp.'[20]

Reflecting contemporary society, the fate of émigré gentlemen is known through their memoirs or other studies devoted to their stories, but those of the men who followed them, sometimes showing unwavering attachment, is largely unknown. Meanwhile, it should be noted that the non-commissioned officers and soldiers who left the army with their officers, disillusioned with events in France and in their regiments, did not always do so with the intention of joining the émigré army. Jean Frédéric Wolf, the *chef de musique* (bandmaster), with the rank of *maréchal des logis*, of the 9e Dragons (ci-devant de La Reine) is one example. He quit the garrison at Laon on 11 April 1792 to cross the Belgian border, with his wife and three children. There he took up a civilian life at Ostende, his wife starting a shop there, however two years later, caught in the tide of war, he joined an émigré regiment in British pay.[21]

Of course, soldiers also deserted from the French army for what can be termed, for want of a better description, as the normal reasons. A list of French deserters in Austrian hands at Huy on 31 May shows, 'a soldier of the Régiment d'Alsace, a fourrier of Vintimille, a dragoon of Schomberg, 2 soldiers of Navarre, a soldier of Royal-Suédois, 2 chasseurs of Gévaudan, a soldier of an unknown regiment.'[22] It was quite common for recruiters to pay the Austrians for some of these French deserters to fill the émigré ranks.

17 Condé, *Journal*, p.238.

18 Condé, *Journal*, p.239.

19 *Courrier français*, 29 February 1792.

20 Brons, *Journal*, p.34.

21 René Trochon de Lorrieère, 'Deux Laonnois au service de l'Angleterre: Jean Frédéric et Pierre Frédéric Wolf 1794–1815', *Fédérations des Sociétés d'Histoire et d'Archéologie de l'Aisne Mémoires*, Tome II, 1955, p.62 and Service historique de la Défense, Vincennes (SHD): 2 Ye 39 82. Wolf joined the Régiment de Mortemart and served with it until it was disbanded in 1802.

22 Grouvel, *Troupes de l'émigration*, vol.II, p.237.

3. The Légion de Mirabeau (Plates 22–24)

Both Mirabeau brothers led a dissolute lifestyle, but, unlike his older sibling, André-Benoît-Boniface-Louis de Riqueti Vicomte de Mirabeau had a successful military career. Having joined the Légion de Lorraine as a *sous-lieutenant* in 1771, he was already *capitaine* in 1780 when he was assigned to the Régiment de Touraine-infanterie. He served during the American War of Independence, being wounded at Saint Kitts in January 1782, and was made a chevalier de Saint-Louis in 1785. Noted for his attention to duty, he was appointed *colonel* or *mestre de camp* of the Régiment de Touraine on 10 March 1788. That same year he married the Comtesse Marie-Louise de Robien, and their son was born in 1789. With a penchant for good food and wine, he was renowned for his stout appearance and so was nicknamed Mirabeau-Tonneau (with tonneau meaning barrel, this related to his figure as well as drinking habits). However, people had to avoid making light of him as he was a fine swordsman, as well as a good horseman. Elected a representative of the nobility of Limoges in the States-General in June 1789, he stood out as an ardent defender of the monarchy and clergy and was dismayed when he learned that the King had accepted the new constitution.[23] After failing to rally his regiment to the royalist cause, as described, he tried to flee with the two cravats of the regimental flags and, after a brief period under arrest, he emigrated, resigning as a deputy in the Assembly from abroad.

On 19 December 1790, Artois agreed that Mirabeau could raise a legion and, on 14 March 1791, the first elements of what was to be the Légion de Mirabeau assembled at Ettenheim. The unit's existence was confirmed on 9 August when its capitulation was signed by the King's brothers, followed by a review by the Comte de Vioménil on 26 August. (see Appendix 2 and 3 for its successive structures).

An officer who joined the legion at an early stage was the Marquis de Toustain, *sous-lieutenant* in the 3e Régiment de Chasseurs à cheval (formerly de Flandre), who emigrated on 30 September 1791. He had been unsure of where to go, but learning his uncle, Vioménil, had been named the legion's inspector, he headed for Ettenheim. On the way, he met another émigré officer, M. de Bellerose, *lieutenant-colonel* of the Chasseurs de la Picardie, and on 11 October they arrived at Ettenheim, where the legion had its headquarters, its men being camped outside the town, Toustain recalled:

> [It] was neither armed, nor dressed, nor trained. It comprised of 6 to 700 men, dressed in canvas smocks and armed with long iron-shod sticks. The cavalry did not have a hundred horses, and the company to which I was attached [the Uhlans] had 6 of them! In fact, we resembled a troop of brigands much more than a militarily organised unit.[24]

23 François-Xavier de Feller, *Dictionnaire historique ou histoire abrégée*, 8ème édition (Lille: Lefort, 1833), vol.XI, p.393.

24 Nieüil (ed.), *Toustain*, p.4.

Toustain found that only a third of the infantry officers had served as such in France; the rest had been NCOs or had other backgrounds. One such was Jean George Roland, from a Swiss military family, who since the age of 18 had served as *sous-lieutenant* in a carabinier company of the forces of his native Vaud/Bern before joining the legion as a *lieutenant* three years later in 1791.[25] Of the legion's cavalry officers, Toustain found, 'all the commanding cavalry capitaines and the greatest part of the officers had served in France in this quality.'[26]

The legion, benefiting from its proximity to Alsace, was soon joined by 250 volunteers from Colmar, and in October Mirabeau created a second company of volunteers who had no service experience. Even he was amused by the heterogeneous character of the men gathered about him:

> The background of this company, at the moment, is quite funny: a canon from Marmoutier, a gentleman glassmaker, 2 abbés, an innkeeper, a well-to-do Auvergnat and 2 councillors of the bailiwick of Langres. I forgot a secretary to the King … A young Breton also arrived at the head of 5 others who are from Rennes and Vannes.[27]

However, on 26 October 1791, the legion only had 730 infantry and 148 cavalry and the Princes considered limiting it to 1,000 men, but after an intervention from Vioménil they decided it should have 1,500 men: 1,120 infantry and 375 cavalry. In fact, the Légion de Mirabeau was to be the only corps to exceed its planned strength, requiring the adoption of a new organisation. The legion's officer cadre was remarkably stable, the vast majority of whom showed great loyalty to their chief and then to his memory until 1795. Officers very rarely left and those that did were senior officers going to better positions. The Marquis de Pange, who had, on 26 August 1791, been *colonel en second* of the infantry before becoming commander of the cavalry, left before the review of 25 January 1792 and was replaced by Alexandre d'Ollonne, one of four brothers in the legion who were relatives of Vioménil. Another senior officer who left was the Comte de Caylus, *colonel* of the legion's infantry, to take effective command of the Régiment de Rohan on its creation on 1 October 1791, and M. de Bergeret replaced him.

In the winter of 1791, the soldiers moved to Renchen, north of Ettenheim, and when, on 11 December 1791, the cavalry's standard and the infantry's flag were dedicated, it was nearby at Ettenheimmünster. It was apparently after this ceremony that a revolutionary correspondent reported on the legion:

> Its *colonel-général propriétaire*, M. de Mirabeau, is at Renchen. At Ettenheim is its *colonel* M. de la Féronière, former *colonel* in France. The rest of the staff is composed thus. *Colonel* of cavalry, M. Alexandre d'Olonne; *lieutenant-colonel*, M. Ducastel, *lieutenant-colonel* of cavalry, the chevalier d'Olonne; *major*, M.

25 Anon., 'Famille Roland', <http://www.davel.vd.ch/qfpdavel/0/D4681.pdf>, accessed 1 June 2015.

26 Nieüil (ed.), *Toustain*, p.5.

27 Grouvel, *Troupes de l'émigration*, vol.II, p.112.

> Le Fort, former *capitaine* of the grenadiers of [the Régiment de] Barrois; *aide-major*, M. Remi de Fribourg; *quartier maître trésorier*, M. Simonaire. This legion is distributed into different companies: The first is composed of volunteers from Alsace, that forms the Cardinal's guard. It is made up of the sons of councillors, lawyers, attorneys, clerks, bakers, butchers, shoemakers, carpenters, servants, beggars, all Alsatians, & above all from Colmar, in all 64 men, who have for their *capitaine* M. d'Orseville, councillor to the grand council. The volunteers from Bourgogne [Burgundy] are charged, at Renchen, with guarding the precious flag, blessed by a monk & which is to be placed one day in the cathedral in Paris. This company is composed of 56 men. That of the mounted volunteers, which has 66 of them, is formed of Frenchmen indiscriminately. The grenadiers are 62 in number, & have as *capitaine* M. de Corsac, formerly *lieutenant* in the Régiment de Touraine. The company of chasseurs à pied, 46 men strong, is formed of vagabonds escaped from the houses of correction, bandits & beggars gathered on the highroads. There are 8 companies at St Landelin, near Ettenheim, & under the sway of Montessa [Montessus], Leclair, Blair, etc. amounting to 380 men. At Reinsen [Ringsheim] are 60 chasseurs à cheval, unarmed, very badly mounted & almost naked; 34 hussars are at Grashousen [Grafenhausen]; & they are also as well equipped as the former. The uhlans, cantoned at Renchen, are a newly formed company, on the basis of the chasseurs à cheval, very badly mounted, to the number of 34 men, who have as *capitaine* M. Belleros [de Bellerose]. A company of 64 men formed of men who were gamekeepers, bears the name of *chasseurs appris*; & it is perhaps the only corps that is capable of something. Unfortunately all those who compose it are patriots on the inside; & they only remain under this dismal standard to have bread. If all these companies are brought together, 926 men will be found.[28]

This number is consistent with the review of 1 January 1792: for the infantry, the two companies of volunteers (Alsace and Burgundy) had 219 men; the grenadier company, 93; eight fusilier companies, 397; the company of chasseurs of the line, 60; two companies of enfants perdus, 93; flanquers, 69; chasseurs appris, 99; and the artillery company, 60, so almost 1,100 men in total. For the cavalry, one company of mounted volunteers, 99 men; two companies of chasseurs à cheval, 98; hussars, 70, and uhlans, 50; with the staff: 150 officers – 1,106 infantry and 317 cavalry.

The uhlan company, although not included in the original capitulation, was one of the first to be mounted and equipped. It often provided honour escorts, for example, Toustain wrote, 'On 6 [January 1792], Princess Louise de Condé passed through our quarter to join her father. I had the honour to command the detachment of 25 uhlans sent to meet her.'[29] It is at this time, early January 1792, that the Prince de Condé hoped to seize Landau with the help of some of the garrison, for which the legion had to prepare, 'For a month, we slept fully dressed, ready to respond at the first signal; but these plans were discovered and the garrison changed.'[30]

---

28 *Courrier Français*, 7 January 1792, publishing a letter dated Regensburg, 27 December 1791.

29 Nieüil (ed.), *Toustain*, p.9.

30 Nieüil (ed.), *Toustain*, p.9.

Threatened by the French Assembly, the Swabian Circle of the German Empire demanded that the legion be either dismissed or disarmed and expelled from the region. However, on 14 February, the Prince de Condé signed a mock treaty with the Prince of Hohenlohe-Waldenburg, who had just agreed to raise a regiment in the émigré service (see below). Under its terms the Légion de Mirabeau was transferred to his service under the name of the Légion de Waldenburg despite the objections from, this time, the Franconian Circle. On 23 February the first of the legion's three columns of 500 men, set off for the estates of Waldenburg, in Upper Baden, to arrive between 28 February and 1 March 1792.

Table 4: Strength of the Légion de Mirabeau at the time it marched from Ettenheim to Waldenburg, February 1792, as given in a 'state copied from the original'.[31]

Général	1
Colonels	3
Lieutenant-colonels	3
Major	1
Field officers	10
Other officers	140
Cavalrymen	320
Infantrymen	650
Volunteers on foot	280
TOTAL	1,408
Waggons, each drawn by four horses	21

The elegant castle of Pfedelbach was made available to the Vicomte de Mirabeau but he installed his staff and the uhlans there while he and his wife chose to live in an adjoining cottage. The rest of the legion was installed in neighbouring villages. A local gazette reported on the arrangements made upon its arrival, 'The Légion de Mirabeau, 1,565 strong, which is quartered in the Hohenlohe lands, was disarmed on the 8th of this month, in the presence of M. d' Eckardt, Major General of the Franconian Circle.'[32] Only the noble companies and the units responsible for discipline in the different quarters retained their weapons, the rest were placed in magazines. The local population were initially hostile towards the Mirabeaus but this was alleviated by scrupulous regulation of their subsistence. To maintain the façade of changed service the legion's uniforms adopted a Palatinate silhouette with so-called Rumford helmets, German bearskin caps, short lapels cut as a plastron, half-gaiters for the infantry and metallic scale epaulettes. The uhlans and hussars retained French-style uniforms, and the other units also kept some French details such as hussar-style waistcoats for the officers and badges of rank worn above the pointed cuffs.

It was difficult for Mirabeau to finance the legion; his wife sold her diamonds to help, which caused him to consider resigning on 16 February. However, the haven in Upper Baden allowed him to complete the training

31 *Mercure universel*, Mardi, 3 avril 1792, p.35

32 Anon., *L'esprit des Gazettes* (1792, no further details), p.282.

Staff of the Légion de Mirabeau, Spring/Summer 1792. (Author's collection)

of his troops so that, on the eve of the declaration of war, they were ready to enter the campaign.

The legion had now received enough volunteers to have, in addition to the Alsace and Burgundy companies, a third, the Méridionaux (southerners), as well as an élite Compagnie générale. Together, they formed an independent volunteer battalion of four companies. The two line infantry battalions were organised more closely to the French model: the first battalion had six companies, one of grenadiers, four of fusiliers and one of enfants perdus or skirmishers, and the second battalion had the same organisation, but a company of chasseurs (or chasseurs appris) replaced the grenadiers.

Some explanation is required for the titles of certain units or functions. Mirabeau, being proprietary *colonel* of the legion, had the rank of *colonel-général* while he was also *capitaine commandant* of two companies, which were named 'de la générale' (of the general) and that qualified as élite companies. The Compagnie générale de l'infanterie wore a strange Oriental-style turban and, serving as a sort of grenadier company, marched at the head of the three other companies of the Bataillon des volontaires. In turn, this battalion took precedence over the two other infantry battalions of paid soldiers. Likewise, in the cavalry, the first squadron was formed of volunteers, and the Compagnie générale à cheval had élite distinctions to its uniform. The Marquis de la Ferronnière was the functional commander and so was called *commandant général*. There were distinctive features of the uniform of each unit, Toustain explained: 'All these different uniforms were quite useful to us in the war, the enemy thinking that each of them was of a different regiment, so that they believed us infinitely stronger than we were really. But that had the disadvantage that they attacked us with more considerable forces.'[33]

The success of the legion was principally due to the personality of its chief, whom his men adored. Toustain, who was to serve on his staff for more than a year, provides a colourful description of him:

> The Vicomte de Mirabeau was a very extraordinary man physically and morally. His appearance was ridiculous, above all when he had the whim to put on a hussar uniform. I saw him once in this costume, waltzing with Madame de Contades. He looked like a rolling barrel! He was, however, very nimble: no officer of the legion mounted a horse more lightly. He had a superb head, but with great moustaches and a royale [a small tuft of a beard under the lower lip] that gave him a grotesque air. His character was a mixture of great qualities and great vices: brave to the point of recklessness, generous to the point of dissolute, frank and loyal; having infinite wit, he was gifted with a rare eloquence, of that suited to electrifying troops. But, to these precious qualities, he unfortunately added very little morality, a great disorder, the fatal passion for wine and strong liquors … and a disposition to extreme anger.[34]

Moreover, he was no tactician: 'The Vicomte had, of all the military virtues, only bravery which he did not even restrain. He possessed no kind of talent, had no idea of the cavalry arm and was, in fact, incapable of commanding an army corps. He knew no other manoeuvre than to go forward, bayonet fixed and would willingly have got himself killed.'[35]

However, it was his character and energy that, despite the difficulties he faced, forged this heterogeneous body into an élite unit. As such, the legion was paid a backhanded compliment by the amount of attention it received from the revolutionary press. Mirabeau was caricatured, his soldiers called hannetons noirs (black cockchafers) and the legion was denigrated: 'The Légion Mirabeau [sic] is composed of a group of animals, which made it rather resemble Noah's Ark. There are people of all nations, all languages, all religions, all ages, all sizes, all opinions. And from this mixture results a confusion that cedes nothing to the Tower of Babel'.[36]

It was also the target of disinformation in the press, an example being:

> From the banks of the Rhine, 8 June. – The Légion de Mirabeau is on its last legs … The pay that it always received a month in advance, no longer arrives. It has been awaited for over a month, as well as another sum of 65,000 livres. But the cashier is a man of the troops, who gives rise to serious concerns; besides, these sums would not be enough … The legion will still be obliged to ask for the cancellation of debts. No more horses, no more fodder, coats with holes in their elbows, their situation is such that these poor brigands are on the verge of dying of hunger. The rumour ran that the chief Mirabeau had blown his brains out.[37]

---

33 Nieüil (ed.), *Toustain*, p.413.
34 Nieüil (ed.), *Toustain*, pp.15–16.
35 Nieüil (ed.), *Toustain*, p.16.
36 *Mercure universeli* 3 April 1792, p.35, letter from Hohenlohe 23 March.
37 *Le Moniteur*, 17 June 1792.

When war was declared, at the end of April, the Légion de Mirabeau had, '257 volunteers, 1,243 men and 401 horses.'[38] It was assigned to the vanguard, commanded by the Comte de Vioménil, of the Armée de Condé.

4. The Noble Companies of Officers and Gentlemen (Plates 1, 9–11)

This category comprises two forms of company that had the same organisation, those of officers and those of other gentlemen, although in practical terms the distinction between such personnel was not as clear as the titles suggest.

The Compagnies d'officiers

As has been described, the cantonments of the Netherlands multiplied rapidly after the first officers were installed at Ath. At the end of July 1791, there were already assemblies of the officers of the infantry regiments Colonel-général, Auxerrois, Viennois, Dauphin, Orléans, Bourbon, Vivarais and Chartres, which were joined in August by those of Vintimille and Penthièvre. This organisation meant an astonishing variety of infantry and cavalry uniforms, still in accordance with the regulations of 1786–1791, was worn. Furthermore, several of these companies clothed their drummer in the old livery of the regiment.

These companies took the name of the regiment from which most of the men came, and then, when one company was merged with another, that of the senior regiment. An example of a company that merged in this way was the one that the Comte de La Tour tried to form from officers of the Royal-Liégeois at Worms, but, due to lack of numbers, his men were incorporated into the Compagnie d'officiers des Régiments de la Marine et Royal-Liégeois. It appears that La Tour was finally joined in that company by 10 officers, of a variety of nationalities, from his former regiment.[39]

The story of the Compagnie d'Orléans-cavalerie, which was in the Armée du Centre from March to July 1792, provides an example of a cavalry company. Officers of the regiment only emigrated from Valenciennes in November 1791, as until then, there was a hope that the King might use it as either an avenue to escape or to hold as a rallying point. They then proceeded to Ath, where their counterparts of Royal-Picardie were forming a company. The first known return for the state for the officers of both regiments is at the Namur cantonment on 1 April 1792. This shows 39 volunteers (of which 17 were absent), including 24 officers from the regiment (five absentees), a trooper named Vauvillers and a trumpeter, Peck. The gathering was commanded by Comte Gibon de Kérisouet, *major* of the regiment. That month, the company moved to Neumagen (Neumagen-Dhron), on the banks of the Moselle, northeast of Trier, and seven officers, trooper and trumpeter, requested a *traitement de route*, a travel allowance to cover the

38 Grouvel, *Troupes de l'émigration*, vol.II, p.114.

39 M. Lecomte, 'Le Régiment Royal-Liégeois au service du Roi de France (1787–1792)', *le Carnet de la Sabretache*, 1938 and 1939 (Nos. 388 and 389) and Champflour (ed.), *La coalition d'Auvergne*, p.297.

eight days from 10 April of the march at a rate of 24 livres for an officer and 12 for a cavalryman. The state of 1 May, at Neumagen, is the first to list the two companies of Orléans-cavalerie and Royal-Picardie separately. After M. de Loulai, transferred to Royal-Picardie, and the Comte d'Apremont left to join the troops with the Prince de Condé, it shows the company of Orléans-cavalerie with 25 officers, 17 other volunteers (including 13 absent), a trooper and a trumpeter (although it appears the last had deserted in April with his travel allowance). On 24 June 1792, the company had 46 men, including 26 officers of the Orléans-cavalerie, the same trooper and a farrier. Gibon remained in command, the second in command was the *commandeur* de Courtebonne, and the *chefs de section* were Baron de Mallet, Comte de Saman, Marquis de Tressan and Chevalier de Bazouges, whose ancestry and military career have been described in the Introduction.

Table 5: Composition of the Compagnie d'Orléans-cavalerie on 14 June 1792 according to the original regiments, excluding the unmounted trooper and the farrier.[40]

26	Orléans-cavalerie	1	Royal-Pologne-cavalerie
5	Chartres-dragons	1	Royal-Lorraine-cavalerie
2	Royal-Normandie-cavalerie	1	Du Roi-infanterie
1	Artois-cavalerie	1	Chasseurs de la Normandie
1	Chasseurs du Hainaut	1	Lorraine-dragons
1	Condé-dragons	1	Barrois-infanterie
1	Chasseurs de la Picardie	1	Colonel-Général-dragons

As the company was considered to contain only 30 maîtres, rather than about 40, it was decided that while it would be retained, it would be completed by men from other companies.[41] Thus, it was finally amalgamated and called the Compagnie de Royal-Lorraine et Orléans-cavalerie, the Royal-Lorraine being ranked 13th and Orléans 24th among the cavalry regiments of the Ancien Régime. The *colonel* of the Royal-Lorraine, the Vicomte Jean-Baptiste de Thumery, took command as he was senior in rank to the Comte de Gibon, who left the company.

Compagnies de gentilshommes

Article I of the regulations specified that companies would also be formed that incorporated officers who had retired from service and gentlemen who had never served. The historian, Muret, states that the maîtres verriers (gentleman glassmakers) of Clermontois, in Argonne between Champagne and Lorraine, emigrated en masse to form almost two infantry companies, 'There were eleven combatants in the Juillot family alone, five in that of Dordolot, eleven among the Brossard, ten among the Bonnay, four among the Foucauld, seven among the Finance, fifteen among the Bigault, eight among the Duhoux.'[42]

40 MCC: Fonds Grouvel 15/6 Compagnies des officiers de cavalerie.

41 Musée Condé, château de Chantilly (MCC): Fonds Grouvel, the latter drew from: SHD, registre matricules 2Y-b-817; SHD, archives administratives X-c-117 and AN, AF-II-391.

42 Muret, *Armée de Condé*, vol.I, p.35.

Either version of the émigré uniform (as described in Section 2 of the Colour Plate Commentary, below) was worn in these companies. Unlike those of officers, the companies took the name of their *capitaine*, and so the name could change as they came and went. Each of the volunteers had the right, after their registration, to transfer to another unit whether to join relatives or friends or to take a more advantageous position. This led to a substantial movement of personnel, which could sometimes result in companies disappearing or merging with others.

Brons described the attempt to form two companies at the village of Bettendordf in Luxembourg, which not only failed, but also illustrates how opaque the differences between the two types of noble company described in this section could be. The attempt was made by the Baron de Coetlosquet, former *colonel* of the Régiment de Bretagne, in May or June 1792.

> This company had been joined by several gentlemen of different provinces, discharged officers, or retired from different corps who, originally, had tried to form two companies [under the command of another senior officer]. But after several months of useless attempts, the majority of these officers had preferred to incorporate themselves in the regular companies, formed of officers of line regiments. Several were admitted to those of Picardie, Languedoc, Royal-Roussillon, and Bretagne, and replaced in these companies the small number of officers who had remained in France, by means of which, these found themselves almost complete, that is to say at the effective number of combatants that they would have had if the officers of the different regiments had emigrated in their entirety, as they had done in the majority.[43]

As has been mentioned, there was also the Compagnie noble de Rouault, which Brons described:

> Among the other companies formed by the nobility of the provinces, I remarked that of the noble poitevin chasseurs the chief of which was the Comte Charles de Rouault. It appeared to me to be of about 70 gentlemen all of the age of strength and full of ardour as well as the means for the type of service for which they were destined, that is to say that of light troops.[44]

It seems that Brons was mistaken about the volunteers being from Poitou as there is no mention of this in Beauchet-Filleau's work on the province's émigrés.[45] It is likely that Rouault, *major en second* of the Chasseurs à cheval de la Lorraine in 1788, was joined by gentlemen from a variety of sources, including officers.[46]

43 Brons, *Journal*, p.32.

44 Brons, *Journal*, p.53.

45 Henri Beauchet-Filleau, *Tableau des émigrés du Poitou aux armées des Princes et de Condé* (Poitiers: Librairie Charles Pichot, 1845).

46 Pinasseau, *Campagne de 1792*, p.13 shows it as being of officers from different regiments.

Military Organisation – Armée du Centre

In early June 1792, as the first organisation of the central division was to take place noble companies were installed across, 'the province of Luxembourg, the Ardennes, the lands of Liège, the Electorate of Trier and other surrounding states, up to the environs of Frankfurt, in a length of about fifty leagues by about fifteen or twenty in width.'[47] Within this area, districts were defined, each commanded by a general. The Comte de Brons described that commanded by Baron de Kinglin, *maréchal de camp*:

> Under his immediate orders, was formed, at Ettelbruck, the squadron of the officers of Artois-Cavalerie, Royal-Normandie and the chasseurs à cheval de Franche-Comté. This very well mounted squadron, perfectly adorned and equipped, was under the command of M. de Montmény, lieutenant-colonel of the chasseurs à cheval, and composed in total of about eighty maîtres ... Each maître was superiorly mounted; almost all had a horse in hand, in case of emergency, and all had in their retinue several servants solidly mounted.[48]

At Ettelbruck, 'resident with the general were his staff, the chaplain, the master saddler, the armourer, the master farrier, the pharmacy and other dependencies of this division of the army.'[49] There were also 'a gathering of officers of diverse regiments of German infantry in the service of France' and, at nearby Mersen, 'officers of the Régiment de Rouergue-infanterie. Émigrés in totality with some bas-officiers and soldiers of their regiment; all to a number of about ninety or a hundred combatants.'[50]

Later that month, companies would be distributed among what would become the Armée du Centre and that of Bourbon. The cavalry would remain with the centre while the company of Rouergue would be allocated to Bourbon. As for the German infantry regiments, two companies would be formed for the Armée de Bourbon, Alsace and Hesse-Darmstadt, while the Centre would have one, formed by officers of Royal-Deux-Ponts and La Marck.

It was at about this time that Pinasseau listed the organisation of the future Armée du Centre.[51] This shows it with 34 noble infantry companies, all of officers except for that of Roualt. However, when, after 23 July 1792, the army's order of battle was prepared, the Compagnie de Chasseurs à pied de Provence et des Ardennes had disappeared.[52] The remaining companies of officers formed four battalions each with eight companies – the first battalion, first brigade, was further divided with four general officers commanding a pair of companies, the other battalions were divided between two general officers each with four companies in the second battalion of the first brigade and first battalion of the second brigade while the last, the second battalion, fourth

47 Brons, *Journal*, p.32.
48 Brons, *Journal*, p.33.
49 Brons, *Journal*, p.35.
50 Brons, *Journal*, p.34.
51 Pinasseau, *Campagne de 1792*, pp.11–30.
52 It is shown by Pinasseau, *Campagne de 1792*, p.12 but missing in the later Order of Battle.

brigade, was allocated in the proportion 5:3. The Compagnie de Rouault was placed on the right flank of the first line of cavalry (see Appendix 5).

More substantial changes took place among the noble cavalry companies between June and July. At the beginning, there were 17 companies, again all of officers, and the changes were:

> The Compagnie des Carabiniers de Monsieur was increased to a squadron of two companies.
>
> The officers of the Monsieur-dragons were joined by those of Angoulême to form the Compagnie de Monsieur-dragons et d'Angoulême-dragons, also known as the Dragons des Princes.
>
> As described above the Compagnie de Chamborant et Lauzun-hussards was also expanded to a squadron by the addition of non-commissioned officers and hussars, as well as volunteers, so included among the units of the former royal army.
>
> The Compagnie de la Reine-dragons, with insufficient personnel, was dissolved into the Gardes-du-corps du Roi.
>
> The Compagnie d'Artois-cavalerie, which, on 11 June, only had 21 maîtres of which eight were absent, was also dissolved and its personnel joined different companies.[53]

When the order of battle was prepared in July, the 15 companies formed the second line of cavalry along with the Royal-Allemand and cavalry companies of provincial coalitions (see Appendix 5).

Military Organisation – Armée de Condé

As the year 1791 drew to a close, it was noted that:

> The French who were gathered at Worms formed sixteen companies … These companies were eight on horseback, eight on foot; twelve were composed of active officers, four of officers retired from the service, and of loyalists not having served at all: all under the orders of Monseigneur the Prince de Condé, his son Monseigneur the Duc de Bourbon, and his grandson, Monseigneur the Duc d'Enghien.[54]

This time saw the establishment of a structure that would essentially remain until the Armée de Condé was finally disbanded, 10 years later. This was of independent corps of noble infantry and noble cavalry, the infantry being organised in divisions of two companies and the cavalry in squadrons of two companies, each division and squadron being commanded by a *maréchal de camp*. These corps would be the very essence of the Armée de Condé, forming between a quarter and a half of the total from 1792 to 1801.

Between December 1791 and January 1792, the strength of the noble infantry grew from 560 to 730 men. So, in the latter month, 'The artillery

---

53 Grouvel, *Troupes de l'émigration*, vol.III, p.83.

54 B.P., *Récit de ce qui s'est passé de plus remarquable à l'Armée de S.A.S. le Prince de Condé en 1791, 1792 et 1793* (Laval: Portier, 1817), p.23.

company [was] cantoned at Oppenau [in the Principality of Ettenheim] with two divisions of the noble infantry corps.'[55]

By June 1792, the companies had been organised, with those that had not been able to raise sufficient men being merged into others. In the infantry, there were 24 companies, 18 of active officers from the line infantry and chasseurs and six of retired officers and gentlemen. These six were named after their *capitaines*: Prédelys, Riollet, Tschudy, Mussey, La Devèze and Corsac. It should be noted that Pinasseau lists the last two as free companies of the Third Estate, but other sources indicate otherwise.[56] While it is quite possible that members of the Third Estate were among their personnel, that of Corsac having originated from the infantry attached to the Chevaliers de la Couronne, they were, in terms of uniform and structure, no different to the other four companies of former officers or gentlemen. The order of battle for the Armée de Condé (Appendix 6) shows the 24 companies of noble infantry forming four battalions, each of three divisions.

There were 10 noble cavalry companies, seven of officers and three of gentlemen, those of Franche-Comté, Saint-Clair and Villers, the last two named after their *capitaines*. The companies of officers included those mainly formed by officers of the Régiment du Roi-infanterie who chose to serve as cavalry (the regiment having been disbanded for insubordination on 28 March 1791). The cavalry wings of the Armée de Condé each consisted of a brigade of four squadrons of two companies; that of the right was made up entirely of noble cavalry while the left had a noble squadron brigaded with those of the Chevaliers de la Couronne and Dauphin-cavalerie (see Appendix 6).

The interchangeability of personnel between the companies of officers and those of gentlemen is clearly illustrated by the later incorporation of the Compagnie de gentilshommes de Franche-Comté into the Compagnie d'officiers de La Reine-cavalerie to complete it in numbers.

Military organisation – Armée de Bourbon

Each of what were to be the émigré armies differed in their composition, and the Armée de Bourbon was remarkable for the number of units from the provincial coalitions (dealt with below), as well as having free companies, instead of those of gentlemen. In the infantry, there were 18 companies of officers in two battalions of eight companies each, with a further two in the reserve. In the cavalry, there were six such companies which formed three squadrons, of two companies, which were allocated separately (see Appendix 7).

There was one free company in the cavalry, that of Maillard, described above. In the infantry, there were six free companies. The Compagnie de Le Seigneur was formed of gentlemen with no military experience but commanded by former officers. It was particularly strong, having at least 80 men, due to having incorporated another similar unit raised by the Chevalier de Floyd, who became Le Seigneur's second-in-command. The other five were generally considered to have been composed of men of the Third Estate

55 Romain, *Souvenirs*, vol.II, p.201.

56 Pinasseau, *Campagne de 1792*, p.64.

or bourgeois, coming from different provinces in the companies of Alheim and Abzac, Artois and Flanders in those of La Rianderie and Laurétan and Normandie and Maine in that commanded by Noury (hence it is sometimes shown as the Compagnie de Normandie). The free companies were posted to serve on the flanks of the cavalry and in the reserve (see Appendix 7).

The story of Bernard de Corbehem shows that the personnel of these last five companies was more varied than may be assumed. His family, having been harassed as aristocrats by revolutionaries in their hometown west of Arras, he and his brother emigrated to the Austrian Netherlands on 24 December 1791. They subsequently joined the Compagnie de La Rianderie after having been refused by the Coalition d'Artois on the grounds that they had not been recognised as gentlemen by the Estates of Artois. The brothers were so well treated in the company that they remained with it throughout the campaign despite having received, from home, a certificate proving their nobility.[57]

Noble Companies – The Campaign of 1792

Table 6: Distribution of noble companies (excluding those of coalitions) within the three armies of the Armée des Princes.[58]

Army	Infantry Companies		Cavalry Companies	
	Number	Men	Number	Men
Bourbon	18	1,026	6	342
Centre	33	1,938	17	969
Condé	24	1,344	10	560
Total	75	4,308	33	1,881
Grand total	108 companies – 6,189 men			

With the average strength of the Armée des Princes being calculated at 23,000 men, these noble companies represented approximately 27 percent, or more than a quarter, of the total force.

5. The Coalitions de province (Provincial Coalitions) (Plates 10–12)

Coalition d'Auvergne – The First

As has been described, this coalition, as a body of volunteers from the same province organised as a military unit, was established as early as 10 April 1791, with its first statement having 134 signatories. In early August 1791, it was at Koblenz and served as a model for subsequent regional coalitions, as well as companies of gentlemen or the Third Estate who also wore the same uniform. After having drawn up the nominal list, the Auvergne gentlemen organised themselves into cavalry companies, dressed, equipped and armed in the same manner. Thus, the Coalition d'Auvergne established one of the

57 Bernard de Corbehem, *Dix ans de ma vie ou Histoire de mon émigration* (Paris: A Phian Delaforest, 1827), pp. 36–41.

58 Pinasseau, Campagne de 1792, pp.34, 44 and Muret, *Armée de Condé*, Vol.I, p.69.

two models of the emigrant uniform; the royal blue double-breasted coat with two rows of six gilt buttons decorated with a fleur-de-lys. It adopted, as a distinction, yellow collars and cuffs. Its members being in the main wealthy, the coalition was superbly mounted, using bearskin shabraques.

Other coalitions followed, under the Regulations of 19 August 1791. All were of volunteers who committed to serving for the duration of a campaign and to only leave at its end or, with the approval of its commander, in the event of absolute necessity. This gentleman's agreement reflected the fact that the volunteers agreed to serve while arming and equipping themselves at their own expense. Even when a salary was offered, from November 1791, many of those who could, did without it.

As with all the volunteer companies, a newcomer had to be vouched for by two of the coalition members and then accepted by the vote of all its members. The Comte de Montlosier joined the Coalition d'Auvergne in April 1792, when it was cantoned at Ehrenbreitstein, a suburb facing Koblenz across the Rhine.[59] Although from a well-known and prestigious family and having been among the first signatories, and so incorporated into the first company, his initial reception was cold as he had supported the constitutional monarchy.[60] What is more he had written a political work recommending the replacement of the old parlements and states-general by a bicameral parliament, as adopted by Louis XVIII at the Restoration in 1814 and 1815.

Table 7: Exact strength of the elements of the Coalition d'Auvergne at the start of the 1792 campaign.[61]

Lieutenant-général	1
Maréchaux de camp	2
Aides majors	2
Porte-étendards	2
Aides de camp	6
First Company	61
Second Company	62
Third Company	66
Fourth Company	57
TOTAL	259

Article X of the Regulation of 19 August 1791 stipulated that, 'the gentlemen may among themselves change companies, after having obtained the agreement of their respective chiefs who will report it to the princes; but the change may only take place once for each gentleman.'[62] Examples of this took place in the Coalition d'Auvergne, such as the Comte de Richardie de Besse, a former officer in the Gardes Françaises who joined his comrades in the Hommes d'armes à pied and M. du Croiset, who joined the guards of the

59 Montlosier, *Souvenirs*, p.70.

60 Montlosier, *Souvenirs*, p.74.

61 Champflour (ed.), *La coalition d'Auvergne*, pp.125–136.

62 Anon., *Règlement définitif*, Article X.

Comte d'Artois.[63] Any gentleman who transferred to another unit, of course had to pay for their uniforms and horse furniture themselves. By the start of the campaign, of the 308 gentlemen who had signed the act, 11 had returned to France and 38 had transferred to other corps; so the Coalition d'Auvergne only formed two squadrons.

Characteristics of the Provincial Coalitions

The coalitions were formed on the basis of the ancient provinces of the Kingdom of France, so their peculiarities ranged from dialect to familial links. In the Coalition d'Auvergne, the families of Bosredon and Fargues each provided a complete section. In the Coalition de Guyenne, distinction was made between companies drawn from different parts of the province. Unlike that of Auvergne, many provincial coalitions found that their elements were widely dispersed, which hampered cohesion. On the other hand, some coalitions were formed by combining volunteers from different provinces, such as that of Artois, which included men from the neighbouring regions of Flanders, Boulogne and Picardie.

The coalitions organised themselves as best suited their members, especially in terms of numbers and means. So, they varied in size and whether they were of cavalry, infantry or both. At the company level, all were organised on the same basis, as established by the regulation of 19 August. All wore the emigrant uniform, but each sought to be different, often having a distinctive feature on their uniform or using a provincial emblem. The strength of companies, infantry or cavalry, varied, but an approximate number of 55 men, including a trumpeter or drummer, was perhaps average. It was considered that as each company had the same organisation, equipment and armament, they were interoperable. When entering the campaign, each cavalry company was to be equipped with 24 carbines.

Of the personnel of the coalitions, the Comte de Brons observed, 'Most of these noble combatants had only served a little or not at all, but almost all were sons or grandsons of former soldiers, some were retired and pensioned officers, there were even in these coalitions a certain number of Chevaliers de Saint-Louis.'[64] However, the celebrated writer and politician François-René de Chateaubriand, who served as a volunteer in the 7th Breton company, later recalled:

> An army is normally composed of soldiers of about the same age, the same height, the same strength. Very different was ours, a confused assembly of grown men, old men, children come down from their dovecotes [nurseries], speaking in Norman, Breton, Picard, Auvergnat, Gascon, Provençal, Languedocien dialect. A father served with his sons, a father-in-law with his son-in-law, an uncle with his nephews, a brother with a brother, a cousin with a cousin. This throwback, as ridiculous as it seemed, had something honourable and touching about it, because it was animated by sincere convictions; it offered the spectacle of the old monarchy and gave a last representation of a world that passed. I saw old gentlemen, of

---

63 Champflour (ed.), *La coalition d'Auvergne*, pp.52, 56.

64 Brons, *Journal*, p.38.

> severe appearance, with grey hair, torn coat, bag on the back, musket slung across, on a sling, dragging themselves along with a stick and supported under the arm by one of their sons ... All this poor band, not receiving a sou from the princes, made war at its expense, while the [Assembly's] decrees managed to plunder it and threw our wives and mothers in dungeons.[65]

Marcillac also paid tribute to the provincial gentlemen, contrasting their position with courtiers:

> Ambition could influence the departure of the man of heart, of the man filled with favours from the monarch and who was to rediscover at Koblenz the elements that he had left behind at Versailles; but this provincial gentleman, unknown to the King, a stranger to all that emanates from his individual bounty, who, after having sold his harvest, abandons his wife, his children, quits his most dear interests, and leaves on foot from the depths of Brittany or the middle of the mountains of Auvergne to go to take up the musket and practice the soldier's profession in Germany, without perspective, without dreaming of a reward which, even if obtained, would always be out of proportion to his sacrifices; there is in this movement what one calls the sublime ideal.[66]

Coalition de Bretagne

On 27 August 1791, Breton gentlemen proposed forming a coalition, on the model of the Coalition d'Auvergne, to the Prince de Condé. Indeed, on 23 December 1791, representatives of the coalition proposed that it come within Condé's command, to which he, diplomatically, replied that he would accept the decision of the King's brothers. Six months later, the Coalition de Bretagne was dispersed, from Flanders to the Rhine, as described by Comte Olivier d'Argens, who registered on 1 February 1792 at Ath in what was later to become the 8th Breton company:

> At Oudenaarde was a party of the Bretons. At Mons a company of gentlemen of the same country also formed. On the 22nd, M. the Comte de La Châtre, commanding the French in the Ath cantonment, passed the company in review and installed, following military form, the two capitaines, M. de Pontavice, from Fougères, capitaine in the Régiment de Chartres, en premier, and M. de Kernesne senior, from Morlaix, lieutenant in the Régiment de —. The four chefs de section, namely: MM. de Lavilléon de Moncontour, lieutenant in Normandie; de Kernesne, junior, from Guincamp, sous-lieutenant in the Régiment de Flandre; de Kermenguy of Saint-Pol-de-Léon, supernumerary officer in the Régiment de Bretagne, and Dondel of Vannes, sous-lieutenant in Auxerrois.[67]

The eight *chefs d'escouade* were chosen by the volunteers themselves.

---

65 François-René de Chateaubriand, *Mémoires d'Outre-Tombe*, new edition (Paris: Librairie Garnier Freres, 1910), vol.II, pp.60–61.

66 Marcillac, *Souvenirs*, p.32.

67 Anon. (ed.), *Olivier d'Argens*, p.14.

Finally, on 17 and 18 April 1792, the Coalition de Bretagne was gathered near Trier, when those from Flanders arrived at Hillesheim. However, the previous dispersion of the companies saw a lack of cordiality among them, as recalled by Argens: 'In the course of June, it was mentioned, in our cantonment, that the gentlemen [in the cantonment] of Wittech [Wittlich] were going to take out a loan; but the division that reigned amongst the gentlemen of Wittech and then between them and the gentlemen from Oudenaarde, and the security that was demanded, caused the loan to fail.'[68] Such loans, sometimes initially needed to clothe and equip the volunteers, until they were paid by the King's brothers from November 1791, ultimately served as funds to allow the poorest to provide for their accompanying families. Although the Coalition de Bretagne finally had eight infantry and two cavalry companies, it is not known if it had a staff, although this is very likely.

Coalition du Poitou

The Coalition du Poitou is known to have had a staff. Its first company was created on 24 September 1791 at Tournai, but the principal gathering of the gentlemen of the province in the following weeks was at Binche.[69] On 1 December, the coalition already had five infantry companies and the nucleus of a cavalry company. In the spring of 1792, the fifth foot company was broken up and distributed among the other four and its second cavalry company was not formed until 17 July 1792 and not completed until August. The Coalition du Poitou was therefore organised as an infantry battalion, of four companies in two divisions, and a cavalry squadron; the staff consisted of two infantry division commanders and a squadron commander, with their respective aides de camp, two *aumôniers* and a *chirurgien-major*.

Coalition de Champagne et de Lorraine

On 26 December 1791, representatives of the nobility of Lorraine, Barrois and the Trois Evêchés (the three bishoprics of Metz, Toul and Verdun) met and renounced the formation of a coalition. However, due to their dispersal in different cities and cantonments in Germany, they would appoint commissioners to maintain links and establish a register of its members. They wished:

> … to renew to the King, in the hands of Monsieur and M. the Comte d'Artois, the oath that it made to die rather than to consent to the destruction of religion, to the alteration of the monarchy & the imprescriptible rights of the royal family, regarding as traitors those who sought to destroy them and those who would oppose the restoration of the rights of the three orders.[70]

In the end, the Lorraine gentlemen joined those of Champagne to form a single coalition.

---

68 Anon. (ed.), *Olivier d'Argens*, p.18.

69 Beauchet-Filleau, *Tableau des émigrés du Poitou*, p.19.

70 *Courrier français*, 28 February 1792.

Coalition de Normandie

On 20 October 1791, Norman gentlemen proposed forming a coalition authorised to wear a badge recalling the coat of arms of their province to the King's brothers. However, they were dispersed between Nivelles in Brabant, where the greatest number had gathered, and various cantonments between the Rhine and the Moselle. At the end of November 1791, those in Germany gathered at Ehrang, near Trier, but they were only joined by those from Brabant at the end of March 1792.

The Third Estate in the Coalitions

Most of the coalitions were formed exclusively by, and of, gentlemen. However, émigrés of the Third Estate from the province of Dauphiné who had gathered at Bern requested to serve as infantry or cavalry at their own expense in the cause of the King were in correspondence with gentlemen from their province at Koblenz on 15 September 1791.[71] This led, two months later, to the drafting of a regulation dated 1 November for the organisation of émigrés from the upper middle class into companies of volunteers, within the coalitions.

Nevertheless, no such company is known to have been in the Coalition du Dauphiné, so it would appear that in this coalition, as in some others, bourgeois volunteers served alongside noble comrades. Indeed, the Coalition de Bretagne is the only one known to have had a company specifically of the Third Estate, along with its seven noble companies, but differentiated from them by having a uniform of a different colour. Chateaubriand was critical of this: 'the iron grey uniform of this last company differed from that of the seven others, royal blue with ermine facings. Men attached to the same cause and exposed to the same dangers their political inequalities perpetuated by odious signs: the true heroes were the plebian soldiers, as no personal interest diluted their sacrifice.'[72]

The provincial coalitions formed about 13 percent of the Armée des Princes.

Table 8: Approximate strength and distribution of the provincial coalitions, summer 1792.

Name	Composition	Units	Strength	Placement
Coalition d'Auvergne	Cavalry only	2 squadrons	260	Armée du Centre
Coalition de Bretagne	Cavalry	1 squadron	110	Armée du Centre
	Infantry	5 companies forming the Bataillon Breton + 3 companies incl. 1 du Tiers.	440	
Coalition de Guyenne	Cavalry	1 squadron (2nd coy. completed with maîtres from Provence)	70	Armée de Bourbon
	Infantry	3 companies	180	
Coalition de Normandie	Cavalry	1 squadron	100	Armée de Bourbon
	Infantry	7 companies	320	

71 Anon., *Règlement pour la Formation en différentes Compagnies, du Tiers-Etats rassemblé auprès de MONSIEUR & de Monseigneur Comte d'ARTOIS* (no details), pp.5–7.

72 Chateaubriand, *Mémoires*, vol.III, p.62.

Name	Composition	Units	Strength	Placement
Coalition de Saintonge, de l'Angoumois et de l'Aunis	Cavalry	1 company	35	Armée du Centre
	Infantry	2 companies	110	
Coalition de l'Anjou et du Maine	Infantry only	2 companies	110	Armée de Bourbon
Coalition de l'Artois	Cavalry	1 squadron	110	Armée de Bourbon
	Infantry	2 companies	110	
Coalition du Dauphiné et de la Provence	Cavalry only	1 squadron	110	Armée de Bourbon
Coalition du Languedoc	Cavalry	1 company	55	Armée du Centre
	Infantry	1 company	55	
Coalition du Limousin	Cavalry	1 company	55	Armée de Bourbon
	Infantry	1 company	55	
Coalition du Périgord	Cavalry	1 company	55	Armée du Centre
	Infantry	1 company	55	
Coalition du Poitou		Staff	10	Armée du Centre
	Cavalry	1 squadron	110	
	Infantry	4 companies	220	
Coalition de Champagne et de Lorraine	Cavalry	1 squadron	110	Armée de Bourbon
	Infantry	2 companies	110	
TOTAL	Cavalry	22 companies	2,995	
	Infantry	34 companies		

6. The Corps de la Marine Royale (Plate 13)

The situation for naval officers in France had become intolerable from the end of 1789, when there was an insurrection by port workers at Toulon against its commander, the Comte d'Albert de Rions, this was followed, from the summer of 1790, by indiscipline from the crews and marines as well as the actions of the clubs established in the ports and arsenals, nevertheless naval officers did not emigrate to join the Princes until the summer of 1791. One was the young Comte de Cacqueray, who left Paris on 11 September 1791, accompanied by the Chevalier de Chièvres, an artillery officer, to join the emigration. After the usual adventures, they finally reached Tournai and presented themselves to the Comte de Montboissier:

> Then 20 or 25 officers of the Navy found themselves there: Monsieur de Vaugirard, capitaine de vaisseau, was the only corps commander and had just written to the Princes on behalf of the émigré sailors to offer their services and especially to ask for the honour of being employed under their eyes in the Artillery service, the cannon being their most familiar weapon. It seemed that one had to wait for their response to make a decision; but it was rather lightly decided that a cavalry corps would be formed. About twenty officers registered themselves in it; the rest decided to serve on foot. Several were already in the companies at Ath. I put myself in the cavalry...[73]

73 Cacqueray, *Mémoires inédits*, p.10.

As the number of officers from the service grew, a cantonment for the Navy was established at Enghien, a fiefdom of the Duke of Arenberg south-west of Brussels and north-east of Ath. There, the Comte de Vaugirard, whose rank was equivalent to *colonel*, took command of the cavalry, among whom was Cacqueray, who bought a horse and all the equipment necessary. Those men who could not provide for themselves remained at Tournai.

The Comte d'Hector, naval commander at Brest, and his brother-in-law, the Comte de Soulange, the first senior officers from this service to leave France, arrived at Tournai on 10 October 1791. Hector soon travelled to Koblenz to see the princes, and on his return, on 15 October, he was greeted before Enghien by a mounted detachment of 20 or so men under Vaugirard. These gentlemen had taken riding lessons from an NCO of the Carabiniers, who had emigrated, but particular care had to be taken not to attract the attention of the Austrian authorities as it was then strictly forbidden for the émigrés to exercise militarily.

On 3 November 1791, La Châtre went to Enghien to organise the officers of the Navy, 'he appointed the capitaines and chefs de section of the two infantry companies and one cavalry company.'[74] However, on 5 November, Hector ordered another organisation due to the influx of fresh volunteers, which necessitated another cantonment at Binche. In December, the number of naval officers present soon meant that a fifth infantry company was formed. Finally, all companies, both cavalry and infantry, were united at Enghien, where two new infantry companies and a second cavalry company were created.

Then, on 17 March, the Corps de la Marine Royale left for the Principality of Stavelot, with the first detachments arriving there on the 26th. Hector joined them three days later, by which time half of the officers had joined. The deadline for the entire corps to arrive had been set as 10 April, and Hector reviewed the cavalry that morning and the infantry in the evening. He then gave orders for training to commence immediately. Cacqueray noted, 'The monks full of attention and honesty for us offered their cloister and garden for the exercise of the infantry, a field was rented outside the town for that of the cavalry.'[75] On 16 April the Corps de la Marine was reorganised into eight infantry companies, forming two divisions, and two cavalry companies. Military training continued, and then, once the declaration of war was known, on 24 April, the émigrés could receive weapons and train as a constituted body. To this end, officers went to Liège to negotiate the purchase of weapons and, since the Princes could not cover the expense, the corps raised a subscription to make an advance to them.

As there then existed a separate company of naval officers at Koblenz that guarded the Princes' headquarters, the corps decided to ask that all the companies share this honour, by rotation. The response to this request, announced on 8 May, was that the officers at Koblenz would form the ninth company of the corps, that the corps could not be divided during the campaign and, finally, that the naval companies would, in turn, serve near

74 Cacqueray, *Mémoires inédits*, p.18.

75 Cacqueray, *Mémoires inédits*, p.33.

the Princes. By then, arms had arrived from Liège, but in insufficient numbers so the first cavalry company could only arm a guard and a picket of eight and 10 men respectively.

Finally, at the end of June, Hector obtained authorisation to publicly exercise the corps under arms. At this time it was briefly designated as the Légion, rather than Corps, de la Marine and, in early July, was increased with the addition of a tenth company. This was because more officers had joined, Cacqueray wrote:

> Many irresolute people ... had decided to finally emigrate. Several of our comrades in this circumstance were quite badly received. The Council sent them to the Princes who, with reason, decided that they ought to be admitted into our ranks. A contrary decision would have been very impolitic and would have had no other effect than to swell the ranks of our enemies.[76]

Vicomte de Kerouartz. (Author's collection)

The Corps de la Marine moved to Malmedy, north-east of Stavelot, where on 24 July, the cavalry standard and infantry flag were blessed in the church of Malmedy Abbey. The order to depart finally arrived on 31 July, and the cavalry set off the following day. Four infantry companies marched on 2 August, followed by the other five the next day; the last, which had continued service with the Princes, then joined them.

The definitive strength for the infantry was more than 600 officers, including a large number of cadets serving as simple soldiers. Each company was to have a *capitaine en premier*, *capitaine en second*, four *chefs de section*, eight *chefs d'escouade*, 46 volunteers, as well as a *tambour* and an *aumônier*. The cavalry formed a squadron of two companies, or about 120 *maîtres*, and had its own staff: a *chef d'escadron*, a *major*, three *aides de camp*, an instructor (the Comte du Trésor, former *colonel* of the Lorraine-dragons), a *porte-étendard*, a farrier and his assistants. With more than 700 men, the Corps royal de la Marine represented three percent of the strength of the Armée des Princes.

To understand the significance of this corps, it must be understood that, 'The navy, composed of more than a thousand officers [half of whom were Breton gentlemen], did not count twenty of its members who took part in the Revolution and more than nine hundred emigrated.'[77] In which case, the Corps de la Marine alone consisted of 70 percent of the service's officers, and, furthermore, there was a company of former naval officers within the

76 Cacqueray, *Mémoires inédits*, p.40.

77 Colbert Turgis (ed.), *Souvenirs maritimes*, p.63.

Coalition de Bretagne (see the illustration of the Vicomte de Kerouartz). Finally, the corps:

> [Was] cited by everyone for its indefatigable zeal to learn a trade, that is to say the mechanics of a task of which it was entirely ignorant and for the meticulous precision that it set to fulfil all duties. One saw general officers learning to do the exercise and handling of weapons with a zeal and a constancy that would be desirable to find in ordinary recruits.[78]

7. The Reconstituted Maison militaire (Plates 14–16)

The reconstitution of the troops of the Royal Household followed a logical process. After Artois emigrated, his guards dispersed and only a handful accompanied him, notably the *capitaine* of his company. Meanwhile, as long as the King and Monsieur remained in France, honour required their guards to stay with them; so, when the latter left the country, his guards could follow. The King's guards of the Maison bleue (Blue Household): the Gardes du corps, de la Porte, de la Prévôté de l'hôtel du Roi and Cent-Suisses, who were all still traditionally called archers, remained attached to his person, until their dismissal or redeployment. The Gardes du corps, as has been seen, were disbanded on 25 June 1791. The official disbanding of his brothers' guards followed, as well as the Gardes de la Porte. Furthermore, as stated, the Compagnie de la Prévôté de l'Hôtel du Roi was requisitioned by the Assembly in the summer of 1789 and then definitively attached to the new Gendarmerie Nationale on 15 May 1791. Finally, the Cent-Suisses were the last to disappear, on 16 March 1792, and dispersed on 15 April.

In the reconstituted Maison militaire, only the Gardes du corps du Roi and those of his brothers would retain their names as they had disbanded when the King was considered a captive. The King had disbanded the other units between 1776 and 1788, and in the case of the Gardes Françaises the name had been dishonoured.

The Compagnies nobles d'ordonnance

The Compagnies Rouges (Red Companies): the company of the Gendarmes de la garde à cheval du Roi, that of the Chevau-légers (Light Horse) and the two of the Mousquetaires, as well as the former *maîtres* of the Gendarmerie de France, all dismissed between 1776 and 1788, were the first to be reorganised. Indeed, apparently in March or April 1791, *maréchal de camp* de Clarac already, 'commanded the corps of gens d'armes and chevau-légers,' assembling at Koblenz.[79] The regulation of 19 August 1791 gave impetus to the establishment of the old Compagnies Rouges as related by the Comte de Brons:

78 Colbert Turgis (ed.), *Souvenirs maritimes*, p.64.

79 La Chapelle, *Souvenirs*, pp.27–28.

> … their Royal Highnesses, wishing nevertheless to leave to the former maîtres of these different companies the possibility of forming new units on the same principles which directed the raising of the other corps of the army, regulated by a particular article of their ordinance [the regulation of 19 August 1791] … that individuals of these different corps who wished to reunite themselves in companies of fifty-five maîtres, would be free to register themselves to this effect and that, under the name of compagnies nobles d'ordonnance, they would be commanded by the former officers of these corps that would come to reunite in them.[80]

On 10 September, a former musketeer, M. de Saint-Victor, presented the Princes with a memorandum on the need to reconstitute the old Compagnies Rouges as well as the Grenadiers à cheval that, although not a noble corps, formerly marched at the head of the Maison militaire. The proposal was accepted, and the regulations for the Compagnies nobles d'ordonnance were published on 21 September. As described, each émigré volunteer was authorised to transfer, just once, between companies so the Marquis du Dresnay, former senior officer of the Chevau-légers de la Garde du Roi, wrote to all the gentlemen dispersed at Ath, Worms and other cantonments. Officers of the other units of the old Maison militaire that were to be reconstituted did likewise. The Vicomte de Vergennes deployed all his energy to accelerate the formation and arming of the brigades, while 'the Marquis de Castérie (du Saillant), colonel, chef de brigade of the carabiniers, had the task of the instruction on foot and on horseback.'[81] As part of his efforts, Vergennes bought 100 troop horses, which he had equipped in a uniform manner. Then, after having them valued, he put them up for sale by lottery; those who did not have a mount could thus secure an equipped horse, undertaking to repay the debt once they returned to France.

The 1ère compagnie noble d'ordonnance was established at Neuwied, and it was so successful that when the Princes reviewed it on 25 April 1792, it already had 600 *maîtres*, including officers. The company carried the old standards of the Gendarmes de la Garde du Roi, which were retained when they were disbanded in 1787 by the *aide-major*, M. de Pompry, whose son brought them with him when he emigrated. The second company was at Andernach and was equally successful, for its standards, those of the two former companies of Mousquetaires, were reconstructed.

Due to the number of volunteers, the two compagnies nobles d'ordonnance had a special regulation, summarised as, 'Each company was composed of eight brigades forming four squadrons. Each brigade was of 2 senior officers, an aide-major, a fourrier-major, two maréchaux-des-logis, four brigadiers, fifty-five maîtres, a trumpeter and a maréchal [master farrier]. There was one porte-étendard per squadron.'[82] The *aides-majors* were responsible for training, the allocation of duties, the inspection of detachments and day-to-

80 Brons, *Journal*, p.44. The text in the cited reference gives the relevant year as 1792 this is a mistake in transcription, the subsequent text making it clear that it was 25 August 1791.

81 Brons, *Journal*, p.44.

82 Brons, *Journal*, p.45.

day order, and, in addition to the *fourriers-majors* on the staff, there was a *major* in charge of the office and detail of the corps, and another in charge of equitation:

> Their royal highnesses had granted in each company two places for superior officers by seniority, the others at their choice. The former officers of the gendarmes, chevau-légers and mousquetaires having as a preliminary to be placed by right provided that they had joined or written to announce themselves before 1 March 1792. The two majors taken in the corps at the choice of the princes. The aides-majors chosen from among the maîtres of the brigades or officers of the troops of the line at the wish of the chief provided that they were able to take charge of one of the parts of the instruction.[83]

All these appointments were made pending confirmation by the King, once he was free and restored to his throne. In accordance with the contemporary custom, four days after the decision to form the two compagnies nobles d'ordonnance, the officers were nominated, Condé writing on 25 September, 'Monsieur received in the plain [near Schönbornslust] the commanders of the Compagnies Rouges, and those of the Auvergnats' company.'[84] Recruitment could then begin.

The structure of the Compagnies nobles d'ordonnance or Compagnies Rouges was:

> *Lieutenant-général* commanding the two compagnies nobles d'ordonnance: Comte de Montboissier (also commander of the second company)
> Comte de Clarac, *maréchal de camp*, commanding the 1ère compagnie noble d'ordonnance (of the former Gendarmes and Chevau-légers de la Garde du Roi)
> 1er escadron (1ère and 5e brigades)
> 2e escadron (2e and 6e brigades)
> 3e escadron (3e and 7e brigades)
> 4e escadron (4e and 8e brigades)
> Comte de Montboissier, *lieutenant-général*, commanding the 2e Compagnie noble d'ordonnance (of the former Mousquetaires de la Garde du Roi)
> Four squadrons and eight brigades organised as in the 1ère compagnie.[85]

The two Compagnies nobles d'ordonnance, with about 1,200 horsemen, including officers, should not have cost the Princes anything since they had been mounted, equipped and armed at their own expense. However, 'in order not to distinguish them from the other noble companies, they received like them the salary that was paid during the campaign.'[86]

83 Brons, *Journal*, p.46.
84 Condé, *Journal*, p.226.
85 Grouvel, *Troupes de l'émigration*, vol.III, p.50.
86 Brons, *Journal*, p.47.

The Gardes du corps

After the Compagnies Rouges, it was decided to re-establish the former Gardes du corps, of the Princes and then of the King. The reconstitution of the first was decided on 19 August 1791, and the final size of each, that of Monsieur and the Comte d'Artois, was fixed in spring 1792. Each corps was made up of two complementary units.

The Guet (the Watch) was to be composed of 32 guards and four *brigadiers*, doing duty in two detachments. At any time, a *brigadier* and eight guards were on internal duty, serving on foot, while a further *brigadier* and eight guards were mounted, on picket, to serve as an escort.

The Cornette was the rest of the guard unit, organised as a war squadron of two companies, each with a trumpeter. This squadron was so named as it carried the guard's standard, formerly called a *cornette*. It was probably of the same design as that of 1789, recreated exactly, and it is known that the Princes paid 1,000 livres for each of the respective standards.[87] Grouvel provides a state of Monsieur's Guards in March 1792:

a) Guet: *capitaine*, a *lieutenant*, a *major*, an *aide-major*, a *sous-lieutenant*, a *maréchal des logis*, two *brigadiers*, two *fourriers*, 33 *gardes*; *secrétaire, trompette, maréchal* (farrier) and his boy, *sellier* (saddler) and his boy, a *piqueur*,[88] 19 *palefreniers* (grooms); 77 horses, not including those of the *capitaine*; a cart, waggon and forge, a *vivandier* (sutler).
b) Cornette: commander (de Damas), 5 senior officers, 5 *maréchaux des logis*, 8 *brigadiers*, 112 *gardes*, a *aumônier*, a *chirurgien-major*; 2 *trompettes*, a *maréchal* and his boy, a *sellier* and his boy, a *piqueur*, 56 *palefreniers*, 3 carters, 2 drivers; 198 horses of which 31 were for the *piqueur* and grooms, 14 for carts and the forge.[89]

At the start of the campaign, after moving towards Trier, the Guet of the Gardes de Monsieur was, 'at the strength of "38 company officers and gardes du corps", and the Cornette at 14 company officers and 124 gardes du corps.'[90] The Guet of the Gardes de Monsieur was commanded by Comte d'Avaray and the Cornette by Comte Charles de Damas, with a *porte-étendard*. The Gardes du comte d'Artois similarly consisted of a Guet commanded by Bailli de Crussol with approximately 40 officers and *gardes* and a Cornette commanded by Chevalier de Puységur, with a *porte-étendard*, of around 120 officers and *gardes* in a squadron of two companies. Pinasseau gives the strength of the two guards units as 360 men conforming with Brons, who wrote, 'they were each complete with 150 maîtres, both former gardes and agrégés [associates].'[91]

87 Grouvel, *Troupes de l'émigration*, vol.III, pp.47–48.
88 Literally translated as huntsman, a *piquer* was in charge of the *capitaine*'s, or in this case Monsieur's, replacement horse should it be needed.
89 Grouvel, *Troupes de l'émigration*, vol.III, p.45.
90 Grouvel, *Troupes de l'émigration*, vol.III, p.46.
91 Pinasseau, *Campagne de 1792*, Part 1, p.19 and Brons, *Journal*, p.56.

One of the latter was the 14-year-old Comte de Neuilly, who emigrated in late 1791, with his widowed mother, his late father having been equerry to the former King and, as commander of the riding school, had taught the young princes to ride. Soon after arriving at Koblenz, when they were presented to the Princes, Artois:

> … expressed to my mother regret at not being able to take me as one of his pages, whose number was complete; but he placed me in the Guet of his Guards, composed of thirty Maîtres, chosen among the best families, mounted on horses with short tails, and attached more particularly to the person of the Prince, although they did duty and manoeuvred with the other guards.[92]

Neuilly was placed in the Compagnie d'Alsace; he began his duties immediately, having already had some military education, which came round every five days. The rest of the time he had to continue his training, this consisted of equestrian skills at the Prince-Bishop's riding school, fencing, weapon handling – the *gardes* being armed with a carbine – and compulsory lessons in German.

The Garde du corps du Roi was reconstituted on the same lines, from former *gardes*, who had mostly emigrated after their final dismissal, as well as volunteers, called, as in all the other corps of the Maison militaire, *agrégés*. The latter arrived from other corps or were relatives of *gardes*. Their organisation was reported in a revolutionary newspaper at the beginning of 1792, 'composed of four hundred former Gardes-du-corps, and three hundred recruits … In the Gardes-du-corps one finds those who drove the King's carriage, disguised as postilions, on the famous journey to Varennes. They say haughtily that the King had ordered them to join his brothers.'[93]According to the same source, the Maison militaire had a total of 2,200 men.

In August 1791, there were already 200 men in the Garde du corps du Roi, and the following month they were joined by 12 *gardes* of the first company who arrived at Koblenz with their standard. The Gardes du corps du Roi were, like those of the Princes, established at Thal, a suburb of Koblenz. In November, the number of registered *Gardes du corps* was around 1,000, but it is necessary to recognise that this included those who were present as well as those registered by a friend or a relative, while they sold what they could in France or borrowed the necessary funds to join the corps. It was reconstituted according to the traditional structure of four companies, which were in precedence, the Compagnie écossaise (Scottish Company) and then those of Noailles, Gramont and Luxembourg.

It can be considered that, except for the infirm, and five or six who favoured the Revolution, all the 1,200 *Gardes du corps* emigrated and, with additional personnel, the corps in emigration exceeded 1,600 horsemen, including officers and supernumeraries. Each of its traditional companies

92 Maurice Barberey (ed), *Dix années d'émigration. Souvenirs et correspondance du comte de Neuilly* (Paris: Charles Douniol, Libraire-éditeur, 1865), p.36.

93 *La semaine politique et littéraire*, 9 January 1792.

was organised into three squadrons of two (regulatory) companies. It was undoubtedly the finest unit, and, with the Coalition d'Auvergne, one of the best mounted. However, its nature meant that the 1,600 *Gardes* came with 860 *piqueurs*, grooms and assorted servants with more than 2,500 horses.

The Compagnie de grenadiers d'ordonnance

The Compagnie des Grenadiers à cheval had been disbanded in 1775. In emigration, it was recreated in a decision of June 1792, as the Compagnie de grenadiers d'ordonnance, with its definitive organisation being decided the following month when it joined the rest of the Maison militaire in the Armée du Centre. By tradition, it was the only Compagnie Bleue that did not attend the King's person but joined the Maison militaire when the latter went on campaign.

Table 9: Organisation of the Compagnie de Grenadiers d'ordonnance.[94]

Staff	1 *capitaine-lieutenant*, 1 *aide-major*, 4 *lieutenants*, 8 *sous-lieutenants*, 1 *adjudant*, 1 *quartier-maître*, 8 *sergents*, 1 *porte-étendard*, 1 commissariat, 1 *aumônier*, 1 *chirurgien-major*, 4 *tambours* (one attached to each peloton), master farrier attached to the first platoon and 3 other farriers attached to the other platoons, master saddler and his boy
Escadron	2 divisions commanded by the 2 most senior *lieutenants* who were attached
Divisions	Each formed of 2 platoons or brigades
Pelotons	Each formed of 2 sections
Sections	Each was commanded by 1 *sous-lieutenant* with 1 *sergent* who were attached and formed of 2 escouades (squads)
Escouades	Each formed of 10 grenadiers, this number included the leaders, 1 *brigadier* and 1 *appointé* (equivalent to a lance corporal or chosen man)

The Comte de Virieu, gentleman of honour of Monsieur, was given the command of the Compagnie de grenadiers d'ordonnance on 1 July and advanced all the costs of forming the unit. Although it never exceeded 70 or 72 men, it was nevertheless considered as a squadron on the states and order of battle of the Armée du Centre. The Comte de Gibon Kérisouet, who came from Orléans-cavalerie (see above), took command of a platoon on 30 July 1792, which was not a demotion as, in the Grenadiers d'ordonnance, a *lieutenant* ranked as *mestre de camp de cavalerie* and a *sous-lieutenant* as a *lieutenant-colonel*.

The choice of grenadiers reflected the traditional role in the Maison militaire of the Grenadiers à cheval, which had been established by Louis XIV. As the Maison militaire marched at the head of the army, he wanted it to be preceded by mounted grenadiers, armed as dragoons and equipped with axes, shovels and picks, who could clear and storm any obstacles in its path. The men were thus traditionally drawn from infantry regiments and, even on horseback, wore gaiters and not boots. In June, Maillard had been asked to indicate suitable men to serve in the new unit, but, on the eve of the campaign, few could be found despite the privileges; for example, the

94 Grouvel, *Troupes de l'émigration*, vol.III, p.55.

sergents and *brigadiers* had the rank of officers. Nevertheless, the Comte de Brons noted, 'The grenadiers who came out of the kingdom to follow their officers and non-commissioned officers of cavalry or dragoons completed these brigades.'[95] This is supported by Grouvel, who found that four NCOs and four men of the Dragons de Bourbon who had emigrated from Dunkirk were assigned to the Grenadiers d'ordonnance.[96] It is known that the corps was armed with infantry muskets supplied from England.

The Hommes d'armes à cheval

Another corps to be reconstituted was the Gendarmerie de France, descended from the old compagnies nobles d'ordonnance raised at the end of the Hundred Years War in the reign of King Charles VII. Unlike the Gendarmes de la Garde du Roi, it did not belong to the Maison militaire, nevertheless, it was traditionally attached to it. It shared the colour of its uniform with the Compagnies Rouges, but unlike them, the corps wore shoulder belts with coloured squares that recalled their traditional status as archers, a distinction shared with the Maison bleue.

Until it was disbanded in 1788, *maréchal* de Castries had been *colonel-général* of the Gendarmerie de France while the Marquis d'Autichamp had effective command. The belated revival of the Gendarmerie was closely tied to the rivalry between Calonne and Castries that dated back to the contorted world of Versailles politics. The former realised that Castries would object to the restoration of the corps on the grounds it had been disbanded on the King's volition and so attracted the displeasure of Monsieur and Artois. Then, on 14 December 1791, Autichamp presented a memorandum proposing that the old Gendarmerie be reconstituted under a new name, that of Hommes d'armes à cheval (mounted men-at-arms). The *maréchal* had gained the Princes' trust, and so, on 1 January 1792, they agreed to the project, and they undertook to ask the King, once he was fully restored, to give it back its former name; therefore, Castries fully supported it.

However, Calonne was only able to provide 50,000 livres to raise the corps when 10 times that was needed, so Autichamp had to find the funds himself, as he recalled in a memorandum to the King in 1816:

> The Princes ordered that different corps be formed at Koblenz, following the example of the Maison du Roi. I joined to me 30 gentlemen to raise one on the basis of the former gendarmerie and to cover the costs. Mgr the Comte d'Artois proposed me to command it. I obeyed his orders and, jointly with the 30 officers, we gathered 600,000 francs and, in the space of 5 months, we had 550 men on horses and 150 on foot, who were armed and equipped at our expense.[97]

Following the same principle as that used for the reconstituted units of the Maison militaire, the principal officers' positions were firstly the reserve

95 Brons, *Journal*, p.101.

96 Grouvel, *Troupes de l'émigration*, vol.III, p.56.

97 Charles-Louis Chassin, *La préparation de la guerre de Vendée* (Paris: Imprimerie Paul Dupont, 1892), vol.I, p.91.

of former officers of the Gendarmerie and then any vacant positions were offered to cavalry officers, while those of *maîtres*, initially intended for former members of the Gendarmerie de France, had to be widely accessible to representatives of the Third Estate, which is why, since the latter were more numerous than the former, the body was finally considered bourgeois.

The establishment of the Hommes d'armes à cheval was:

Staff:
Duc d'Angoulême – (nominal) *commandant général en premier*
Marquis d'Autichamp – *commandant général en second*
Marquis d'Apchier – *major général*
1 *aide de camp*, 2 *aides-majors*, 2 *sous-aides-majors*, 1 *quartier-maître trésorier*, 2 *adjudants-majors*, 1 *aumônier*, 4 *chirurgiens-majors*, 1 *fourrier-major*, 1 *timbalier* (kettle drummer)

4 squadrons, each of 2 companies:
Each squadron commanded by a *maréchal de camp*

Companies:
Each would have – 1 *capitaine-lieutenant*, 1 *lieutenant*, 1 *sous-lieutenant*, 1 *porte-étendard*, 2 *maréchaux des logis*, 1 *fourrier*, 4 *brigadiers*, 6 'former' *hommes d'armes*, 49 *hommes d'armes*, 1 *trompette*: 64 men

1er escadron, Marquis d'Autichamp:
1ère Compagnie – écossaise (Scottish)
5e Compagnie – de la Reine

2e escadron, Comte de Lambertye:
2e Compagnie – anglaise (English)
6e Compagnie – du Dauphin

3e escadron, Comte de Bassompierre:
3e Compagnie – bourguignon (Burgundian)
7e Compagnie – de Monsieur

4e escadron, Comte de Montsoreau:
4e Compagnie – de Flandre
8e Compagnie – d'Artois[98]

The names given to the companies were those used when the original corps had been dissolved. They contained many supernumeraries and it was much easier to get recruits than mounts. However, being established in the Principality of Nassau, at Diez on the Lahn in particular, it was close to Holstein where horses could be bought. In April, Autichamp complained that all his personal money had been spent, without having acquired weapons –

98 Grouvel, *Troupes de l'émigration*, vol.III, p.68.

the muskets and pistols from Liège and the sabres from Solingen – while the corps' debts already amounted to 60,000 livres.

At the end of June 1792, the Hommes d'armes à cheval numbered, '590 maîtres (not including senior officers and staff), with 88 grooms and servants.'[99] However, this does not include a foot detachment of 150 men.[100]

The cavalry of the Maison militaire, with the Hommes d'armes à cheval

Regulations issued in the name of the Princes governing equipment and camps on 19 June 1792 used a strict hierarchy of ranks and units.[101] The order of precedence among the cavalry units of and connected to the Maison militaire was, 'Gardes du corps [du Roi], gardes des Princes, compagnies nobles d'ordonnance, compagnies des Hommes d'armes à cheval, compagnies des chevaliers dragons de la Couronne.'[102] However, an issue arose when, due to the size of the Gardes du Corps, the compagnies nobles d'ordonnance were placed on the left wing, rather than on the right with the rest of the Maison militaire. The senior officers of the Hommes d'armes à cheval refused to give them precedence, respectfully recalling that:

> The former Gendarmerie was always brigaded in war with the Gardes du corps; the first company, known under the name of Ecossaise, and created in 1422 for the guard of Charles VII, had the honour of mounting the guard of the King's quarters before the second company of the Mousquetaires. When the Gendarmerie was not encamped with the *Gardes du Roi* and the Maison militaire was in a line, the Gendarmerie formed the left of it.[103]

The point was conceded, so in the order of battle of the Armée du Centre, the Hommes d'armes à cheval were at the head of the cavalry of the left wing, in front of the two compagnies nobles d'ordonnance.[104]

Table 10: The strength of the mounted units of the Maison militaire and the Hommes d'armes à cheval.

Corps	Strength (men)	Squadrons
Gardes du corps du Roi	1,600	12
Gardes du corps des Frères du Roi	320	2
Compagnies nobles d'ordonnance	1,200	8
Grenadiers à cheval d'ordonnance	100	1
Hommes d'armes à cheval	550	4
Hommes d'armes, foot detachment	150	–
Total	3,920	27

99 Grouvel, *Troupes de l'émigration*, vol.III, p.71.
100 Pinasseau, *Campagne de 1792*, p.19.
101 Anon., *Règlement concernant les Equipages de l'Armée, les Effets de Campemens, leur Distribution, la Forme & les Dimensions des Camps d'Infanterie & de Cavalerie* (dated 19 June 1792, no further details).
102 Grouvel, *Troupes de l'émigration*, vol.III, p.71.
103 Grouvel, *Troupes de l'émigration*, vol.III, pp.70–71.
104 Pinasseau, *Campagne de 1792*, pp.55–56.

The Infantry of the Maison militaire

The infantry of the reconstituted Maison militaire consisted of three elements: the Cent-Suisses, which finally had between 20 and 30 men, including officers, as described above, the Compagnie de l'Institution de Saint-Louis and the Hommes d'armes à pied (not to be confused with the foot detachment of the Hommes d'armes à cheval).

The Compagnie de l'Institution de Saint-Louis

The ancient company of the Gardes de la Porte was revived in a provisional decision of 1 February 1792 under the name of the Compagnie de l'Institution de Saint-Louis. Its *capitaine* was the Comte de Vergennes, who had commanded the Gardes de la Porte and had been minister plenipotentiary at Koblenz in 1787. The established strength of the company was to be:

> 216 gardes, divided into 4 brigades of 54, including 2 brigadiers and 2 sous-brigadiers, nominated by the capitaine-colonel; the officers will be 12 in number (capitaine-colonel, major, 4 lieutenants, 4 sous-lieutenants, aide and sous-aide-major) with a quartermaster, a surgeon-major and a chaplain. Attached to the company will be 4 drummers, 4 fifers and an armourer.[105]

Pinasseau indicates the Compagnie de l'Institution de Saint-Louis had 200 men, however, with supernumeraries, it was closer to 270 or 280 and was considered as a half-battalion of infantry.[106]

The Hommes d'armes à pied

By the end of 1791, two-thirds of the former officers of the Gardes Françaises had joined the Princes, and in December, the most senior of them raised 80,000 livres and proposed to create 32 companies, matching the number of the proposers. However, the new corps could not take the name of their former regiment, which was forever tarnished by the role its soldiers had played in Paris on 13 and 14 July 1789. Nevertheless, after some interruptions, the project to form the corps got underway and former officers had to have joined by 28 February 1792 in order to have their rights recognised. The formal order to create it was given on 2 March and, finally, on 28 March, it took the name of the Hommes d'armes à pied.

The Hommes d'armes à pied, after the order of 2 March 1792, was to have 1,798 men and its establishment was:

> Staff:
> Baron de Coys, *maréchal de camp, capitaine* in the former Gardes Françaises – *commandant du corps*
> 2 *maréchaux de camp*, commanding two united brigades
> 4 *maréchaux de camp*, each commanding a brigade
> Marquis d'Argoult, *maréchal de camp, major* in the former Gardes Françaises – *major*

105 Grouvel, *Troupes de l'émigration*, vol.III, pp.59–60.
106 Pinasseau, *Campagne de 1792*, p.18.

1 *aide-major*, 4 *aides-majors de brigade*, 4 *sous-aides-majors*, 1 commissariat, 1 *quartier-maître*, 1 *fourrier-major*, 4 *fourriers de brigade*, 4 *porte-drapeaux*, 1 *aumônier*, 1 *chirurgien-major*, 4 *chirurgiens de brigade*, 1 *tambour-major*, 1 master armourer, 1 master tailor, 1 master shoemaker.

4 brigades each of 4 divisions, each formed of 2 companies:
Companies:
Each was to have – 1 *capitaine* (with the rank of *colonel*), 2 *lieutenants* (*lieutenant-colonel*), 3 *fourriers* (*lieutenant*), 4 *brigadiers* (*sous-lieutenant*), 8 *chefs d'escouade*, 36 *fusiliers d'ordonnance*, 1 *tambour*

1er and 3e brigades, Comte de Lubersac:
1er brigade, Marquis de Chasteloger:
Compagnies des Dorides, du Dreneuc, du Cluzel, de Thuisy, de Beauvoir, de Tourdonnet, de Chatignonville, de Prunelay
3e brigade: Vicomte de Saint-Blancard:
Compagnies de Mazancourt, du Boisbéranger, d'Artignosc, des Reaux, de Brache, de la Rochelambert, de Bartillat, du Chesneau

2e and 4e brigades, Marquis de Champigny:
2e brigade, du Moncel:
Compagnies d'Ancourt, de Vassan, de Maubec, de Marconnay, de Laurières, de Hocquart, de Roideville, de Trenquelléon
4e brigade, de Sainte-Maries:
Compagnies du Dreneuc, de Romance, d'Obsonville, de Chailly, de Manneville, de Saint-Martin, de Cotte [NB only seven listed][107]

The Comte de Brons noted that:

> The foundation of the companies was formed of the small number of non-commissioned officers and soldiers of the Gardes Françaises remaining faithful to the laws of duty and honour. They were joined by many volunteers taken in part from the poor nobility but for the greatest number from the upper third-estate and that loyal bourgeoisie whose principles and conduct gave them so just a right to see themselves admitted to the heart of the order whose devotion they imitated.[108]

Madame de Bennes, who used her maiden name to call herself the Chevalier de Haussay, and her husband joined the corps on 20 March 1792 and were registered the following day in the 31e Compagnie (du Chesneau).[109] The couple then spent three months training at Bendorf, just north of Koblenz.[110]

107 Grouvel, *Troupes de l'émigration*, vol.III, p.62
108 Brons, *Journal*, p.49.
109 SHD: GR1 YI 3. Dossier de Louise de Bennes, certificate of service signed by former senior officers and dated Hamburg, 18 July 1796. In it the captain of the company is written as Duchesmeau, the name given here is that in all other documents.
110 Bennes, *A narrative*, p.17.

Their placement in the 31st company might suggest that the corps was nearing completion, which would have been 1,798 all ranks, but it seems each company was severely understrength, with Grouvel stating it had 700 to 800 men during the campaign, and Pinasseau 920 men.[111]

Table 11: The strength of the infantry units of the Maison militaire and the Hommes d'armes à pied.

Corps	Strength (men)	Units
Cent-Suisses	30	
Hommes d'armes à pied	800	12–14 companies ?
Compagnie de l'Institution de Saint-Louis	270	½ battalion
Total	1,100	

The Maison militaire, excluding the Chevaliers de la Couronne, therefore represented a force of 5,000 men, or more than a fifth of the strength of the Armée des Princes.

8. The German Corps in the Service of the Princes and King (Plates 18, 19 & 24)

The French royal army of 1789 and 1790 had eight regiments of German infantry: Alsace (in 1789 numbered 54), Salm-Salm (63), La Marck (79), Royal-Suédois (91), Royal Hesse-Darmstadt (96), Nassau (99), Bouillon (101) and Royal Deux-Ponts (102). Although mainly recruited from Germans, any nationality was included except for French (save men from Alsace or Lorraine, especially if they were German-speakers), Swiss and Irish. The German regiments wore a uniform coat that was bleu céleste (celestial blue, a blue-grey hue, as opposed to bleu ciel, sky blue) in colour. Along with the colour of the coat, the other distinction was that the drapeaux d'ordonnance carried by the second battalions displayed the regiments' German identity, except for the Régiment d'Alsace, which had a flag that was identical in design to those of the French infantry. All the other distinctive emblems, such as the arms of France on the officers' gorgets and the white cravats attached to the flags, were French.

Except for minor differences in their staffs, the regimental structures were the same as for the rest of the infantry. Each was composed of two battalions, the first with a grenadier and four fusilier companies and the second with a chasseur and four fusilier companies. This structure disappeared in the French army in 1791, the chasseurs being replaced by another grenadier company; however, it was retained as the model for the new regiments raised in the military emigration.

German service in the army of France reflected old and, therefore, privileged dynastic or political relationships between German rulers and the French monarchy. So, by ending it in January 1791, when all the foreign

111 Grouvel, *Troupes de l'émigration*, vol.III, pp.63–64 and Pinasseau, *Campagne de 1792*, p.18.

regiments, except for the Swiss, lost their identity, the Assembly sought to both sweep away France's former foreign policy and move towards a national army. Given the pressure from the new French regime, in January and February 1792, as well as from Emperor Leopold, it is understandable that very few German princes agreed to raise new units in the service of the King of France. Furthermore, none achieved their intended size.

The Régiment de Rohan

On 1 October 1791, Cardinal de Rohan was the first to sign an agreement to raise a German infantry regiment for the Armée des Princes. Its depot was placed at Ringsheim, just outside Ettenheim and opposite Strasbourg. It was to be identical to a German regiment formerly in French service with 1,500 men, on the war footing of 1789–1790, in two battalions organised as described above. The process of raising such a regiment was always the same: the *colonel-propriétaire* advanced the money for the levy, armament, clothing, equipment, pay and subsistence of the corps. Once it was complete, he was reimbursed, and the Princes took financial responsibility for it. In the event that the entire corps could not be raised, or there was a need to deploy the troops available as quickly as possible, the Princes could decide to take it into their service as it was, rather than wait for it to be complete. Each soldier enrolled for a period of four years, and the officers applied directly to the Princes for their commissions, the first being dated 1 October.

Composed of Catholic soldiers, German or French including some former soldiers of the royal army, the Régiment de Rohan, or Rohan-étranger (Rohan Foreign), had barely 385 men in July 1792. From then on it never exceeded 400–450 men, organised as one company of grenadiers, two of fusiliers and one of chasseurs. Nevertheless, it had a very fine cadre of experienced officers, from different German regiments in French service as well as a large number of Frenchmen, several from the Régiment d'Enghien. Almost half had experience of active service. When Condé's troops moved to the area of Bingen in March 1792, the Rohan-étranger moved to Horchheim, near Worms, to be nearer before being incorporated into the Prince's army.

The Régiment de Wittgenstein

Again in October 1791, the young Comte de Sayn-Wittgenstein-Hohenstein offered to raise a German infantry regiment in his name and a provisional ordonnance was signed at Koblenz, on 3 November 1791.[112] It was to take the number 105, as if it were part of the French royal army, and had a uniform according to the 1786 regulations, but with the fusiliers adopting the new Model 1791 infantry helmet. It was formed at Schloss Meerholz, about 20 kilometres from Hanau on the Main.[113] Again, the regiment was initially to

112 Grouvel, *Troupes de l'émigration*, vol.III, p.141. The French rendering of the names of these German and Swiss noblemen and officers has been retained.

113 Grouvel, *Troupes de l'émigration*, vol.III, p.142, identifies the location as Marienborn, which was in a very different location, but the additional details he gives shows it to be Meerholz, now in Gelnhausen.

have 1,500 men, but this was reduced to 1,100 when the company of chasseurs carabiniers was detached in March 1792, as noted by Brons:

> I also saw the German regiment of Wittgenstein, raised by the count of that name for the service of their Royal Highnesses. It appeared to me to fine and well-trained. The grenadiers in particular were of the finest type. This regiment had as colonel the Comte d'Erlach who, I believe, was previously a capitaine in the Gardes Suisses. The division of chasseurs which was part of it had been detached for outpost service under the orders of the Marquis de Gerduk [sic].[114]

However, the regiment never had more than 575 men and so formed one battalion, with a grenadier company and four companies of fusiliers. The soldiers were a heterogeneous group, the majority being from Liège, joined with men of all nationalities, particularly Hessians. However, there was also a solid core of former soldiers of the King and recruits from Alsace and Lorraine. Serving in the Armée du Centre, the regiment was placed on the flanks of the cavalry of the first line with the chasseurs carabiniers in the vanguard.

The Hussards de Salm

The third German regiment was that of the Hussards de Salm, the capitulation for which was signed at Koblenz on 15 December 1791 and completed on 1 January 1792. Retaining proprietary interest in the regiment, the Prince de Salm had a clause in the capitulation by which the corps could pass into the service of another power.

It was to be a corps of German hussars in the service of the King of France, so initially it was not to accept recruits from Alsace or Lorraine. Its *colonel propriétaire* was Prince Maurice-Gustave-Adolphe de Salm-Kyrbourg, former *colonel* in the Régiment d'Esterhazy-hussards, whose brother had joined the patriot revolution in the United Provinces. The *colonel-commandant* was his nephew, Prince de la Trémoille, or de la Trimouille, and the *lieutenant-colonel* Baron de Grünstein, previously *major* of Royal-Liégeois.[115] The corps was to have four squadrons with two companies, each of 72 hussars, 89 men in all, or around 730 sabres, with a staff of 20. However, it could only raise 200 to 220 men, in two squadrons, and so, on 3 August 1792, it was joined by the hussars of the Légion de Mirabeau to form the cavalry of the Armée de Condé's vanguard. Recruitment was more difficult than expected, but the regiment received troopers and officers from the émigré hussar regiments, other than Saxe and Bercheny. One was Henry Schmitt, born in 1769 at Biblis, near Worms, who had joined the Régiment d'Esterhazy-hussards as a volunteer on 1 April 1788 and was named *sous-lieutenant* on 15 May 1791 after emigrating, before joining the Hussards de Salm in 1792.[116]

114 Brons, *Journal*, p.53.

115 Grouvel, *Troupes de l'émigration*, vol.I, p.74.

116 A. Pernot (ed.), *Mémoire sur l'arrestation du duc d'Enghien* (Dôle: Typographie L. Bernin, 1891), p.4.

The Régiments de Hohenlohe-Bartenstein and Hohenlohe-Schillingsfurst

Finally, on 3 February 1792, despite the opposition of Prussia, Austria and the Franconian Circle to which they belonged, the reigning princes of Hohenlohe-Waldenburg signed capitulations for the raising of two infantry corps, one of chasseurs – the Régiment de Hohenlohe-Bartenstein of 644 men – and the other of line infantry – the Régiment de Hohenlohe-Schillingsfurst of 1,148 men. Each had a different organisation from that of the other German regiments. The Bartenstein Chasseurs was to have 10 companies: one of grenadiers-chasseurs, one of chasseurs appris (experienced) and eight of line chasseurs, in two battalions. The Régiment de Hohenlohe-Schillingsfurst was also to have two battalions, each with one grenadier and eight fusilier companies. In all other ways, the organisation of the two regiments was to be the same, each with 14 officers on the staff and three officers and 60 men per company.

The Chasseurs were commanded by Prince Louis-Aloys-Joseph of Hohenlohe-Waldenburg-Bartenstein, born 1765, who had begun his military career in Austrian service in 1784 before transferring to that of Bavaria two years later. Hence, he chose a Palatinate/Bavarian, or Rumford, style uniform for his chasseurs while Hohnelohe-Schillingfürst wore that of the French regulations of 1786, with celestial blue coats, like Rohan and Wittgenstein.

The project was ratified on 14 February 1792 by the Princes, who undertook not to recruit any troops in the territory of the Princes of Hohenlohe. In return, as has been seen, the latter provided a refuge for the Légion de Mirabeau to complete its organisation, clothing and equipment, a treaty that King Louis XVI had to denounce on 31 March 1792. Both Hohenlohe regiments were to recruit Germans or Alsatians, but, in the summer, neither had more than 260 men, including officers, and this number soon slipped to 220 to 230 due to desertion. Both, like the majority of the new corps, served within the Armée de Condé.

Table 12: The strength of the newly raised German units.

Corps	Date	Strength	Deployment
Rgt. de Rohan	1 October 1791	400	Armée de Condé
Rgt. de Wittgenstein	October 1791	575	Armée du Centre
Hussards de Salm	15 December 1791	200	Armée de Condé
Rgt. de Hohenlohe-Bartenstein	3 February 1792	250	Armée de Condé
Rgt. de Hohenlohe-Schillingsfurst	3 February 1792	250	Armée de Condé
Total		1,575	

These units, therefore, accounted for seven percent of the total strength of the Princes' forces in the summer of 1792. However, it should be recognised that as well as the two companies of German officers, German soldiers also served in other corps, such as the Royal-Allemand-cavalerie, the different hussar units, as well as the Irish Brigade and those raised for the vanguard.

9. Light Troops (Plates 19–21)

Units of light troops, raised for the duration of the campaign, formed stand-alone units, such as regiments, or legions with companies of different arms. The success of these units varied greatly, often depending on the personality, ambition or even the honesty of their proprietors.

Table 13: The light troops of the Armée des Princes, according to when they were formed.

Corps	Formation	Strength	
		Theoretical	**Actual (approx.)**
Chasseurs royaux des Princes	15 October 1791	Regiment, 1,200	200
Légion de Breuilpont	January/February 1792	Chasseurs-carabiniers	
		6 companies: 200	200
		Uhlans	
		1 company or squadron ?	50 then 100
Chasseurs impériaux russes or Chasseurs étrangers de Polignac	17 February 1792	Regiment of 2 squadrons: 704	200
Chasseurs-carabiniers de Wittgenstein or de Goerduck	25 March 1792	Battalion of 8 companies: 424	2 companies: 140
Chasseurs flamands de Calonne	March/April 1792	2 companies: 100	100
Légion de Normandie or Légion de Carneville	19 April 1792	Infantry	
		6 companies: 1,100	450
		Chasseurs à cheval	
		2 companies: 268	100
Total			1,440–1,490

The Chasseurs royaux des Princes

The first capitulation signed by the Princes for raising such a corps was on 15 October 1791, for a light infantry regiment that was to have 1,200 men in two battalions each of eight companies of 75 men.[117] It was to be called the Chasseurs royaux des Princes, although the term Légion des Chasseurs royaux may have also been used.[118] The instigator of the project was John Gordon Sinclair, known in France as Baron Gordon de Sinclair. He claimed to have fought as a volunteer in the British Army at Bunker's Hill in the American War of Independence before continuing his career as a captain in the Polish army, then a volunteer again, this time in the Prussian army. He stated that in his opinion his career only really began with, 'the civil war in Brabant, in which I served as colonel, and adjutant-general to Gen. Schoenfield [sic], commander in chief.'[119] Then, according to him, in June 1791 he proposed to La Fayette and Duportail, then Minister of War, to raise

117 Grouvel, *Troupes de l'émigration*, vol.III, p.149.

118 John Gordon Sinclair, *Colonel Sinclair's Letters to his Enemies* (London: privately published, 1796), p.62, letter from Maréchal de Broglie.

119 Sinclair, *Letters*, p.11.

a corps of riflemen, which was immediately accepted, hence his brevet as a French officer, signed by King Louis XVI on 17 June.[120] After the failure of the King's flight, he threw in his lot with the Princes and, in September, made them the same offer, which was considered by a council of general officers, 'the result of which was, that the Princes not only honoured me with the first capitulation in the new army, but also created me Proprietor of the Corps of Chasseurs Royaux des Princes.'[121]

However, according to Sinclair, his project was opposed by a former controller of finances and counsellor of the Parlement de Paris, named Saint-Morys, who was in league with Calonne. He blamed them for taking advantage of the difficulties encountered in raising the corps to have him dispossessed of his proprietorship when the capitulation was cancelled on 30 July 1792. Nevertheless, Sinclair apparently continued to serve the Princes and he was later to publish certificates testifying to his, 'activity, will & courage … zeal & intelligence'.[122] It should be recognised, however, that he published these at a time when he sought to bolster his character, being involved in a number of legal battles, including bitter divorce proceedings with his wife, who, on his own admission, he had married on the expectation that she would be a wealthy heiress.[123] His conduct in one of these actions finally saw him found guilty of perjury and, in June 1798, imprisoned.[124]

Given Sinclair's origin, the regiment was to have been raised on British lines, and its equipment came from Britain, including its arms from Birmingham, via Ostende, which Sinclair arranged with more or less success. Meanwhile, the corps itself was raised in Liège by the *colonel commandant*, the Chevalier Maynard de La Valette. It is notable that among the first commissions sold by Sinclair, in October 1791, was that of *lieutenant-colonel* to George Ramsay, a former captain in the 30th Foot, who would, in 1793, raise the York Rangers, the uniform of which had similar features to those of the Chasseurs Royaux des Princes. By the summer of 1792, however, Ramsay was not in the regiment, and the first *lieutenant-colonel* was, 'Harris Power, former lieutenant in the British infantry, captain in the Dutch Bylandt dragoons, then Brabant général-major' and the other *lieutenant-colonel* was the Marquis de Mesmon, formerly *lieutenant* in the Gardes Françaises.[125] Finally, as Grouvel recounted:

> On 12 September, … the Princes dispose of the property of the corps of the Chasseurs royaux des Princes and pass a capitulation with the Comte de Saint-Morys, son of the Comte de Saint-Morys cited above, former aide de camp of the Comte de Maillebois in Holland and of the maréchal de Broglie. He has just married at 19 Calonne's niece, Mlle de Valicourt. It seems that Saint-Morys has

120 Sinclair, *Letters*, p.15.
121 Sinclair, *Letters*, pp.18–19.
122 Sinclair, *Letters*, p.56, from Broglie, dated 21 August 1793, one of several such certificates.
123 Sinclair, *Letters*, p.16.
124 *Oxford Journal*, 30 June 1798. He committed the offence in evidence he adduced in proceedings he had brought against Calonne.
125 Grouvel, *Troupes de l'émigration*, vol.III, p.151.

> again paid great sums to the Princes and Sinclair to obtain the ownership of the regiment for his son ...[126]

Despite its proprietorship and insufficient numbers – only 200 men but still organised on the basis of eight companies, so of 25 men – the unit was well trained and thought of. The men were a mixture of Dutchmen, Germans, Liégeois and French, some former soldiers, with good non-commissioned officers.

The Chasseurs impériaux russes or Chasseurs étrangers de Polignac

The Chasseurs impériaux russes were raised at the beginning of 1792, and their name appears to have been in recognition of the financial and political support Empress Catherine provided the King's brothers. The unit was initially intended as a light cavalry regiment of 700 horse but, as this could not be achieved it was renamed the Chasseurs étranger de Polignac or Chasseurs à cheval de Polignac and never exceeded 202 men, including 59 officers. Its *colonel propriétaire* was the 73-year-old Marquis de Polignac who had been Artois's first equerry. On his death later in 1792, it passed to his son, Jules, who was then aide de camp to Monsieur. Jules and his wife, Gabrielle, Marie-Antoinette's favourite, had been among the first émigrés to leave France, two days after the storming of the Bastille, being particular targets of so-called popular anger. The unit was considered as German and was to have three squadrons each of four companies, the capitulation being based on the organisation of the Royal-Allemand. Article 17 stipulated that, 'The regiment will be raised by the care of the colonel and no Frenchman may be admitted in it, if he is not an Alsatian and Lorrainer.'[127] However, exceptions were made as 30 dragoons from the Régiment d'Artois who had emigrated with their officers, were incorporated. The corps served in the vanguard of the Armée du Centre.

Chasseurs de Flandre or de Calonne

In February 1792, the Chevalier Louis-François-Alexandre de Calonne-Billemont, a former officer of the German Régiment de La Marck-infanterie, raised a free company of men from Artois or Flanders. 'The company began to recruit on 5 February at Ronse [or Renaix in French, northeast of Tournai and northwest of Ath], doubtless by the intermediary of the "depot of the émigré non-commissioned officers and soldiers" formed at Ath.'[128] It was designated as the Compagnie des Chasseurs de Flandre or Chasseurs de Calonne. In March, the company was complete and placed under the command of François-Ignace-Dominique de Calonne-Beaufayt, nephew of the owner and previously an officer in the Régiment de Brie. Recruitment was aided by the Calonne family's presence in the region, Calonne-Billemont being a cousin of the minister Calonne, so there were hopes of raising further companies, on 10 April 1792, 'one finds traces of purchases for the corps of "300 carbines,

126 Grouvel, *Troupes de l'émigration*, vol.III, p.152.
127 Grouvel, *Troupes de l'émigration*, vol.III, p.124.
128 Grouvel, *Troupes de l'émigration*, vol.III, p.233.

348 pistols and sabres'".[129] A second company was indeed raised in May, and its command was given to Calonne-Beaufayt's brother, Philibert-Philibert-Louis.[130] Although a third company was not raised officers were appointed and its command was given to the Chevalier Philippe de Bourgogne, with his brevet dated 11 September 1792. Bourgogne had been first page to Louis XVI and distantly related, by an illegitimate line, to the royal family and the former counts of Flanders.[131] The two existing companies formed part of the vanguard of the Armée de Bourbon.

Chasseurs-carabiniers de Wittgenstein or de Goerduck

This unit was formed after the chasseurs were detached from the Régiment de Wittgenstein, on the instigation of their *capitaine*, André-Frédéric de Goerduck, to form a battalion of Chasseurs carabiniers.

Goerduck, was experienced and ambitious, born in France the son of a bandmaster, he had been in a Hessian regiment in British pay in America before becoming an officer in the Salm Legion and then serving in the patriot forces in the Netherlands, before coming to France to enter the Royal-Liégeois as *capitaine*.[132] Then, in 1789, he was seconded as an instructor to an experimental course to train chasseur-carabiniers in the French infantry, probably due to his experience in America.[133] After emigrating, he sought to make a profit by the purchase of 3,000 German carbines, which he intended to resell to all the light corps of the royalist army.

The capitulation for the new unit was formalised on 24 March 1792, and, two days later, Goerduck was appointed to its command as *lieutenant-colonel*. His second-in-command was the Chevalier Prudhomme de Borre, also with the rank of *lieutenant-colonel*, who was another former *capitaine* in the Royal-Liégeois. The unit was to be a battalion of 424 men in eight companies. It was intended to serve as a German jäger corps, so the officers were to be 'all Germans or Alsatians, save for 6 French.'[134] The soldiers, principally recruited in the territory of Liège, were to have been former hunters or accredited marksmen, for which they received the pay of a *caporal*. However, as Goerduck's business enterprise faced difficulties and his debts piled up, the Chasseurs-carabiniers de Wittgenstein, or de Goerduck, never exceeded 150 men, with 105 chasseurs in two companies, which were placed in the vanguard of the Armée du Centre.

The Légion de Breuilpont

The Marquis de Breuilpont, *capitaine* in the Dragons de Monsieur in 1786, refused the rank of *major* in March 1791 as he considered that the King was

129 Grouvel, *Troupes de l'émigration*, vol.III, p.234.

130 Paul Armand du Chastel de la Howardries-Neuvireul, *Notices généalogiques tournaisiennes* (Tournai: Vasseur-Delmée, 1881), vol.I, pp.343–344.

131 M.E. Saint-Maurice Cabany, *Le Nécrologie Universel du XIXe Siècle* (Paris: Le Nécrologie Universel du XIXe Siècle, 1845), vol.I, p.69.

132 Grouvel, *Troupes de l'émigration*, vol.III, p.147.

133 Léon Hennet, *Les compagnies de cadets gentilshommes et les écoles militaires* (Paris: L. Baudoin et Cie., 1889), p.157.

134 Grouvel, *Troupes de l'émigration*, vol.III, p.147.

no longer free. The following month, he emigrated and joined his former regimental commander, the Comte de La Châtre, at Ath and became his aide de camp. Breuilpont was very wealthy from the estate of his mother's late husband, who had been a rich tax farmer. Breuilpont, born almost six months after his death, was regarded as a natural son of the late King Louis XV. Using his money and connections, as well as his position on the staff of La Châtre, he had supported the raising of a free company by M. d'Ormesson, formerly *capitaine* in the Dauphin-infanterie. He had then sought recruits for further companies, 'at Courtrai [Kortrijk], Ypres, Diksmuide, Roulers [Roeselare] and in other localities on the extreme border of maritime Flanders.'[135] The men of Ormesson's company, like those of Calonne, were excellent, made up of former soldiers, farmers, ploughmen, craftsmen, and volunteers from Flanders and Artois, intelligent and particularly suited to their role of reconnaissance or harassment.

From March 1792, Ormesson's company was at Marchin in Luxembourg, in front of the cantonment of Huy. The levy was successful, and in June it had 130 men. The Princes gave the Comte de La Châtre official authorisation to raise a corps of chasseurs carabiniers. On 1 August, Breuilpont received a brevet as *colonel* of this corps, which was organised as four companies, and, two days later, the Duc de Bourbon appointed him to lead them in the vanguard of his army. As well as holding the outposts, Breuilpont was charged with, 'several reconnaissance missions which he drove, with a detachment of 60 horse and 15 chasseurs, up to 35 leagues (140 kilometres) beyond the outposts, despite the continual pursuit of the French.'[136] In the meantime, he decided to raise a legion in his own name, but without a capitulation from the Princes, to consist of the chasseurs carabinier companies, now raised to six each with 20 to 25 chasseurs, and a cavalry detachment of 100 uhlans. The colour of the uniform was iron, or pike, grey as worn by the Austrian light troops.

The prestige of the Légion de Breuilpont was such that it was one of the very few units to continue to recruit until November 1792. On 17 September, there were 169 chasseurs carabiniers and 48 uhlans, which increased to 230 and over 100, respectively, the latter forming a squadron. An example of the recruitment was, 'on 13 [October], a sergent, a brigadier, a caporal, three chasseurs with horses and 3 hussars, 2 dragoons, an artillery driver, and 2 fusiliers on foot, deserters coming from the Ath depot, joined the corps (they came from the Régiments de Royal-Auvergne, Auxerrois, Navarre, Beauce, Esterhazy, etc.).'[137]

The Légion de Normandie or de Carneville

On 19 April 1792, the day before war was declared, agreement was reached to raise the Légion de Normandie, it and that of Mirabeau were the only such units to be formed under a capitulation. This was with the Vicomte de Carneville, a Norman gentleman and former *lieutenant-colonel*, since 1790,

135 Grouvel, *Troupes de l'émigration*, vol.III, p.237.

136 Grouvel, *Troupes de l'émigration*, vol.III, p.238.

137 Grouvel, *Troupes de l'émigration*, vol.III, p.239.

of the Régiment d'Artois-cavalerie, who had left the service of France on 21 June 1791.

The legion was to have two infantry battalions with five companies, one of grenadiers and four of fusiliers, plus four companies of chasseurs à cheval (although the capitulation suggested that these latter could initially serve on foot); the second battalion was to be raised only once the first battalion and the first two companies of light cavalry were complete. 'The total strength will be 1,100 infantry and 268 cavalry, in all 1,368 men.'[138] Initially formed from Norman gentlemen who had assembled since the end of 1791 at Baden-Baden, the Légion de Normandie obtained a depot in Tienen in April, with subsidiary posts at Tournai, Mons and Mechelen. At the end of June, it was assigned to the vanguard of what was later to be the Armée de Bourbon. Although the men recruited were similar to those of the free companies, the Comte de Brons specifies that, 'almost all the officers were Normans as well as a large number of its soldiers.'[139] It seems that the legion never had more than 400 men and, on 11 August, it was organised as a staff, a free company, one of grenadiers, two of fusiliers and one of foot chasseurs, armed with German carbines, along with a company of chasseurs à cheval.

10. The Staff, Administration and Services (Plates 8 & 17).

While, of course, personnel from the staff, administration and other services, were present from the start of the military emigration it was not until June 1792 that these elements were organised in the Armée des Princes.

Table 14: The staff, administration and services of the three parts of the Armée des Princes, July 1792.[140] (Pinasseau, Campagne de 1792, pp.30, 39 & 48).

	Armée du Centre	Armée de Condé	Armée de Bourbon
Princes du sang	2	1	2
Maréchaux de France	2	–	–
Lieutenants-généraux	16	6	2
Lieutenants-généraux de Marine	4	–	–
Maréchaux de camp	116	31	25
Chefs d'escadre	12	–	–
Army staff	28	12	6
Infantry staff	20	8	6
Cavalry staff	19	8	5
Aides de camp (approx.)	370	74	56
Administration	22	7	3
Medical officers	3	4	2
Total	614	151	107

138 Grouvel, *Troupes de l'émigration*, vol.II, p.225.

139 Brons, *Journal*, p.191.

140 Pinasseau, Campagne de 1792, pp.30, 39, 48

The Staff

There were five Princes du sang (princes of royal blood of the House of Bourbon): Monsieur, the Comte de Provence; his brother the Comte d'Artois; their cousin the Prince de Condé; his son, the Duc de Bourbon, and the latter's son, the Duc d'Enghien. The Duc d'Angoulême and his brother the Duc de Berry, Artois's two sons, were then too young to serve in the army.

The title *maréchal de France* was a distinction, not a rank. The two *maréchaux* were the Duc de Broglie, who commanded the Armée du Centre, and the Duc de Castries, at the head of its cavalry. The next in seniority were *lieutenants-généraux* and *maréchaux de camp*, and their naval equivalents, the latter corresponding to a brigadier general. Some had command roles such as the Comte de Vioménil, of the vanguard of the Armée de Condé and the Comte de Béthisy at the head of the German brigade. On the staff of the infantry, they served as *major général* and *aides* and on that of the cavalry as *maréchal général des logis* and *aides*. The army's chief of general staff was also designated *maréchal général des logis*, so the term was used at army level as well as in the cavalry, assisted by *aides-maréchal général des logis*, such as the Comte de Brons. There was also the rank of *maréchal des logis*, equivalent to sergeant that still exists today in the cavalry and related arms.

Attached to the various staffs were specialists: artillery officers, commissaries, administrative and medical personnel. Those from the Corps royal du Génie (engineers) were also distributed among the general staffs as well as fighting units to, for instance, draw maps and plans, or supervise field works. With the armies were an engineer *colonel*, a *lieutenant-colonel*, a *major*, 25 *capitaines*, 35 *lieutenants en premier* as well as students – four of whom were *sous-lieutenants* before 1789, six of this rank since 1789 and two *élèves aspirants* (candidate students) appointed *sous-lieutenants* by the princes in 1792.[141]

A unit of guides, serving as dispatch riders, could also be formed, the headquarters of the Armée du Centre having a unit of around 10 men. In addition, there were units for security and policing. Staff officers were attached to the Austrian or Prussian forces, and then there were the multitude of aides de camp. Brons described the sight of them when the King of Prussia reviewed the Armée du Centre in early August 1792, 'Each of the general officers had with him the number of aides de camp fixed by their Royal Highnesses, namely four for the lieutenants-généraux and two for the maréchaux de camp. The Maréchaux de France had twelve and the Princes twenty-four each.'[142] With each peloton of two companies having at its head a *maréchal de camp*, and each battalion, of four pelotons, commanded by a *lieutenant-général*, 'the truth obliges me to admit to you that the number was really too considerable.'[143]

141 Brons, *Journal*, pp.238–239. He also listed another student who had joined the corps in 1789 but who had been unable to join the training school at Mézières

142 Brons, *Journal*, p.48.

143 Brons, *Journal*, p.48.

The Administration

The supporting services dealt with the logistical, health and spiritual needs of the combatants. Thus, they fell within the intendance (literally, stewardship), responsible for the camp, the equipment and the food of the soldiers, the health service, and finally the chaplaincy.

At the head of the administration was a *commissaire des guerres* (war commissary), possibly assisted by a *commissaire ordonnateur* (ordering commissary), in charge of the office administration. His responsibility was financial: pay, recruitment or advances, as well as the purchase of weapons, equipment, or fodder. In addition, the commissary serving with an inspector general was responsible for the *contrôle des effectifs* (equivalent to muster rolls) and the detailed review of the equipment, clothing and weapons. The *intendant*, of the same rank as the *commissaire des guerres*, was responsible for supplying the army and had several clerks under him, responsible for the stores.

From the beginning of 1792, with the prospect of being joined by many more troops and volunteers, the Princes devoted a significant part of their funds to establishing, near the frontiers, 'considerable depots of arms, powder, tents, saddles, cartridge pouches, blankets, uniform coats, helmets and shoes. In a word, all kinds of camping effects, weapons, clothing and equipment.'[144] The largest was at Remich on the Moselle, 'where the surplus of arms, tents, camping effects and ammunition of all kinds had been deposited.'[145] It was maintained until the end of the campaign, and the stored powder was valued at 1,000 louis, and there were also 4,500 British muskets, of a model for officers, that had cost 30 to 35 louis each. Unused ordnance was kept there along with the stores of individuals and some regiments, including Berwick. Two artillery *capitaines* were responsible for the depot, assisted by clerks and a number of gunners. Furthermore, a strong detachment of Hommes d'armes à pied was assigned to guard it.

Ultimately the army relied, for its financial management, on one man, as an émigré not prone to flattery observed, 'Calonne exercised his wits to subsist an army of twenty-two thousand men, to arm it, equip it, provision it, and have it march, after having maintained it dispersed in three hundred cantonments over 200 leagues of country.'[146]

The Medical Services

Although relatively little known, the medical services of the émigré army were essential elements, maintaining the morale of the personnel and its effective strength both by preventive measures and the care given to the sick and wounded. The doctors and pharmacists of the hospitals or armies and *chirurgien-major* and their assistants in the hospitals, regiments and ambulances were civilians but wore distinctive uniforms. They served what was perhaps the foremost military health system, with every unit having a *chirurgien-major* on its staff. This was not the case for all armies, and the

---

144 Brons, *Journal*, p.146.

145 Brons, *Journal*, p.146.

146 Champflour (ed.), *La Coalition d'Auvergne*, p.272.

inadequate medical resources in the Prussian army was to have terrible consequences during the campaign.

The limited funds available to the Princes were focused on acquiring troops, weapons and equipment. The lack of medical and surgical facilities had to be remedied by goodwill and generosity, with donations from, for example, the Empress of Russia and the Princess of Monaco, Condé's mistress, solid organisation, and finally the best use of skills.

On the eve of the campaign, when the émigré army was static for a prolonged time, a distinction was made between first aid hospitals, local to the cantonments, and auxiliary hospitals.[147] As soon as the campaign began, the service was organised between travelling and resident hospitals. The first provided field ambulances for first aid and triage, so analogous to the current British military term rather than a vehicle, and the field hospital, which was established as close as possible to the combat zone. This required, among other things, suitable shelter from the elements, routes to receive and evacuate the wounded and a reliable source of water. The resident hospital met the same criteria as an auxiliary hospital, often housed in a requisitioned or rented building, such as a lazaretto or former convent. It had to be located far enough from the operational zones to provide long-term and convalescent care for the wounded by auxiliary staff, an *infirmier-major* and assistants, ecclesiastics and women nurses, as well as have a depot for such resources as bandages and medicines. In both cases, the hospital was headed by a director, several doctors and surgeons, even student surgeons, and at least one pharmacist, an apothecary-major with assistants.

The Chaplaincy

Finally, it should be recognised that the Armée des Princes was based on the principle of unwavering loyalty to the King and to the Catholic Church. The representatives of the latter were present in armies in peacetime, performing the divine service within each unit or cantonment or blessing standards before their presentation delivery. In war, they blessed the soldiers, who bowed with one knee on the ground and their hats in their hands before an engagement. Their number, however, was almost tenfold due to the exodus of ecclesiastics from France, so, as a result, each company had an *aumônier*. On the battlefield they were often employed to recover the wounded and provide first aid with the *frater*, a soldier serving as both barber and nurse. Finally, these chaplains could grant extreme unction to dying soldiers and entrust the bodies of the deceased to consecrated ground.

147 Jean des Cilleuls, 'Le service de santé des forces armées de l'émigration et particulièrement de l'armée de Condé (1791-1801)', *Société française d'Histoire de la Médecine*, 29 March 1969, pp.89–105.

5

The Émigrés in the 1792 Campaign

The Armée des Princes Divides

Considering the difficulties that they had faced, by June 1792, the émigrés must have thought that things were looking promising for them. They had benefited from the time the French Assembly had needed between December 1791 and July 1792 to organise the nation in arms, as well as the initial setbacks suffered by the new regime's armies. These made it possible to complete the formation of the Armée des Princes so that it could make a realistic military contribution in the coalition. This was aided by the release of the money sent by the Empress of Russia in July, a million livres, for the Armée des Princes.

On the French side, confusion reigned, with a succession of four Ministers of War in five months, including Dumouriez resigning on 26 June after three days in post, and commanders swapping places without the minister even being informed. There was no overall plan, and the Austrian counter-offensives were difficult to contain; the last of which, on 19 July, saw the recapture of Bavay.

On 21 June, the first state for the Armée des Princes was drawn up. It was divided into three corps or divisions, two of them based on where the troops were. That under the orders of the Duc de Bourbon consisted of all the troops then present in the Netherlands around Huy. While the Prince de Condé's forces were made up of the troops formerly stationed in the regions of Worms and Ettenheim, and in the German states located on the right bank of the Rhine. However, three factors influenced the division under the orders of the King's brothers; the first was their prestige, so it needed to be the largest. The second was that it should be a rallying point to the royalist cause, which was to be encouraged by including most of the former royal troops and the reconstituted Maison militaire. The companies of officers with it were to provide the cadres for units made up of soldiers who would flock to join them. Thus, the Corps royal de la Marine, although stationed around Malmedy, in the Ardennes, moved to join this division. The last criterion was mobility, so the division had the largest and best cavalry force, in order to move as quickly as possible on Paris, once the enemy positions had been bypassed or breached.

The summer saw troop movements throughout the regions. For instance, on 29 June, after the Bishop of Saint-Omer had blessed the standards of the two squadrons of the Coalition d'Auvergne at Thal, near Koblenz, where they had been since August 1791, they marched for Treis-Karden on the banks of the Moselle. From 2 July, Prussian and Austrian troops began to arrive at Koblenz.[1] The Duke of Brunswick, having established himself at Horchheim, met the Princes at Bingen where he assured them: 'on behalf of the two Sovereigns who honour me with their confidence, and, if I dare say so, after my personal sentiment and attachment, that no one has ever conceived the slightest idea of their not playing the brilliant role that is due to them on so many counts, and which we need for our own interest.[2]

Furthermore, at a further meeting, at Horchheim on 4 July, Brunswick denied a report that the Princes were to be placed in the second line of any invasion force:

> He interrupted and exclaimed with vehemence that he gave his word of honour that never, never had the Powers even conceived the idea. We know, moreover, that the Empress put it as a condition of her accession to the project of the two Kings that the Princes would have a place in the front line appropriate to the eminence of their rank and the nobility of their conduct.[3]

The coronation of Emperor Francis II at Frankfurt on 14 July provided an opportunity for the members of the coalition to meet for three days. Also present was an agent of Louis XVI, Mallet du Pan, a journalist and fervent supporter of the counter-revolution, who had been sent to negotiate the terms of the intervention of the armed coalition. These were summarised as, 'to insist with the powers to obtain from them that the émigrés should never be employed in the first line, but only in the wake of the armies and to guard the places which would be seized.'[4] However, Mallet du Pan also had to hear the complaints of the Emperor's minister about, among other things, the Princes whom he accused, 'not only of intentions contrary to the wishes of the King, but also of wanting to become independent and create a regency.'[5] These last were certainly justified but all the signs were that the fate of the French monarchy was already sealed.

Leaving Frankfurt, Frederick William II, the King of Prussia, went to Mainz on 21 July, where Brunswick was appointed commander-in-chief of the coalition forces and the plan for the invasion of France was decided upon. Frederick William then went to Bingen, where, on 26 July, he reviewed part of the émigré troops. The next day, the definitive organisation of the Armée des Princes was confirmed:

---

1 Cacqueray, *Mémoires inédits*, p.47.
2 Crétineau-Joly, *princes de Condé*, vol.I, pp.47–48.
3 Crétineau-Joly, *princes de Condé*, vol.I, p.51.
4 Montlosier, *Souvenirs*, p.88.
5 Montlosier, *Souvenirs*, p.89.

> It was agreed in these conferences that the army of the émigrés, twenty to twenty-five thousand men strong, would be divided into three corps; the most considerable will be of twelve thousand, under the command of the Princes brothers of the King, and of maréchal de Broglie; it is to be part of the Prussian army which will occupy the centre. The second, of five or six thousand, having as general the Prince de Condé, is to move to the left, to act with an Austrian division. The third, commanded by Monseigneur the Duc de Bourbon, who is to have his son with him, is destined for the country of Liège, where the prince will be able to gather under him five thousand émigrés.[6]

These were soon designated as the Armée du Centre, Armée de Condé and Armée de Bourbon, at the end of July or early August 1792 (see Appendices 4, 5 and 6). The Armée du Centre was to enter France from the province of Luxembourg, while the Armée de Condé remained as part of a corps of observation on the right bank of the Rhine, and the Armée de Bourbon would be in the Ardennes to provide cover against any French troops that might emerge from Alsace or Lorraine.[7] Each was a royalist army in miniature, with a staff, administration, medical services, provost, artillery, engineers, advance guard, main body and reserve. Did the dispositions mean that Monsieur and Artois were keeping the Condés, father and son, at a distance to prevent them from taking some of the glory that was to come the way of the King's brothers? Condé himself clearly implies it in his correspondence. The explanation provided by the Allies, which the Marquis de Bouillé repeated, was that this deployment offered deserters or supporters of royalty a chance to rally to a Bourbon on each front. The Duc d'Enghien provided another:

> One can regard as a great misfortune for our cause this dispersion of the émigrés; they were divided so as to leave them no strength, to make them passive beings: one feared their ardour, the moral effect, perhaps that too great a force would have been produced on minds. One wanted to render them null, and this plan was scrupulously followed. Many other reasons, called political, opposed the use of the émigrés during this campaign. The only one that was given to us was that we could not wage war with equality; that if taken, we were hanged and massacred, and that we were not people to take reprisals on our prisoners, which was for us a great disadvantage.[8]

The belated authorisation to arm, equip and train their troops meant that the Armée des Princes was not as prepared as it could have been for the forthcoming campaign. It was necessary to act quickly to find recruits for the paid regiments, issue new regulations, contract for weapons, tents, camping equipment, and horses, and to establish and organise depots, hospitals, and ambulances. It was at this time that the companies of gentlemen completed their equipment and armament in the cantonments of the province of Luxembourg:

---

6 Romain, *Souvenirs*, vol.II, p.235.

7 Montlosier, *Souvenirs*, p.89.

8 Jean-Paul Bertaud, *Le duc d'Enghien* (Paris: Librairie Arthème Fayard, 2021), p.136.

Caricature Armée de Condé, anonymous, 1792. (Author's collection)

> The arms had meanwhile arrived. These weapons that an uncertain or tortuous policy had made the hands of the French nobility wait so long, and that they had feared more than once to not obtain. One exercised in all the infantry cantonments weapon handling, loading, and firing of all kinds. The companies of officers in active service needed only very few days to get back to all the manoeuvres and the precision of the march as well as the tone of command. It took a little longer for the companies of gentlemen of the various provinces to reach a certain point of instruction.[9]

At the same time, some units finished recruiting and adopted a definitive organisation.

On 23 July, the King's brothers had the latest regulations for the next campaign published, in particular the regulation concerning the order of battle. Table 15 presents the highest strength of the three armies, probably in September, when they were joined by the survivors of 10 August, the last émigré officers, deserters, recruits from depots in the Austrian Netherlands and Germany, as well as Switzerland and Alsace.

9 Brons, *Journal*, p.38.

Table 15: Strength of the three armies comprising the Armée des Princes.[10]

Units	Armée du Centre	Armée de Condé	Armée de Bourbon	Total
Staff	589	140	102	831
Administration	22	7	3	32
Health	3	4	2	9
Infantry	6,525	3,739	3,077	10,571
Cavalry	6,816	1,482	1,036	9,334
Provost	15	7	20	42
Artillery (officers)	226	100	50	376
Engineers (officers)	23	8	14	25
Gunners and workmen	30	15	12	57
Total	14,249	5,502	4,316	24,067

At first, the coalition army was only to be composed of 50,000 Prussians, but it was subsequently decided that they would be joined by six thousand Hessians. It had long been established that the Austrian army would not be part of the first line, but act on the flanks as a corps of observation to try to scotch suspicions that the Queen was plotting with the Emperor. It is estimated that at the beginning of the campaign the coalition forces amounted to around 130,000 men distributed as follows:

- 42,000 Prussians commanded by the King of Prussia and the Duke of Brunswick, to march in a single column on Longwy.
- 12,000 to 14,000 Austrian and Imperial troops were to march from the Moselle valley under the orders of the Prince of Hohenlohe-Kirchberg, including those commanded by *Feldmarschalleutnant* Wallis, along with 6,000 Hessians on the left flank of the Prussians, while a contingent of 2,000 men from Mainz remained on the Rhine. Hohenlohe, 'was to menace Sarrelouis [sic] and Landau, besiege Thionville and keep Metz in check, while the Prussians marched on Longwy and Verdun, crossed the Argonne, to emerge into the plains of Champagne, and take the road to Paris.'[11]
- 32,000 Austrians under the orders of Sachsen-Teschen, maintained the security of the Netherlands, from Flanders to the Ardennes. *Feldmarschalleutnant* Baillet de Latour was in the northeast, *Feldmarschalleutnant* Beaulieu de Marconnay in the centre and *Feldzeugmeister* Clerfayt de Croix ready to march into France.
- 7,000 to 10,000 Austrians in the Breisgau, the region between the Rhine and the Black Forest, to guard the river under the orders of the Graf Esterházy de Galántha and 6,000 under the Graf zu Erbach-Schönberg around Speyer.
- 23,000 émigrés.

10 Jean Pinasseau, *Campagne de 1792*, pp.11–72.

11 Léonce Grandin, *Les Prussiens en France Longwy – Verdun – Thionville – Valmy 1792* (Paris: Delhomme et Briguet, 1892), pp.98–99.

From the Brunswick Manifesto to the Siege of Thionville

In May 1792, Louis XVI, concerned about the manifesto the coalition was rumoured to be preparing for publication, entrusted Mallet du Pan to ensure that *maréchal* de Castries knew his wishes. Finally, when the two met, Mallet du Pan delivered the King's instructions regarding the drafting of the document:

> The manifesto must threaten the factious and not France; it must not introduce any sentiment of animosity, nor of vengeance … His Majesty particularly requests that the Princes endeavour, by the style and tone of their manifesto, to persuade the multitude that no personal resentment animates them, nor the nobility, and that they only enter France with the intention of re-establishing the monarchy, of placing the King back on his throne, of restoring order, justice and peace.[12]

Consequently, four points were to be included in the text, echoing the new Emperor's response to the Assembly in March:

1. The security of the King, Queen and the Royal Family.
2. The free and complete liberty of the King and his family.
3. The security of the members of the clergy and nobility, and of all good citizens remaining in the kingdom, as well as the conservation of their property.
4. The restoration of the apostolic and Roman Catholic religion.

It is known that the princes did not have, or did not seek, the opportunity to address the Duke of Brunswick about the manifesto, the writing of which was ultimately entrusted to the Marquis de Limon, who had formerly been a confidant of the Duc d'Orléans. It was published at Koblenz on 25 July and then by the French press on 3 August. Its preamble seemed to respect Louis XVI's wishes quite well. The legitimacy of the war was recalled, conducted by two sovereigns who had 'no other goal than the welfare of France, without claiming to enrich themselves by conquests.'[13] Furthermore: 'convinced that the sound part of the French nation abhors the excesses of a faction which subjugates it, & that the majority of the inhabitants, waits impatiently the moment of relief to openly declare themselves against the odious enterprises of their oppressors.'[14] The goals of the war were simply to reestablish the throne and altar and to end the anarchy in France.

However, half of the manifesto was devoted to a long list of threats against those who refused to submit or who represented a danger to the royal family. Indeed, Paris was promised, 'exemplary and forever memorable vengeance'

12 Duc de Castries, *Maréchal de Castries, serviteur de trois rois* (Paris: Editions Albatros, 1979), p.173.

13 Duke of Brunswick, *Déclaration que Son Altesse Sérénissime le duc régnant de Brunswick-Lunebourg, commandant les armées combinées de Leurs Majestés l'Empereur & le Roi de Prusse, adresse aux Habitans de France*, p.3.

14 Brunswick, *Adresse aux Habitans de France*, p.2.

if anything untoward happened to them and, explicitly, if the Tuileries Palace was 'forced or insulted.'[15] So that the King could exercise his sovereignty, he was invited to indicate to the coalition:

> ... the city in his kingdom closest to his frontiers, in which he will judge it appropriate to retire with the Queen & his family, & under a good and trusty escort ... in order that His Most Christian Majesty can in complete safety call to Him the ministers & counsellors who he pleases to designate, make such summons as he deems appropriate, provide for the restoration of good order, & regulate the administration of his kingdom.[16]

Whether by Louis XVI, his wife or some other agency, the return to the earlier project of 1789 side-stepped the Princes and émigrés, none of whom were mentioned in the manifesto's text. The refusal to rely on the nobility for the restoration of the monarchy would continue even at this juncture.

The day after the conference of 21 July, the troops that were to form the Armée du Centre were to start to concentrate in the Trier region, with Monsieur and Artois establishing themselves at Bingen, where they would join with the Prussian troops. Although numerically the strongest of the émigré forces, they were scattered, lacked cohesion and were the least prepared, some units lacking tents, vehicles, and even weapons, and were the worst trained. The Armée du Centre was short of money, having spent a lot on rebuilding the Maison militaire, so individual units had to make their own arrangements. Already anticipating problems, the Comte Hector had informed the Prince of Nassau that the Corps de la Marine Royale would not be able to leave its cantonment due to the lack of funds. The Prince provided 24,000 livres in bills of exchange to be drawn on banks in Holland, to which a member of the corps added 1,000 livres. The sailors, the most distant unit being at Malmedy, only learned of the movements on 27 July, and orders to depart arrived four days later. The Corps de la Marine's cavalry set off for Trier, and the nine infantry companies followed over the next two days.

In the meantime, the Prussian army was concentrating around Koblenz before setting out in three columns along the left bank of the Moselle for Trier on 30 July. Frederick William, accompanied by his sons, went ahead to join the two princes at Bingen and the émigré troops who were present paraded:

> The review of honour of His Prussian Majesty took place in the plain found at the gates of Trier between the abbey of St-Maximin (where the headquarters of the French princes then were), and that of Sainte-Marie-des-Martyrs. A party from the royal line infantry was under arms there, having at its head the general officers who were employed with it. M. de Martanges was the senior of the lieutenants-généraux and commander in chief the whole of this infantry of which each

15 Brunswick, *Adresse aux Habitans de France*, p.5.

16 Brunswick, *Adresse aux Habitans de France*, p.6.

> peleton formed of two companies was under the orders of a maréchal de camp and each battalion formed of four pelotons under those of a lieutenants-général.[17]

The Prussians reached Trier on 5 August, having taken six days to march the 90 or so kilometres from Koblenz, the excessive heat having added to the difficulty of crossing the Eifel massif. They camped a league outside the city, and, on 7 August, the two French princes placed their headquarters nearby. It was from here, on 8 August, that they published their declaration in which they recalled the causes of their just crusade, and exhorted all repentant subjects or soldiers to join their ranks.

Three days later, Frederick William witnessed the émigré cavalry parade at their camp at Pellingen. The Marquis de La Maisonfort, serving in the squadron of the Dragons des Princes, named after its senior company, recalled, 'Twenty-five to thirty squadrons paraded before Frederick William who, his hat off for an hour, saluted so to speak each horseman. We all wore white sashes and cockades of the same colour.'[18] Another émigré explained the use of the first distinction, 'The army of Monsieur and the Comte d'Artois wore a white sash, because, serving with the Prussians and Austrians, one had wanted to give them a sign distinctive from the patriots, to avoid accidents, misunderstandings.'[19]

While the émigrés were around Trier, on 13 and 14 August, they began to hear about the events of 10 August at the Tuileries and the coup d'état that removed Louis XVI from his throne. Finally, orders were given to be ready to move. It was now that the polymath Johann Wolfgang von Goethe encountered émigrés as he travelled to join the hussars of the Duke of Saxe-Weimar, his patron, in the Prussian army:

> I found there the corps of the émigrés which was composed entirely of nobles, most of them Chevaliers de Saint-Louis. They had neither servants nor grooms, and they took care of their persons and their horses themselves. I saw several of them lead them to the watering place and hold them in front of the forge. But what made the most singular contrast with this humble conduct were the carriages and vehicles of all kinds which cluttered a large meadow.[20]

The march was towards Luxembourg, where a military hospital and supply magazine were to be established for the Prussian and Hessian troops, and, on 15 August, the Prussians set up camp at Moutfort, outside the city, where the Hessians joined them. Perhaps it was inevitable that these movements would cause congestion, so the Corps de la Marine had to halt for a week at Bitburg, 30 kilometres north of Trier, to let the Prussian vanguard pass. The Corps de la Marine then moved towards Luxembourg, the infantry on 14 and 15 August and the cavalry on 17 August, to join the army. The effects of the

17 Brons, *Journal*, p.48.

18 La Maisonfort, *Mémoires*, p.112. In error he placed this at the end of July when it was, in fact, on 11 August.

19 La Rochefoucauld, *Souvenirs*, p.111.

20 Johann Wolfgang von Goethe, *Campagne de France* (Lausanne: La Guilde du Livre, 1968) p.36.

congestion were compounded by confused staff work, as related by Olivier d'Argens, in the Coalition de Bretagne still cantoned near Trier:

> On 15 August, an aide-de-camp had brought us, in the morning, an order to leave the next day for the army of the Prince de Bourbon, and we were to return to Liège or Huy; but in the evening, an order arrived from the princes to go to Trier, and from there to the camp of Saint-Maximin; which disconcerted our captain. We left Trier on the 18th, around eight o'clock in the morning for Grevenmachen or Grevenmaker [Grevenmacher]. The Armée des Princes, which arrived there at the same time as us, had, for three weeks, camped twice at Saint-Maximin and Penbren [Pellingen], three or four leagues from Trier. The company did not have tents; it slept under the stars, and fortunately the night was not bad. On the 19th, from Grevenmaker [sic] we went to the town of Statbredimus or Bredemie [sic]. The rain began an hour after our departure, was heavy and rendered the march difficult; our company still did not have tents that day, but the next day. This camp lasted ten days.[21]

The camps were formally laid out and, in the Armée de Bourbon at least, 'the tents were made of all sorts of colours; the name of the company was written on each of them.'[22] Each arm had a place and, 'behind were the servants' tents, the small kitchens and the baggage.'[23] In general, the cavalry were more fortunate, being quartered in neighbouring villages, 'the volunteers slept in the barns, the stables; their servants, in the attics, often next to their masters.'[24]

The Prussian reconnaissance troops had entered France at dawn on 12 August, soon followed by those under the Marquis de Breuilpont. The bulk of the forces followed and as they did the weather changed, the rain poured down accompanied by a dramatic drop in temperature. On 19 and 20 August, Austrian and then Prussian forces appeared under the walls of Longwy, elsewhere Prussians commanded by Hohenlohe attacked the French camp of Fontoy, west of Thionville in the Moselle valley, commanded by *maréchal* Luckner.

Longwy had been reinforced, so its garrison was of almost 2,600 men, with 72 guns. After the Austrian commander, Clerfayt, had his initial summons rejected, howitzers opened up on the town on the night of 21/22 August. Despite limited damage having been caused, the stronghold capitulated on the morning of 23 August. It had hardly been a siege as neither of the coalition forces had any heavy artillery. Nevertheless, the Prussians and Austrians had already been astonished by the resistance they had encountered from the local population. In particular, when they entered Sierck-les-Bains, they had been fired upon by villagers. Then on the morning of 24 August, when the garrison of Longwy emerged onto the glacis to lay down its arms, not a single soldier of the 34e Régiment d'infanterie (ci-devant Régiment d'Angoulême) left the ranks to take the white cockade. The Prussians and Austrians had been led to believe

21 Anon. (ed.), *Olivier d'Argens*, p.21.
22 La Rochefoucauld, *Souvenirs*, pp.108–109.
23 La Rochefoucauld, *Souvenirs*, p.109.
24 La Rochefoucauld, *Souvenirs*, p.109.

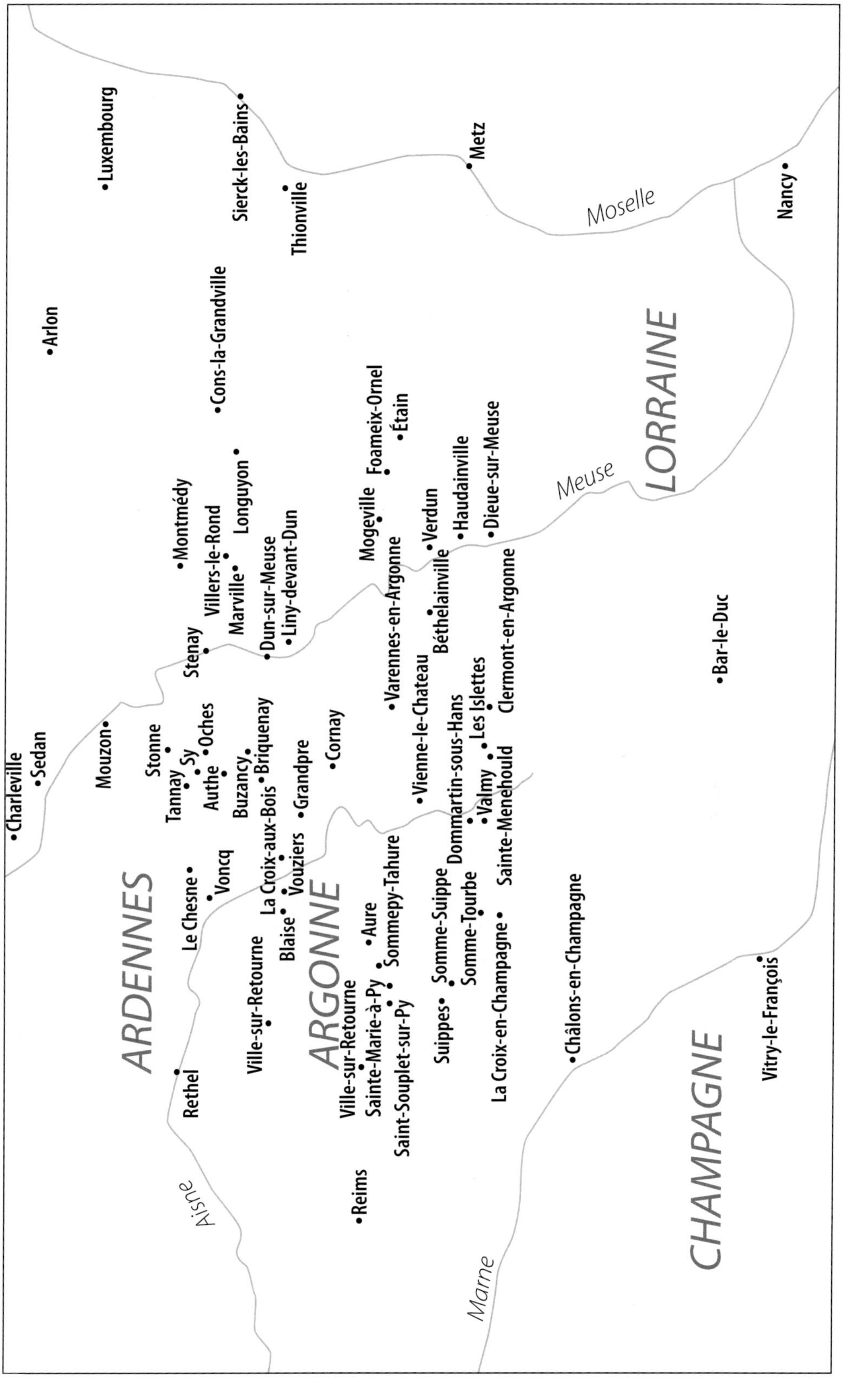

The 1792 Campaign.

that the population would greet the coming of the émigrés with enthusiasm; instead, the majority exhibited a cold hatred towards their countrymen and either avoided them or sought to assassinate them if they could.

The immediate consequence of the fall of Longwy was that Luckner abandoned the camps at Fontoy and Richemont to fall back behind Metz, leaving the way to Thionville open. Goethe, who joined the Prussian army outside Longwy on the afternoon of 27 August, wrote that the allied camp was, 'Established on a plain, it could be taken in with a glance, but one could not reach it without difficulty. The wet ground, broken down, stopped the horses and carriages.'[25] On the morning of 29 August, the army resumed its advance. Frederick William and the Duke of Brunswick, taking post on high ground, saw their army march in front of them. Only regimental commanders were authorised to precede it in a carriage; all others had to follow the artillery and the trains, despite the state of the roads after 10 days of rain.

The Princes had remained three days at the castle of Stadtbredimus before re-entering France on 29 August at the head of their army, which now took the name of the Armée Royale. They were to join their allies before the walls of Thionville. Argens in his journal described the enthusiasm of the émigrés at the time:

> We set off on the march with great satisfaction, the most complete joy painted on all faces. We were all, or almost all, convinced that we were going to march directly on Paris; that all obstacles would be easily removed; that the troops of the line only awaited our entry, as well as the brave allied royalists in the interior, and above all in Brittany, to join us. The day of our entry into Paris was even fixed.[26]

However, marching behind the Prussian troops who were accustomed to living on the country and therefore systematically pillaging it, the émigrés could not find much to eat for themselves or their horses. Individuals had to buy what they could at a high price, as the assignats the Princes intended for requisitions once on French soil were not accepted. The few buildings in the area offered little in the way of shelter, and the army's administration aroused a lot of resentment due to its inadequacy, while the entourage surrounding the Princes diverted, not to say devoured, a large part of the scarce provisions:

> One saw with pain the Princes surrounded by a crowd of general officers, aides-de-camp, staff officers who would have been far too numerous for an army of two hundred thousand men and who uselessly devoured part of the provisions that were so difficult to obtain. But these gentlemen would have thought to have dishonoured themselves in following the fine example of the Marquis de Monlozet, maréchal de camp, who, not wishing to be a burden to the Princes, had become a simple cavalryman in the Compagnie de Saintonge, considering, more, at this moment, his quality as a gentleman, than that of General Officer in which all his émigré colleagues wanted, absolutely, to be employed and, above all to receive the

25 Goethe, *Campagne de France*, p.38.

26 Anon. (ed.), *Olivier d'Argens*, pp.21–22.

> numerous rations that the regulations of the Princes granted them. They were, moreover, followed by a truly frightening number of carriages and baggage carts [forming a procession of more than 4 kilometres] which clogged all the roads and consumed the fodder that the unfortunate companies of émigrés had so much trouble obtaining; also, there arose from all sides a general cry against this abuse which, nevertheless, lasted the entire campaign and was, perhaps, not one of the least causes of its result.[27]

Throughout the campaign, the cavalry had to bivouac, and most did not have tents, 'The gardes du corps are almost the only ones to whom they were provided.'[28] The other exception was the Royal-Allemand that, having emigrated as a regiment, was properly equipped with tents and camp equipment.

The siege of Thionville was to be left to the Austrians and émigrés while the Prussians advanced on Verdun. *Maréchal de camp* (formerly Baron de) Wimpfen, who commanded Thionville, had a garrison of 5,900 men, and they were warned of the allied advance by a deserter, who from the style of his uniform may have been from Breuilpont's corps. Denis Bélot of the second battalion of the Volontaires de Seine-et-Marne, wrote:

> Yesterday, the 28th, several officers of our battalion walking in the vicinity of the place, perceived a Tyrolean chasseur coming towards them with the butt of his carbine in the air and shouting: 'Vive la nation!' … He replied that he had deserted the Army of the Princes and that he was pursued by a detachment, that the enemy army was only two leagues away…
>
> On the 29th, at noon, we saw in the woods large parties of troops, and having recognised them as enemies, we fired several cannon shots at them to drive them off. During this time, we worked with as much zeal as courage to complete the fortifications and put them in a state of defence. On the morning of the 30th, 600 men left Thionville, all armed and equipped with sharp tools; half firing in order to protect the other half who cut down the trees, both in the fields and the gardens surrounding the city on the side of the Metz gate and hiding the besiegers' progress from us. In the evening of the 30th, we put another six hundred out through the Luxembourg gate, to also bring down the plantations concealing the operations of the attackers. The latter fired on us but the cannonballs did us no other harm than cover us with earth. We retired without loss, after having accomplished the task that we had been given by the general.[29]

On 31 August, the émigrés arrived, and Monsieur proclaimed himself Regent; he had already been recognised as such by Catherine of Russia and the Allies finally and reluctantly agreed. However, militarily, what the émigrés found

---

27 Cacqueray, *Mémoires inédits*, p.57. The regulation he mentioned was the *Règlement Concernant les Equipages de l'Armée, les Effets de Campemens, leur Distribution, la Forme & les Dimensions des Camps d'Infanterie et de cavalerie,* of 9 June 1792.

28 Ernest d'Hauterive (ed.), *Journal d'émigration du comte d'Espinchal publié d'après les manuscrits originaux* (Paris: Perrin et cie., 1912), p.409.

29 Louis Bonneville de Marsangy (ed.), *Journal d'un volontaire de 1791* (Paris: Perrin et cie., 1888), pp.37–47.

was disappointing, 'No battery either of cannons or mortars, no preparations for entrenchment, no siege tools, no precise disposition for investment.'[30]

The city was dominated to the northwest by high ground around Œutrange from where it would have been possible to bombard it effectively. Wallis's Austrian corps, of about 6,000 men, camped at the foot of this elevation and the émigrés to its left; the Princes' headquarters were established nearby at Hettange-Grande. Chateaubriand, with the infantry of the Coalition de Bretagne, noting: 'Near our destitute and gloomy camp, existed another glittering and splendid. At the headquarters, one only saw waggons full of victuals; one only saw cooks, valets, aides-de-camp. Nothing better represented court and province.'[31]

Maréchal de Castries was on the opposite, right, bank of the Moselle to the northeast of Thionville, around the villages of Métrich and Malling. He had with him an infantry corps, consisting of the Brigade irlandaise, Chasseurs royaux des Princes and Chasseurs de Polignac, and some cavalry, including the Hommes d'armes, in all 3,000 to 4,000 men. The rest of Hohenlohe-Kirchberg's troops, 12,000 strong, were deployed at Richemont, south of Thionville, to block the main road to Metz.

The émigrés were ridiculously short of artillery themselves: six 4-pounder cannons and two defective 10-inch mortars, served by 50 officers and gunners of the Royal Corps of Artillery. Despite the shortage, the army staff had the guidance of a *major général de l'artillerie,* the branch's senior officer, *Lieutenant-colonel* de Pertius of the Régiment d'Auxonne. In the end, 'After many requests and many delays, the princes finally had 2 cannons of 12 [pounds] sent to them after the surrender of Longwy, and 2 mortars of 12 inches, but the bombs were of 10'.[32] Construction of the batteries was slow, as Chateubriand explained, 'for we were all, officers young and old, little accustomed to wield the shovel and pick. We lacked wheelbarrows, and we carried the earth in our coats, which served us as sacks.'[33]

The Prussian army advanced through Longuyon and Étain to arrive before Verdun late in the afternoon of 30 August. The summons to surrender was refused the following day, and Prussian batteries, established in the afternoon, commenced a bombardment at midnight. It lasted until 8:00 a.m. on 1 September and, 'Around noon, the city was summoned a second time; it requested a delay of twenty-four hours.'[34] After this expired, on 2 September, the city surrendered, but its commander, *général* Beaurepaire, blew his brains out at the end of the meeting held at the town hall to sign the act of capitulation. Once again, none of the French soldiers joined the émigré ranks. This and the hostility the Allies were encountering, now made the Prussian King consider that he had been deceived by Monsieur, that the French troops and wider population would readily rally to their cause.

30 Brons, *Journal*, p.67. Brons was also an eyewitness, travelling to Thionville on several occasions.
31 Chateaubriand, *Mémoires*, vol.III, p.73.
32 Brons, *Journal*, p.71.
33 Chateaubriand, *Mémoires*, vol.III, p.77.
34 Goethe, *Campagne de France*, p.61.

Most of the troops in front of Thionville remained idle, enjoying a brief spell of fine weather that lasted until 4 September. The Princes issued their first summons that day and, following form, the besieged requested a delay of 24 hours to consult. The imperial troops used this time to prepare for the bombardment that would take place the following night, 5/6 September. Wimpfen's answer was that he would never surrender. Supported by the municipal committee, he informed the Princes that he was unaware of what was happening elsewhere, at Longwy and Verdun, but he had always been faithful to the Nation and the Law and would remain so. Nevertheless, a further summons was delivered at 2:00 p.m. on 5 September, which began by announcing the news of the massacres that had just taken place in Paris and Versailles, on 2 and 3 September. The Princes believed that on learning this news, the population of Thionville would want to dissociate themselves from those responsible.

In Paris, Nicolas Ruault gave his brother a summary of these events:

> Oh crime, oh shame, oh height of horrors and political crimes! All the prisoners have been massacred these last days, without remorse, with infernal cold-bloodedness. These massacres were committed at the same time at the Chatelet, the Abbaye, La Force, Bicêtre, La Salpêtrière, Saint-Firmin, the Carmes and the Conciergerie du Palais. They lasted several days; the victims numbered in the thousands, they were piled up in carts as they were slaughtered. Those who ordered these assassinations were the Commune called on 10 August, it is Danton, Marat and consorts; the pretext is the King of Prussia at Verdun, it is the Prussian army that advances in Champagne. They call them measures of public safety; the Fatherland in danger; they did not want all these so-called aristocrats detained in the prisons of Paris to remain alive if the Prussian army approached Paris. They took the lead by massacring them all. No one opposed this execution which lasted five days ...[35]

The people of Thionville, if they were informed, were unmoved. Elsewhere, as news of the September massacres spread like wildfire, others sought to emulate them, such as at Reims, Charleville and Châlons, where:

> Luckner cannot contain the undisciplined hordes of volunteers of 92. They decapitate Lieutenant-Colonel Immonier, of the Régiment de Vexin [32e]; they go to the Town Hall to slit the throat of the mayor and to the prisons to massacre the aristocratic prisoners; they assassinate an old man who is carrying a book of mass under his arm; they kill the lieutenant-colonel of the 38e d'infanterie, on the pretext that he has too aristocratic an appearance ...[36]

The second summons having been rejected, Thionville was attacked on the night of 5/6 September. Without properly constructed batteries, the Austrians took advantage of the complete darkness of the first part of the

35 Ruault, *Gazette*, p.306, letter of 8 September 1792.

36 Antoine Lapierre, *Campagne des émigrés en Argonne en 1792* (Sedan: Librairie Genin, 1911), p.38.

night and brought their artillery into the plain, to half-range of the walls, and opened fire. Meanwhile, Castries moved to Distroff and Yutz, closer to the town, at the head of '3,000 gentlemen on foot, including the Bretons, the Irish brigade, the light troops, the hussars and the Gendarmerie.'[37] Using the guns with him, two Austrian 18-pounders with their crews and two 4-pounders of the Artillerie royale des Colonies, he launched a false attack from his side:

> … the outposts of the Armée Royale numbering 250 to 300 men [a corps of noble infantry and part of the Infanterie de la Marine], were ordered to move forward and marched under cover of darkness [and fog] to the glacis. Having reached it, without having been discovered, they stopped and, shortly afterwards, an aide-de-camp came to give them the order to return as quickly as possible. They were perceived in their retreat by the advanced works that fired some cannon shots at them without causing them any harm.[38]

Some allied guns were dismantled and around 20 Austrian soldiers killed. Other casualties of this useless attack were the Prince of Waldeck, who had an arm carried off by a French cannonball and, among the émigrés, the *major* of the Régiment de Wittgenstein, who was killed. In the morning, at 6:00 a.m., the column that had reached the glacis fell back to, 'the castle of Distroff, spent the day of the 7th there, and on the 8th returned to Mittrich [Métrich], from where, on the 9th, it went to the Hettange [-Grande] camp.'[39] Without proper equipment, the siege was reduced to skirmishes among the forward posts while the rest of the Austrian and royal troops, without a trench, sought to protect themselves as best they could from the defenders' artillery. The company of the Hommes d'armes à pied in which Madame de Bennes served did not come under fire during the siege, nevertheless she summed up the situation succinctly: 'The besieged ridiculed us, as really they well might, for there was not the least probability of success on our side. Their powerful artillery kept us at a distance, from which our shot could not reach them.'[40]

The émigrés had pickets in the vineyards and hedges of the village of La Grange, in front of Hettange-Grande, provided by the light troops as well as the Institution de Saint-Louis and the Coalition de Bretagne. Indeed, on 8 September, during one of the skirmishes, a Breton officer, de la Baronnais, was among the first émigrés killed in the campaign, along with *Major* de Potot, of the Chasseurs de Goerduck, and one of the chasseurs who was carrying the *major*'s body back to camp.[41]

The same day, at 5:00 p.m., 'the garrison sent a reconnaissance (100 cavalry with 4 cannons) in the direction of Manom; it fell back before the advance of the Hommes d'armes à cheval and Hussards de Saxe, who were in turn halted

---

37 Grouvel, *Troupes de l'émigration*, vol.III, p.17.

38 Cacqueray, *Mémoires inédits*, p.61.

39 Anon. (ed.), *Olivier d'Argens*, p.23.

40 Bennes, *A narrative*, p.19.

41 Brons, *Journal*, p.69; Brons mistakenly gives the date as 27 August that it was 8 September is confirmed by Cacqueray, *Mémoires inédits*, p.61.

by the fire of the artillery of the place.'[42] The following day, a convoy with food, as well as mortars and larger calibre cannons, for the Armée Royale arrived from Koblenz via the Moselle. The Castries's detachment received two 18-pounders, 'The Austrians were also expecting some from Luxembourg. We were working on building a battery on a height 800 toises from the place which, all day long, fired very heavily on the workers.'[43] Nevertheless, the only casualty of the day was one Austrian officer who was killed.

The Princes Ride out into Champagne

While a large part of the émigré infantry and some of the Austrian army remained in front of Thionville, Frederick William had left Verdun to head towards Châlons. His northern flank was covered by Clerfayt's corps while the Hessians established themselves at Clermont-en-Argonne, facing Les Islettes. Despite the weather, a rapid advance could have been expected, but a week was lost in procrastination. This allowed Dumouriez, who had succeeded La Fayette on 29 August (and four days earlier, Kellermann had replaced Luckner at the head of the Armée de la Moselle), time to hold a council of war in Sedan to decide on strategy. One of those present was *maréchal de camp* John Money, who left an account.

Having been persuaded to remain in French service by *lieutenant général* Arthur Dillon, they both travelled to Sedan. A plan to try to divert the Austrians by advancing on Brussels was discussed, but Money objected, adding that the Assembly would never consent to a plan that would, 'leave the road to Paris, open.'[44] Money advised taking a position between Verdun and Sedan to support whichever was attacked first, as well as to dispute the crossing of the Meuse, and, if this was not possible, to withdraw to defend the passes in the Argonne through which the road to Paris ran. Having learned that the enemy was advancing on Verdun, Dumouriez adopted this plan, and, on 30 August, his vanguard was at Mouzon on the Meuse. The following day, news arrived that Verdun was invested, and Dillon was sent south on a reconnaissance with a strong detachment of cavalry. However, he was driven from Stenay by a larger enemy force; some of Clerfayt's Austrian troops. In response, Dumouriez brought his army across the Meuse and then, hearing of the fall of Verdun, he continued to fall back until 3 September when he established himself at Grandpré, in a fortified camp, with his vanguard, with Dillon and Money, securing his right flank at Cornay. Although coalition troops were only two leagues away, Dumouriez's movements took place unhindered. Grandpré stands in a strategic pass in the heart of the Argonne forest east of Reims. The Argonne:

> … was then a wooded massif, 60 kilometres in length, and the width of which varied from 2 to 14 kilometres; it constituted a fortress at the gates of Champagne.

---

42 Grouvel, *Troupes de l'émigration*, vol.III, p.17.

43 Cacqueray, *Mémoires inédits*, p.61.

44 Money, *Campaign of 1792*, p.39.

Officer, Chasseurs à cheval, en surtout, 1786–1791 by Benigni. (Courtesy of La Sabretache)

> Its dense forests, interspersed with pools; its narrow and deep gorges where sleeps the treacherous water of the marshes; its steep heights, where bluffs and spurs with sharp edges follow one another; it with rare, bad roads, full of quagmires, formed a set of strategic defences ...[45]

To the east, the Meuse had three key crossing points, from north to south, Sedan, Stenay and Verdun, the last two of which were now in the hands of coalition forces. The roads running west from Stenay and Verdun converged on four passes through the Argonne. As well as Grandpré, those from Stenay went through either Le Chesne (or Le Chesne Populeux) or La Croix-aux-Bois to join at Vouziers. From Verdun the road ran through Les Islettes, in front of which was Clermont-en-Argonne, Sainte-Menehould behind and to the north was the village of La Biesme, overlooking the pass. All these essential positions were to be subject to coalition offensives to break through the French defences.

On 4 September, Dillon and Money, at the head of the vanguard, received orders to march through Varennes-en-Argonne, on the east side of the Argonne ridge, for Sainte-Menehould to secure the pass at Les Islettes. Approaching Varennes, scouts warned that it was held by enemy troops, but they quickly withdrew. However, soon afterwards, Dillon, wary of being ambushed, received information that the enemy held the pass and so ordered his troops to cross the high forest of the Argonne to reach Vienne-le-Château. The coalition troops at Varennes may have been a patrol from the Prussian 2nd Cavalry Division of Graf von Kalckreuth, who had tried in vain to convince Brunswick to seize the Argonne passes. The Comte de Montlosier claimed that some émigrés were present, 'The first body of émigrés ... immediately began to advance. It entered Varennes ... I cannot say what led this body of Prussians and émigrés to suddenly leave'.[46] Given the dispositions of the émigré troops on this date, this element may have been from the Légion de Breuilpont.

Dillon's troops only managed to reach Vienne-le-Château at 10:00 p.m., and so it was the next morning that they reached Sainte-Menehould. There, they found that the information that had led to the previous day's testing march had been false, and *maréchal de camp* Galbaud du Fort held La Biesme, overlooking Les Islettes pass, with two infantry battalions. Dillon then posted his men in Les Islettes and the surrounding area, with his headquarters at Sainte-Menehould; Clermont-en-Argonne was not secured, and when Dumouriez finally gave the order to seize it, it was already occupied by Hessian troops. Goethe noted in his journal:

> The Argonne forest, a chain of wooded hills ... stretched out immediately before us and stopped our movement. There was much talk of Les Islettes, an important passage between Verdun and Sainte-Menehould. Why was it not occupied? This was what could not be agreed on ... While we had marched on Verdun and

45 Lapierre, *émigrés en Argonne*, p.35.

46 Montlosier, *Souvenirs*, p.102. In his *Mémoires*, (vol.II p.155), Louis-Philippe also mentions, 'the arrival of a detachment of Prussians and émigrés.'

> bombarded that town, Dumouriez had sent troops across country to fortify Les Islettes and cover the right wing of his position behind Grandpré, and thus oppose the Prussians, the Austrians and the émigrés with new Thermopylaes ... while the army ought to have marched forward without respite, it was necessary ... to assault at any costs the fortified defiles ...[47]

If the Allies could not cross the Argonne forest, Dumouriez would force them to make a detour of about 60 kilometres, which would make their supply chain vulnerable to attacks by his forces, who still retained Montmédy and Sedan. Conversely, if the barrier was forced, he would have to abandon his camp at Grandpré and hastily withdraw behind the Marne to block the road to Paris. His 23,000 men, dispersed in several positions, would not be enough for such a task, so he called for reinforcements from the armies of Beurnonville, at the camp of Maulde, north of Valenciennes, and Kellermann. On their arrival, they would amass at least 50,000 men to face Brunswick on the plains of Champagne. Brunswick would stretch his lines of communication and disperse his troops to retain a strategic position along them should he attempt to dislodge Dumouriez from his position, leaving the latter the opportunity to fall on his rear. Brunswick, from 7 September, recognised that Dumouriez sought to make a firm defence of the Argonne forest to gain time to gather as many troops as possible for a decisive battle. Brunswick's plan initially showed him to be the better strategist.

This involved bringing up troops in the centre and south to fix Dumouriez, before attacking the more northerly position at La Croix-aux-Bois, which defended the camp at Grandpré, to clear the way to Sainte-Menehould and the highroad between Verdun and Châlons. To this end, he ordered Hohenlohe-Kirchberg to join the Hessians at Clermont-en-Argonne. This left Wallis's corps and the émigré infantry, supported by part of the 1ère compagnie noble d'ordonnance, the squadron of the gentlemen of Languedoc, Saintonge and Angoumois and the Hussards de Saxe, to continue the siege of Thionville. The besiegers were to be reinforced by Graf zu Erbach-Schönberg's corps, which would come from Speyer, a move which would prove to be an error.

The Armée Royale before Thionville was divided on 10 September. The Princes with the bulk of the cavalry and an infantry detachment, preceded by a vanguard corps, were to join the Prussian army at Verdun for the march on Paris. Orders were given for their departure the following morning. The news of this division of the royalist forces aroused anger; Prince Xavier de Saxe, who commanded the émigré infantry, refused to remain at Thionville, and *maréchal* de Broglie took his place, 'Subordination did not reign much in the camp among the provincial gentlemen ... they testified their discontent, and murmured a great deal. They raged loudly against the Monarchiens who surrounded Monsieur, accused him of being one himself.'[48]

Given the lack of means available to the émigrés left before the walls of Thionville, Wimpfen retook the initiative as soon as the Princes had left. That very day, 11 September, he led a cavalry sortie to reconnoitre the

47 Goethe, *Campagne de France*, pp.68–69.

48 Olivier d'Argens, *Mémoires*, p.24.

enemy's positions and communication was reestablished with Metz. Thus, the defenders of Thionville received a letter from Metz exhorting their resistance, combining a shameless lie about support coming from Paris with justification for the bloodshed in that city: 'Your town is the theatre of liberty! It is upon you that all France turns its gaze. Always hold firm. One hundred thousand Parisians have arrived at Châlons and are with Lückner's army. Before leaving Paris, they wanted their women to be safe, during their absence, so they slaughtered eight thousand prisoners and aristocrats of the capital.'[49]

The eight days following their departure from Thionville were trying and difficult for the Princes' cavalry as they marched 20 to 30 kilometres per day in consistently atrocious weather; the rain was accompanied by cold that surprised everyone. The vanguard consisted of the hussar squadrons of Bercheny-Lauzun and Chambord and the Chasseurs de Polignac, to which was added the Brigade de Monsieur of noble cavalry – 1,200 horsemen, with 200 infantry. It was under the orders of *maréchal* de Castries and commanded by the Marquis de Jaucourt. The army corps itself, with the King's brothers, was organised in two columns, that on the right commanded by the Duc de Coigny, with the Princes, and that on the left by the Marquis d'Autichamp. The infantry detachment of 1,500 men at the head of the Prince's column consisted of the Brigade irlandaise, the so-called Régiment de Vexin, the Compagnie des gentilshommes chasseurs de Rouault, and the infantry companies of the Corps de la Marine. It was followed by the Princes' baggage and then the cavalry, that of the Corps de la Marine forming a reserve. In all, there were 6,000 men and 8,000 horses, including the Princes' suites.

Despite the state of the roads, the Princes' column, marching one or two days behind the vanguard, reached the suburbs of Verdun on the afternoon of 13 September. Part of the infantry, including that of la Marine, was left at Verdun, and the rest continued, arriving at Dun-sur-Meuse at 6:00 p.m. the following day.[50] Meanwhile, the vanguard was already being deployed, 'It was at Béthelainville [about 14 kilometres west of Verdun] that the Marquis de Jaucourt received the order to join Clerfayt, who needed reinforcements.'[51]

Meanwhile, from 10 September, Brunswick's forces had commenced a series of attacks on Dumouriez's outposts along the line of the Argonne ridge. The position in the defile of La Croix-aux-Bois secured the camp of Grandpré, and, since 7 September, work had been done to defend it. On 11 September, the officer responsible reported that retrenchments and abattis had been completed, making the position impregnable and asked for his men to be relieved by a volunteer battalion. The following morning, on Dumouriez's orders, he left the post guarded by a hundred men and withdrew to the Grandpré camp. Having learned of this movement, Clerfayt, reinforced by Kalckreuth's Prussian vanguard, advanced from Buzancy and seized the pass during the night of 12/13 September.

49 Marsangy (ed.), *Journal 1791*, p.70.

50 Maleyssie, *Mémoires*, p.351.

51 Lapierre, *émigrés en Argonne*, p.597.

Early the following morning, the French retook La Croix-aux-Bois, but two hours later, an Austrian column led by Clerfayt himself arrived and forced them to retreat to Vouziers. This second attack by Clerfayt's troops coincided with another carried out by émigré troops on Le Chesne.[52] This was driven off by the French, who held the post, but learning that that of La Croix-aux-Bois was lost, they withdrew. Although from the vanguard, the specific units of the Armée Royale that were in action at Le Chesne are not known. Émigré reinforcements arrived after Le Chesne had been abandoned by its defenders, as one of their number relates, 'However, the émigrés and among others the companies of Auvergne who had been brought up by forced marches to support the attack [on La Croix-aux-Bois] arrived. They immediately moved to another defile or gap which led to Le Chêne-Populeux [sic].'[53]

The seizure of La Croix-aux-Bois was the breakthrough that forced Dumouriez to abandon his camp at Grandpré with the intention of reaching Sainte-Menehould, where he was to be joined by Beurnonville, who was marching from Rethel with 10,000 men, and Dillon was directed to hold the pass of Les Islettes to cover this concentration. Brunswick sent forward a column of light troops, mainly hussars but supported by horse artillery, in pursuit. Catching up with the troops that had retreated from La Croix-aux-Bois, the Prussian guns opened fire, which caused a wave of panic not only among this column but also the main body of Dumouriez's troops. While some went in the greatest disorder towards Sainte-Menehould, others fled to Châlons, where Kellermann arrived at the head of the Armée du Centre. As Dumouriez himself reported, 'There was no action, but a flight of 10,000 men before 1,500; if the enemy had pushed his point, he could have disordered all the army.'[54] As for his large force of artillery:

> The cannoneers went off with their guns as expeditiously as the roads would admit, even till they became a column of cannon … and had it not been for the extraordinary bravery of the Chamborant [2e] regiment of hussars (which, when complete, is about five hundred men) all the cannon of the army would have fallen into the enemy's hands.[55]

Nevertheless, breaking contact with the pursuit, Dumouriez managed to establish his camp northwest of Sainte-Menehould, at Dommartin-sous-Hans, near the village of Valmy.

Meanwhile the émigré troops remained to the east of the Argonne; indeed, the vanguard that had reached La Croix-aux-Bois was sent back. Contades, in the Monsieur Brigade, recalled arriving there but, 'After having

52 Despite Dumouriez himself confirming the émigré attack (François Barrière (ed.), *Mémoires du Général Dumouriez* (Paris: Firmin Didot Frères, 1848), p.277); some historians (Arthur Chuquet, *Campagne de l'Argonne (1792)* (Paris: Librairie Léopold Cerf, 1886), p.91 followed by Lapierre, *émigrés en Argonne*, p.54) have sought to deny this, apparently ignorant of their formations.

53 Montlosier, *Souvenirs*, p.103.

54 Quoted in Money, *Campaign of 1792*, p.76.

55 Money, *Campaign of 1792*, p.77.

waited some time on the main road, we fell back to Authe'.[56] The Hussards de Bercheny arrived on 15 September but withdrew to Buzancy.[57] The same day, Espinchal, of the Coalition d'Auvergne, was with part of the main column:

> The weather is fairly fine ...We are on the march at midday, all for the same point by the high road that leads from Verdun to Dun[-sur-Meuse], where the headquarters of our Princes will be. A short league before arriving there, we halt at the village of Ligny-sous-Dun [Liny-devant-Dun], a large place where the brigade is lodged and under cover entirely, men and horses.[58]

It is there that they learned of the success at La Croix-aux-Bois. The following day was also fine, a rarity that year. At 2:00 p.m., the brigade was on the march again, but had difficulty crossing the river at Dun-sur-Meuse as the road and bridge were obstructed by the train of the Princes' headquarters. That night, the brigade arrived at the village of Nouart, east of Buzancy, but there was little arrangement when it came to its quartering.

Orders were received to move on to Vouziers, so the troops were on the march at 6:00 a.m. on 17 September. However, after passing through Buzancy, they were halted in the plain west of the town as the Austrians still occupied the area around Vouziers, so the Princes established their headquarters at Buzancy. Espinchal was quartered at the village of Briquenay, which was almost empty as the inhabitants had fled pillaging by French and Prussian troops. The villagers slowly returned, although interactions with the émigrés were strained as they supported the revolution.

The Princes' corps had now joined up with the émigré vanguard, which had remained around Buzancy, Espinchal's entry for 19 September began: 'Fine weather all day... After the precise orders that we received the previous evening, the brigade is mounted at three o'clock in the morning and we are on the march for Vouziers. We cross the wood of La Croix where the combat of the 15th took place. We still see all the abattis made by the patriots'.[59]

The march may have been preceded, as far as Vouziers, by the Hussards de Bercheny, as Grouvel suggests that they marched there on 18 September but halted, presumably waiting for the rest of the vanguard to catch up.[60] Contades, in the Monsieur Brigade, marched from Authe on 19 September:

> To arrive in time, we had to leave Authe well before day. We had a halt of three hours, and we set off on the march to arrive at Saint-Souplet. Unfortunately, our advance guard took the guide with it and, the night becoming very dark, we lost sight of them. We found ourselves lost in the immense plains of Champagne and very near a camp of six thousand patriots. M. de Jaucourt had the column halted, recommended silence, sent hussars to reconnoitre the countryside and attempt

56 Gérard de Contades (ed.), *Coblenz et Quiberon Souvenirs du Comte de Contades* (Paris: E. Dentu, 1885), p.60.

57 Grouvel, *Troupes de l'émigration*, vol.III, p.279.

58 Champflour (ed.), *Coalition d'Auvergne*, p.182.

59 Champflour (ed.), *Coalition d'Auvergne*, p.187.

60 Grouvel, *Troupes de l'émigration*, vol.III, p.279.

> to find a guide. After having waited a very long time, an adjutant of Bercheny brought one, who he had taken by force in a village.[61]

Arriving at Saint-Souplet-sur-Py, they found it still contained a post of patriots, the hussars fell upon them with the flats of their sabres and the revolutionaries fled, discarding their muskets in doing so.

Once the main émigré column had reached Vouziers, there were delays as units waited to cross the Aisne by the single bridge. Espinchal's company, after several hours, finally received the order to cross at 11:00 a.m.. Once over the river, the company reached a plain: 'All the corps arrive here successively and each takes the rank indicated by the order of battle. We make a halt here that lasts all day. Our baggage trains having crossed Vouziers, place themselves in our rears; the generals assuring us that according to all the probabilities we are at the moment of an action'.[62]

Cacqueray, with the Escadron de la Marine, was in the reserve at the rear of this march:

> Having arrived at the Aisne bridge near Vouziers, we found there the Princes and maréchal de Castries who made new dispositions. All the corps that arrived in succession were ordered to make a halt in the fields on the other side of Vouziers to await new instructions ... At three o'clock, the Princes left Vouziers and, in passing through the middle of the army, they even gave us with a very energetic spirit, the hope of soon seeing the patriots up close. At 4 o'clock, the army set off on the march in two columns.[63]

The right-hand column – Gardes du Roi and des Princes, Colonel-général Brigade (that included the Coalition d'Auvergne) and the Régiment de Royal-Allemand – marched along the road while the left marched across the plain. The latter consisted of, in order, the 2ème Compagnie noble d'ordonnance (Mousquetaires), Hommes d'armes à cheval (Gendarmerie), the Carabiniers Brigade and finally the Escadron de la Marine.

In the right-hand column, Espinchal wrote:

> ... we march exactly in order observing, as was prescribed, the greatest silence. It is not known where one is going. At midnight, in the blackest night and after having crossed quite smartly seven to eight leagues of the Champagne Pouilleuse plain, we all halted at the village of Sainte-Marie-à-Py, where despite the darkness, we were placed in line behind the corps that had already arrived; we dismount and bivouac all night. Fires are lit on all sides ...[64]

At about midnight, the columns united and halted at Sainte-Marie-à-Py, about three kilometres east of the vanguard at Saint-Souplet-sur-Py. There, everyone, including the Princes, snatched some sleep on the ground.

---

61 Contades, *Coblenz et Quiberon*, p.62.

62 Champflour (ed.), *Coalition d'Auvergne*, p.188.

63 Cacqueray, *Mémoires inédits*, p.64.

64 Champflour (ed.), *Coalition d'Auvergne*, p.189.

The Battle of Valmy, 20 September 1792, by Horace Vernet. (Public domain)

Meanwhile, an attack on 17 September to secure the gorge of Les Islettes for the coalition forces failed. This meant that Dumouriez's position at Dommartin-sous-Hans was secure, and the following day, 18 September, Kellermann joined him there, just to the north of the direct road from Verdun. So, the mass of the French forces was to the south of that of the émigrés at Sainte-Marie-à-Py. That night, 19/20 September, the émigré vanguard, after bivouacking for four hours at Saint-Souplet-sur-Py, shifted south to Somme-Suippe, where, as Contades explains, 'We threw ourselves on straw, impatiently awaiting the day that was going to decide the fate of France and of us.'[65]

The Battle of Valmy

At dawn, 20 September, the day of the Battle of Valmy, the main body of the émigré cavalry resumed its march on Suippes in a light cold rain.[66] The vanguard was about four and half kilometres away at Somme-Suippe, where the Princes took breakfast with the Marquis de Jaucourt. The Armée Royale was north of the French positions, which could easily be turned and isolated, but, without other orders, it seemed that it had been placed there to prevent French troops coming from Châlons.

Given the movements that had taken place, instead of barring the way to the capital, the troops of Kellermann and Dumouriez faced west, towards Paris.

65 Contades, *Coblenz et Quiberon*, p.63.

66 Today Suippes is the site of one of the French army's main training camps.

Kellermann's position was foremost in the form of an arc, a windmill marking his centre, on the ridge just to the west of Valmy, with Dumouriez behind across the Verdun-Châlons road west of Sainte-Menehould. The fighting began about 7:00 a.m. when a regiment of Prussian hussars, taking advantage of the fog, surprised the 1er Dragons still in bivouac, in front of the mill, before withdrawing. At 9:00 a.m., two 12-pounder batteries were deployed on the ridge at the most advanced point of the French defensive line and, as the fog began to dissipate, began to fire on the advancing Prussian troops who were gradually revealed. Brunswick, who has been criticised for having wasted time before attempting to seize the passes of the Argonne, now did not wait for Clerfayt's Austrians, who could not arrive before dawn on 21 September. It is for this reason that Dumouriez, for one, did not expect the main attack. Hearing the cannonade, which intensified by 10:00 a.m., he went forward to discover that while the Prussians sought to break through to the north to reach Braux-Sainte-Cohière, in the plain immediately east of Valmy, Kellermann had left the southern flank quite exposed. He thus brought up the reserve of the Armée de la Meuse to Braux while securing the road to Sainte-Menehould with cavalry. Dumouriez was astonished by the scale of the cannonade, which, from 11:00 a.m., set the battlefield ablaze, the smoke partly masking the view, while the Prussians massed on the heights opposite the mill.

When the cannonade ceased, Kellermann had to retreat, abandoning the Valmy hill to fall back on Dumouriez, and this retrograde movement led the Prussian infantry to move forward a second time. However, their artillery, often firing at the limit of their range, was unable to support this offensive movement, which stopped in front of the French troops. The French army, seeing the enemy immobile again and waiting for the order to launch an assault, let out an immense clamour with shouts of 'Vive la nation!' Brunswick, however, broke off the action. Despite all the noise and expenditure of ammunition, the two armies are estimated to have expended 20,000 rounds in the cannonade, the French suffered no more than 300 killed and wounded, and the Prussians even fewer.[67]

It is certain that the health and, therefore, operational effectiveness of the Prussian army weighed heavily on Brunswick's decision. It had, since the siege of Longwy, been suffering from the consequences of its negligence, with the military hospital already full of victims of dysentery. Soldiers, ill-prepared for the rain and cold that they encountered, had died of disease, exposure or exhaustion during the march from Longwy to Verdun. With barely any food, they lived on what little the country had to offer; after pillaging the houses, the Prussians could only feed on unripe grapes and potatoes with any fat they could find, even candles. One émigré described the situation at Grandpré, now occupied by the Prussians, which, '… was no longer a camp, it became a cemetery. There was barely time to bury the dead there. Even in the cesspools men died. They were left there.'[68] The army was encumbered by a convoy of carts serving as ambulances.

---

67 Money, *Campaign of 1792*, p.90, he estimated the French had 250 killed and wounded and the Prussians perhaps 300 to 400.

68 Montlosier, *Souvenirs*, p.112.

The émigrés were in the Champagne Pouilleuse, the 'countryside [had] the saddest appearance in this season when the land is completely bare. As far as the eye can see, only fields and not a single bush.'[69] Such country favoured the deployment of this formidable cavalry force, numbering more than 5,000 horses. However, after remaining inactive all day on 20 September, they were then dispersed in cantonments late in the afternoon. The main body remained between Somme-Suippe and Suippes, the vanguard was at La Croix-en-Champagne, and the Marquis d'Autichamp had been sent, with 400 Hommes d'armes à cheval (Gendarmes) and 100 hussars, to Auve to monitor the high road between Châlons and Sainte-Menehould.

The two armies were now camped, immobile but facing each other out of cannon range. The advantage Brunswick had gained by forcing Kellermann back and seizing the Châlons to Sainte-Menehould road had come to nothing because the initiative was now lost. The French cavalry secured the supply routes, not only from Châlons but also from Vitry-le-François and Bar-le-Duc, further to the south. The French were now well provided for, while, as Money writes: 'We were soon informed by deserters, of the distressed situation of the enemy, that they were without bread, that the men were obliged to eat the horses killed in the cannonade, that they had eaten all the poor peasants cows and hogs in the country, and were dying fast of the dysentery.'[70]

Although Brunswick had the Prussian position strengthened with entrenchments, his situation only worsened after another attack on Les Islettes by the Hessians failed on 22 September. He was reduced to opening negotiations with the new regime in Paris through Dumouriez. However, the longer these lasted, 'Every day the Prussian army diminished, it melted away so to speak and had no means of making amends.'[71]

The coalition army was always only fit for its task if it was immediately joined by counter-revolutionary supporters. This had not happened, and now, faced by a population that might rise up to expel the invaders, it was clearly inadequate. With the prospect of an upcoming retreat, the Prussians sought to isolate their allies. The Austrians wanted to withdraw to the Netherlands to forestall expected French offensives. The situation for the émigrés became more dangerous. They were excluded from the exchange of prisoners that was negotiated with the Convention, a negotiation that served as a cover for other, more important matters, as new measures were being taken by the French regime to execute any captured émigré. In time, the Duke of Brunswick would be suspected of having negotiated shameful terms to ensure that the Prussian army would not be pursued in its retreat, a retreat that would nevertheless turn into a humiliating rout.

Excluded from these negotiations, as they had been from the strategic decisions of the commander-in-chief since the beginning of the campaign, the émigrés were eager for action. On 21 September all the émigré cavalry deployed according to the order of battle:

69 Cacqueray, *Mémoires inédits*, p.65.
70 Money, *Campaign of 1792*, p.90.
71 Montlosier, *Souvenirs*, p.112.

> We are formed in two columns, first by companies, then by squadrons. These movements are made with as much precision as one could expect from troops who only had very little training. It is in this order that we advance across the plain. The weather is getting fine, and makes us enjoy a spectacle that I will never forget in my life, the sight of 36 to 40 squadrons, forming a corps of about 5,000 cavalrymen, almost entirely composed of the élite of the French nobility and almost all the great seigneurs of the Kingdom, having at their head four sons or grandsons of France. These squadrons march in the best order, and mounted as no cavalry has ever been … in the belief that the patriots attacked by the Prussians on one side, and on the other by the Austrians, the noble cavalry was only placed in this plain to cut them off in their retreat, or pursue them in their flight. The order to fold the coats was given. The white plume floats on all heads, and the white cockade adorns all headdresses, everyone is decorated with his white sash.[72]

No one knew that *maréchal* de Castries had proposed to charge the French batteries at the head of the émigré cavalry, but this had been rebuffed by the Frederick William, on the grounds that the French nobility was too precious to be exposed in that way. Unaware of the real state of the Prussian army, the émigrés could imagine that Brunswick was reorganising his forces for a decisive attack supported by Clerfayt. In reality, the latter's bid to attack alone had just been refused.

By 21 September, the émigrés occupied La Croix-en-Champagne while the Prussians were now installed at the camp at Hans, previously occupied by Kellermann. Hohenlohe-Kirchberg was to the north of the Prussians while Clerfayt had replaced the patriots at Valmy. Dumouriez had withdrawn his army towards Les Islettes. On 23 September, an incessant to-and-fro of officers began between the camps of the Prussians and the patriots and one of Dumouriez's aides-de-camp was seen at Brunswick's headquarters.

Separated from the main troop concentration, the émigrés were at first a little better off than the Prussians. They were mostly cavalry, so they could scour the countryside in search of food and fodder and send detachments to thresh grain and, under a strong escort, have it ground at a mill. Much of the infantry was attached to the Princes' headquarters, so they managed to find shelter from the bad weather, delaying the onset of dysentery. Some of the cavalry at Somme-Tourbe, which had been devastated by the Prussians, was dispersed. On 24 September, the Escadron de la Marine and the Colonel-général Brigade went to the adjacent village of Saint-Jean-sur-Tourbe, as it was in a better condition. The Régiment de Berwick, at least, remained at Somme-Tourbe, and was there on 28 September when it had 458 soldiers present under arms, out of a total strength of 73 officers and 616 soldiers, along with 38 domestics, 43 horses, 36 carters and 87 train horses.[73]

On 20 September, the day of the Battle of Valmy, the émigré troops left before Thionville under the command of *maréchal* de Broglie had set off to join the Princes' corps. Their stay, soaked by the rain and largely inactive, had been far from comfortable, Chateaubriand recalled:

72 Champflour (ed.), *La coalition d'Auvergne*, pp.192–193.

73 Grouvel, *Troupes de l'émigration*, vol.III, p.135.

> The siege continued, or rather there was no siege, as the trench was not opened and troops were lacking to regularly invest the place ... Our few resources were exhausted; Paris seemed further away. The bad weather did not cease; we were inundated in the middle of our works; I woke up sometimes in a ditch with water up to my neck: the next day I was stiff.[74]

Olivier d'Argens, also in the Coalition de Bretagne's infantry, reached Rouvres-en-Woëvre, two kilometres east of Etain, on 23 September, to await further orders. On the march, it had been announced that the Prussians had gained a great victory over the patriots in the Argonne passes.[75]

According to Grouvel, it was during this march that the Comte de Ruays, an officer of the Chasseurs royaux des Princes, who was therefore in the vanguard of these reinforcements, was taken prisoner.[76] Without an act of condemnation against him, it can be assumed that he was simply killed. The German Régiment de Wittgenstein, responsible for securing the rear of the march, reached Etain on 24 September. There was now a rumour that Custine, at the head of a French army, was on the march to attack the émigrés, so the infantry of the Corps de la Marine that had already left Etain for Verdun, 'received the order to retrace its steps.'[77]

The 1ère compagnie noble d'ordonnance marching ahead of the émigré infantry met resistance from the inhabitants of the village of Voncq, 11 kilometres north of Vouziers. The municipality had been summoned twice to provide it with bread and fodder, and the Comte de Sémallé ordered a reaction:

> It is I who, upon the refusal of the inhabitants of Voncq-en-Ardennes to deliver the necessary provisions to us, gave the order to occupy by full force. This large bourg was turned, while M. de Chambrun, who commanded a brigade of chevau-légers and gendarmes, advanced in a straight line. The inhabitants did not perceive the movement we were making to take them from behind. They had poorly barricaded the roads, with carts and farming tools. A representative of the people, living in this bourg, had convinced the population to resist, then had fled through the vineyards, abandoning the defenders. His house was set on fire, and as all the others were made of wood, and the harvests had just been brought in, everything was consumed, the fire lit up the night for two leagues around. It seems that some inhabitants, who had shut themselves in the barns to shoot at us, were in part burned or asphyxiated by the smoke; the others, to escape the flames, threw themselves into the vineyards with their wives and children. I nearly perished in this affair. My mare, hit by a bullet in the mane, reared up and threw me off just as the gable of a barn fell on the square. I was not injured; my mare, surrounded by fire on all sides, remained trembling without moving, until I was able to get back in the saddle.[78]

---

74 Chateaubriand, *Mémoires*, vol.III, pp.97–98.
75 Anon. (ed.), *Olivier d'Argens*, p.24.
76 Grouvel, *Troupes de l'émigration*, vol.III, p.152.
77 Anon. (ed.), *Olivier d'Argens*, p.25.
78 Jean-Réné-Pierre de Sémallé, *Souvenirs du comte de Sémallé, page de Louis XVI* (Paris: Alphonse Picard et fils, 1898), pp.40–41.

The historian Arthur Chuquet wrote that in retaliation for shots that allegedly killed an émigré and two horses:

> Two hundred out of three hundred houses were reduced to ashes. The attackers immediately went towards the houses of the main notables ... They forbade the peasants from taking the horses out of the stables. They prevented a mother from saving her three children who perished in the flames. The house of the member of the Convention Robert was made of cut stone and did not burn quickly enough; they forced the family's old nurse to carry straw to the attic. Eighteen inhabitants of Voncq were tied up and led to Vouziers.[79]

The company continued to Vouziers, reaching it on 24 September, before going on to Sommepy-Tahure where it remained for a week without orders.

The invaders now faced increasing defiance from the local population and, on 27 September when the Breton battalion was at Haudainville, just south of Verdun, '... a part of the Armagnac brigade ... was sent with a detachment of Prussians to collect food and forage from the patriot bourg of Dieu [Dieue-sur-Meuse], that had refused.'[80]

Meanwhile, on the Champagne plain, the émigrés convinced themselves that a new attack was imminent. On 27 September, there was a staff meeting that the Princes had been invited to, at which it seemed that Brunswick's opposition had finally been overcome. Dumouriez had built new redoubts at Gizaucourt, south of Valmy, but it was learned that they were not yet palisaded, so Clerfayt proposed to attack them with his troops supported by the émigrés. In addition, Brunswick published a new manifesto that he had addressed to Dumouriez. Furious, the latter suspended the armistice and declared hostilities resumed. On 28 September, orders were given for the coalition forces to prepare for battle. Nevertheless, these aggressive displays ran counter to other developments, as Goethe observed, 'one already perceived some signs of understanding and accommodation; for example, the postmaster of Sainte-Menehould had been exchanged for the people of the King's entourage, taken on 20 September between the carts and the army.'[81]

The anticipation of action was shattered when, on 29 September, it was learned that the army was to retreat. The Prussians broke camp at the end of the day and, once evening came, the baggage convoy set off, followed by the rest of the army after midnight. The decision could be considered a deliverance from the weather and the difficulties encountered in finding supplies. Once in the Netherlands, the members of the coalition could rebuild their forces, and optimists even anticipated a new campaign. No one imagined the fate that awaited the émigrés.

---

79 Chuquet, *La campagne de l'Argonne (1792)*, p.489.

80 Anon. (ed.), *Olivier d'Argens*, p.25.

81 Goethe, *Campagne de France*, p.57.

The Armée de Condé, Arms at the Ready, Behind the Rhine.

Capitaine Romain of the artillery, listed the elements in the Armée de Condé at the end of July 1792 when it was on the point of leaving Bingen:

> 1. The Légion de Mirabeau, fifteen hundred men strong, of infantry and cavalry, commanded by the Vicomte de Mirabeau.
> 2. The infantry Régiment de Rohan, raised by the Cardinal, commanded by Prince Louis de Rohan, that amounts to four hundred men.
> 3. Two Régiments d'Hohenlohe that are few in numbers, forming together six hundred men; they were raised and are commanded by two princes of this name.
> 4. A company of non-commissioned officers all émigrés, who serve to guard the headquarters: it is of about a hundred men.
> 5. A regiment of noble infantry, composed of twenty-four companies, making fourteen hundred men.
> 6. Two artillery companies [since May], formed of officers and pupils of this corps, having attached some workmen, and pontonniers [bridge makers] de Strasbourg, who made it their duty to follow their officers.
> 7. Five squadrons of noble cavalry, making six hundred horse.
> 8. The Régiment des chevaliers de la Couronne, an élite corps composed in great part of individual émigrés who did not adhere to the order of nobility; they amount to three hundred.
> 9. A squadron of the Régiment de Dauphin, cavalry, of which the troopers came away almost en masse with their officers.
> 10. The Régiment des Hussards de Salm, raised by the Prince de Salm-Kirbourg, having two hundred horse.
> 11. About fifty troopers of the Provost.
>
> In total: three thousand five hundred infantrymen, fifteen hundred cavalry, and two hundred of artillery.[82]

With the addition of the staff and other services, the total would be close to 5,500 men.

The period between 21 and 31 July was spent in arranging the logistics for the marches of the royalist troops. The Prince de Condé was unhappy about how the funds for the armies were distributed: 'those that were given to my son [the Duc de Bourbon] and I were almost nil … we all separated on 1 August, my son left for Liège that day, I for Flonheim [northwest of Worms] with my troops, and the Princes left on the 2nd for Simeren [Simmern, on the road to Trier].'[83]

On 1 August, the Armée de Condé was attached to the corps commanded by *Feldmarschalleutnant* Esterházy de Galántha, and the Prince moved south from Flonheim towards the Breisgau. On 6 August, at the request of *Feldzeugmeister* Hohenlohe-Kirchberg, he established himself at Neustadt,

82 Romain, *Souvenirs*, vol.II, pp.254–255. The vicomte de Mirabeau dying on 15 September 1792 it can be ascertained that this was copied between the end of July and early September that year.

83 Condé, *Journal*, p.304.

bringing his troops closer to the French border. In the first days of August, the Prince planned to seize the nearby stronghold of Landau, knowing that some of the troops there, including the Swiss Régiment de Steiner, were ready to defect. A Madame de Sartory travelled there incognito and met officers in the garrison who agreed to hand the place over, the only condition being that it was to be to the Prince de Condé and the Austrians should not be present.

Condé informed Hohenlohe-Kirchberg of these arrangements and ordered Mirabeau to join him with his legion before Landau. The Mirabeaus marched on 2 August 1792, crossed Heilbronn (Baden-Württemberg), then headed for Speyer before turning south to reach Philippsburg, where they hoped to link up with the Austrians under Hohenlohe-Kirchberg. However, when they arrived there, on 5 August, Hohenlohe had already left. On 3 August, the latter's vanguard arrived before Landau and his troops had the best of an encounter with the Republicans, who lost 100 men killed and 30 captured, as well as a standard. In response, elements of the enemy forces withdrew to the heights of Wissembourg, behind the Lauter, while *lieutenant général* Custine, who commanded the southern element, entered Landau, raising the strength of the garrison from 3,500 men to 7,000 or 8,000. For Condé, the opportunity to seize Landau by surprise was lost.

After camping for a day and a half, the Mirabeaus crossed the Rhine on 7 August, via the pontoon bridge at Philippsburg, and joined the Armée de Condé the same day. It was attached to the vanguard, commanded by Vioménil, as one of the legion's officers wrote:

> One can say, to the glory of the legion, that, in the difficult march that we had just made, the soldiers not having received pay, having often lacked bread, the officers not having had their salaries for three months, not a single complaint was heard, there was not a single deserter. The princes could not pay us the arrears; we were granted thirty sous per day which were soon reduced to twenty. At least there was with that enough to not die of hunger![84]

Hohenlohe-Kirchberg is sometimes criticised for failing to support Condé, but there is no indication of this in the Prince's correspondence, indeed, on 11 August, Condé informed his son:

> We have just been told that the Duke of Brunswick had delayed his entry until the fifteenth, and that the Princes would not enter until seven days after him; I do not know if that is true. It seemed to me that the Prince of Hohenlohe bore with some impatience being at his orders; if he had been the master, we would have entered by lower Alsace, and his fingers were itching to go and attack Biron and Kellermann, retired behind the lines of the Lauter after having abandoned without reason that of the Queich; but he claimed that the Duke was pressing him to go to the Saar, and consequently withdrew himself from Heidelsheim to Neustadt, where however he is still, but from where he must leave tomorrow or the day after tomorrow.[85]

---

84 Nieüil (ed.), *Toustain*, p.13.

85 Crétineau-Joly, *princes de Condé*, vol.I, p.72, Condé to Bourbon.

The Duke of Brunswick, concentrating his forces on the Saar and the Ardennes, required Hohenlohe's 18,000 men to enter France. Unable to act against Landau alone, on 9 August Condé crossed the Rhine at Speyer with his cavalry, the infantry and baggage followed the next day. That day, he wrote to Artois describing the difficulties he faced.[86] In the first place, Esterházy had tasked him with monitoring the Rhine from Philippsburg to Kehl (opposite Strasbourg), more than 60 kilometres with less than 5,000 combatants, to which he had replied that he could at most monitor the 40 kilometres, from opposite Fort-Louis to Kehl. Moreover, Esterházy informed him that he would be supplied with bread and fodder for up to 5,000 men, and his only remaining funds were 26,000 livres, barely enough for the transport and vehicles of his baggage. On 11 August, Condé wrote again to Bourbon, from Blankenloch, 10 kilometres north of Karlsruhe:

> We managed, not without difficulty, to cross the Rhine at Speyer. It took two days, the Nobility is well and is marching wonderfully; never a straggler. We quit the sight of Landau with some regret, but not the smallest murmur, not the smallest cooling in the zeal that you know. We are in full march, without tents, without cannons, without money, and that is fine. Tomorrow we will be at Etlingen, the day after tomorrow at Kuppenheim [six kilometres southeast of Rastatt]; I have received news from the Prince of Esterházy … We take, starting today, bread and fodder from the Austrians … The Régiments d'Hohenlohe have joined me, they have about five hundred men between them, which makes, with the Legion, about four thousand five hundred.[87]

The numbers given by the Prince are of the combat units. The army continued to be joined by more émigrés and volunteers, including several officers who had fled Landau. The arrival of the two regiments of Hohenlohe-Bartenstein and Hohenlohe-Schillingsfurst, the two sons of the Prince of Hohenlohe-Waldenburg, led to the definitive organisation of the Armée de Condé (see Appendix 6).

After marching through Ettlingen and Rastatt, on 15 August the Prince established his headquarters at Bühl, behind but in the centre of the front facing the Rhine between Strasbourg and Fort-Louis. It was there, the following day, that the news of the assault on the Tuileries and the massacre of the Swiss and the last defenders of the throne on 10 August arrived. Without other activity, it was very difficult to prevent hotheads such as the Mirabeaus from responding to provocation from the Sans-Culottes, as the Prince de Condé confided to his son:

> Although I have forbidden my posts to fire first, these gentlemen have not done the same. They snipe at us, so we must return the fire; two of Mirabeau's chasseurs killed two officers the day before yesterday; they had one wounded yesterday. All this is useless, and I would like to prevent it; but how to persuade people who have a musket to let themselves be shot at without doing anything?[88]

86 Condé, *Journal*, pp.307–309.

87 Crétineau-Joly, *princes de Condé*, vol.II, p.71.

88 Crétineau-Joly, *princes de Condé*, vol.II, p.74, letter of 14 August 1792.

Mirabeau had his band play *Ça ira* and *On va leur percer le flanc* on the dyke opposite Fort-Louis and the antagonised revolutionaries responded with artillery, wounding an officer and, the following day, killing a local villager. It was estimated that the patriots fired more than 500 musket and 200 cannon shots in five days. Mirabeau continued to show a lack of restraint, for example, raiding the village of Neuhaeusel, just north of Fort-Louis, on 17 August:

> Mirabeau did an escapade for which I removed him from the command of his post and placed him under arrest, from which I only had him released today [24 August]. Imagine that, against my orders, he crossed the Rhine one night with fifty men, killed two sentries and brought back seven prisoners, without having fired a musket shot. One cannot help but say that this is vigorous and that it proves how these people guard themselves; but I punished him none the less, as I ought, for his lack of subordination. He is a brave man, but a very dangerous head.[89]

It is clear that Condé had little idea of the wider operations and was reduced to guessing what might happen based on the orders he received. At the end of August, he wrote:

> As for us, I really believe that we will not be long without making some movements, and I am charged with having all the boats removed from all the places that I guard on the banks of the Rhine. ... what is being asked of me is not very easy, given that the Nationals are shooting at them like the devil and the boatmen are afraid ... The appearance of some of these boats caused the general alarm to beat in their camp, the night before last; they only shoot out of fear ... The day before yesterday they were still firing a lot of cannon on the Legion which serves wonderfully and which is all the less upset because the shots go over and never hit anyone.[90]

Finally, on 5 September, the Armée de Condé received the order to move south to be opposite Strasbourg, and there was talk of crossing the Rhine with the Austrians.[91] The Légion de Mirabeau received a terrible blow when, on 15 September, after eight days of fever, the vicomte died of an apoplexy at Freiburg. Condé, in a letter the next day, wrote, 'We mourn with all our soul and we will bury the unfortunate Vicomte de Mirabeau tomorrow.'[92] Esterházy wished to honour him by having Austrian troops in the ceremony: 'proof of the particular esteem in which he held the Vicomte de Mirabeau. All our [legion's] officers went to Freiburg to attend the procession. Four grenadiers of the legion and 400 Austrians [four companies of Nr.7 (Schröder) Regiment] with four pieces of cannon accompanied it. Prince Esterházy and the Prince de Condé were at the ceremony.'[93]

---

89 Crétineau-Joly, *princes de Condé*, vol.II, pp.75–76, Bühl, 31 August 1792.

90 Crétineau-Joly, *princes de Condé*, vol.II, pp.54–55.

91 Romain, *Souvenirs*, vol.II, p.243.

92 Père Sommervogel, *Une correspondance pendant l'émigration 1792-1797* (Paris: Charles Douniol, Libraire-éditeur, 1867), p.13. The letter was written from Bad Krozingen (given as Grötzingen).

93 Nieüil (ed.), *Toustain*, pp.16–17.

Mirabeau's men were permitted to have his heart, enclosed in a small lead box, attached to the infantry flag, carried by the volunteer battalion.

The months of August and September were spent watching the banks of the Rhine but the duty also made the troops accustomed to military service as one of the noble volunteers summed up, 'The campaign was reduced to making marches, taking up positions, making counter-marches, ensuring against surprises and traps. The French troops that were to be found in Alsace were more numerous than the Condé corps.'[94] Then the Armée de Condé was sent even further south, towards Basel, where, again, there was a suggestion of crossing the Rhine. It was here that the Condéens learned that the Armée du Centre, the bearer of all hopes, was in Champagne, a few days from Paris, and so they supposed that the liberation of the royal family was imminent.

Retreat and the Disbanding of the Armée Royale

The retreat of the Armée Royale began at dawn on 30 September, although the Armagnac brigade, which had been at Haudainville since 27 September, remained there until 4 October. The first night, 30 September/1 October, was exceptionally mild, but then, two days later, the rain and wind returned. After halting at the village of Aure, the columns of cavalry and carriages met at Blaise, west of Vouziers, to march towards Stenay. Although Clerfayt's army marched in parallel, alerts multiplied. The Comte d'Espinchal wrote: 'one runs risks going to the neighbouring villages [of Mars-sous-Bourcq, just west of Blaise] where the patriots come to forage … We learn that in recent days, several émigrés, including some serving in the gardes du corps, having had the imprudence to halt in villages to buy food, were seized by armed patriots and handed over.'[95]

That same day, 4 October, Cacqueray was designated with his squad to go ahead to prepare accommodation and fodder for the escadron de la Marine, which was marching with the Princes and had set off at 5:00 a.m. in the morning. A guide led him to:

> Le Chêne le Pouilleux … I took another guide there to take us to Oteh [Oches], our destination. Half a league from Chêne le Pouilleux, we encountered M. Archambaud de Périgord, aide-de-camp to the Comte d'Artois, he warned me that 600 patriots were lying in ambush in a wood; he was going to report it to the Princes and advised me to halt and await their orders.[96]

After some hesitation, Cacqueray decided to continue but avoid the threat by leaving the main road to reach Sy where the Princes' headquarters were to be. When he reached Oches, he saw his squadron, having taken a shortcut, was going to enter at the same time. The inhabitants of the village preceding Oches fled into the woods while a shot was fired towards the

94 B.P., *Récit*, p.65.

95 Champflour (ed.), *La coalition d'Auvergne*, pp.211–212.

96 Cacqueray, *Mémoires inédits*, p.69.

squadron. However, reassured by the émigrés, the inhabitants of Oches, who had at first taken them for Prussians who had pillaged and molested them, returned, and the Royal-Allemand established themselves in the neighbouring village. Early in the evening, the squadron of the Auvergne coalition (the second squadron in the Colonel-général brigade) also arrived around the castle of Sy. 'After having crossed the Vouziers bridge,' it had taken lanes through the village of Chêne-le-Pouilleux before reaching the main road again.[97] When the brigade reached Tannay, just west of Sy, it was learned that a group of local armed patriots, reinforced by a detachment from the Sedan garrison, were in the surrounding woods. Monsieur de Caraman asked *maréchal* de Broglie:

> for the help of a few infantry, with authorisation to search the wood, jointly with the Commissaire-général brigade which is near us, in view of the woods and the patriots' fires. But maréchal de Broglie refused the attack of the woods; he nevertheless sent the company of gentlemen chasseurs formed by the active efforts of the Comte Charles de Rohault [Rouault]. They arrived with us with the best will, they were placed with our picket, but they only had very few cartridges and many lacked carbines. A dozen were found in the brigade and they were lent to them.[98]

On 5 October, the column of La Marine and Royal-Allemand mounted at dawn and headed east for Stonne. Arriving there, they found the Hommes d'armes à cheval had fallen back to the village, having received reports that patriots were again lying in ambush in the woods at the foot of the road descending from this town and leading to Stenay. Cacqueray recalled:

> We all formed up in battle formation, in the fields, on the sides of the road, awaiting orders from maréchal de Broglie. Shortly after our arrival, we heard a dozen cannon shots and a some discharges of musketry; we learned almost immediately that it was a body of patriots, established with three pieces of cannon, in a wood near the headquarters [at the castle of Sy], who were firing on the Colonel Général Brigade and on the column of the Gardes du Corps which was marching on the main road … the Brigade irlandaise and the hussars were made to enter the woods, which forced them to leave their posts. They only killed three horses of the Gardes du Corps and there was no one wounded. During this cannonade, we were in battle lines with the Gendarmerie and Royal-Allemand near Ston [Stonne], in the plain which is at the bottom of this village, we heard a fairly lively fusillade, and on a height opposite us, a body of patriots who observed us. Maréchal de Broglie, for what reason I do not know, did not want to have it attacked by the Brigade irlandaise and some cavalry corps; it would have been very easy to surround them and seize their cannons. One contented oneself to have the woods in front of the army searched by the hussars and some detachments of infantry; many nationals and peasants who had joined them were killed and taken. The hussars, with a light heart, set fire to three fine villages. This useless, and even impolitic, barbarity

97 Champflour (ed.), *La coalition d'Auvergne*, pp.213.
98 Champflour (ed.), *La coalition d'Auvergne*, pp.214–215.

> was generally disapproved of in the army. Moreover, this was the first and last time that we found ourselves in the presence of the enemy in this ridiculous and disastrous campaign.[99]

Another account of this encounter reads:

> On the fourth day, the French princes slept at the castle of Scy [Sy], on the Sedan to Le Chêne le Pouilleux road. The garrison of the city, which was said to number six thousand men, came at night to seize them, which was all the easier since this castle was only guarded by a small detachment of Royal-Allemand [in the rearguard of the Marquis de Jaucourt]. The garrison had been followed by the national guards of the neighbouring villages. They had four pieces of cannon which were put in battery 150 paces from the castle where the princes were, before the arrival of the émigrés. An entire rank of horses of the gardes du corps was killed at point-blank range, without those who were riding them being killed. At that moment, the forest was surrounded by the maison du Roi who took many prisoners. An aide-de-camp of the Marquis d'Autichamp, named the Chevalier de La Porte, from Bordeaux, having been killed by one of these wretches, whose life he had just saved, all those who, following the example of this brave patriot, wished to pick up their muskets after surrendering were cut down. Ninety-two of them were killed, and the commander who was a forge master was taken … This was the only affair during the retreat.[100]

The Princes' column, reunited, passed through Stonne on 5 October and crossed the Meuse at Stenay in the afternoon. Headquarters were established there, and the troops dispersed in the surrounding villages, where they lingered until 9 October. Meanwhile, the infantry that had originally been left at Thionville remained around Verdun. Also, on 5 October, the Armagnac brigade moved to Mogeville, north of the Etain-Verdun road, and in the absence of any orders, stayed there until 10 October when it retreated to Foameix-Ornel, northwest of Etain.

On 8 October, the Régiment de Wittgenstein set off on the march from Etain to Longwy, where the Prussians still maintained a garrison, and its *colonel*, the Comte d'Erlach, had 'weapons loaded to defend against brigandage … and placed 50 men to escort the vehicles with the order to fire on their allies if they approached.'[101] Although forced to protect themselves from the Prussians, the émigrés could rely on the Austrians and Clerfayt's army, having taken the direct route from Vouziers to Stenay, covered their retreat. Republican cavalry clashed with the Austrian infantry in the forests around Montmédy.

Two of the escadron de la Marine, *lieutenants de vaisseau* de Derval and de Thibeau, apparently believing themselves safe, decided to go to Stenay alone,

99 Cacqueray, *Mémoires inédits*, pp.70–71.

100 Anon., *Explication de l'énigme de la Révolution européenne* (London: Schuler, 1826), vol.I, pp.189–190. The date was given as 3 October, however this is likely to have been a mistake in transcription.

101 Cited in Grouvel, *Troupes de l'émigration*, vol.III, p.144.

where they were arrested by the Republicans and immediately massacred. Having been volunteers, they may have had leave to quit their unit, a request that would have been readily given as the Princes no longer had the means to pay the troops. The volunteers who departed with permission were joined by others, of all ranks and status, who straggled and deserted. For example, a return from the Régiment de Berwick stated that, '61 men were taken prisoner at Le Chêne le Pouilleux …' in the first fortnight of October.[102] The scale and timing indicate that they were stragglers taken by Kellerman's vanguard after the royalist army passed through the village on 3 and 4 October. Indeed, it is known that three Gardes du Corps were taken at Le Chesne on 5 October by elements of the 1er Chasseurs and 3e Hussards.

These three émigrés, two brothers named Godefroy and the younger brother of the Comte de Béon, were brought before a military commission of the Criminal Tribunal at Paris.[103] The latter had been established by the law of 17 August 1792 to judge conspirators, and, by a decree of 11 September 1792, its remit was extended to émigrés. A military commission of five members was created to judge the émigrés who were taken prisoner following the decree of 20 October. Along with these three émigrés, six others appeared before the same commission, along with four of their servants who were all acquitted. The émigrés often asserted their ignorance of the new laws against them; perhaps reasonably given how recently they had been implemented. Three appear to have been arrested on 23 September at La Croix-aux-Bois, these were Jean-Alexandre Dumesnil, formerly *capitaine* in the Esterhazy Hussards, serving as a volunteer in Bercheny, Jean-Louis Mirambel, a Garde du corps de Monsieur, and a servant.[104] Another three émigrés, from units of the Maison militaire, were arrested at Auberive, north of Dijon, perhaps on their way to Switzerland. The nine émigrés were guillotined on 23 October on the Place de l'Hôtel de Ville in Paris. The fate of the Berwick soldiers is not known, but there were several instances of royalist troops being summarily executed. On 5 October, four deserters from the Chasseurs de Polignac, taken by the National Guard at Ville-sur-Retourne, were massacred by the populace and Parisian volunteers.[105]

Coinciding with the retreat of the Armée du Centre, the corps commanded by the Prince de Condé had set off on 4 October to march northwards to Mahlberg, just outside Ettenheim, which they reached three days later. It was then, 7 October, that the Condéens received the news of the failure at Valmy and the subsequent retreat. Fearing the worst, the Prince de Condé was ordered to Kehl to defend the Breisgau from any attempt by the revolutionaries to cross the Rhine from Strasbourg.

The retreat of the Armée du Centre continued through Marville, Villers-le-Rond and Cons-la-Grandville, by sideroads in which the horses sank to their hocks, 'All along the road one could see nothing but stuck or broken

102 Grouvel, *Troupes de l'émigration*, vol.III, p.135.

103 *Bulletin du tribunal criminel, 27 octobre 1792*, pp.149, 151 and Madival & Laurent, *Archives parlementaires*, vol.LII, pp.593.

104 *Bulletin du tribunal criminel, 24 octobre 1792*, pp.143–144.

105 Grouvel, *Troupes de l'émigration*, vol.III, p.125.

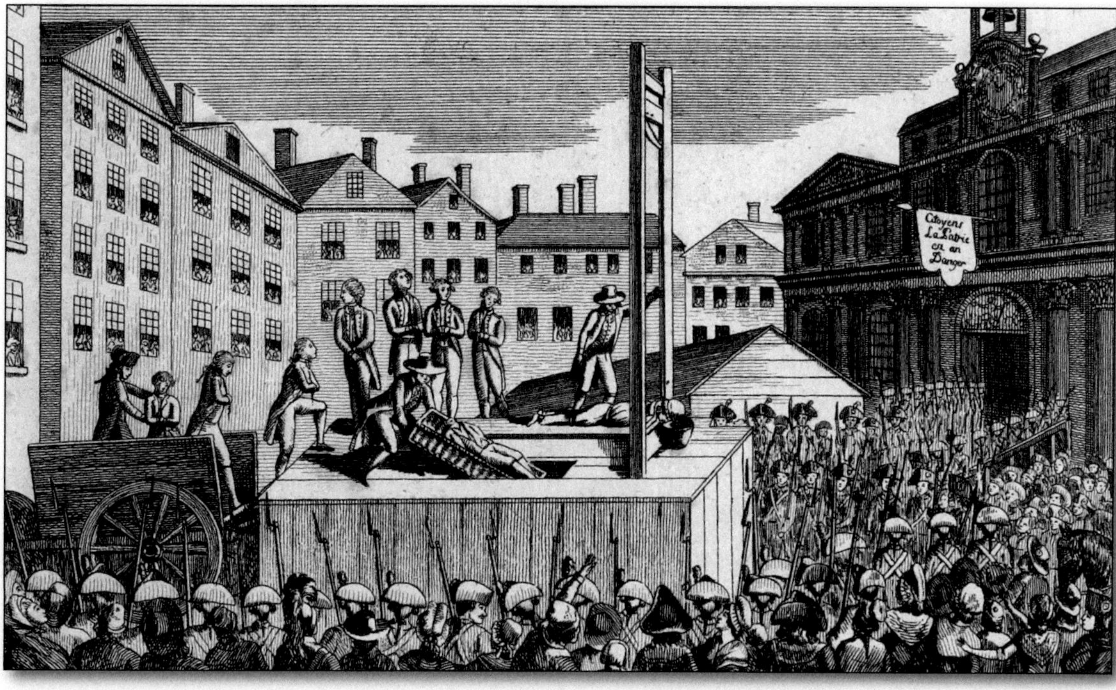

'Nine emigrants at the guillotine,' 1792, by an unknown artist. (Collection Musées Ville de Paris, licence CCØ)

carriages, or horses dead from fatigue.'[106] The following day, 12 October, the émigré column finally reached the main road leading to Longwy and, having bypassed the town, it took the road to Luxembourg around midday. Having crossed the frontier, they dispersed that evening around Arlon, where the Princes established their headquarters.

Behind them came the émigré infantry. In the Armagnac brigade, Chateaubriand had contracted dysentery, and he struggled to keep up with his company of the Coalition de Bretagne that was already dispersing: 'The rains had broken up the roads; one encountered everywhere caissons, gun-carriages, bogged down cannons, overturned carts, sutleresses with their children on their backs, soldiers dead or dying in the mud.'[107] Argens described the brigade's route:

> … on the 14th, we brought ourselves to the walls of Longwi [sic]; we halted there for a quarter of an hour near the gate which opens onto the main road to Luxembourg; after the moment of rest, we continued our march, and a quarter of a league further, we made with the greatest regret our exit from France, to go to Musson where we stayed.[108]

In the 31e compagnie of the Hommes d'armes à pied, Bennes and a comrade were left at Cons-la-Grandville to escort the unit's sick. There they obtained four horses and a good waggon for the sick, and were preparing to leave when

106 Cacqueray, *Mémoires inédits*, p.72.
107 Chateaubriand, *Mémoires*, vol.III, p.114.
108 Anon. (ed.), *Olivier d'Argens*, p.26.

the rearguard of the Hussards de Bercheny warned them that Republican troops were not far off:

> … and that we might be overtaken by them, unless we used the utmost dispatch. We exerted ourselves, and in order to proceed faster, my companion, after my example, threw his musket into the waggon and took a whip. The poor horses we lashed most unmercifully to be sure, but we heard a dreadful firing, which made it necessary for us to go on full speed.[109]

On reaching Longwy, they found that their unit had already left, so, without stopping, they continued to drive for 24 hours, night and day, until they caught up with it at Arlon. The émigrés' retreat from France, although difficult and perilous, had been achieved, certainly by the cavalry, in good order with few losses.

Some hoped that Arlon would be a new rallying point, but many of the émigrés had had enough. Some simply quit, without bothering to request leave, although most sought it. One of these was Chateaubriand, who obtained a certificate of honourable service from his *capitaine* on 16 October before leaving for the Channel Islands, where family members had taken refuge. The sheer number of those granted leave by *maréchal* de Broglie made it clear that the army would be dismissed imminently. On 14 October, Cacqueray and his uncle went to Arlon to take their leave from the escadron de la Marine, it was granted. They set off for Liège, which they only reached on 20 October, as their horses were exhausted from the previous campaign.

On 13 October, the coalition garrison of Verdun capitulated, and Republican troops entered at noon the following day. The Republican volunteer Denis Bélot, who had left Thionville in pursuit of the retreating enemy, saw for himself the state of the Prussian army:

> The hospitals are overflowing with enemy sick; it is impossible to transport them without putting their lives in danger. The Prussian army that I saw provides the most lamentable appearance. The soldiers are without bread, without clothes; three-quarters suffer from a terrible disease known as dysentery. We encounter them pale, defeated, eyes dull and haggard, staggering with each step that they try to take. What a pitiful state![110]

Brons confirms the effect it had on the Armée Royale:

> … dysentery … brought from this disastrous camp of Grand-Pré by the unfortunate Prussian army, had also spread to the armée des princes where it began to wreak daily ravages. Many gentlemen, officers, volunteers and soldiers died on the way during the first days of the retreat. Many others arrived at Luxembourg suffering from this frightful disease and the city was soon full of these unfortunates who had neither the strength nor the means to travel any further.[111]

109 Bennes, *A narrative*, pp.21–22.

110 Marsangy (ed.), *Journal 1791*, p.80.

111 Brons, *Journal*, p.102.

Throughout their retreat, the émigrés' baggage had been subject to plundering by the Prussians. This did not cease after they had crossed the frontier as a garde du corps recalled, '... finding us formed up on the square of Arlon 4 leagues [16 kilometres] from Luxembourg, they robbed us, seized out portmanteaux, ordered us with sabres, bayonets and other weapons, to give them money, saying that we had caused the war.'[112]

Once the Princes had been joined by their infantry, it was decided to move on to the Liège region in three columns. On 25 October, the Princes established themselves at Val Saint-Lambert, a large abbey located six kilometres southwest of Liège. Their remaining troops were scattered in the principality, as well that of Stavelot and the Duchy of Jülich, between the Meuse and the Rhine, north of Aachen and west of Köln. Placed in winter quarters, the émigrés were charged with monitoring the banks of the Meuse. Meanwhile, to the south, the Armée de Condé took up winter quarters behind the Black Forest from 27 October, with its headquarters at Villingen-Schwenningen, and the infantry distributed from there northwards to Rottenburg am Neckar, while the cavalry was sent to Württemberg.

The move to the Liège region by the 13,000-strong Armée du Centre had the aim of linking up with the Armée de Bourbon. The latter was estimated to have at most 5,000 men, but combined, they would still constitute a significant force, which could be of use in the defence of the Netherlands and Liège, or even to conduct a unilateral but limited offensive in northeastern France. However, in early November, the coalition Allies informed the Princes that they would no longer be able to provide support for their troops after 1 December. This news increased the authorised departures, and desertions also grew in number. The number of sick also grew, and Brons, the Princes' commissioner, was only allocated 300 to 400 livres for their care so had to use his own money the cover the difference.[113]

The Armée de Bourbon, Providing Unexpected Assistance

When the Armée de Bourbon was deployed to the Ardennes, it was not fully operational. Indeed, the Prince de Condé wrote on 11 August to his son, 'I see with pleasure that you have found money elsewhere, since you have managed to obtain weapons and to have tents delivered to you. I find it excellent that you have taken those that you found on hand, even if they were intended for me.'[114] Stationed in a region bound by Huy, Namur and Liège, the army had a certain cohesion given that it was limited in size and most of its units had been stationed in the Luxembourg region. As for its organisation:

> The Picardie company ... by its rank took the head of the infantry of this army and headed the first battalion of the first brigade. It was this which, after the total

112 Jorgen Green, *Jean-Baptiste Xavier Carpentier de Colbaut, un émigré loyal et son combat contre la Révolution 1792-1794* (Denmark: Editions Grifo, 2011), p.5.

113 Brons, *Journal*, p.107.

114 Crétineau-Joly, *princes de Condé*, vol.I, pp.74–75.

> assembly of the Armée de Bourbon furnished the first guard of honour … and the first war detachment at the opening of the campaign. The other companies of line regiments, French or foreign, took the rank of seniority of their respective corps in the brigades.[115]

It is striking how little information there was about the invasion of France and the progress of the Armée du Centre, despite the Prince de Condé sharing what little he knew with his son. On 22 August, he wrote, 'It is incredible that I am not sent couriers for news of this importance. I have not received the slightest word from the Armée des Princes since I left them.'[116] After some delay, the Armée de Bourbon moved further to the south, around Marche-en-Famenne, and with the lack of communication from the Austrian allies, Bourbon was concerned that he may be left isolated in the midst of the enemy. If he failed, it would perhaps have dramatic consequences on the rest of the operations. On 16 September, he wrote to one of his correspondents, 'if by chance General d'Erbach makes a move, which could well occur, you would please me by giving me details in a positive manner.'[117] François de La Rochefoucauld, survivor of the massacre of 10 August, joined the Armée de Bourbon at Marche-en-Famenne, or Marche-en-Famine as the émigrés referred to it, on 17 September:

> … the first sight of the little town did not reassure me at all. The day I arrived there, the weather was bad; it had rained heavily for several days; there was everywhere a terrible rain. The town is encircled with an old wall which makes the air damper; it is composed of a single street which goes in turns, and very badly built. It was there that the headquarters of our little army and the general staff were established. The Duc de Bourbon was lodged in the principal house; as there were not enough stables for all the horses, many were picketed in the courtyard, some under a roof, others out in the open …[118]

The infantry was camped in tents north of the town, along the road leading to Namur. Although small, the Armée de Bourbon had good commanders, at its head was the Comte d'Egmont who had served in command positions, despite his youth, in the War of the Austrian Succession and then the Seven Years War. Its vanguard was led by the Comte de La Châtre, a valiant and experienced soldier, until he was replaced by the Marquis de Breuilpont as a reward for his exploits. Furthermore, the army had some artillery as described by the Duc de Bourbon, 'The Duc de Saxe [Saxe-Teschen] has granted me four cannons and a howitzer with their caissons and utensils that I requested from him; he gave them to me with infinite grace. They are pieces taken at Quiévrain from the French patriots.'[119] The cannons, probably

---

115 Brons, *Journal*, p.42.

116 Crétineau-Joly, *princes de Condé*, vol.I, p.75, Condé to Bourbon 22 August 1792.

117 Louis Joseph de Bourbon-Condé, *Une correspondance en émigration (1792-1797)* (Paris: C. Douniol, 1867), p.13.

118 La Rochefoucauld, *Souvenirs*, pp.102–103.

119 La Rochefoucauld, *Souvenirs*, p.109.

12-pounders, named *Modeste*, *Favorite*, *Assassine* and *Coco*, and the howitzer were supplied on 4 September and so armed a full artillery company.

La Rochefoucauld gave the strength of the army as, 'For the General Staff: 128 officers, etc. (including the Duc de Bourbon), 285 servants, 489 horses; for the army: 4,000 men, 1,392 servants, 2,093 horses.'[120] He also described the Duc de Bourbon, who he encountered on several occasions, as having, 'an extremely cold nature, he had a diffident air, and was hardly appropriate to arouse enthusiasm and zeal, but he took infinite trouble to procure to each what they needed.'[121] He gained his troops' esteem through his actions rather than his personality, like his father, being assiduous in his military duties. Although his table was frugal, he hosted about 40 people to eat every day, including his guard. In addition, his personal household carried out additional duties in the army, 'one was in charge of letters, another was a surgeon, etc.'[122]

On 24 September, the Armée de Bourbon moved towards Namur, and two days later it deployed on the Meuse southwest of Dinant with its headquarters at the Abbey of Géronsart. It was there that it was learned that there had been a battle in France and, as was too often the case, after great joy from false expectation and news, the émigrés had to digest the unthinkable; that after a fight, about which nothing was known, the Allies were in retreat. All were unaware of the extent of the debacle and how the operational situation had suddenly become calamitous. Unlike the coalition, constantly hindered or thwarted by the opaque policy of Prussia, the young French Republic, with the unity of decision and vision of the Military Committee and the Convention, was to strike with strategic audacity.

Since 19 September, *lieutenant-général* Custine commanded the French army in the Vosges and when the Austrian troops moved to reinforce those besieging Thionville, the Military Committee decided to take advantage of their absence to have him penetrate the Palatinate and drive towards the Rhine to threaten the coalition troops' line of retreat. On 29 September, Custine left Landau at the head of 13,000 men, and the following day, he captured Speyer, nearly 2,500 prisoners, and 55 pieces of artillery. From there, he had access to the Palatinate and could threaten the Rhine valley, from Mainz to northern Alsace. Appointed to the command of the Armée du Rhin on 6 October, Custine seized Worms and part of the émigrés' magazines on the same day.

On 15 October, Dumouriez arrived in Paris a national hero to report his victory and seek approval for his plan to invade the Austrian Netherlands. In Paris, Nicolas Ruault summed up the situation:

> The King of Prussia and his army no longer exist in France: we now run on the foreigners who had begun by running on us. The little princes of Germany flee before our cockade and our tricolour hats. Their cities, their strongholds surrender to us without striking a blow. Savoy, the country of Nice are liberated.

---

120 La Rochefoucauld, *Souvenirs*, p.112. Unfortunately, the order of battle La Rochefoucauld provided was not included in the published journal by the editor (pp.111–112).

121 La Rochefoucauld, *Souvenirs*, p.130.

122 La Rochefoucauld, *Souvenirs*, p.130.

> The frontiers of France on Germany are set free of their prince-bishops. It will not be long before Brabant is [liberated] from the House of Austria to unite itself with us.[123]

Once again, his analysis was to be proved accurate. After seizing Philippsburg, on the right bank of the Rhine, Custine moved on Mainz, which fell on 21 October. The Prince de Condé had, on 15 October, sent four of his artillery officers to Mainz to assist in its defence; however, this aid was declined.

Meanwhile, negotiations took place between the court of Vienna and that of Potsdam with dreadful consequences for the émigrés, as revealed by a letter from Count Thugut, the Austrian Minister of Foreign Affairs, dated 23 October 1792:

> The experience of this campaign appears to have proved that the very nature of the émigrés renders them hardly combinable with our troops and as well only renders them subjects to often become encumbrances in the subsistence, mobility and the operations of the armies of His Majesty, so that in considering the little service that had been got from them and might be promised for the future, it seems evident that in this regard, any future expense for them, even was it to be less considerable, will be always badly spent. It appears, in consequence, that one should know not to hesitate to cut them off, for the future, from all hope whatever of help, if until now it was impossible to imagine some means to break them up or to disencumber the allied courts of them by whatever other means.
>
> But these émigrés find themselves in so deplorable a misery that a great part, ready to perish from hunger in the full force of the term, without coats, without shoes, will be, I think, not physically in a state to follow the order which may be given to disperse them. It is to be feared that despair and absolute destitution of everything will soon lead them to great excesses, to throw themselves into the woods, to infest the highways, and if one wished to take the steps to expel them by armed force, the neighbouring States refusing to receive them, one would end up by being forced to exterminate them.
>
> As it appears desirable that one should avoid coming to such disagreeable extremes, I can only submit to Your Excellence's consideration if it would be possible to reach an agreement with the Prussian court to still provide in these circumstances, with the strictest and most severe economy, for the most pressing needs of the émigrés who make up the former royal army until it is possible to settle upon some sort of project to rid His Majesty's States of them.[124]

On the same day, the French entered Frankfurt, and the Convention adopted a law for the perpetual banishment of émigrés and decreed the death penalty for those who returned.

It was only on 2 November that the Armée de Bourbon learned of the situation of the Armée du Centre, or at least of what was left of it. Having been inactive until then, it was now exposed to the greatest danger. Dumouriez,

123 Ruault, *Gazette*, p.317, letter of 18 October.

124 Cited in Ernest Daudet, *Histoire de l'Émigration pendant la Révolution Française* (Paris: Hachette, 1905), vol.I, p.212.

back on the frontier, gathered his forces around Valenciennes to launch a major offensive against the 25,000 Austrians under Coburg entrenched in the Borinage and in front of Mons. On 6 November, the Austrians were defeated at Jemmapes and forced to retreat to Brussels. The Armée de Bourbon had been deployed west of Namur, on the plain of Fleurus, but had not been brought up to support the Austrians, and the following day it was ordered to withdraw on Liège. However:

> Instead of beating a retreat, by the road that had led us to Namur, we made a rather perilous march to bring us to Brussels; we passed close to the French outposts. We could have alerted them and attracted considerable forces upon us that would have put us in the greatest perplexity. This hazardous march [which passed through Genappe and Waterloo] was a gallantry of the Duc de Bourbon. He wished to gain merit with the Archduchess-Governor of the Netherlands, by covering the retreat to which she was forced by the enemy. We marched all night making as little noise and display as possible. The next day, on the journey, we only made two stops and arrived, around nine o'clock in the evening, on the glacis of Brussels where we remained in bivouac until midnight. During this time, the carriages and baggage of the Archduchess marched by; and when she had passed with all her retinue, we set off again.[125]

The irresistible advance of the Republicans into what was to be Belgium caused the retreat to become a headlong flight, throwing Austrian and royalist troops pell-mell onto the roads of Holland and Germany along with thousands of émigrés who had taken refuge there:

> The road was covered with people, the carriages followed one another and formed a line; they were full of people and often harnessed to two horses, for in this moment of debacle one could not find any to hire, again they were very expensive. I saw carriages harnessed with two or three saddle horses that had never drawn before. The confusion was very great and the desolation at its height, as there was fear. The women wept. One feared the passage of towns and pillage, because in this terrible moment of reverse we could neither complain of nor obtain protection against violence.[126]

A little further on, when the Armée de Bourbon had reached Tienen, the Austrian command informed the Duke that he could no longer provide for the needs of the émigré troops. It was there, on 9 November, that La Rochefoucauld was granted leave to quit as a volunteer in the Compagnies des gentilhommes de Champagne. He headed to Maastricht, where many émigrés, preferring to remain together in adversity, sought safety.[127] They placed their trust in protection from the stronghold's garrison but, above all, Dutch neutrality. However, on 10 November, Custine's forces beat a

125 Mautort, *Mémoires*, p.422.
126 La Rochefoucauld, *Souvenirs*, p.195.
127 La Rochefoucauld, *Souvenirs*, p.209.

Prussian corps on the Lahn, and the noose seemed to be tightening around the émigrés.

On 11 November, the remainder of the Armée de Bourbon reached the small town of Tongeren, La Rochefoucauld had passed through it two days before:

> It was so packed with carriages and people from Brussels that all the inns, all the houses were full, and what is more the square was covered by more than 200 carriages whose horses had passed the night attached to the traces; many people had slept in their carriages and had only been able to procure some bread to eat and a little wine to drink. The corps of Gendarmerie had been based there since its retreat from France; it was paid and fed by the Emperor. It was commanded by M d'Autichamp.[128]

On 15 November, all hopes of subsistence vanished, and five days later, the King's brothers decided to disband their troops. What remained in the coffers was shared between them – 15 francs to each volunteer with some assignats – and the following two days were devoted to issuing the certificates of service and dismissal. The final discharges took place on 23 and 24 November, and the émigrés immediately dispersed on the roads to exile, often destitute, having sold their weapons, uniforms and horses for next to nothing.

There was no alternative, as Dumouriez returned in triumph to Brussels on 14 November and then Liège on 28 November, dangerously close to the frontier with the United Provinces, right up to the walls of Maastricht. He then took winter quarters in Belgium.

128 La Rochefoucauld, *Souvenirs*, pp.206–207.

Epilogue

As early as 25 October, when the Armée des Princes had disintegrated and its final disbanding was inevitable, *maréchal* de Broglie gloomily concluded:

> The rest that will leave me distant from all military details and affairs is strangely troubled by reflections that one cannot prevent oneself from making on the end of this campaign and on the disastrous consequences that will result from it for Religion, for our unfortunate King, for our unlucky Nobility, finally for all Europe which is going to be infected with the contagion that has discomfited and ruined France. We have been unfortunate for more than three years, hope nevertheless remained to us and appeared finally to be realised soon when the finest armies entered the Kingdom. This hope vanished like a dream, and we can no longer see anything but a bottomless abyss in which Kings, Princes and individuals are going to be engulfed … But, at the final reckoning, it is always necessary to revert to resigning ourselves to the will of God and submitting to what he commands.[1]

As a result of the disaster, the émigrés, proscribed and condemned in their native land, faced the dangers of surviving abroad, attempting to return home to protect their loved ones or joining the revolts in the west of France. From the day after Valmy, the nobility began to disperse, the majority in a state of destitution. Some died, the captured émigrés being murdered immediately or subsequently executed, while others preferred to take their own lives rather than fall into the hands of the Republicans or because they had lost everything, including their faith. Very few died from combat, more from dysentery. Of the 11,000 noble officers who were in the army and navy in 1789, it can be estimated that at least 7,000 to 8,000 served in the Armée des Princes. Many of them had not been able to flee with their families, so those who survived were to find themselves separated from their loved ones for many years, or divorced from their wives by force of law. Their errant life would arouse sympathy across Europe. As Madame de La Ferronays wrote:

> We took … the road of exile in the poor brown berline that I can still see, very pretty for its time, with its panels and doors encircled with golden arabesques …

1 Grouvel, *Troupes de l'émigration*, vol.III, p.21.

> It was to make all our journeys of emigration … For us, it was like the clothes of the Israelites in the desert … until our embarkation for England…[2]

Most of the émigrés tried to keep away from the theatres of war, in Britain and the Channel Islands, or even the West Indies. Those that remained on the continent headed for the United Provinces, Germany, Switzerland and Italy, unaware that the advancing revolutionary armies would drive them even further, even to Russia, the United States or Canada.

The disbanding of the Armée du Centre was not instant, and some units survived a little longer: 'The two squadrons of the princes' Gardes du corps were kept for a month and sent to the Pays de Juliers [Jülich], a principality of the Elector of Bavaria. Ours [Gardes de Monsieur] came to be quartered in the small town of Rauderat [Randerath] and was disbanded fifteen days later.'[3]

The Comte de Brons maintained the hospice at Luxembourg and, for a while, 'the convalescent depot previously established in Trier, etc.'[4] In November, the Comte d'Artois provided him with 175 louis, three-quarters of what the Prince possessed, to provide care for the sick, wounded and convalescents as well as destitute émigrés. Soon, against expectations, the King's brothers received relief from Empress Catherine of Russia, who gave them 750,000 roubles, of which they kept a fifth, 'a part was put in reserve, another served to give advances to the most pressing creditors and the most needy émigrés.'[5] On 15 December, the Princes issued a final regulation for the assistance of émigrés who had participated in the campaign, classifying them according to the state of their health or family, particularly those with young children. The Prince de Condé and *maréchal* de Broglie, now at Düsseldorf, were appointed to organise this assistance and designate the commissioners who would be in charge of it. Brons, with financial support from the sisters of Francis II, Archduchesses Maria Clementina and Maria Amalia of Austria, was able to continue the work of the hospice until the summer of 1794.

The Prussian army, particularly the infantry, continued to disintegrate:

> The Prussian's route was strewn with thousands of corpses. They did not even wait for the unfortunate soldiers piled on the carts to render their last breath to be thrown into the ditches that bordered the roads … A no less rapid mortality had spread among the horses of this army, above all among those of the artillery, the train and the provisions of which a prodigious number had perished in Champagne and on the return journey and of which several thousand still perished from Arlon to the Rhine.[6]

Brons estimated that of the Prussian army's 50,000 men who had entered the campaign, just 30,000 were still alive at the beginning of November, only

2 Costa de Beauregard (ed.), *Souvenirs tirés des papiers du comte de La Ferronays* (Paris: Librairie Plon, 1901), pp.21–22.
3 La Chanonie (ed.), *Tercier*, p.93.
4 Brons, *Journal*, pp.102–103.
5 Castries, *Le maréchal de Castries*, p.181.
6 Brons, *Journal*, p.106.

half of whom would have been able to fight. Prussia's military reputation was ruined. In France its soldiers had behaved as if in a conquered country, and they had not spared the émigrés in these excesses. The latter were described as, 'unfortunate victims of Prussian pillage. All very well supplied with the necessary clothing when they commenced to fight with these troops, they had barely enough to cover themselves with when they left them.'[7]

The relationship between the émigrés and Prussians had broken down during the retreat, each blaming the other. As the Régiment de Wittgenstein marched through Longwy one of its officers approached some Prussian officers and told them, in their own language, 'that perhaps one day we would go to Berlin with those who had just beaten their army at Valmy, to ask them the reason for its defeat.'[8] A threat that was to prove a premonition. It appeared that Frederick William had sacrificed the émigrés to save what remained of his own forces. Sick émigrés, facing certain death, were abandoned at Verdun; one such was Baron Klopstein, a volunteer in the Régiment de Wittgenstein, who was taken by the patriots on their entrance and shot. The dishonoured Prussian king would never be forgiven by the émigrés. Furthermore, the secret agreements that ensured his army would not be disturbed as it withdrew from France enabled the revolutionary forces to focus their efforts against the Austrian Netherlands. Whatever the Austrian commanders felt about the émigrés, the latter could provide them with motivated and experienced troops.

As soon as their disbanding became imminent, the commanders of Royal-Allemand, Saxe and Bercheny Hussards, as well as the Légions de Carneville and Breuilpont, made approaches for their units to transfer to Austrian pay. Despite being much smaller than Austrian regiments, the three cavalry units transferred under the command of their *colonels* and retained their uniforms, attracting a large number of gentlemen as cadets. The Légion de Normandie, or Carneville, was reorganised into a corps of light infantry, chasseurs à pied, and hussars with Austrian arms, equipment and clothing but in their previous colours. Although the Marquis de Breuilpont failed to have his legion taken into Austrian pay, his 100 or so uhlans joined the Hussards de Saxe and Bercheny, and the around 200 chasseurs carabiniers were incorporated into the Le Loup Jägers. As for the Chasseurs de Polignac, a few remained as a guard for the Princes in January 1793 during their residence at Hamm, only disappearing in the summer of 1794. Furthermore, many gentlemen, officers or volunteers joined the Austrian army individually, perhaps more than 1,000 in the Walloon regiments, while others joined various cavalry regiments.[9] The Marquis de Breuilpont himself was wounded at the Battle of Jemmapes on 6 November while attached to Clerfayt's staff. Furthermore,

7 James Money, *Histoire de la campagne faite en 1792 par les Armees Françaises* (London: E. Harlow, 1794) p.46. This passage is missing (it would have appeared at p.57) in the English edition of the same year. It is also missing from the 1849 French edition which had been translated from German by Paul Mérat and published at Paris by Librairie militaire, maritime et polytechnique de J. Corréard.

8 Grouvel, *Troupes de l'émigration*, vol.III, p.144, the officer was a M. de Norvins.

9 Hughes de Bazouges, 'La carrière autrichienne de Philippe de Brons', *Carnet spécial de La Sabretache 'L'émigration militaire 1791-1801'*, pp.28–34.

Portrait of Louis XVIII. (Author's collection).

Charles-Eugène de Lorraine, Prince of Lambesc, former *colonel* of Royal-Allemand, was appointed colonel-proprietor of the Kurassier No.7 regiment in 1794, a post which he held until his death in 1825.

Meanwhile, the Prince de Condé refused to disband his army and obtained the minimum required to sustain it from the Austrians during the months of November and December. Nevertheless, its fate remained uncertain, which prevented him from accepting other volunteers. After 26 December, he was joined by his son, the Duc de Bourbon, and grandson, the Duc d'Enghien.

As stated above, many émigrés had taken refuge in Maastricht, where they were soon drawn into the conflict again. On 4 February 1793, France declared war on Britain and the United Provinces and two days later Maastricht was besieged. Émigrés, who had formerly served in the Armées du Centre and de Bourbon, formed an infantry regiment of 1,200 men wearing the orange cockade of the United Provinces. The siege was raised on 2 March, and the Régiment de Maëstricht, although often ignored, would be the first of the émigré corps raised from 1793 to continue the fight under different cockades for God and the King.[10] Certainly, such émigrés served as soldiers of fortune but did so guided by honour.

It is not known how many of the 13,000 to 14,000 officers and gentlemen who served in the Armée des Princes survived to see their homeland again. However, perhaps 2,000 of them died of disease, were killed in combat, or were executed after being taken prisoner during the Revolutionary Wars. Others of them continued the fight in the Armée de Condé, in foreign service or with the Grande Armée catholique et royale, as the insurgents of western France called themselves. For some, this continued until 1815, when the west rose up again to tie down 15,000 men who would otherwise have been available to fight at Waterloo. The majority of the survivors of the Armée des Princes, however, returned to France in 1801–1802 after Bonaparte granted them an amnesty.

Had their fight been in vain? It is often forgotten that the Bourbon Restoration, from 1814 to 1830, lasted longer than the First Empire. British support for the émigrés, from 1793 until the Congress of Vienna in 1815, forged a new relationship between the two countries. This not only saw a break with centuries of war but also, for example, them taking leading roles in ending the transatlantic slave trade. Louis XVIII was criticised for his measures to appease the very different France that he returned to.

10 See Hughes de Bazouges & Alistair Nichols, *For God and King*.

This included his refusal to be crowned, but also for failing to reconcile the émigrés with those who had dispossessed them or massacred their families. However, until his death in 1824, he wore only one outfit, that of an émigré volunteer in the Armée des Princes, in recognition of all the sacrifices those gentlemen endured to restore their King and Religion.

Colour Plates Commentaries

Section 1

The Armée des Princes was very much influenced by the heritage and uniforms of the royal army at the end of the reign of Louis XVI. Thus, the old uniform of the Ordinance of 1 October 1786, sometimes modified in accordance with the provisional regulations of 1 April 1791, was worn. Alongside these were those wearing the habit d'émigrant (Section 2), the newly-raised German troops wearing uniforms largely modelled on the old royal army (Section 3), the light troops with a palette of new uniforms (Section 4) and the Légion de Mirabeau (Section 5).

Uniforms of the Former Royal Army

About a third of the men in the Armée des Princes, between 7,000 and 8,000, still wore the French uniform of the end of the reign of Louis XVI. The modifications made by the Provisional Instruction of 1 April 1791 would have only affected those of all ranks, and in particular the cavalry, who had emigrated at the beginning of 1792. However, there is evidence that the Assembly's decrees were slow to be implemented due to the disorganised state of the army or lack of money.

For parade, service or campaign dress, infantry officers wore their coats fastened, without the shirt-frill, with the gorget bearing the arms of France (11b). Only senior officers were mounted while company officers served on foot, in cuffed boots for *capitaines*, and in gaiters for *lieutenants* and *sous-lieutenants*. These gaiters were, for all ranks, white in parade dress as well as service and campaign dress in summer, while, for these last two orders of dress, they were black or grey in winter.

In tenue de société (society dress) or when travelling, the coat was unfastened, with the shirt-frill and a white tie, worn with white breeches and stockings in summer and both black in winter, buckled shoes or cuffed boots, a fancy sword and cane. Petite tenue de quartier (quarter undress) consisted of a coat without weapon, boots or gaiters and a bonnet de police (equivalent to a fatigue cap). A bonnet de police of a *capitaine* of the Colonel-Généralinfanterie is illustrated at 9b.

The rank insignia of the NCOs were worn on the forearm, a simple horizontal lace, of silver or gold for *sergents*, depending on the button colour and two for *sergents-major*. Those of *caporaux* and *fourriers* were of the same form, on both forearms for the former and higher on the left arm for the latter, but in the regimental facing colour.

Fusiliers had shoulder straps of the colour of their coats and fleur de lys, in the regimental facing colour, on their coat turnbacks. The colour of the pompon, or houppe ronde, identified a soldier's company easily and so aided counting in quarters. Chasseurs had green epaulettes and green hunting horns on their turnbacks. Grenadiers wore bearskin caps, with a brass plate at the front bearing a grenade, red élite epaulettes and grenades of the facing colour on the turnbacks. The turnback badges of the officers were in gold or silver thread.

In this period, only grenadiers and chasseurs were equipped with a sabre briquet, but this soon extended to all infantrymen, contrary to what the provisional regulation of 1 April 1791 stipulated.

Plate 1: Chevaliers-dragons de la Couronne.

Plate 1 illustrates the uniforms in the Chevaliers-dragons de la Couronne with a habit à la française (1a). The new uniform of the Chevaliers de la Couronne (1c) was not simply the replacement of the habit coat by a frac with a folded-over collar and 10 buttons, but included various elements specific to the noble cavalry, such as black leather equipment. The helmet was, however, unique to the Chevaliers de la Couronne. It was manufactured in Germany in the spring of 1792 and appears to have been inspired by that of the Régiment du Roi (see commentary on Plates 18 & 19 below). The front brass plate was embossed with the crown of the royal arms. The white metal buttons bore the same crown and the motto Dieu et le Roi (God and the King).

The rank distinctions were, at first, strictly of the French model. With the new uniform, the epaulettes for the simple cavaliers were gilt, and those of the officers used crimson silk instead of that of feu (literally fire, as used on the ribbon of the Cross of Saint-Louis) red.

Some units that had emigrated or were reconstituted used lapels of facing colours, as in the case of the trooper of the Maréchaussée (1b) serving as a *prévôté* (provost). His uniform only differs from that of the new Gendarmerie nationale by the absence of white piping on the collar, lapels and cuffs, the retention of the white aiguillettes worn on the left shoulder, and the use of the fleurs de lys on the turnbacks as well as the horse furniture.

Rank Distinctions (Plate 1d–o)

The epaulettes were those of 1786–1791:

d) *Cadet-gentilhomme*: contre-epaulettes of gold or silver according to the button colour, edged with vivid red called feu.
e) *Adjudant*: red silk shoulder-strap on the right and epaulette on the left, with two lines of gold or silver; the epaulette fringe is of red and gold or silver.[1]

1 Raoul Quarré de Verneuil, *L'armée en France depuis Charles VII jusqu'à la Révolution* (Paris: Dumaine, 1880), p.325.

f) *Porte-drapeau*: red silk shoulder-strap and epaulette, edged with gold or silver; the fringe is of red and the particular metal colour.
g) *Sous-lieutenants de remplacement*: as for the *sous-lieutenant*, but with a gold or silver central line of gold on the straps.
h) *Sous-lieutenants*: red silk shoulder-straps and epaulettes with three square lozenges outlined in button colour lace; fringes are a mix of threads of silk and gold or silver.
i) *Lieutenants en premier*: shoulder-strap on the right and epaulette of gold or silver lace on the left, each with three square lozenges outlined in red silk lace. Two-thirds of the epaulette fringe is gold or silver, and a third of red silk thread. *Lieutenants en second* wore the same but with a red silk line along the centre of the straps (as seen in g above) and the fringe is two thirds red silk and one third metal.
j) *Capitaines de remplacement*: as for the *capitaines commandants* but the contre-epaulette strap has one red silk line down the centre, and that of the epaulette has two such lines.
k) *Capitaines en second*: as for the *capitaines commandants*, but both straps have a single central line of red silk along their length.
l) *Capitaines commandants*: contre-epaulette on the right shoulder and epaulette on the left shoulder. *Majors* wore the same but their epaulettes fringes were thicker being formed of so-called graines d'épinards (spinach seeds). Until 1788 *majors* had worn these epaulettes on both shoulders but when the cavalry rank of *chef d'escadron*, to command two companies, was introduced that year they were to wear the epaulette on the left while *majors* wore theirs on the right.
m) *Lieutenant-colonel*: epaulette as for the *mestre de camp*, but on the left shoulder only.
n) *Mestre de camp en second*: as the *mestre de camp* but with a red silk line along the length of the straps on both shoulders.
o) *Mestre de camp, colonel* from 1791: epaulettes on each shoulder, of gold or silver, according to the buttons, with fringes of graines d'épinards and cordes de puits (lit. well ropes, what in the British army was referred to as bullion).

Volunteers in the Coalitions and free companies of the Third Estate did not wear epaulettes, unlike those in such units as the Corps de la Marine Royale and Légion de Mirabeau. In addition, volunteers of the Chevaliers de la Couronne, although ranked as dragoon *sous-lieutenants* did not wear officers' distinctions but embroidered epaulettes or those of scales of the type called à la Piémontaise, as worn by Bavarian and Palatinate troops. Former officers, when serving in companies of former officers or of gentlemen, were, however, authorised to retain their epaulettes (9c). Moreover, all the officers, whatever the unit, wore the same rank distinctions and other symbols, gorgets (11b) and sword knots (11d), as the 1786 regulation.

The symbols preserved or adopted by the royalist émigrés, such as the King's cypher on sabretaches, fleur-de-lys on portmanteaus and headgear, etc., were not only to display attachment to the monarchy but also for identification. The distinctive white armband was particularly important. It had been used by the King of Sweden and his supporters during and after the Swedish revolution of 1772 (where it was known as the Armkládet), and its adoption was a means to pay homage to him. He was assassinated in March 1792. With the addition of the fleur-de-lys, at first in the distinctive sky blue facing colour of the Légion de Mirabeau (22f), it became a counter-revolutionary symbol. In particular, it (11c) identified individual personnel such as couriers and commissaries as émigrés, in addition to the fleurs-de-lys, the white plumes, cockades and finally sashes, the latter worn by all the officers and volunteers. However, it is known that on the march, these royalist insignia were not worn. Finally, in combat, particularly during sieges and the incursion into Champagne, the émigrés placed oak leaves in their headgear, between their cockades and plumes, a field sign traditionally used by Austrian troops.

Plate 2: Brigade irlandaise (Irish Brigade)

The three Irish regiments are shown in order of seniority: Dillon, the only one, since its creation in 1688, to not have changed name, Berwick and Walsh, with their respective drapeaux d'ordonnance (2a, 2b, 2c) carried by the second battalions. The first battalions carried the white drapeaux colonel, and that of Berwick had the motto 1691 SEMPER ET UBIQUE FIDELES 1791 embroidered in the vertical bar, parallel with the staff, in a similar manner to that of the Régiment de Vexin (see 3d).

The distinctive red of their uniform coats was similar to that of British troops; indeed the Régiment de Walsh were descended from the Irish Guards of James II, hence the use of the royal crown on its flag. The regiments were also alone in wearing four lace buttonholes on the lower sleeve in a herringbone pattern.

The figures are a *capitaine* and fusilier of the Régiment de Dillon (2d & 2e), subaltern officer and chasseur of Berwick (2f & 2g) and a fusilier of Walsh (2h).

Plate 3: Régiment de Vexin

The uniform of the Régiment de Vexin was that of 1786, and the facing colour was a shade of orange called aurore (3h). The regiment's *colonel*, the Chevalier de Damas-Crux, is illustrated (3g). The officer on foot (3a) is in summer campaign dress with the oak leaves of the Austrian troops with which Vexin served in Champagne. The fusilier (3b), shown from the back, has the fleurs de lys in the facing colour on the turnbacks; the chasseur (3f) had green epaulettes (3e) and green hunting horns on the turnbacks. The sword knot for the sabre briquet, if worn, would have been white for fusiliers, green for chasseurs and red for grenadiers (although the grenadiers were not reformed in Vexin, due to their dishonourable conduct at Marseille). The regiment's drapeau d'ordonnance (3c) and drapeau colonel (3d) are shown, the latter bearing the motto awarded to it by the King's brothers.

Plate 4: Compagnie française and compagnie suisse de garde du quartier-général

The Compagnie française guarded the headquarters of the Armée de Condé and was formed by NCOs and soldiers of proven loyalty and valour. It wore the white uniform of the 1786 regulations with facings of royal blue. The drummer wore the King's livery (4a). The fusilier (4b) wears a waistcoat and bonnet de police, as in quarters or camp, while his comrade (4c) is illustrated in tenue d'exercice. The *sergent* (4d) has a gold lace, matching the button colour, across each forearm.

The two Swiss companies that carried out the same functions in the Armée de Condé and the Armée de Bourbon were formed of officers (4e), NCOs and soldiers (4g) from the Régiment de Châteauvieux for the first and from Diesbach and Reinach for the second. Given that the latter was called the Compagnie franche de Porrentruy it is reasonable to assume that it adopted the white facings of Reinach.

The fanion (4f) is taken from photographs of the original. Unlike the units of the Maison du Roi, who had their emblems brought away from France, the new corps had theirs made during the emigration. These were white and bore three golden fleurs de lys, the name of the units and, if applicable, a characteristic symbol, such as a crown for the Chevaliers de la Couronne or an anchor for the Corps de la Marine.

Plate 5: Artillery and Engineers

When the Royal-Artillerie was formed in 1693, it was entitled to both a royal blue uniform, Louis XIV being *colonel*, and the red facings and piping reserved for élite troops due to its history. It also meant that it was listed among the infantry until 1791, when it became an independent specialist arm. Since 1776, it had been organised in seven regiments of 20 companies, five companies forming a brigade and two brigades a battalion; each regiment had the name of the city where it was stationed, in which there was also an artillery school: Strasbourg, Metz, Grenoble, Besançon, La Fère, Toul and Auxonne.

The artillery worked siege guns, 24 and 16-pound cannons, howitzers and mortars, and field guns, 12 and 8-pounders. Depicted are a gunner in training (5c), serving a gun (5e) and on guard (5g). The colour of the gun carriages and caissons was blue-grey (5d). The artillery was also responsible for all related units – workshop craftsmen and miners (5b). Each artillery regiment had a company of miners who were thus commanded by artillery officers; they were specialists in siege work but could be required to assist the gunners. The miners were distinguished by black facings, and, even today, the sappers, created in 1792, have black velvet distinctions.

In addition, each infantry regiment had two 4-pound guns in an artillery company whose soldiers were not part of the Royal-Artillerie but of the regiment.

In this period, the Corps du Génie was only comprised of officers, called *ingénieurs*, instructed at the school at Metz, and also had black facings. The *ingénieur* represented (5a) is in full dress, with a red waistcoat and breeches, like staff officers, while in service dress he would wear the same as the artillery officer (5f), with blue breeches and cuffed boots. The belts could be white or black.

In July 1791, the artillery was strengthened with an eighth regiment, the former colonial regiment that had been raised in 1784. Nevertheless, the Armée des Princes retained a distinction between the Corps royal de l'Artillerie and that of the Artillerie des Colonies. The uniform and flags hardly differed but the latter had, on their turnbacks, fleur-de-lys on the forward ones and anchors on the rear.[2]

Plate 6: Hussars of the Régiments de Bercheny and Saxe.

The hussars, except for the trumpeter of the Régiment de Saxe (6e), are illustrated in the 1786 uniform. The Régiment de Bercheny wore light blue dolmans, pelisses and breeches, red cuffs and white (silver for officers) buttons, lace and cords. The *colonel* (6a) is distinguished by the rank distinctions over his cuffs, both on the dolman and pelisse, as well as his breeches and the white fur trimming of his pelisse. Red breeches were customarily adopted by officers of this regiment. The hussar (6b) wears the regulation uniform.

The Régiment de Saxe, which until 1789 had been Conflans, wore dark green dolmans and pelisses and red breeches, red cuffs and yellow (gold for officers) buttons, lace and cords, as illustrated for the hussar (6c). The fur trimming of the hussars' pelisse was black, that of the *colonel* was white, and for the other officers it was of gorge de renard (fox throat so off-white) and NCOs dos de renard (fox back, a dark red-brown).[3] The subaltern (6d) is in tenue de société or de route, with a senior officers' style waistcoat, as an alternative to the breeches shown, these could be of nankin or de fantaisie (fancy) style, with lace on the front, on the thighs, but without rank stripes. For duty in quarters and petite tenue, the officers wore, with the hat or bonnet de police, this surtout, with one or two rows of buttons, in the colour of the regimental dolman. Underneath was worn a waistcoat of the same colour as the surtout, with a single row of buttons for subalterns and with three rows of buttons and braided cords in hussar style for more senior officers. The trumpeter (6e) wears a uniform according to the provisional regulations of 1 April 1791, a royal blue coat with a turned down collar, worn by drummers and trumpeters in the Armée des Princes, decorated with lace of the petite livrée du Roi (small or lesser King's livery) also called galon d'ordonnance (see 12h). He is distinguished by having the regiment's cuffs and breeches. In the hussars, the trumpeters' shabraque was in reverse colours; a black sheepskin.

In these regiments, the hussars carried the cloak rolled in front of the saddle, with the pistol holsters. On campaign, quarters or on marches,

2 For full details see Anon., *Ordonnance du Roi, Concernant le Corps-royal de l'Artillerie des Colonies, du 1er janvier 1786* (Paris: Imprimerie Royale, 1786), Articles XI and XII.

3 Anon., 'Régiment des hussards de Conflans (Louis XVI)', in *Tenues des troupes de France n°15* (Paris: H.E. Martin, 1903), p.17.

overall trousers were worn. They were the same colour as the breeches, with black leather reinforcements on the inner legs and crutch, and lateral bands of the facing colour with small regimental buttons. They could be replaced by leather breeches, often the colour of chamois.

Plate 7: Cavalry of the Régiments Royal-Allemand and Dauphin.

The cavalry was, without doubt, the arm of the royal army that underwent the most reform between 1776 and 1791. As well as the dragoons, hussars, and chasseurs à cheval, there were 26 regiments of heavy cavalry, referred to simply as cavalerie. These included the carabiniers, split into two in 1788 and treated as a separate corps from 1791. The others were distinguished by their titles: three honorific – Colonel-général, Commissaire-général and Mestre de camp-général; five des Princes – La Reine, Dauphin, Berry, Artois and Orléans; the rest were considered royal, of the King or with their names prefixed with Royal, such as Royal-Allemand or Royal-Cravates.

On 1 January 1791, the names ceased to be used, and the regiments were numbered according to the date they had been created (Mestre de camp-général had been disbanded after Nancy). Subsequent regulations sought to standardise the regiments. However, as described above, such regulations were slow to be adopted, so the Régiment Royal-Allemand (trooper 7d, *sergent* 7e, officer 7f) retained its traditional bearskin and the 1786 version of its distinctive uniform. The coat was called à la polonaise, with white Brandenburg buttonholes instead of lapels, vertical pockets (the French regiments had horizontal ones), and on the coat tails curious triple laces ending, like the Brandenburgs, in tassels. It also had a turned-down collar, a distinction shared with the Maison militaire. Finally, the Royal-Allemand was, at the time, the only regiment to have crimson facings. The other cavalry regiments wore a uniform coat that was similar to that of the infantry, with a stand-up collar, distinguished by facing colours.

Both the Royal-Allemand and Dauphin-cavalerie (officer 7a, trumpeter 7b, trooper 7c) are illustrated in what they would have worn in 1792; the 1786 uniform but with the saddlery adopted in 1791, namely the sheepskin half-shabraque. However, they retain the old rectangular portmanteau, as confirmed by a picture of 1793–1795 in the Berlin Album (Anne S.K. Brown Military Collection). The new portmanteaus were to be round with the new regimental number, which was also displayed at the corner of the blue saddle cloth.

The troopers' waistcoats were of white tricot and the breeches of leather. The trumpeter (7b) retains the 1786 uniform, rather than the 1791 replacement (see 6e). Like the infantry:

> Each company is distinguished by a woollen pompom, worn above the cockade, scarlet for the 1st company, celestial blue for the second, pink for the third, marigold yellow for the fourth. The adjudants, master farrier, saddler and armourer wear white pompoms being attached to the staff; the officers' pompom

is of goat hair in the colour allocated for their company. That of the officers of the unit's staff was white.[4]

Finally, troopers wore an ample cloak, which was grey-white flecked with blue, with three white Brandenburgs on each side. Those of the officers were blue with silver lace on the collar.

Plate 8: Medical Services, Administration and Chaplaincy

The *chirurgien major* (surgeon major) of hospitals or military posts (8a) is identifiable by the 12 golden buttonholes or tabs worn on both sides of the coat front. His assistants had six buttonholes, worn from bottom to top, 3, 2 and 1. The coat is a grey-blue, quite close to a cornflower blue. He is distinguished from the *médecin major* (doctor major) of hospitals (8b) by his red waistcoat and breeches. The other distinction was that the *chirurgien major* has black cuffs and a grey-blue collar, the *médecin* having them the other way around. The depiction of a *chirurgien aide-major* (8c) is taken from a contemporary picture; instead of the cuffed boots shown, called à l'américaine, black gaiters could be worn. Due to his rank, he only wears one golden tab on each side of the collar, and his cuff buttons have no vertical tabs. Within each regiment or corps, such as a provincial coalition, the *chirurgien major* and his assistant wore the unit's uniform with black and gold distinctions on the collar, cuffs and hat; only the *chirurgien major* was part of the staff and was mounted. In the hussar and chasseurs à cheval regiments the surgeon wore the surtout coat. For a long time, the *chirurgien major* was forbidden to be armed, so had no sword knot, epaulettes or even a cockade. The *infirmiers* (nurses or orderlies) (8d) were rare and more often stationed within hospitals, or with the ambulance to assist the surgeon, but there were none to collect the wounded.

The *commissaire des guerres* (war commissary) (8e) still wears the uniform from 1786–1791, with the hat bearing gold lace. It only differed from that of the *commissaire ordonnateur*, by the amount of embroidery on the collar and cuffs. On duty on foot or parade, he would wear, like the waistcoat, red breeches instead of those of leather shown here.

Finally, an *aumônier* (chaplain), a common sight throughout the émigré armies is illustrated (8f).

Section 2 – Corps Dressed in the *habit d'émigrant*

There were two versions of the habit d'émigrant, single-breasted (11e), with one row of buttons down the front, or double-breasted (11f) with a double row of buttons and a turned-down, or reversed, collar.

The doubled-breasted style was strongly influenced by British and American fashion, and, like the uniform coat, it was cut so that the colour

4 Verneuil, *L'armée en France*, p.326.

of the waistcoat was visible. Monsieur, later King Louis XVIII, is portrayed wearing this style throughout his reign until his death in 1824. It should also be noted that the provisional instructions of 1 April 1791 for the uniform for generals mentions its adoption for the first time in what was still the French royal army. It was to be the petit uniforme, worn on campaign, 'made with a reversed collar, lapels, [round] cuffs ... & cuff flaps cut in the same proportions as those of the infantry.'[5] It also specified that: 'Aides-de-camp [17a] may wear daily a coat with a reversed collar & fashioned lapels, both for the collar and lapels, the cuffs and cuff flaps, in the shapes and proportions prescribed above for Generals; but the reversed collar will be made of chamois cloth & the coat cannot be decorated with any braid or embroidery.'[6]

With this coat, the aides-de-camp wore a plain black hat, the same sword as the generals, the 1788 model, and a shabraque in the style of the cavalry officers, which was crimson embroidered with gold. Furthermore, 'The waistcoat & breeches will be in chamois cloth, & likewise without embroidery or braid. The buttons of the coat and waistcoat will be gilded, & conform to the design of the model prescribed by the regulation of 1786.'[7] Therefore, the uniform adopted by some of the émigrés was that prescribed by one of the last regulations of the royal army, signed by Louis XVI while still King of France.

The single-breasted version was the frac or tailcoat, and was initially the more widespread. It was also inspired by British civilian clothing; indeed, the French word originated from the English frock coat. Having a single row of buttons, it did not have lapels. This model had been introduced for the French cavalry and was called a surtout in the regulation of 21 February 1779. 'This surtout will be made in the form of a frac & decorated with eight large buttons like the uniform coat, six at the opening, placed one at the top, two in the middle & three below; & two at the hips.'[8] It had an upright collar, round cuffs and lining of the same colour as the coat. Intended to be economical, it was to be worn on the march, campaign and in quarters, so that the full-dress coat would last for six years. It was discontinued on 22 December 1788 for the cavalry and dragoons but retained for the hussars. However, at the start of the Revolution, it was still being used by troopers as quarters or service dress.

In addition, in 1788, three infantry regiments, the Régiment de Provence and the Swiss Régiments de Salis-Samade and Diesbach, that formed the Artois division, had been chosen to try a new experimental uniform, which included a surtout with an upright collar and cuffs of the distinctive colour for subalterns and reversed collars for the senior officers. It was planned that all regiments were to adopt this uniform in 1790, but the project was abandoned

5 Anon., *Instruction provisoire sur l'uniforme des officiers généraux et des aides de camp. Du 1er avril 1791* (Paris: Imprimerie Royale, 1792), p.6.
6 Anon., *Instruction provisoire généraux et des aides de camp*, p.8.
7 Anon., *Instruction provisoire généraux et des aides de camp*, p.8.
8 Anon., *Règlement arrêté par le Roi pour l'Habillement et l'Equipement de ses Troupes. Du 21 février 1779* (Paris: Imprimerie royale, 1779), p.26 also *Règlement du 1er Octobre 1786*, p.63.

due to financial difficulties.[9] Nevertheless, the term frac was still in use in the French army, as seen in an instruction of 1791: 'The Trumpeters of the Chasseurs à Cheval regiments, will wear a frac à la française, like that of the hussar trumpeters.'[10] A painting 1790 of chasseurs à cheval officers shows one in a frac and hat, so this coat, subsequently worn by the émigrés, already existed at the end of the reign of Louis XVI, with the cuffs and reversed collar in the facing colour (10c).

Senior Officer, Régiment de Provence-infanterie, experimental uniform 1788, by Hoffmann-Millot. (Hoffmann-Millot, Tenues d'essai 1788, courtesy of La Sabretache)

What became known as the emigrant uniform, of whichever version, was the most commonly worn style within the Armée des Princes, including by the generals and staff. The first unit to adopt it was the Chevaliers de la Couronne (1c). One of the corps wrote that at the end of June 1791 (so two months before the appearance of the Princes' regulation of 19 August that established the habit d'émigrant), 'at Mannheim a uniform was adopted: it was a blue frac with fleurs-de-lys on the buttons.'[11] The first two companies of the Coalition d'Auvergne, formed from 20 August 1791, would also appear to have been wearing the habit d'émigrant when they were presented to Monsieur and the Comte d'Artois, near the castle of Schönbornslust, on 27 September 1791.[12] An illustration in Champflour's *La Coalition d'Auvergne* shows a double-breasted coat, although it is described elsewhere as simply a 'blue coat without lapels.'[13] This double-breasted coat appears to have also been worn by the companies of retired officers and gentlemen of Condé's corps.

The habit d'émigrant, in its various forms, was worn by about 10,000 to 12,000 men in the army, not only in the companies of former officers or gentlemen volunteers but also those of the Third Estate as well as, for example, the Chevaliers de la Couronne, units of the Maison militaire, and the Corps de la Marine.

9 See Anon., 'Essai d'une nouvelle tenue (1788)', *Carnet de La Sabretache*, No. 79, 1899, pp.398–399, which includes three plates illustrating the uniforms and the La Sabretache collection holds a set of such plates by the artist Hoffmann.

10 Anon., *Instruction l'Habillement*, p.5.

11 La Maisonfort, *Mémoires*, p.184.

12 Champflour (ed.), *La Coalition d'Auvergne*, pp.120, 124.

13 Champflour (ed.), *La Coalition d'Auvergne*, p.124.

However, whatever uniform was worn, the émigrés wanted above all to be the custodians of the traditions of the former royal army through the maintenance of different orders of dress (quarter, marching, service, campaign, parade, etc.) and emblems such as rank distinctions, gorgets (11b), titles, flags, guidons, standards, sword knots (11d) etc..

Plates 9–11: Companies of officers and gentlemen (infantry and cavalry).

Officers who had emigrated generally wore their existing uniforms, for example, 9a – *lieutenant*, chasseurs à pied des Ardennes, 9d – Comte de La Tour, *colonel* of the Royal-Liégeois, 10c – officer, unnamed chasseurs à cheval regiment, from a contemporary painting, and 10e – officer of the Orléans-cavalerie, campaign of France. These were sometimes copied by volunteers who joined the companies of officers, such as 9c – volontaire, Régiment de Provence. The Regulations of 19 August 1791 were intended primarily for the new companies of officers or retired officers and gentlemen, so men who did not have a uniform. Article XX defined the clothing that had already been adopted:

> The uniform of all the companies will be a blue coat, red waistcoat, yellow breeches; buttons of gilded brass, with a fleur-de-lys in the middle. White plume on the hat, white cockade & black collar … And in the case where some companies had already adopted a different uniform than that prescribed by the regulation, the Princes permit that they provisionally retain them.[14]

It should be noted that the collar mentioned above was a separate piece worn inside the coat and not that of the coat. The coat was lined with serge of the same blue colour as the coat which had horizontal pockets with three buttons.

Nevertheless, it is clear that all ranks in the cavalry companies of retired officers and gentlemen in the Armée de Condé wore the double-breasted frac with a red folded down collar. This is attested by at least two miniatures, including that of the Duc d'Enghien, as a volunteer, in the Musée de l'Empéri, Collections Raoul et Jean Brunon, Salon-de-Provence. Given that the Prince de Condé was particularly strict regarding regulations, it can be assumed that this was consistent across all such units. However, the infantry may not have worn the same double-breasted frac; indeed, the officer of such a compagnie noble illustrated (9e) wears a single-breasted coat.

Although it cannot be said for certain, it is reasonable to assume that the similar companies in the other armies wore more or less the same uniform, but with the regulation royal blue collar (11g). For all the companies of officers and gentlemen, the shabraque from this period was of black sheepskin, with

14 Anon., *Règlement définitif*, Article XX.

royal blue furniture, and one can assume that red lace was adopted by the noble companies.

Grouvel states that the drummers wore the same coat as the rest of the company but with their collar, cuffs and pockets edged with the lace of the petite livrée du Roi. Their waistcoats would have been white or yellow, and their breeches white, yellow or blue.

The trumpeters of the mounted companies of officers and gentlemen were similarly dressed, but with white or buckskin waistcoats and breeches and white boot cuffs. Grouvel describes the coat: 'turned down collar in crimson cloth over a upright collar; cuffs and shoulder straps of royal blue cloth. The coat is laced, in wool, in the King's livery, all around the collar, the cuffs, the pocket flaps and at the top of the sleeve, in the form of swallow nests on a crimson background.'[15] As this is clearly an adaptation of the regulation trumpeter's uniform for the habit d'émigrant, it is reasonable to assume that the cuffs were also crimson.

The commanders of the companies of officers, however, could choose to dress their drummers (and so by implication the cavalry trumpeters) in other liveries, such as that of Bourbon as described in a statement:

> … hat, with white cockade and plume; ventre de biche [a soft ochre colour] cloth for the coat, scarlet linen and serge for the lining and breeches, crimson velvet for the collar, cuffs and livery lace; yellow wire buttons, blackened gaiters, white stockings, shoes with brass buckles, sabre, shoulder belt, [drum] case barrel of brass with crimson rims, sticks, holder and drum-cover …[16]

It should be noted that in the companies of retired officers and gentlemen while former officers were authorised to wear their epaulettes (as by 11e), no other rank distinctions were worn, unlike other units such as the Chevaliers de la Couronne or Marine royale.

Plates 10–12: Provincial Coalitions, Compagnies franches and Compagnies du tiers.

Without evidence to the contrary, it is to be believed that the companies of the coalitions, free companies and those of the Third Estate wore the uniform described in the Regulation of 19 August 1791. However, the red waistcoat would have been worn by the coalitions and not the others. The only exception was the Compagnie du Tiers in the Coalition de Bretagne that wore grey, with red collars (12f). All the buttons were gilded with a large fleur de lys in the centre (11a); the 10 buttons down the front being larger than those for the waistcoat and the cockade strap on the hat. The hat was uniform for all companies wearing the habit d'émigrant.

Several of the coalitions (unfortunately, information is not available for all) sought to be distinctive. So, the first such uniform, that of the Coalition

15 Grouvel, *Troupes de l'émmigration*, vol.II, p.197.

16 Grouvel, *Troupes de l'émigration*, vol.II, p.202.

d'Auvergne (10b) was described as: 'Blue coat without lapels. Yellow cuffs and collar, red piping, yellow breeches, yellow waistcoat. Buttons with the fleur de lys, scaled epaulettes, *à la Piémontaise*, without distinction of rank. Plain hat, white cockade and plume, green sprig. Sabre of choice, white sash. Horse furniture: bearskin shabraque edged in yellow.'[17] Although the epaulettes à la Piémontaise were not retained, the rest of the uniform remained. Across the companies of officers and gentlemen, as well as the provincial coalitions, these were:

- Differences in the cut of the coat, single or double-breasted, with or without turnbacks.
- Particular colours, or materials, on the collar and cuffs. As has been seen those of the Coalition d'Auvergne were yellow and they were sky blue for the Coalition de Champagne (former officer 12b & drummer 12g). The collar and cuffs of the Coalition de Normandie were of false leopard skin (10a).
- Insignia or lace, such as the lace worn on the red collar and cuffs and blue turnbacks of the Coalition d'Artois et de Flandre (12c, 12d). While the inner turnbacks of the coats of the Coalition de Normandie had gold fleur-de-lys on them, the outer ones were decorated with gold leopards.
- Waistcoats could be single or double-breasted. Red ones were associated with staff officers and so-called learned branches of the army, the artillery and engineers, as well as noble officers in the navy. As foreseen by the regulation, there were variations and Grouvel described compagnies d'officiers as wearing yellow waistcoats with a double row of buttons.
- The standards carried by units, although all were white and followed a similar pattern, were unique. The obverse bore the arms of France and, in the case of the coalitions, those of the province while the reverse had emblems and other devices specific to the unit. The only example of a standard carried by a coalition that is known is that of Champagne, showing the arms of France attached to those of Champagne on the observe and the other side has the date 1358 (when Champagne became part of France) with a cross of Lorraine on a azure field in each corner, denoting the coalition included gentlemen from Lorraine and Barrois.[18]
- Finally, all companies of the Coalition de Bretagne, including the Compagnie franche du Tiers (12f), wore a white sash scattered with ermine symbols, the heraldic emblem of Brittany.

Plate 13: The Corps royal de la Marine

The uniform of this corps is well established due to the existence of at least seven portraits of officers serving in it. Five of the paintings represent members of the cavalry squadron, on foot beside their horses, and the others

17 Champflour (ed.), *La Coalition d'Auvergne*, p.124.
18 Grouvel, *Troupes de l'émigration*, vol.III, p.210.

are bust portraits of men serving with the infantry.[19] All are dressed in a royal blue frac, with a single row of 10 buttons, a turned-down collar, and round cuffs, with two or three buttons, also of royal blue. The waistcoat was French scarlet in colour, as worn throughout the army by the noble corps, and all the portraits confirm the orange tint of this shade.

The uniform was identical in every way for the infantry and cavalry companies. The officers' epaulettes were of those of the army, but royal blue replaced feu red for the distinctions (13b). The gilded buttons bore the fleur-de-lys like the other companies.

The cavalry, or chasseurs à cheval, (13f) wore a black leather waistbelt over the waistcoat that carried the straight sabre, of the émigré model, with a guard of three branches, in a leather scabbard with brass reinforcements at each end. The waistbelt bore a naval anchor superimposed with a silver fleur-de-lys and the words Mon Dieu, above, and Mon Roi, below.

Article XXI of the Regulations of 19 August 1791 stated that: 'In companies of mounted gentlemen, saddles that can be obtained will be used indiscriminately; but holsters will be adapted to them, and they will be covered with a shabraque of red wool, or such other colour adopted by the company, the aforesaid shabraque plain and without lace.'[20]

However, it is certain that no known units conformed to this, and the five surviving paintings representing cavalrymen of the Navy squadron show the form illustrated here. The trumpeter (13g) wears the uniform prescribed for the émigré companies; the royal blue uniform of the rest of the unit, but with the collar, cuffs and pockets edged with a lace of the King's livery.

The infantry is represented by an *élève* (pupil) or *aspirant* (midshipman) (13a) and a mounted officer (13e). The rank of the first is denoted by his wearing a hat that is smaller than those of his seniors and the badges of rank on his shoulders being reversed: a contre-epaulette on the left and an epaulette on the right. The latter also has a shoulder belt of black leather, but with a brass plate of the same design as the cavalry. An alternative to this, which may have been reserved for the naval élèves, was a black leather sheath bearing a white fleur-de-lys in the centre and the words Mon Dieu above and Mon Roi below. The officers on foot carried an infantry sabre, but with the hilt of a 1780-model ship's officer's sabre with a bronze lion's head above the brown leather grip, as shown in the portrait of François-Yves de la Roche Kerandron.[21]

Another contemporary portrait shows a naval officer (13c) wearing the regulation greatcoat of the end of the reign of Louis XVI, which is blueish slate grey in colour.

While several sources clearly attest that the infantry was provided with a flag and the cavalry with a standard, the exact description is not given.

19 One, a full-length portrait of horseman, in the collection of the Society of the Cincinnati, Washington D.C., USA, is wrongly identified as being of the Comte d'Estaing.

20 Anon., *Règlement définitif*, Article XXI.

21 See <https://fr.wikipedia.org/wiki/Fran%C3%A7ois-Yves_de_la_Roche_Kerandraon>, accessed 10 June 2024.

However, the trumpet banner (13g) is known.[22] Thus, following the tradition of the cavalry, it can be assumed that the emblems on the standard were identical. Furthermore, the author Henri Servien described a fanion (13d). However, he wrote that this was 'of the colonel's company of the Régiment Marine royale destroyed at Quiberon (1795).'[23] In this, he confuses the Régiment d'Hector, which was also sometimes called the Royal-Marine, an infantry unit raised in July 1794 in British pay, with the Corps de la Marine royale. The Régiment d'Hector, as with all such units, only had one flag, which was white with three golden fleurs-de-lys.

So, it can be concluded that the flag and standard, like the trumpet banner, were white with the arms of France on the obverse and the name of the corps on the reverse, both sides having anchors and fleur-de-lys in the corners. Both the flag and standard would have had a white cravat and alternating gold and silver cords and tassels.

Plates 14–16: The Reconstituted Maison militaire.

A leading principle in the reconstitution of the Maison militaire was that its units, considered the élite of the royal army, should set an example and not be distinguished by ostentatious dress. It was by the quality of their mounts and armament, and by their buttons and organisation, that they were to be recognised. Unfortunately, their cost was to be a considerable burden on the available funds, in particular to the detriment of the Armées de Condé and Bourbon.

The reconstituted corps, even if under new names, wore the habit d'émigrant in the colour of its forerunner, the only exception to this being the Hommes d'armes à pied. Within corps, companies were identified by different colours or buttons and lace of gold or silver.

At the time of the Revolution, the dress of the Gardes du corps du Roi consisted of a grand uniforme (full dress) and a lesser-known petit uniforme (service dress). The first was unchanged since Louis XIV, except for some details reflecting the style of the day, and consisted of a dark blue coat with red folded-over collars, cuffs, waistcoat and breeches with extensive silver lace decoration. The petit uniforme was identical to that of the cavalry, according to the regulation of 1786, with scarlet, or orangey-red, lapels, collars and cuffs. The coat lining was white, as were the waistcoats, and buckskin breeches were worn. The turnbacks bore the symbol of the Gardes, a radiant sun with a face in silver thread on a blue cloth background.[24]

In emigration, the Gardes du corps du Roi wore a black hat without lace, with a white cockade and plume; blue habit d'émigrant with red turned-over collar and cuffs which were edged with plain one-inch-wide silver lace as were the flaps of the horizontal pockets; red waistcoat; nankin breeches; cavalry boots with white inner cuffs. Unlike the earlier petit uniforme, the

---

22 Grouvel, *Troupes de l'émigration*, vol.III, p.93.

23 Henri Servien, *Petite histoire des guerres de Vendée* (Niort: Editions de Chiré, 1983), p.144.

24 An example of this uniform is displayed in the Musée de l'Armée, Paris.

Table 16: Distinctions in the Maison militaire of the Armée des Princes.

Corps	Coat	Waistcoat and breeches	Collar and cuffs	Distinctions
Gardes du corps du Roi	Royal blue	Red on foot duty, white on campaign	Red for all companies	Silver shoulder belts with squares in the company colour:
1ère Cie	Compagnie écossaise			White
2e Cie	1ère compagnie française, de Noailles			Red
3e Cie	2e compagnie française, de Gramont			Green
4e Cie	3e compagnie française, de Luxembourg			Yellow
Gardes du corps de Monsieur	Scarlet red	Blue waistcoat; red breeches on service on foot and white on campaign	Blue	Silver shoulder belts with squares in the company colour:
1e Cie	Cte d'Avaray – guet			Aurore
2e Cie	Cte de Damas – cornette/escadron			Violet
Gardes du corps du Comte d'Artois	Saxon green	Crimson, white on campaign	Crimson; crimson and silver waistbelt	Silver shoulder belts with squares in the company colour:
1e Cie	Bailli de Crussol – guet			Sky blue
2e Cie	Chevalier de Puységur – Cornette/escadron			Pink
1ère Cie noble d'ordonnance	Red	White waistcoats, whitened leather breeches	Red	Gilt buttons, epaulettes and lace
2e Cie noble d'ordonnance	Red	White waistcoats, whitened leather breeches	Red	Silver buttons, epaulettes and lace
Hommes d'armes à cheval	Red	White waistcoats, whitened leather breeches	Red	Silver shoulder belts with squares in the company colour:
1ère Cie	Ecossais			White
2e Cie	Anglais			Violet
3e Cie	Bourguignons			Royal blue
4e Cie	Flandre			Yellow
5e Cie	La Reine			Puce red
6e Cie	Dauphin			Sky blue
7e Cie	Monsieur			Black
8e Cie	Artois			Light green
Hommes d'armes à pied	Red	Red waistcoat, white breeches	Sky blue	White metal buttons
Cie de l'Institution de St Louis	Royal blue	Red waistcoat; white breeches	Red	Gilt buttons with a silver fleur de lys, corps lace
Grenadiers d'ordonnance	Royal blue	White waistcoats, whitened leather breeches	Red	Bearskin

coat lining and turnbacks, with the same decoration, were blue. The buttons were silver; 'The war cry of the gardes du corps is UN ROI OU LA MORT [a King or Death], and this motto is engraved on their button.'[25] The waistcoat bore little silver buttons of the same description, and the greatcoat was of the regulation type for the cavalry, but of royal blue with white lace at the base of the cape.

Knowing that the uniforms were to be simpler, as an economy measure, it is likely that the coats of the Gardes of Monsieur and Artois were lined in a similar fashion while retaining their distinctive colours.

25 Louis Blanc, *Histoire de la Révolution française* (Paris: Librairie internationale, 1869), vol.II, p.55.

For indoors duty, service d'appartement, and in the immediate vicinity of the palace, when red stockings were worn, the Gardes du Corps were armed with a sword as well as a small musket (mousqueton). Mounted, they carried the 1787 model sabre, which served as the model for the noble émigré cavalry through to the disbanding of the Armée de Condé in 1801.

As seen in Table 16, each company was distinguished by the squares of their shoulder belts being of different colours. The respective colours could have also been used for the waistbelts used on duty on foot, but the figures illustrated are all shown wearing black leather waistbelts. The figures are:

Garde du corps du Roi (14a) and trumpeter (14b) of the compagnie de Luxembourg, both on mounted duty.
Garde of the same company on service d'appartement (14c).
Gardes de Monsieur, officer (14d).
Garde de Monsieur, compagnie d'Avaray service d'appartement (14e).
Garde du comte d'Artois, compagnie de Crussol, service d'appartement (14f).

The other members of the Maison militaire that are illustrated are:

1ère Compagnie noble d'ordonnance, standard bearer (15a).
1ère Compagnie noble d'ordonnance, standard (15b); this was formerly carried by the Gendarmes de la Garde du Roi, the reverse was the same.
1ère Compagnie noble d'ordonnance, officer (15c).
1ère Compagnie noble d'ordonnance, *maître* (15d).
Hommes d'armes à cheval, 4e Compagnie, Flandre, *maître* (16d).
Hommes d'armes à cheval, 6e Compagnie, Dauphin, *maître* (16e).
Hommes d'armes à pied, *fusilier d'ordonnance* (16a).
Compagnie de l'Institution de St Louis, *garde* (16b). The collar and cuffs of the coat are edged with white lace with alternate gold and silver diamond shapes. Brass scaled epaulettes with gold and silver, mixed, fringes on the left shoulder and a contre-epaulette on the right.
Grenadiers d'ordonnance, grenadier (16c); the corps retained the traditional grenadier cap of its forerunner.

Plate 17: Princes, *maréchaux*, *généraux* and Staff

The princes retained previous uniforms, as described by the Comte d'Espinchal, who on 19 September 1790 attended a dinner at Milan held by the Archduke Ferdinand: 'Today, each of us changes costume and puts aside the frac for uniform. The Prince de Condé puts on that of colonel-général of the infantry and the other two princes that of their infantry regiments; du Cayla, d'Autichamp, Choiseul and the Chevalier de Virieu have the uniform of maréchal de camp and I that of supernumerary colonel of cavalry.'[26]

26 Hauterive (ed.), *Espinchal*, p.49.

1a

1c

1b

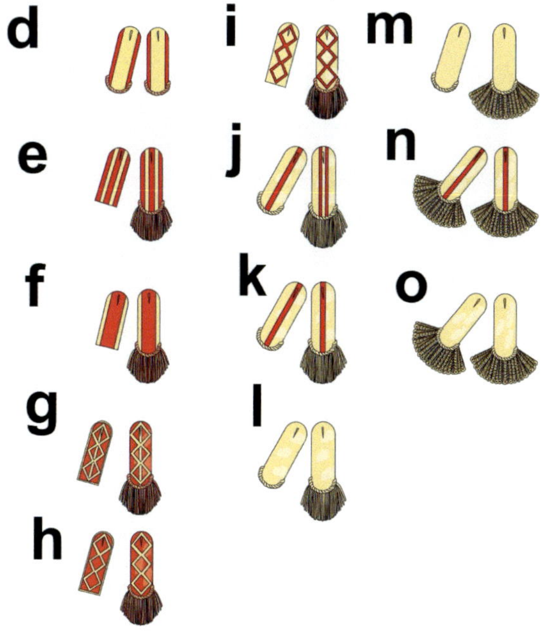

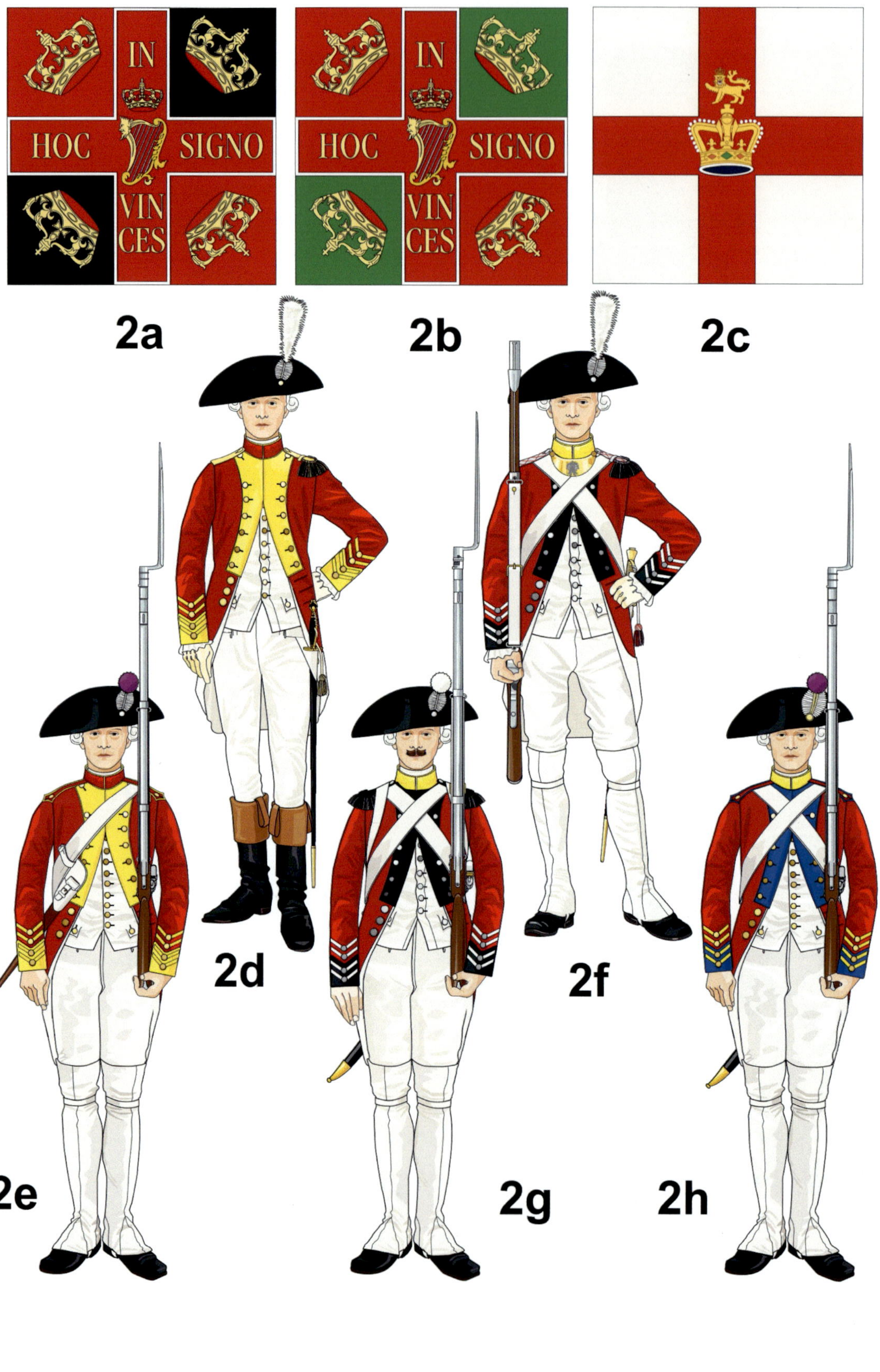
IN
HOC SIGNO
VIN
CES
IN
HOC SIGNO
VIN
CES
2a
2b
2c
2d
2f
2e
2g
2h

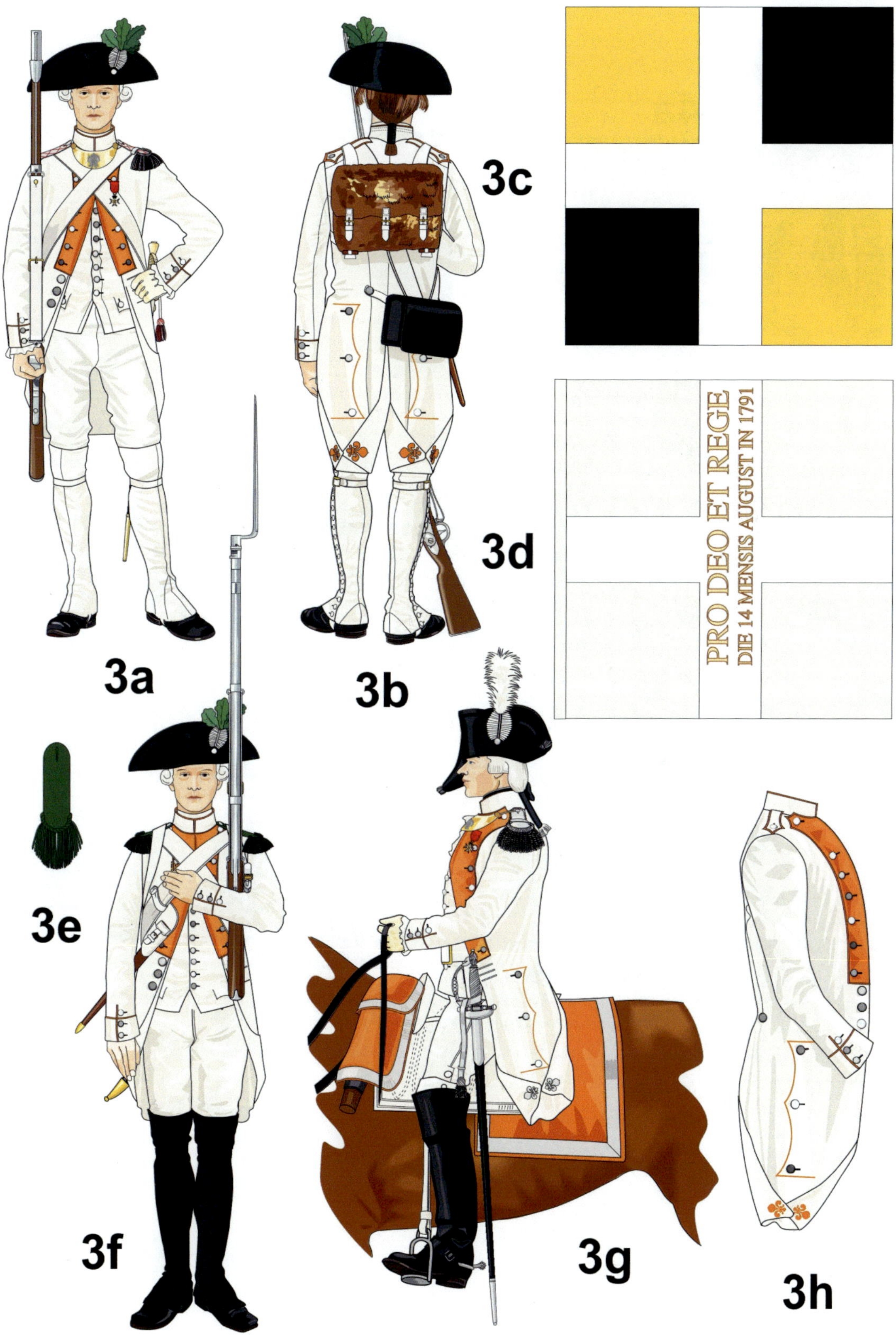
3a
3b
3c
3d
PRO DEO ET REGE
DIE 14 MENSIS AUGUST IN 1791
3e
3f
3g
3h

4a
4b
4c
4d
4e
4f
4g
CORPS DE CONDE
COMPAGNIE
SUISSE

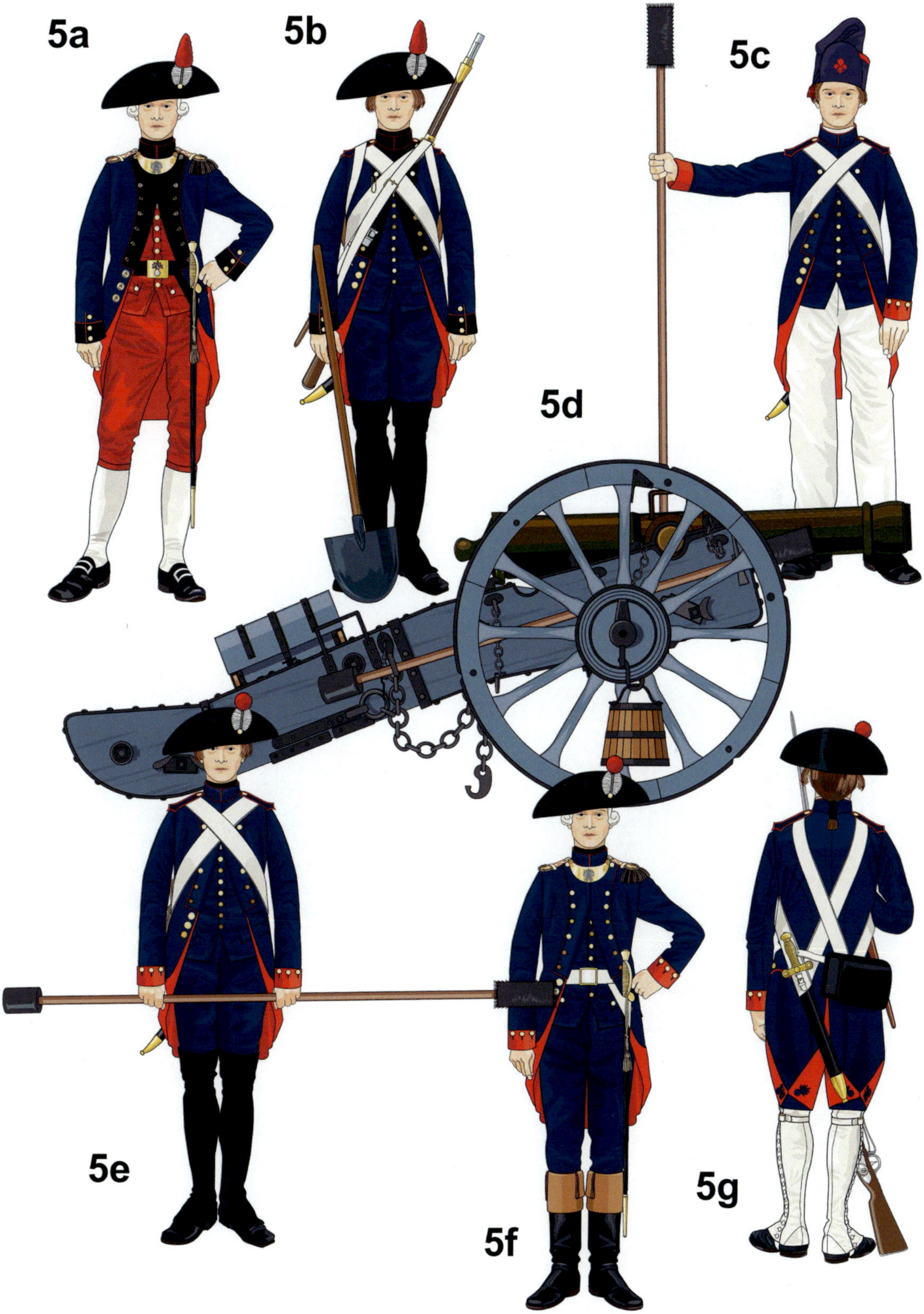
5a
5b
5c
5d
5e
5f
5g

6a

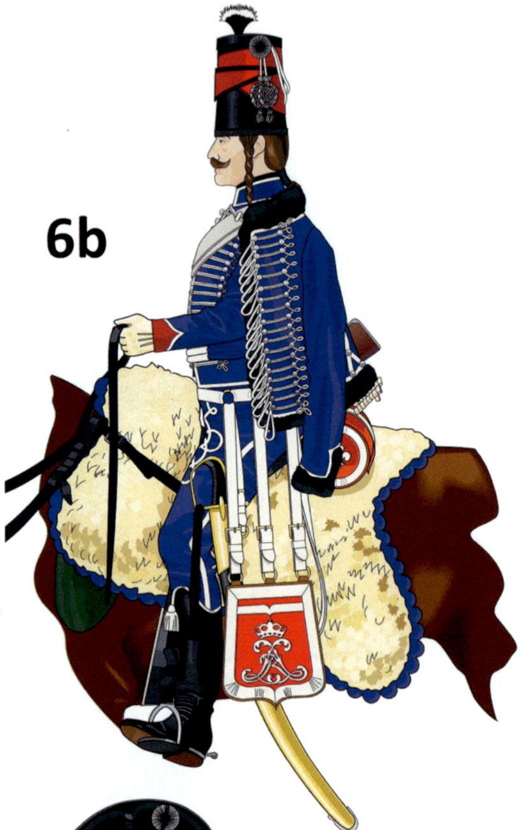

6b

6c

6d

6e

7a
7b
7c
7d
7e
7f

8a

8b

8c

8d

8e

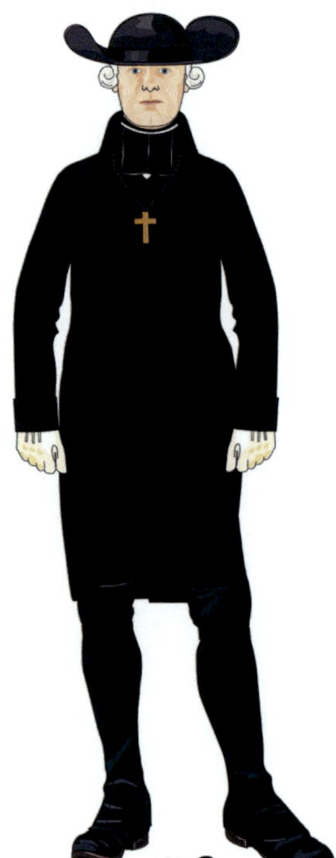
8f

9a

9b

9c

9d

9e

10a

10b

10c

10d

10e

11a

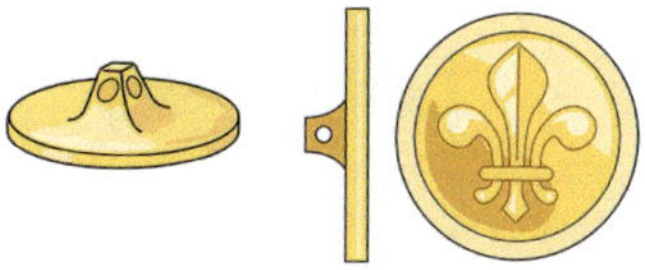

11b

11c

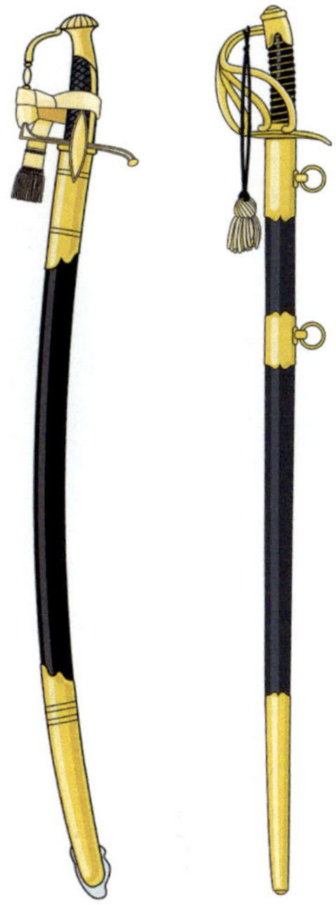

11d

11f

11g

11e

12a
12b
12c
12d
12e
12f
12g
12h

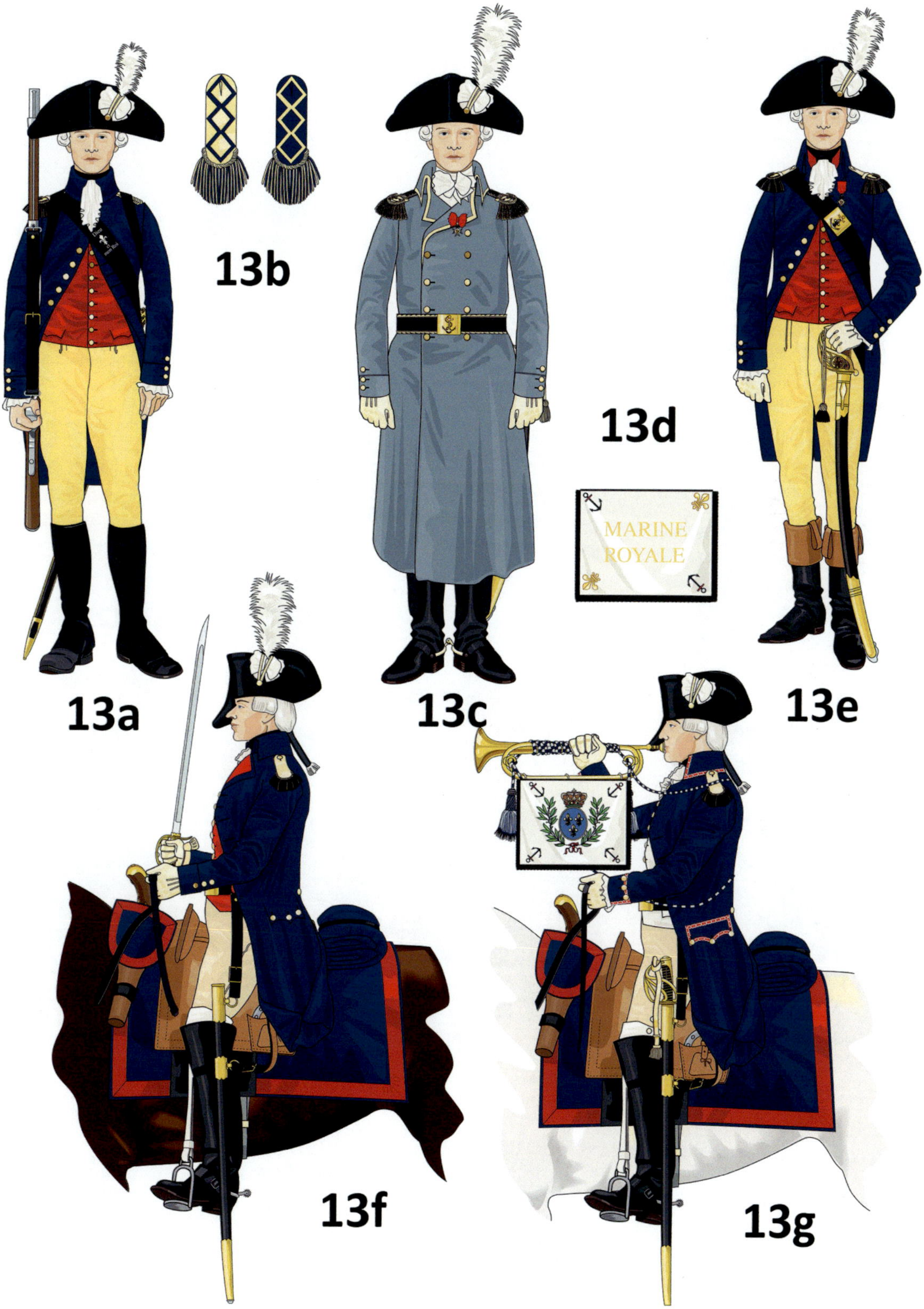
13a
13b
13c
13d
MARINE
ROYALE
13e
13f
13g

14a
14b
14c
14d
14e
14f

15b

15a

15c

15d

16a

16b

16c

16d

16e

17a
17b
17c
17d
17e

18a
18b
18c
18d
18e
18f

19a
19b
19c
19d
19e
19f

20b
LES CHASSEURS ROYAUX DES PRINCES
20a
20c
20d
20e
20f

21a
21b
21c
21d
21e

22a
22b
22c
22d
22e
22f

23a

23b

23c

23d

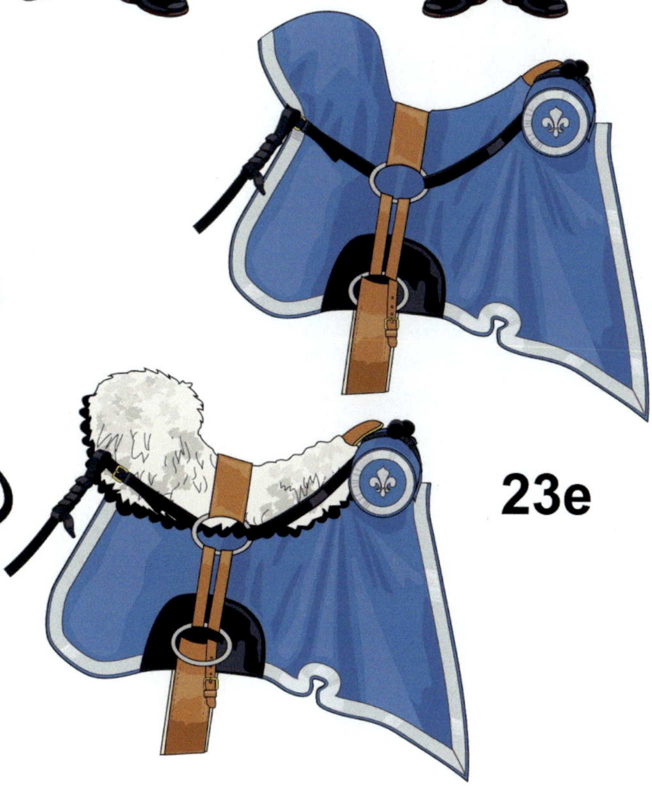

23e

24a
24b
24c
24d
24e

Aide de camp, petit tenue, 1789. (*Le Passepoil* 1936/5, Le duc d'Orléans, colonel-général des hussards, 1789, courtesy of La Sabretache)

The Prince de Condé continued to wear this uniform when appearing at court during his later exile in Britain. Furthermore, Monsieur wore his 'full dress uniform of colonel of the carabiniers,' when the Armée du Centre paraded for the King of Prussia on 11 August 1792.[27]

However, the uniforme d'émigrant was adopted by all; not only was it more practical on campaign, but it was also shared by the other gentlemen in the army. The aide de camp (17a), here a *colonel*, wears a uniform conforming to the Provisional Instruction of 1 April described above, with folded down collar and chamois coloured waistcoat and breeches; his sash was that used by the staff of the Armée du Centre and his sword and sword knot is of the 1788 model for officers on general duty.

Monsieur (17b) is shown wearing the habit d'émigrant with the distinctions of the Coalition de Normandie; the details, including the unusual ceremonial sword, are based upon a miniature of 1795. The wearing of the distinctions of this coalition alludes to him being Regent for the Dauphin, the Duc de Normandie. The horse furniture in a soft shade of green is taken from an illustration showing him in the uniform of *colonel-général* of the carabiniers on the eve of the Revolution, although used for a half, or rump, saddle cloth, and the pistol holster covers. The uniform worn by the Prince de Condé (17c) is well known. He is depicted in full dress. His service dress was the

27 Brons, *Journal*, pp.53–54.

same, but then he wore the blue sash of the Order of Saint-Esprit under his coat. His epaulettes have three stars added to those of a *colonel*, showing, like his saddlecloth, the rank of *lieutenant-général*. His French-style saddle is covered with crimson velvet, and his baton of command has a sheath of copper or brass. The sword that is reproduced is based on the original at the Musée Condé, Chantilly, which was presented by Louis XVI to mark his appointment as *colonel-général* of the infantry in 1780.

The depiction of *maréchal* de Castries (17d) is based on, 'A miniature … [which] represents him in a royal blue coat with upright collar and lapels the same, gold embroidery (which is not that of generals), on the collar and lapels; a colonel's gilded epaulettes charged with two crossed bâtons de maréchaux, in blue and gold enamel.'[28] Features known to have been worn by émigré generals have been incorporated, so the embroidery lace is shown edging the collar, the lapels are turned over and the cuffs are round. The baton of command is of the pattern for *maréchaux*, with a royal blue sleeve scattered with gold fleurs de lys. The last figure is of the Duc de Bourbon (17e), taken from a contemporary miniature, wearing a brown riding coat without a brassard, which dates the portrait from 1792.

Section 3 – Plates 18 & 19: The German line regiments raised for the service of the Princes.

These three regiments, Rohan, Wittgenstein and Hohenlohe-Schillingsfürst, wore the uniforms of the French army of 1786–1791. The peculiarity of the German infantry regiments was the colour of their coats, which was bleu céleste, sometimes given as bleu céleste foncé (dark celestial blue), not to be confused, as mentioned above, with bleu ciel (sky blue).

Wittgenstein is represented by fusiliers (18a & 18b) and a fusilier *capitaine* (18c), while Rohan is represented by a chasseur (18d), a grenadier (18e) and a fusilier officer (18f). Hohenlohe-Schillingsfürst is represented by a fusilier officer (19d), a fusilier (19e) and a grenadier drummer (19f). This regiment's traditions were continued in 1815 in the Légion royale étrangère and then through the Légion (1818) and Régiment de Hohenlohe (1821) to today's Légion étrangère, created in 1831.

Table 17: The German line regiments in the service of the Princes.

Regiment	Facing colours	Headdress	Companies
Rohan étranger; yellow metal buttons	White collar White lapels White cuffs	Hat	Fusiliers
		Hat	Chasseurs
		Bearskin	Grenadiers
Wittgenstein; yellow metal buttons	Yellow collar Red lapels Red cuffs	1791 model helmet	Fusiliers
		Bearskin	Grenadiers
Hohenlohe-Schillingsfürst; white metal buttons	Collar, lapels and cuffs, black with white piping.	Hat	Fusiliers
		Bearskin	Grenadiers

28 Grouvel, *Troupes de l'émigration*, vol.III, p.29.

Only the fusiliers of the Régiment de Wittgenstein adopted the fur crested French 1791 model helmet; the others wore hats that were still tricornes, but with the front corner less protruding than in earlier times, part of the evolution to the bicorne.

The 1791 helmet was distinct from the dragoon helmet, a version of which was worn in the French infantry from 1771 to 1776. This model differed from that of the dragoons in that the crest was further back but had the same horse mane. It was generally abandoned in 1776 for the tricorne described above. Only the Régiment du Roi retained the helmet, decorated on the front by an oval brass plate bearing the arms of France, held by two chains on the side. The other peculiarity was that all the officers and the entire Compagnie-colonelle wore it with a white, rather than black, mane, a tradition that was adopted by the Légion de Mirabeau to distinguish volunteers and staff officers. When the Régiment colonel-général infanterie was created in 1780 for the Prince de Condé, it was equipped with a similar helmet but, unlike the earlier model, the crest was further forward with a Medusa head and the embossed frontal plate, with the arms of Colonel-général, descended from the crest to the crown. The mane was, however, white for the whole regiment.

After having considered equipping the French infantry with a shako in 1788, in 1791 the helmet with a central fur crest, described in French as à chenille (with caterpillar), was adopted. However, among the émigré units, it was only used by the Régiment de Wittgenstein.

Section 4 – Light Troops (Plates 20 & 21)

The units in the Armée des Princes, created specifically for a reconnaissance role, to conduct raids on the enemy or to harass them with accurate fire, wore a variety of uniforms. These were not influenced by French patterns or the habit d'émigrant but by German, Austrian, British or Polish styles. The dominant colours were green, black, brown and grey as seen in Table 18.

In contrast, there is no reason to consider that the clothing of the free companies, although their uniforms would have been decided by their respective proprietors, was not based on the habit d'émigrant. Although it is of note that the Compagnie de Rouault, in the Armée du Centre, was considered as a unit of chasseurs à pied, or light infantry, however there is, unfortunately, no information about its uniform.

Table 18: Uniforms of the Light Troops (Uhlans, chasseurs à cheval, light infantry, chasseurs carabiniers)

<table>
<tr><th>Corps</th><th>Headgear</th><th>Jacket</th><th>Distinctions</th></tr>
<tr><td>Chasseurs royaux des Princes (20a)
Armée du Centre</td><td>British light infantry style cap, with white crest and red plume</td><td>Scarlet red jacket; waistcoat likewise, with 8 yellow buttonholes on each side. Yellow buttons. White breeches. Black studded boot and half-gaiters</td><td>Black collar with a yellow buttonhole on each side, black lapels with yellow buttonholes. Black pointed cuffs with yellow lace.</td></tr>
<tr><td colspan="4">Equipment and uniforms bought in England; British style oval breast plate (20b); black leather crossed shoulder belts; rifled carbines with or without sabre-bayonet.</td></tr>
<tr><td>Chasseurs-carabiniers de Goerduck (20c)
Armée du Centre</td><td>Black top hat, white cockade and green plume</td><td>Brown jacket and breeches; half-gaiters</td><td>Grass green collar, pointed cuffs, lapels and lining; golden yellow lace on the cuffs and buttonholes; yellow metal buttons.</td></tr>
<tr><td>Chasseurs flamands de Calonne (20d)
Armée de Bourbon</td><td>Tyrolean jäger style hat with turned up rim to the side; yellow cockade strap</td><td>Iron grey short jacket and breeches; black half-gaiters; yellow metal buttons with a fleur de lys</td><td>Collar, Bavarian style lapels, cuffs, turnbacks and shoulder straps dark green with scarlet piping. Officers' gorgets, rank distinctions and sword knots in the French style</td></tr>
<tr><td colspan="4">Equipment of black leather; rifled carbine with sabre-bayonet; black leather waistbelt with pouch and two pistol holsters on the front.</td></tr>
<tr><td>Chasseurs étrangers de Polignac (20e,20f)
Armée du Centre</td><td>Celestial blue czapka, turban of black sheep skin, orangey yellow cords and raquettes</td><td>Celestial blue jacket, celestial blue Hungarian style breeches with orangey yellow lace bastions</td><td>Scarlet red collar, pointed cuffs, turnbacks and heart-shaped plastron lapels; orangey yellow lace on the cuffs, turnbacks and buttonholes</td></tr>
<tr><td colspan="4">White leather equipment; gilded button with a fleur de lys; cavalry horse furniture: Hungarian style with white sheepskin, celestial blue schabraque with red wolf's-teeth edging, celestial blue portmanteau the ends of which had red lace edging and a white fleur de lys in the centre.</td></tr>
<tr><td>Légion de Normandie or de Carneville
Armée de Bourbon</td><td colspan="3">The uniforms of some elements – the free and grenadier companies – are not known. However, a company of foot chasseurs and two of light infantry (formerly fusiliers) were taken into Austrian service late in 1792. Their uniforms, which are known, would have been those of the original corps.</td></tr>
<tr><td>Light Infantry (21a)</td><td>Black leather hat, rim raised at the front; red turban; brass plate on the front with a hunting horn; yellow cord</td><td>Green short jacket; white waistcoat; blue breeches; black half-gaiters</td><td>Yellow metal buttons; black collar with yellow lace; black Bavarian plastron lapels with yellow piping and lace buttonholes; inverted pointed cuffs black with red piping and, above, three buttons with yellow herring-bone buttonholes; black turnbacks pied red</td></tr>
<tr><td colspan="4">White leather crossed belts with cartridge pouch and sabre briquet; musket and bayonet.</td></tr>
<tr><td>Chasseurs à pied (21b)</td><td>As above</td><td>As above</td><td>As above but the collar was red (with no lace) and the lapels were piped red instead of yellow</td></tr>
<tr><td>Black leather crossed belts; rifled carbine and sabre-bayonet.</td><td></td><td></td><td></td></tr>
<tr><td>Chasseurs à cheval (21e)</td><td>Black helmet of boiled leather; brass reinforcements; red turban; brass fleur de lys on the front of the crown; black mane</td><td>As above</td><td>As for the chasseurs à pied above</td></tr>
<tr><td colspan="4">Green schabraque with yellow lace; portmanteau likewise with a yellow fleur de lys in the centre; chasseur à cheval sabre and pistols.</td></tr>
<tr><td colspan="4">Légion de Breuilpont
Armée de Bourbon</td></tr>
<tr><td>Chasseurs-carabiniers (21d)</td><td>Chapska of white felt with black fur</td><td>Iron or pike grey short jacket fastened by ten yellow metal buttons with a fleur de lys; breeches of the same grey; black half-gaiters</td><td>Black turned down collar and round cuffs; white serge lining and turnbacks; vertical pockets with three buttons; Palatinate scaled epaulettes. Sergents had crimson piping on the jacket and cuffs as well as the edges of the front flap of the breeches</td></tr>
<tr><td colspan="4">Black leather equipment – cartridge pouch on the waist belt; rifled carabine and sabre-bayonet.</td></tr>
</table>

Corps	Headgear	Jacket	Distinctions
Uhlans (21c)	As above	As above, Hungarian style boots and breeches	As above; black lance pennant; black sheepskin saddle cover with iron grey edging
Régiment des Hussards de Salm (24b) Armée de Condé	The French style mirliton is black with the inside of the flame red bordered with black; colback for the officers	Red dolman with white cords and lace; black breeches and pelisse with red cords and lace, white sheepskin edging on the pelisse	Black waistband with red loops; red sabretache with black lace edging and King's cypher; white sheepskin saddle cover with red edging
Equipment and uniform of the French 1786 model, so pelisse fur edging for the officers and NCOs was as described for the other hussar regiments, above. Trumpeters had reversed colours and a black sheepskin saddle cover.			
Régiment de chasseurs Hohenlohe-Bartenstein (Armée de Condé)			
Chasseurs (19a)	Palatinate helmet with black mane and the arms of France on the front	Green jacket and breeches; yellow metal buttons; black half-gaiters shaped to a point at the front	Red collar; yellow lemon Bavarian style plastron lapels, round cuffs and turnbacks; officers had French model gorget, rank distinctions and sword knots
Grenadiers-chasseurs (19b)	German sugar loaf bearskin	As above	As above
Chasseurs-appris (19c)	Tyrolean jäger style hat with turned-up side	As above	As above
Black leather equipment; German muskets and, for the chasseurs-appris, Austrian model 1779 carbines 1.1/4 löthiges Tirolerjäger Stützen			

Section 5 – Légion de Mirabeau (Plates 22–24)

While the legion can be considered as light troops, it is dealt with separately due to its size, organisation and diversity of uniforms. In addition, it was the first to introduce a distinctive armband which would serve as a model for the rest of the Armée de Condé from 1793 (see Volume II). Study of the uniforms is aided by the descriptions in the memoirs of the Marquis de Toustain and versions of a picture of the Vicomte de Mirabeau with his son and members of his staff wearing a variety of the legion's uniforms.[29]

Officers

Rank distinctions were shown by the number of silvered white laces on the sleeves and breeches; senior officers had fleurs de lys embroidered on their lace. The officers wore epaulettes with scales à la Piémontaise. Several sources show officers armed with two pistols carried in holsters on a waistbelt which was covered by a sash. The colour of the sash was sky blue for the infantry, black for the foot chasseurs and red for the cavalry and enfants perdus.

While subalterns had plain waistcoats with a single row of buttons, those of more senior officers were of hussar-style with three rows of buttons with silver cords between them and silver lace on the edges.

29 Nieüil (ed.), *Toustain*, pp.412–413 and Arnaud de Gouvion Saint-Cyr, 'Les gravures de l'état-major de la légion de Mirabeau (1792)', *Carnets de la Sabretache, Carnet spécial 2021*, pp.8–20. Two further versions were sold by Bertrand Malvaux in 2023.

The tails of the officers' coats, except in the uhlans, were long, while other ranks, including volunteers, had short tails. Gorgets were not worn, and officers did not have a loop or knot on their sword or sabre, the corps not having been part of the Royal Army. Officers and, probably, all volunteers wore sky blue and black neck cravats or scarves.

Infantry

The infantry wore black coats with a sky-blue collar, Palatinate-style plastron lapels, pointed cuffs and lining with white metal buttons with the device 'Honneur aux preux' (Honour to the brave). Their waistcoats and breeches were sky blue, and they wore short black gaiters and white leather belts.

Bataillon des volontaires

Lieutenant, Compagnie Générale (22a) – This company had black felt hats decorated with a white fleur de lys on the front, with a sky blue turban.

Lieutenant, other three companies (22c) – Black Palatinate helmet with brass trim, bearing the arms of France on the front; white mane. This officer has the distinctive black and sky-blue scarf at the collar and a belt plate of copper or brass with a sky-blue base on which was placed a gilt fleur de lys. Sometimes, the letters L and M were added for the Légion de Mirabeau (22e). Companies were distinguished by plumes of different colours, the officers having white at the top and the other ranks white bases; green is the only colour that has been identified as being used. Another feature which seems to have been specific to the volunteer companies was the scalloping to the bottom of the lapels, apparently representing a French heraldic shield.

Regular battalions

Lieutenant, Grenadier company (22b) – Black bearskins and red epaulettes were worn.

Enfants perdus – All ranks had pistols and holsters, as described for the officers, with a red sash over which was placed the cartridge pouch worn at the front. Originally, a bearskin, shorter than that of the grenadiers, was worn but it was replaced, according to two engravings, in 1792 by a cylindrical black felt hat.

Fusiliers – Palatinate helmet as worn by the volunteers but with a black mane.

Capitaine, Chasseurs (22d) – The company wore green coats with black collars, Palatinate-style plastron lapels, pointed cuffs and lining. Waistcoats and breeches were green, gaiters and belts were black. The hat was of the Henri IV style with the left side turned up. Instead of haversacks the chasseurs had hunters' bags.

Artillery

The artillery wore the same uniforms as the infantry, but with yellow metal buttons with the same device.

Cavalry

The two versions of horse furniture used throughout the legion's cavalry (23e) had sky blue shabraques with white lace borders, or silver for officers.

Capitaine, Compagnie Générale, hussards nobles (24e) and Hussar, Hussar Company (24a & 24c) – Both companies had black dolmans with sky-blue collars and pointed cuffs; sky blue pelisse with black sheepskin trim; sky blue breeches, while leather breeches appear to have been worn on the march. Cords and lace were white; the sash was sky-blue with white barrels (silver for officers). They wore hussar boots and sabres, with black leather belts. Toustain stated that the sabretache bore the royal cypher and was red, but it is shown here as sky-blue in accordance with the Fonds Grouvel. Their cloaks were grey.

The Compagnie Générale was distinguished by a galon d'élite, a lace that surrounded the dolman cords, which had been worn by the Régiment Colonel-général-hussards at its creation in 1783. The headgear was the bonnet à la talpache or à la tolpache, derived from the Balkan form of kalpak, with a sky-blue bag piped white. Their waistcoats were sky-blue.

The Hussar Company wore black and sky-blue mirliton shakos and had red waistcoats.

Capitaine, Volunteer Company (23d) – Coat as for the infantry, black waistcoats, yellow leather breeches and hussar-style boots. They carried dragoon sabres, carbines and pistols with black leather belts, and had grey cloaks. Initially, they had grenadier bearskins, as illustrated, but in March 1793, these were replaced by the Palatinate helmet as the chasseurs à cheval, but with a white mane.

Capitaine, Uhlan Company (23a) – Black single-breasted jacket with short tails, sky blue collar, pointed cuffs and piping. Sky blue waistcoat and breeches; all ranks wore a red sash over the two pistol holsters; hussar style boots. Sky blue czapka with white on all the edges and a black top with a white cross, around the head was a band of fur four inches wide of sable for the officers and bear for the other ranks. A wide lace, white or silver, ran down the right side of the czapka. The sabre was of the French chasseur pattern. No carbine was carried. The lance was seven feet long and had a red pennant bordered in white, with, at the end of each tail, white tassels with bells attached.

Capitaine, Chasseurs à cheval companies (23c) – Same coat, waistcoat and helmet as the infantry fusiliers; yellow leather breeches; hussar boots, dragoon sabres, carbines and pistols with black belts. Grey cloaks. The *capitaine* had a white mane on his helmet, whereas the rest of the company would have had black.

Trumpeters etc.

Trumpeter, Hussar Company (24d) – All drummers, trumpeters and musicians wore the livery colours of the Vicomte de Mirabeau. Those with jackets wore red with green facings.

Staff

Capitaine, staff (23b) – These officers wore the infantry coat and the Palatinate helmet with a white mane. The officer shown wears the alternative black surtout with 10 buttons, sky-blue turned-down collar and leather breeches.

All the staff and attached officers had a white brassard on the left arm, with a sky-blue fleur de lys and both edges piped in the same colour, onto which a white cockade was fixed (22f). When worn with this cockade, the brassard was positioned so that the fleur de lys were visible to the front of the arm.

Flags

See Volume II.

Appendix A

The Règlements (Regulations) of the Armée des Princes

The Armée des Princes was, above all, considered as the depository of the traditions of the former royal army, as well as of the regulations and orders which governed it. So the main texts, that were still implemented, were complemented by those that were specific to the new corps as well as the exceptional situation, namely an army of which half was composed of officers and gentlemen (of which a certain number had never served), the adoption of a so-called emigrant uniform for those not possessing one, and the raising of new French and foreign corps, including several legions or coalitions each possessing its own organisation.

Despite the Armée des Princes being dispersed in three corps, each was subject to the same rules decreed by the brothers of the King, the latter being considered, from 21 July 1791, a prisoner of the Constituent Assembly and then its successor, the National Convention, from 21 September 1792.

There is no exhaustive list of these regulations, but this inventory aims to be as complete as possible by drawing on various sources, both primary and secondary. Among the most interesting and exceptional printed documents is undoubtedly the order book of the Hommes d'armes à cheval, found in Champagne by the patriots during the 1792 campaign and sent to Paris, to be used against the émigrés due to the names it contained. At the time, each company maintained two types of order book.[1] One was kept by the captain and the other by the fourrier-clerk. There were also two types of orders, on the one hand the permanent general orders, copied in alphabetical order by theme (discipline, daily service, organisation, duties of NCOs, uniforms, etc.), and on the other, special orders, as in a circumstance on campaign, designating men for guard, escort or even reconnaissance duty. The order book of the Hommes d'armes à cheval follows and supplements the 1788 regulations for the organisation and manoeuvres of cavalry regiments on campaign and is undoubtedly unique for this period. The regulations being 'the ordinance of the King bearing regulations on the constitution

1 Clément de La Jonquière, *Le livre d'ordre d'un régiment d'infanterie en 1781* (Paris: Lavauzelle, 1899), provides a comprehensive study of the subject.

& especially the training & pay of the cavalry, of 17 March 1788' and 'the provisional regulations on the service of mounted troops on campaign, 12 August 1788.'

The Prince de Condé's journal entry for Saturday 8 October 1791, recorded an, 'assembly of company commanders at my quarters in the morning; I tell them to exercise their companies in accordance with an extract from the ordinance of 1788, which I gave them.'[2]

Although knowing neither the title nor the date, Champflour considers that an initial regulation would have dealt with questions of admission and verification of ranks. 'It starts from this principle that all ranks granted and all decorations obtained since 17 July 1789 will be considered null and void, the King, from this date, no longer truly enjoying his freedom.'[3] Consequently, it was the King's brothers who reserved for themselves the right to confirm them.

The following regulations and other instructions are known to have been made:

'Regulation for the Légion de Mirabeau. At Schönbornslust Castle, 9 August 1791. Signed, Louis-Stanislas Xavier.'

'Definitive regulation for the formation into different Companies of the Nobility assembled about Monsieur & Monseigneur the Comte d'Artois. At Schönbornslust, 19 August 1791. Signed Louis-Stanislas Xavier, for myself and my brother, the Comte d'Artois.'

'Letter addressed by the Princes to the Commanders of the cantonments, on sending them the new regulation. Louis-Stanislas Xavier. Charles-Philippe. At Schönbornslust, 30 October 1791.'

'Promulgation of the Sentiments of the Princes, brothers of the King. Louis-Stanislas Xavier. Charles-Philippe. At Schönbornslust, 30 October 1791.'

'Regulations for the Cantonments, with the Letter of sending from the Princes, brothers of the King, and declaration of their sentiments. At Schönbornslust, 30 October 1791.'

'Regulation for the formation in different companies of the Third Estate assembled about Monsieur and Monseigneur the Comte d'Artois. At Schönbornslust, 1 November 1791.'

The *Gazette nationale* from Koblenz, 19 November 1791, stated that, 'the organisational regulations for the émigrés, coming out from the chancellery of the princes, were very well received; they are being printed at this time; it will not take long to be distributed.'[4] It had been decreed that the émigré

2 Condé, *Journal*, p.227.
3 Champflour (ed.), *La Coalition d'Auvergne*, p.162.
4 *Gazette nationale*, no.331, Sunday 27 November 1791.

army was to be organised by 1 November 1791, but this is in fact a reference to the regulation of 30 October.

'Treaty concluded between the Princes brothers of the King and the Prince of Hohenlohe-Waldenburg-Schillingsfürst for the levy of a regiment, 31 March 1792.' This was made following a treaty concluded at Bartenstein on 3 February for the raising of an infantry regiment.

'Regulation of the Princes Brothers of the King, concerning the instructions and manoeuvres on horseback, for the companies of gentlemen. Made at Koblenz, 15 May 1792. Louis-Stanislas Xavier. Charles Philippe. The *Maréchal* Duc de Broglie below.'

'Provisional regulation of the Princes brothers of the King on the duties of cavalry on campaign, 1792.'

'Regulation concerning the Army train, the Camping equipment, its Distribution, the Forma & Dimensions of the Infantry & Cavalry Camps. At Koblenz, 19 June 1792. Signed Louis-Stanislas Xavier, Charles Philipe.'

Four issued at Bingen, 23 July 1792: 'Regulation concerning the order of battle', 'Instruction to make the distribution of camp equipment', 'Regulation concerning the rights of the different ranks composing the army', and 'Regulation concerning the determination of the equipment, camp equipment and quality of the food rations and forage'

'Extract from an Order Book or Military Journal, found on an émigré, and of which the National Convention ordered the printing and distribution to the 83 départements, by decree of 4 |October 1792.' This covered the period from 7 August to 18 September, with the nominative roll of the company at the end of the publication.

Appendix B

Regulation for the Légion de Mirabeau (9 August 1791)

This is the oldest known regulation for the émigré forces. It endorsed the Vicomte de Mirabeau's proposal to raise a corps, which he would command, at his own expense. It shows the initial formation and contrasts with that in which the legion entered the campaign in 1792:

> Monsieur and Mgr. the Comte d'Artois wishing to establish on fixed bases the organisation of the first corps formed under their auspices, under the name which they confirm and which it will keep of 'Légion du Vte Mirabeau' and desiring to attribute to it the advantages which are expected of it by putting it in a position to serve usefully have decided and decide what follows:
>
> 1st Article: – The composition of the Légion du Mirabeau will be of 1,500 men in the first stage of its formation, that is 1,200 infantrymen divided into 16 companies, and 300 cavalrymen divided into 4.
>
> In the infantry there will be 6 companies of a specific denomination, being a company of Alsatian volunteers of 100 men, another of Burgundians of 100 men: one of chasseurs appris [experienced] of 100 men: 2 of enfants perdus [literally lost children, indicating voltigeurs or skirmishers] each of 65, so 130: one of gunners of 70 men. Total 500 men
>
> The rest of the infantry forming 10 companies of which one is of grenadiers, one of chasseurs and 8 of fusiliers each of 70 men. Total 700 men.
>
> Total of infantry – 1,200 men.
>
> The cavalry will be composed of 4 companies, thus: one of hussars of 75 men, one of volunteers of 75 men, 2 of chasseurs à cheval each of 75, so 150 men
>
> Grand total – 1,500 men
>
> The legion thus organised will be likely to be raised to 2,000 men following its first destination, when the Princes will give it the order at the time of its entry into France.
>
> Article 2: – The number and rank of the officers. This legion will keep, from now on, the number of officers which was originally set on the basis of 6 per company.

The Princes, informed of the devotion that all have shown, well convinced of their zeal and sure of the usefulness of their services, are far from wishing to reduce this number.

These places will only become vacant through their death or resignation.

Article 3: – Staff – in addition to the 6 officers per company and the senior officers which they nominated, the Princes approve the formation of the staff proposed by the Vte. De Mirabeau. That is to say a *major* for the corps, 2 infantry *aides-majors*, one cavalry *aide-major* and as many *sous-aides-majors*.

The *aides-majors* will be ranked among the *capitaines* and the *sous-aides* among the *lieutenants en second.*

[There will also be] a *quartier-maître trésorier* [quartermaster treasurer], 2 *porte drapeaux*, an *aumônier*, a *chirurgien major* and an assistant.

The designation of the ranks stated above will be the basis of the brevets that the Princes propose to give to the officers of the Legion according to the table which will be sent to them.

Article 4: – Pay – The pay will be in the customary state, on the basis of that granted in France to foreign troops, but, as for present and until entry into France … [part missing]

Payment for issued items will be likewise discharged on a particular account and it will be provided for according to the arrangements which are to be made shortly with Monsieur Guais or other suppliers, it will be then placed together for maintenance.

Article 5: – Dress, equipment and armament – The Princes approve the models of dress, equipment and armament presented to them by the Vte de Mirabeau and they gave their orders so that the Legion will very shortly be provided with the important objects.

Article 6: – Artillery – The legion is due to be provided with 2 cannons à la suédoise and 2 howitzers, the Princes occupy themselves as to the means of procuring them, as soon as possible, as well as the caissons necessary for the transport of the ammunition.

Made at Schönbornslust Castle, 9 August 1791
Louis-Stanislas Xavier

Appendix C

Definitive Establishment of the Légion de Mirabeau (summer 1792)

Staff

M. de Mirabeau, *colonel général* [proprietor]
M. de la Féronnière, *capitaine commandant* [second in command with rank of *colonel*]
Victor-Claude-Dymas de Riquetti de Mirabeau, *major*
1 *aide-major général* [chief staff officer]
2 infantry *aides-majors* [infantry staff officers]
2 cavalry *aides-majors* [cavalry staff officers]
2 infantry *sous-aides-majors* [assistant infantry staff officers]
2 cavalry *sous-aides-majors* [assistant cavalry staff officers]
2 *porte-drapeaux* [in fact one standard bearer and one guidon bearer]
5 *adjudants* [aides de camp]
1 *capitaine interprète* [interpréter]
1 *quartier-maître* [quartermaster treasurer]
1 *chirurgien-major* [surgeon-major]
1 *aumônier* [chaplain]

Petit état-major [other ranks on the staff]

Tambour-major [Drum major]
Tambour-mâitre [Drum master]
Chef de musique [band master]
Caporal musicien [band corporal]
21 musiciens [musicians]
Sergent major écrivain [sergeant major clerk]
Facteur [Postman]
Charpentier [Carpenter or pioneer]

Infantry – 3 battalions

M. de Bergeret, *colonel commandant*
M. du Hautoy, *colonel en second*
M. Lefort or de Faure, *colonel à la suite* [supernumerary]
M. de Pelissier, *lieutenant-colonel*
M. de Charmoille, *major*
M. Conygham, *major*

Bataillon de Volontaires – 4 Companies

La Générale à pied (u/k) [the General's infantry company]
Compagnie d'Alsace (Baron d'Escorbiac)
Compagnie de Bourgogne (Marquis de Conygham)
Compagnie de Méridionaux (de Martinet) [of Southerners]

First (Regular) Battalion – 6 companies

1 Grenadier Company (Baron de Corsac)
1 Company of *enfants perdus* (Chevalier de Marcombes) [voltigeurs or skirmishers]
4 Fusilier Companies (Baron de Weissenstein, de Charmoille, Comte de Barjon, Chevalier de Blair)

Second (Regular) Battalion – 6 companies

1 Chasseur Company[1] (Baron de Kreuchely)
1 Company of *enfants perdus* or *voltigeurs* (de Jacob)
4 Fusilier Companies (de Saint-Georges, de Rouillac, de Thomasset, de Montessus)

Artillery Company

4 x 4-pounder cannons (Prévot, *capitaine* in the Régiment de Metz)

Cavalry – 3 squadrons

M. Alexandre d'Ollone, *colonel commandant*
M. de Chasseloir, *colonel en second*
M. Max d'Ollone, *colonel en second*

---

1 Successively named chasseurs appris, chasseurs de ligne and finally chasseurs carabiniers, so sharpshooters armed with German carbines (with so-called forced balls) and sword bayonets.

M. d'Eslon, *major*
M. de Séguier, *major en second*

First Squadron – 2 companies

La Générale à cheval (hussards nobles) (de Gobert) [The General's company of cavalry (gentlemen serving as hussars)]
Volontaires à cheval (Comte d'Eberstein)

Second Squadron – 2 companies

Hussar Company (Comte de Perrin)
Uhlan Company (de Bellerose)

Third Squadron – 2 companies

2 companies of chasseurs à cheval (de Douhet and de Jasson)

Appendix D

Precedence of the 69 compagnies d'officiers of the Infantry Regiments in the Three Armies

This has been compiled by comparing the information provided by Grouvel and Pinasseau.[1]

Armée du Centre

33 companies

1. Colonel-général-infanterie
2. La Reine-infanterie
3. Normandie-infanterie
4. Vintimille-infanterie
5. Flandres-infanterie
6. Vivarais-infanterie
7. Lyonnais-La Sarre-infanterie
8. Beaujolais-infanterie
9. Champagne-infanterie
10. Dauphiné-infanterie
11. Agenois-infanterie
12. Lorraine-infanterie
13. Poitou-infanterie
14. Languedoc-infanterie
15. Royal Deux-Ponts-La Marck-infanterie[2]
16. Bouillon-infanterie
17. Armagnac-infanterie

1 Grouvel, *Troupes de l'émigration*, vol.II pp.85–90 and Pinasseau, *Campagne de 1792* vol.I pp.11–72.

2 Pinasseau, *Campagne de 1792*, vol.I, p.54, gives it as La Marck et Royal-Deux-Ponts, reflecting the regiments precedence in the old royal army, namely 79th and 102nd respectively.

18. La Couronne-infanterie
19. Béarn-infanterie
20. Vermandois-infanterie
21. Brie-infanterie
22. Royal-Comtois-infanterie
23. Anjou-infanterie
24. Chartres-infanterie
25. Navarre-infanterie
26. Royal-des-Vaisseaux-infanterie
27. Forez-Angoumois-infanterie[3]
28. Royal-Roussillon-infanterie
29. Dauphin-infanterie
30. Bourgogne-infanterie
31. Limousin-infanterie
32. Penthièvre-infanterie
33. Chasseurs nobles de Rouault – there was a short-lived company of Chasseurs à pied de Provence et des Ardennes, the officers of which appear to have joined Rouault[4]

Armée de Condé

18 companies

1. Piémont-infanterie
2. Aquitaine-infanterie
3. Austrasie-infanterie
4. Soissonnais-infanterie
5. Neustrie-infanterie
6. La Fère-infanterie
7. Condé-infanterie
8. La Marine-Royal Liégeois-infanterie
9. Bourbonnois-infanterie
10. Beauvoisis-infanterie
11. Auvergne-infanterie
12. Médoc-infanterie
13. Monsieur-infanterie[5]
14. Chasseurs bretons-Guyenne-infanterie
15. Royal-infanterie
16. Saintonge-infanterie
17. Bresse-infanterie
18. Enghien-infanterie

---

3 Grouvel gives it as Forez only.

4 Neither Grouvel nor Pinasseau include the Chasseurs à pied de Provence et des Ardennes in their OOB for the Armée du Centre, (vol.I, pp.53–61). It would appear the company was short-lived and the chasseur officers joined Rouault's company. Pinasseau gives Rouault's company as 'Différents régiments: Cte de Rouault, major' (vol.I, p.13).

5 Given as 'Monsieur et Chasseurs bretons' by Pinasseau, vol.I, p.32.

Armée de Bourbon

18 companies
1. Picardie-infanterie
2. Auxerrois-infanterie
3. Royal Auvergne-infanterie
4. Viennois-infanterie
5. Perche-infanterie
6. Touraine-infanterie
7. Duc d'Angoulême-infanterie
8. Maréchal de Turenne-infanterie
9. L'Isle de France-infanterie
10. Orléans-infanterie
11. Bretagne-infanterie
12. Alsace-infanterie
13. Bourbon-infanterie
14. Rouergue-infanterie
15. Beauce-infanterie
16. Conti-infanterie
17. Foix-infanterie
18. Hesse-Darmstadt-infanterie

Appendix E

Armée du Centre, Summer 1792

Composition

INFANTRY	CAVALRY
Compagnies nobles	**Compagnies nobles**
Compagnies d'officiers: Infanterie (34), Marine royale (10)	Compagnies d'officiers: Cavalerie (7), Carabiniers (1), Dragons (3), Dragons/ Chasseurs (1), Chasseurs (4), Marine royale (2)
Coalitions de provinces (15)	Coalitions de provinces (11)
Compagnies de gentilshommes: Bretagne (7), Périgord (1), Poitou (4), Saintonge/Angoumois/ Aunis (2), Languedoc (1)	Compagnies de gentilshommes: Auvergne (4), Périgord (1), Saintonge/Angoumois/Aunis (1), Bretagne (2), Languedoc (1), Poitou (2)
Compagnie franche du Tiers	**Compagnie mixte de hussards**
Bretagne (1)	Chamborand / Lauzun / Esterhazy (1)
Paid Troops	
Régiment de Vexin	Régiment de Royal-Allemand
Régiment de Berwick	Régiment de Saxe Hussards
Régiment de Dillon	Régiment de Bercheny Hussards
Régiment de Walsh	**Prévôté**
Light Troops	
Régiment de Wittgenstein	Chasseurs étrangers de Polignac
Chasseurs royaux des Princes	
Chasseurs carabiniers de Wittgenstein/Goerduck	
Maison du Roi and Gardes des Princes	
Suisses and Cent Suisses	Grenadiers d'ordonnance
Compagnie de l'Institution de St Louis	Gardes du corps du Roi
	Compagnies nobles d'ordonnance
	Gardes des Princes
Hommes d'armes à pied	Hommes d'armes à cheval
Officiers du corps royal de l'artillerie	
Officiers du corps royal de l'artillerie des colonies	
Officiers du corps royal du Génie	

State of the Armée du Centre, 28 July 1792[1]

Infantry	
Active compagnies d'officiers (31)	1,643
Marine royale [see note below]	528
Compagnies de gentilshommes (16)	806
Régiment de Vexin	58
Régiment de Berwick	600
Régiment de Dillon	101
Régiment de Walsh	106
Régiment de Wittgenstein	500
Chasseurs royaux des Princes	180
Chasseurs de Garduck [sic]	200
Régiment de Waldek [sic, see note below]	400
Gardes de la Porte [Compagnie de l'Institution de Saint-Louis]	200
Hommes d'armes [à pied]	500
Cent-Suisses	28
Artillerie des Colonies	66
Corps royal d'artillerie et parc	259
Corps royal du Génie	290
Cavalry	
Active compagnies d'officiers (17) [including one of mixed hussars]	890
Compagnies de gentilshommes (10)	507
Régiment de Royal-Allemand	420
Régiment de Saxe Hussards	500
Régiment de Bercheny Hussards	236
Chasseurs étrangers de Polignac	240
Gardes du corps du Roi	1,800
1ère compagnie noble d'ordonnance	593
2nde compagnie noble d'ordonnance	609
Gardes du corps de Monsieur	144
Gardes du corps de Mgr Comte d'Artois	144
Hommes d'armes [à cheval]	590
Total infantry	6,465
Total cavalry	6,635
Grand total	13,100

Notes: The Régiment de Waldek (or Waldeck) is noted as not yet in the Princes' service, it would not be raised.

The two cavalry companies of the Marine, the Prévôté, the foot detachment of the Hommes d'armes à cheval and the Grenadiers d'ordonnance were missing from this document.

1 Félix Feuillet de Conches, *Louis XVI, Marie-Antoinette et Madame Elilsabeth Lettres et documents inédits* (Paris: Plon, 1864), vol.VI, p.235, copy of documents made by Calonne.

Nevertheless, with the exception of the numbers given for the Corps royal du Génie (doubtless 29 instead of 290), the figures coincide with the numbers given in Chapter 4, so a strength of more than 14,000 men in August-September 1792.

Order of Battle

Princes du sang – Duc d'Angoulême; Duc de Berry
Maréchaux de France – Duc de Broglie, commanding the army; Marquis de Castries

Vanguard
Marquis de Jaucourt, *lieutenant-général*
Infantry – Duc de Laval, *maréchal de camp*
Chasseurs royaux des Princes (1 bn.)
Chasseurs carabiniers de Wittgenstein/Goerduck (½ bn.)
Cavalry
Bercheny hussards (2 sqn.)
Saxe hussards (4 sqn.)
Chamborand et Lauzun hussards (1 sqn.)
Chasseurs étrangers de Polignac (2 sqn.)

First Line
Right Wing
Infantry acting on the flanks of the cavalry
Régiment de Vexin and the (½ bn.) – Baron de Boistel, *maréchal de camp*
Cavalry – Duc de Coigny, *lieutenant-général*; Duc de Guines, *lieutenant-général*; Comte d'Agoult, *maréchal de camp, aide-major général des Gardes*
Grenadiers d'ordonnance à cheval (1 sqn.)
Gardes du corps du Roi: Compagnie Ecossaise (3 sqn.); Compagnie de Noailles (3 sqn.); Compagnie de Gramont with the Dragons de la Reine (3 sqn.); Compagnie de Luxembourg (3 sqn.)
Gardes des Princes: Gardes de Monsieur (1 sqn.); Gardes du Comte d'Artois (1 sqn.)

Infantry
Prince Xavier de Saxe, *lieutenant-général*, commanding
Comte de Martanges, *lieutenant-général*, second-in-command
1st Division – Marquis de Juigné, *lieutenant-général*
1st Brigade (Colonel-général) – Marquis de La Salle, *maréchal de camp*
1st Battalion: Compagnies d'officiers de Colonel-général and La Reine; Normandie and Vintimille; Flandre and Vivarais; Lyonnais/La Sarre and Beaujolais
2nd Battalion: Compagnies d'officiers de Champagne, Dauphiné, Agénois and Lorraine; Poitou, Languedoc, La Marck/Royal Deux-Ponts and Bouillon

2nd Brigade (Armagnac) – Marquis de Janson, *maréchal de camp*
1st Battalion: Compagnies d'officiers Armagnac, La Couronne, Béarn and Vermandois; Brie, Royal-Comtois, Anjou and Chartres
2nd Battalion: Coalition de Bretagne – Compagnies de gentilshommes (7) and Compagnie franche du Tiers (1)[2]
2nd Division – Marquis de Pérusse, *lieutenant-général*
3rd Brigade (Brigade irlandaise) – Duc de Fitz-James, *maréchal de camp*
1st Battalion: Régiment de Dillon; Régiment de Walsh
2nd Battalion: Régiment de Berwick
4th Brigade (Navarre) – Duc de Luxembourg, *maréchal de camp*
1st Battalion: Compagnies de gentilshommes des Coalitions: Saintonge/Angoumois/Aunis (2); Poitou (4); Périgord (1); Languedoc (1)
2nd Battalion: Compagnies d'officiers de Navarre, Royal Vaisseaux, Forez/Angoumois, Royal Roussillon and Dauphin; Bourgogne, Limousin and Penthièvre

Left wing
Cavalry – Comte de Montboissier, *lieutenant-général*; Marquis d'Autichamp, *maréchal de camp*
Hommes d'armes: Gendarmes Ecossais & de la Reine (1sqn.); Gendarmes Anglais & du Dauphin (1sqn.); Gendarmes Bourguignons & de Monsieur (1sqn.); Gendarmes de Flandre & d'Artois (1sqn.)
Compagnies nobles d'ordonnance: Seconde compagnie (4 sqn.); Première compagnie (4 sqn.)
Infantry acting on the flanks of the cavalry
Régiment de Wittgenstein (1 ½ bn.) – Comte de Lowendal, *maréchal de camp*

Second line
Right wing - cavalry (only) – Comte de Caraman, *lieutenant-général*
1st Brigade (Colonel-général) – Vicomte de Beaune, *lieutenant-général*
1st Squadron: Compagnies d'officiers de Colonel-général/Royal Champagne; Royal Piémont (2)
2nd Squadron: Compagnies de gentilshommes du Coalition d'Auvergne (2)
3rd Squadron: Compagnies de gentilshommes du Coalition d'Auvergne (2)
4th Squadron: Compagnies d'officiers de Royal-Lorraine/Orléans; Royal-Guyenne (2)
2nd Brigade – Chevalier de Durfort, *lieutenant-général*
Régiment de Royal-Allemand (3 sqn.)

Left wing - cavalry (only) – Duc de Villequier, *lieutenant-général*
1st Brigade (Monsieur)
1st Squadron: Compagnies d'officiers de Monsieur/Angoulême-dragons (Dragons des Princes); Artois-dragons/Chasseurs de Flandre (2)
2nd Squadron: Compagnies d'officiers de Chartres/Penthièvre-dragons; Compagnie des gentilshommes du Coalition de Périgord (2)

2 Pinasseau does not list this last company in his OOB but it is known that it was attached to the battalion at Verdun in September 1792.

3rd Squadron: Compagnies d'officiers des chasseurs de Franche-Comté; chasseurs de la Picardie (2)
4th Squadron: Compagnies d'officiers des chasseurs du Hainaut; chasseurs de la Champagne (2)
2nd Brigade (Commissaire-général) – Comte de Rouault, *lieutenant-général*
1st Squadron: Compagnies d'officiers de Commissaire-général-cavalerie; Royal-Picardie-cavalerie (2)
2nd Squadron: Compagnies de gentilshommes du Coalition de Poitou (2)
3rd Squadron: Compagnies de gentilshommes du Coalition de Bretgane (2)
4th Squadron: Compagnies d'officiers des régiments de Carabiniers (2)

Reserve
Comte d'Hector, *lieutenant-général de marine*

Infantry

Compagnies des officiers de la Marine royale (10 forming 1½ bn.)
Hommes d'armes à pied (2 bn.)
Institution de Saint-Louis (½ bn.)

Cavalry

Compagnies des officiers de la Marine royale (2 forming 1 sqn.)
Compagnies des gentilshommes des Coalitions de Languedoc; de Saintonge/Angoumois/Aunis (2 forming 1 sqn.)

Artillery
Engineers
Headquarters
Prévôté
Also, General Staff, aides de camp, Suisses, Administration générale, Service de santé

The brigades were titled after the most senior regiments; those which were Royal, took precedence over those of the Princes (and Queen's). This would be reflected in the order of march, with the exception of the Gardes du Corps of the Households of the King and Princes, preceded by the Horse Grenadiers.

Appendix F

Armée de Condé, Summer 1792

Composition and Strength[1]

Units	Infantry (men)	Cavalry (men)
Infanterie noble (two bn. – 24 co. of 56 officers and gentlemen)	1,344	
Cavalerie noble (five sqn. each of two co. of 56 officers and gentlemen)		560
Légion de Mirabeau	1,200	330
Régiment de Rohan	400	
Régiment de Hohenlohe – Schillingsfurst Régiment de Hohenlohe-Bartenstein	600	
Compagnie de sous-officiers (garde du quartier-général)	100	
Chevaliers de la Couronne		300
Dauphin-cavalerie (1 sqn.)		100
Hussards de Salm		200
Prévôté		50
Artillery and pontonniers	200	
Total	**3,844**	**1,510**
Grand Total		**5,354**

With the addition of the general staff and services, the strength of 5,502 men given by Pinasseau is correct for the end of the campaign, October-November, although his numbers were incomplete, for example, for the artillery.

1 Muret, *Histoire de l'Armée de Condé*, vol.I, p.69 and Romain, *Souvenirs d'un officier royaliste* vol. II, Part 1, p.201; Champflour (ed.), *La coalition d'Auvergne*, pp.293–299.

Order of Battle

Vanguard

Comte de Vioménil, *maréchal de camp*, commander
Comte de Béthisy, *maréchal de camp*, second-in-command

Infantry

Légion de Mirabeau (3 bn.)
Chasseurs d'Hohenlohe-Bartenstein (½ bn.)

Cavalry

Légion de Mirabeau (3 sqn.)
Hussards de Salm (2 sqn.)

Right wing – cavalry (only) – Comte de Turpin, *lieutenant-général*
Brigade Royal
Compagnies d'officiers de Royal-cavalerie; Royal-Navarre/Royal Etranger-cavalerie (1 sqn.)
Compagnies d'officiers de Dauphin-dragons; Du Roi-infanterie (1 sqn.)
Compagnies d'officiers retirés and gentilshommes de Saint-Clair; de Villers (1 sqn.)
Compagnie d'officiers de Condé-dragons; Compagnie des gentilshommes de Franche-Comté (1 sqn.)

Infantry

1st Division – Marquis de Vaubécourt, *lieutenant-général*
1st Brigade
1st Battalion: Compagnies d'officiers de Piémont; Aquitaine (1ère division);
Compagnies d'officiers de La Marine/Royal-Liégeois; Condé (5e div.); Compagnies d'officiers de Guyenne; Monsieur/Chasseurs bretons (9e div.)
2nd Battalion: Compagnies des gentilshommes de Prédelys ; de Tschoudy (3e div.); Compagnies des gentilshommes de La Devèze, de Mussey (7e div.); Compagnie des gentilshommes de Riollet, de Comte de Corsac (11e div.)
2nd Brigade
1st Battalion: Compagnies d'officiers d'Austrasie; de Soissonnais (2e div.);
Compagnies d'officiers de Bourbonnais; Beauvaisis (6e div.); Compagnies d'officiers de Royal; Saintonge (10e div.)
2nd Battalion: Compagnies d'officiers de Neustrie; La Fère (4e div.); Compagnies d'officiers d'Auvergne; Médoc (8e div.); Compagnies d'officiers de Bresse; Enghien (12e div.)
2nd Division
Régiment de Hohenlohe-Schillingsfürst; Régiment de Rohan étranger

Left wing – cavalry (only) – Comte de Wall, *lieutenant-général*
Brigade de La Reine
Compagnies d'officiers de La Reine-cavalerie; Chasseurs de différents régiments (1 sqn.)

Chevaliers dragons de la Couronne (2 sqn.)
Régiment de Dauphin cavalerie (1 sqn.)

Artillery
(2 companies)

Engineers
Headquarters
Garde du Quartier-général: Compagnie française; Compagnie suisse
Prévôté
Also, General Staff, aides de camp, Suisses, Administration générale, Service de santé

Appendix G

Armée de Bourbon, Summer 1792

Composition

Infantry	Cavalry
Compagnies nobles	**Compagnies nobles**
Compagnies d'officiers de régiments (18)	Compagnies d'officiers de régiments (6)
Compagnie de gentilshommes de différentes provinces (1)	
Compagnies de gentilshommes des Coalitions (16)	Compagnies de gentilshommes des Coalitions (10)
Compagnies franches	**Compagnies franches**
Compagnies de carabiniers de Calonne or Chasseurs flamands (2) Compagnies de l'aile gauche (2) Compagnies de l'aile droite (2)	Compagnie franche de Maillard
Infanterie soldée	**Cavalerie soldée**
Légion de Normandie	Légion de Normandie
Légion de Breuilpont	Légion de Breuilpont
Compagnie de Bas-officiers	
Officiers du corps royal de l'artillerie	**Prévôté**
Compagnie d'artillerie et d'ouvriers	
Officiers du corps royal du Génie	

Strength

Units	Infantry	Cavalery
Compagnies d'officiers de régiments (18 and 6)	1,026	342
Compagnies des Coalitions (16 and 10)	969	570
Compagnie de gentilshommes (1)	56	
Compagnies franches de gentilhommes (7)	399	
Compagnie franche du Tiers (1)		60
Légion de Normandie	300	90
Légion de Breuilpont	250	50
Officiers du corps royal de l'Artillerie	50	

Officiers du corps royal du Génie	14	
Compagnie de bas-officiers	57	
Canonniers et ouvriers	12	
Prévôté		20
Total	**3,077**	**1,132**
Grand Total		**4,209**

ORDER OF BATTLE

Vanguard

Comte de La Châtre, *maréchal de camp*

Infantry – Comte d'Ozé, *maréchal de camp*

Compagnie de bas-officiers; Chasseurs flamands (2)

Légion de Normandie, infantry

Légion de Breuilpont, carabiniers[1]

Cavalry – Comte de Valory, *maréchal de camp*

Compagnies d'officiers de Royal-Bourgogne-cavalerie; Conti-dragons (1 sqn.)

Compagnies des Coalitions de Provence (1); Guyenne (1) (1 sqn.)

Compagnie franche du Tiers de Maillard (1)

Légion de Normandie, chasseurs à cheval (1 co. plus)

Légion de Breuilpont, uhlans (1 co. plus)

Right wing

Infantry acting on the flank of the cavalry

Compagnies franches de La Rianderie and de Laurétan (2)

Cavalry – Comte de Coigny, *maréchal de camp*

Compagnies d'officiers du Roi-cavalerie; différents corps (1 sqn.)

Compagnies (2) du Coalition de Champagne (1 sqn.)

Compagnies (2) du Coalition de Normandie (1 sqn.)

Infantry

Comte d'Egmont, *lieutenant-général*, commander

Comte de Blangy, *lieutenant-général*, second-in-command

1st Brigade (Picardie) – Marquis de Sommery, *maréchal de camp*

1st Battalion: Compagnies d'officiers de Picardie; Isle de France; Royal-Auvergne; Bretagne; Perche; Rouergue; Duc d'Angoulême; Conti

2nd Battalion: Compagnies des Coalitions de Normandie (6); Anjou/Maine (2)

2nd Brigade (Auxerrois) – Duc de Duras, *maréchal de camp*

1st Battalion: Compagnies d'officiers d'Auxerrois; Orléans; Viennois; Bourbon; Touraine; Beauce/Cambrésis;[2] *maréchal* de Turenne; Foix

1 Only the Marquis de Breuilpont's six companies of chasseurs carabiniers are included as his squadron of uhlans was not raised until mid-August.

2 Both Grouvel and Pinasseau show the company as 'Beauce et Canbrésis' although this is inconsistent with the regiments' precedence, in 1791 their respective numbers were 68 and 20.

2nd Battalion: Compagnies des Coalitions de Champagne/Lorraine (2); Artois (2); Limousin (1); Guyenne (Haute-Guyenne 2, Basse-Guyenne 1)

Left wing

Cavalry – Marquis de Vogüé, *maréchal de camp*

Compagnies d'officiers de Bourbon-dragons; Noailles/Schomberg-dragons (1 sqn.)

Compagnies (2) du Coalition d'Artois (1 sqn.)

Compagnies des Coalitions de Limousin (1); Dauphiné (1) (1 sqn.)

Infantry acting on the flank of the cavalry

Compagnies franches d'Abzac and d'Alheim (2)

Reserve

Compagnies des officiers d'Alsace; Hesse-Darmstadt-infanterie

Compagnie noble de Le Seigneur (or de gentilshommes de différentes provinces)

Compagnie franche de Noury[3]

Artillery

Engineers

Headquarters

Prévôté

Also, General Staff, aides de camp, Suisses, Administration générale, Service de santé.

3 The Comte Palme d'Estaing, in his memoirs, only listed the infantry compagnies franches du Tiers on the flanks of the cavalry; however Grouvel and Pinasseau show that of Noury within the reserve. Grouvel, *Troupes de l'émigration*, vol.III, pp.186, and Pinasseau, *Campagne de 1792*, vol.I, p.71.

Bibliography

Archives

France:
Archives départementales de l'Eure, Evreux (ADE): I J 240: *Mémoires de Jacques de Chambray*
Archives municipales de Valenciennes (AMV): EE404 report
Archives Nationales, Paris (AN): AE II 2983, cote d'origine C 31
Service historique de la Défense, Vincennes (SHD): dossiers individuels: GR1; registre matricules 2Ye
Musée Condé, Château de Chantilly (MCC): Fonds Grouvel

The Netherlands:
National Archief, The Hague (NAN), 2.21.008.01/IN – 19: *Journal de Constant Rebecque*

Russia:
State Archive of the Russian Federation, Moscow (GARF): Collection 728, Inventory 2, Dossier 18, *Armée de Condé/Chevaliers de la Couronne.*

United Kingdom:
British Library (BL): Add MS 37858 Windham Papers

Contemporary Newspapers and Journals

Courrier Français
Journal de la Cour et de la Ville
Journal des débats et des décrets
Journal historique et politique de Genève
Journal militaire
Journal politique de Bruxelles
Le Moniteur (Gazette nationale ou Le Moniteur universel)
La semaine politique et littéraire
Mercure universel
Oxford Journal
Rédaction du journal de Paris

Contemporary Registers

Collection générale des décrets rendus par l'Assemblée Nationale (1791–1792)
Etat militaire de France (1753–1793)
Register der Resolutien van de Hoog Mog. Heeren Staaten Generaal der Vereenigde Nederlanden

Published Works

Albrecht, Joseph, *Archiv für Hohenlische Geschichte* (Dehringen: Ph. Haumann, 1857–1860)

Anon., *Archives parlementaires de 1787 à 1860, Volume XXVI, du 31 mai 1790 au 8 juillet 1790* (Paris: Société d'Imprimerie et Librairie administratives et des Chemins de fer, 1883)

Anon., *Collection complète des Lois, Décrets, Ordonnances, Règlements, Avis du Conseil d'Etat* (Paris: Librairie Guyot, 1834)

Anon., *Collection générale des Lois, décrets, ordonnances, réglemens et avis du Conseil-d'Etat, depuis 1788 jusques et y compris 1824* (Paris: no pubisher, 1824)

Anon., *Copie du Manifeste attribué à Louis-Joseph de Bourbon, dit Condé* (No location or publisher, 1790)

Anon., *Correspondance et écrits de Sa Majesté Louis XVIII* (Paris: Rapilly, 1824)

Anon., *Discours de J.P. Brissot, Député, sur les causes des troubles de Saint-Domingue. Prononcé à la séance du Ier Décembre 1791* (Paris: Imprimerie Nationale, undated)

Anon., *Discours de Maximilien Robespierre, sur le parti que l'Assemblée nationale doit prendre relatviement à la proposition de guerre, annoncée par le pouvoir exécutif : prononcé à la société, le 18 décembre 1791* (Paris: Société des Amis de la Constitution, 1791)

Anon., 'Essai d'une nouvelle tenue (1788)', *Carnet de La Sabretache*, no.79, 1899, pp.398–399

Anon., *Etat des Officiers généraux & de leurs Aides-de-camp déserteurs ou émigrés …* (Paris: Imprimerie Nationale Exécutif du Louvre, 1793)

Anon., *Explication de l'énigme de la Révolution européenne* (London: Schuler, 1826)

Anon., *Instruction provisoire sur l'Habillement des Troupes. Du 1er avril 1791* (Paris: Imprimerie Royale, 1792)

Anon., *Instruction provisoire sur l'uniforme des officiers généraux et des aides de camp. Du 1er avril 1791* (Paris: Imprimerie Royale, 1792)

Anon., *Journal militaire contenant tout ce qui est relatif à l'Organisation et à l'Administration de la force publique, 1ère Partie,* (Paris: unknown publisher, 1792)

Anon., *L'esprit des Gazettes* (No location or publisher, 1792)

Anon., *Le Tribunal criminel extraordinaire, Livre I* (Paris: unknown publisher, undated)

Anon., *Loi relative au serment à prêter par les officiers de tous grades, & Soldats de l'Armée Françoise, & contenant en outre des dispositions particulières au ci-devant Prince de Condé* (Rouen: L. Oursel, 1791)

Anon. (ed.), *Mémoires d'Olivier d'Argens et Correspondances des Généraux* (Paris: Baudouin Frères, 1826)

Anon., *Ordonnance du Roi, Concernant le Corps-royal de l'Artillerie des Colonies, du 1er janvier 1786* (Paris: Imprimerie Royale, 1786)

Anon., *Recueil général des lois, décrets, ordonnances, etc. Depuis le mois de juin 1789 jusqu'au mois d'août 1830* (Paris: Journal des Notaires et des Avocats, 1839)

Anon., 'Régiment des hussards de Conflans (Louis XVI)', *Tenues des troupes de France n°15* (Paris: H.E. Martin, 1903)

Anon., *Règlement arrêté par le Roi pour l'Habillement et l'Equipement de ses Troupes. Du 21 février 1779* (Paris: Imprimerie royale, 1779)

Anon., *Règlement arrêté par le Roi pour l'Habillement & l'Equipement des Troupes. Du premier octobre 1786* (Metz: Imprimerie Collignon, 1786)

Anon., *Règlement concernant les Equipages de l'Armée, les Effets de Campemens, leur Distribution, la Forme & les Dimensions des Camps d'Infanterie & de Cavalerie* (19 June 1792)

Anon., *Règlement définitif, Pour la formation en différentes Compagnies, de la Noblesse rassemblée auprès de Monsieur & de Monseigneur le Comte d'Artois* (Paris: Senneville, Libraire au Palais-royal, 1791)

Anon., *Règlement pour la Formation en différentes Compagnies, du Tiers-Etats rassemblé auprès de MONSIEUR & de Monseigneur Comte d'ARTOIS* (no details)

Anon., *Table générale par ordre alphabétique des matières des lois, sénatus-consultes, décrets, arrêtés, avis du Conseil d'Etat, etc. publiés publiés dans le Bulletin des Lois …* (Paris: Imprimerie royale, 1816)

Attar, Frank, *La Révolution française déclare la guerre à l'Europe* (Bruxelles: Editions Complexe, 1992)

Aulard, François Alphonse, *La société des Jacobins* (Paris: Librairie Jouaust, 1889)

B.P., *Récit de ce qui s'est passé de plus remarquable à l'Armée de S.A.S. le Prince de Condé en 1791, 1792 et 1793* (Paris: Picard, 1817)

Bacourt, Ad. de (ed.), *Correspondance entre le comte de Mirabeau et le comte de La Marck pendant les années 1789, 1790 et 1791* (Paris: Librairie Ve Le Normant, 1851)
Barberey, Maurice (ed.), *Dix années d'émigration. Souvenirs et correspondance du comte de Neuilly* (Paris: Charles Douniol, Libraire-éditeur, 1865)
Barrière, François (ed.), *Mémoires du Général Dumouriez* (Paris: Firmin Didot Frères, 1848)
Barruel, Augustin, *Mémoires pour servir à l'histoire du jacobinisme* (Hamburg: unknown publisher, 1797)
Barthou, Louis, *Mirabeau* (Paris: Librairie Hachette, 1920)
Bazouges, Hughes de, 'La carrière autrichienne de Philippe de Brons', *Carnet spécial de La Sabretache 'L'émigration militaire 1791-1801'* pp.28–34
Bazouges, Hughes de, and Nichols, Alistair, *For God and King. A history of the Légion de Damas (1793-1798)* (Warwick: Helion, 2021)
Beauchet-Filleau, Henri, *Tableau des émigrés du Poitou aux armées des Princes et de Condé* (Poitiers: Librairie Charles Pichot, 1845)
Beauregard, Costa de (ed.), *Souvenirs tirés des papiers du comte de La Ferronays* (Paris: Librairie Plon, 1901)
Bennes, Louise-Françoise de Houssay de, *A narrative of the sufferings of Louise Françoise de Houssay, de Bennes, who served in the army as a volunteer, from 1792 to July 21, 1795, when she was made a prisoner at Quiberon* (London: author, 1796)
Bertaud, Jean-Paul, *Le duc d'Enghien* (Paris: Librairie Arthème Fayard, 2021)
Berville, _, and Barrière, _, (ed.), *La vie et les mémoires du Général Dumouriez* (Paris: Baudouin Frères, 1822)
Besenval, Pierre-Victor Baron de, *Mémoires du Baron de Besenval* (Paris: Baudouin frères, 1821)
Bittard des Portes, René, *Histoire de l'Armée de Condé (1791–1801) pendant la Révolution française* (Paris: E. Dentu-Editeur, 1896)
Blanc, Louis, *Histoire de la Révolution française* (Paris: Librairie internationale, 1869)
Blondin d'Abancourt, Gabriel-Isidore, *Onze ans d'émigration: mémoires du chevalier Blondin d'Abancourt* (Paris: Alphonse Picard et fils, 1897)
Bouillé, François-Claude-Amour de, *Mémoires du marquis de Bouillé avec une notice sur sa vie, des notes et de éclaircissements historiques* (Paris: Baudouin frères, 1821)
Boulanger, Henri, 'L'Affaire des Belges et Liégeois unis, 1792-1793', *Revue du Nord*, 1e année, n°1, 1910, pp.3–40
Brons, Jean-Antoine de, *Journal d'émigration* (Saint-Quentin-de-Baron: Chez Entre-deux-mers, 2014)
Brunswick, Duke of, *Déclaration que Son Altesse Sérénissime le duc régnant de Brunswick-Lunebourg, commandant les armées combinées de Leurs Majestés l'Empereur & le Roi de Prusse, adresse aux Habitans de France* (1792)
Buchez, Philippe Joseph Benjamin, *Histoire parlementaire de la Révolution – Histoire de l'Assemblée Législative* (Paris: Edition Hetzel, 1846)
Buttner, Général F., 'Gardes nationales 1790-1871', *Carnet de La Sabretache*, No. 50, 1979, pp.133–135
Cacqueray de Valmenier, Charles-Georges, *Mémoires inédits, Tome II « L'émigration » 1791-1794 »*, (Cholet: Editions Pays et Terroirs, 2006)
Caron, Pierre, 'Les comités militaires des assemblées révolutionnaires (1789 -an VIII)', *Revue d'Histoire Moderne & Contemporaine*, 1904, pp.689–711
Carré, Henri (ed.), *Journal d'émigration de Louis, marquis Aymer de la Chevalerie (1791-1797)* (Poitiers: Société française d'imprimerie et de librairie, 1933)
Castries, Duc de, *maréchal de Castries, serviteur de trois rois* (Paris: Editions Albatros, 1979)
Cauna, Jacques, 'La Révolution à Port-au-Prince (1791-1792) vue par un Bordelais', *Annales du Midi: revue archéologique, historique et philologique de la France méridionale*, Tome 101, N°185–186, 1989, pp.169–200
Champflour, Jean Martial (ed.), *La Coalition d'Auvergne, Avril 1791. Carnet du Comte d'Espinchal* (Riom: Imprimerie U. Jouvet, 1899)
Chapron, Marcel, *Mirabeau-Tonneau* (Paris: Les Editions Haussmann, 1956)
Charrié, Pierre, 'Les étendards des régiments de hussards', *Carnet spécial de La Sabretache* (Paris: La Sabretache, 1971), pp.118–124
Chassin, Charles-Louis, *La préparation de la guerre de Vendée* (Paris: Imprimerie Paul Dupont, 1892)
Chassin, Charles-Louis, and Hennet, Léon, *Les Volontaires nationaux pendant la Révolution* (Paris: Librairie Léopold Cerf, 1899)

Chastel de la Howardries-Neuvireul, Paul Armand du, *Notices généalogiques tournaisiennes* (Tournai: Vasseur-Delmée, 1881)
Chateaubriand, François-René de, *Mémoires d'Outre-Tombe* New edition (Paris: Librairie Garnier Freres, 1910)
Chavaray, Etienne, *Le général La Fayette (1757-1834) – Notice biographique* (Paris: Société de l'Histoire de la Révolution française, 1898)
Chuquet, Arthur, *Campagne de l'Argonne (1792)* (Paris: Librairie Léopold Cerf, 1886)
Chuquet, Arthur, *Les guerres de la Révolution, Jemmapes et la conquête de la Belgique (1792-1793)* 2e édition, (Paris: Librairie Léopold Cerf, 1890)
Colbert Turgis, G. de (ed.), *Souvenirs maritimes de Scipion de Castries* (Paris: Mercure de France, 1997)
Condé, Louis-Joseph de Bourbon-, *Journal d'émigration du Prince de Condé 1789–1795* (Paris: Georges Servant, 1924)
Condé, Louis Joseph de Bourbon-, *Une correspondance en émigration (1792-1797)* (Paris: C. Douniol, 1867)
Contades, Gérard de (ed.), *Coblenz et Quiberon Souvenirs du Comte de Contades* (Paris: E. Dentu, 1885)
Corbehem, Bernard de, *Dix ans de ma vie ou Histoire de mon émigration* (Paris: A Phian Delaforest, 1827)
Corfield, Penelope J., *The Georgians: The Deeds & Misdeeds of 18th-Century Britain* (New Haven and London: Yale University Press, 2022)
Crétineau-Joly, Jacques, *Histoire des trois derniers Princes de la Maison de Condé* (Paris: Imprimerie Lahure, 1867)
Crouz-Tornare, Alain-Jacques, 'Les formations suisses en France, substituts aux gardes nationales dans les capitales provinciales en 1789-1790', in *La Garde nationale, entre nation et peuples en armes. Mythes et réalités, 1789-1871* (Rennes: Presses universitaires de Rennes, 2006)
D****, Le Duc de (ed.), *Mémoires de Louis XVIII* (Brussels: Louis Hauman et Cie., 1832)
Dalmas, Antoine, *Histoire de la Révolution à Saint-Domingue* (Paris: Mame Frères, 1814)
Daudet, Ernest, *Histoire de l'Émigration pendant la Révolution Française* (Paris: Hachette, 1905)
Daudet, Ernest (ed.), *Mémoires du comte Valentin-Ladislas Esterhazy* (Paris: Plon, 1903)
Deschard, Bernard, *L'armée et la révolution* (Paris: Librairie Desjonquières, 1989)
Doisy, Félix-Martin, *Manuscrit inédit de Louis XVIII* (Paris: I.G. Michaud, 1839)
Doyle, William, *The Oxford History of the French Revolution* (Oxford: Oxford University Press, 1990)
Dumas, Mathieu, *Souvenirs du Lieutenant Général comte Mathieu Dumas de 1770 à 1836* (Paris: Librairie de Charles Gosselin, 1839)
Dumouriez, Charles-Antoine Du Périer, *La vie et les mémoires du général Dumouriez* (Paris: Baudouin frères, 1822)
Enghien, Louis-Antoine-Henri de Bourbon Duc d', *Mémoires et Voyage de Monseigneur le duc d'Enghien* (Moulins: P-A. Desrosiers, 1841)
Estourbeillon, Régis de l', *Les familles françaises à Jersey pendant la Révolution* (Nantes: Imprimerie Vincent Forest et Emile Grimaud, 1886)
Espinchal, Hyppolite d', *Souvenirs militaires du comte Hyppolite d'Espinchal 1792–1814* (Paris: Librairie Paul Ollendorff, 1901)
Feller, François-Xavier de, *Dictionnaire historique ou histoire abrégée* 8ème édition (Lille: Lefort, 1833)
Feuillet de Conches, Félix, *Louis XVI, Marie-Antoinette et Madame Elilsabeth Lettres et documents inédits* (Paris: Plon, 1864)
Folletête, C., *Le régiment de l'Evêché de Bâle au service de la France, 1758-1792* (Fribourg: Imprimerie Catholique Suisse, 1882)
Funcken, Liliane and Fred, *The Lace Wars* (London: Ward Lock, 1977)
Gachard, Louis Prosper, *Documents politiques et diplomatiques sur la Révolution belge de 1790* (Brussels: H.Rémy, 1834)
Goethe, Johann Wolfgang von, *Campagne de France* (Lausanne: La Guilde du Livre, 1968)
Grandin, Léonce, *Les Prussiens en France Longwy – Verdun – Thionville – Valmy 1792* (Paris: Delhomme et Briguet, 1892)
Granié, Pierre, *Histoire de l'Assemblée Constituante de France* (Paris: Chez Desenme, An VI)
Green, Jorgen, m*Jean-Baptiste Xavier Carpentier de Colbaut, un émigré loyal et son combat contre la Révolution 1792-1794* (Denmark: Editions Grifo, 2011)

Grimoard, Philippe Henri de, *Tableau historique de la guerre de la révolution de France depuis son commencement en 1792, jusqu'à la fin de 1794* (Paris: Treuttel et Würtz, 1808)
Grouvel, François, *Histoire des Gardes du corps du Roi pendant la période révolutionnaire, 1789–1801* (France: FGC, 1998)
Grouvel, Vicomte Robert, *Les corps de troupes de l'émigration française* (Paris: Les Éditions de La Sabretache, 1957–1964)
Hardman, John, *The Life of Louis XVI* (New Haven and London: Yale University Press, 2023)
Hauterive, Ernest d' (ed.), *Journal d'émigration du comte d'Espinchal publié d'après les manuscrits originaux* (Paris: Perrin et cie., 1912)
Hennet, Léon, *Les compagnies de cadets gentilshommes et les écoles militaires* (Paris: L. Baudoin et Cie., 1889)
Héricault, Charles d', *La Révolution, 1789-1882* (Paris: Librairie Dumoulin, 1883)
Jomini, Antoine Henri de, *Histoire critiques des guerres de la Révolution* (Brussels: J.-B. Petit, 1840)
Juste, Théodore, *Histoire de la Révolution belge de 1790* (Brussels: A. Jamar, 1846)
La Chanonie, Charles de, 'Le Costume à l'Armée de Condé', *Revue de Bretagne, de Vendée & d'Anjou*, An 36, 1892, pp.184–196
La Chanonie, Charles de, *Mémoires historiques et politiques du général Tercier (1770-1816)* (Paris: Librairie Plon, 1891)
La Chapelle, Jean Edme Xavier de, *Souvenirs d'Edme de La Chapelle de Bernarès, de Bergerac à Quiberon* (Paris: Librairie Plon, 1913)
La Fayette, Gilbert Du Motier de, *Mémoires, correspondance et manuscrits du général Lafayette* (Paris: H. Fournier ainé, 1837 & 1838)
La Jonquière, Clément de, *Le livre d'ordre d'un régiment d'infanterie en 1781* (Paris: Lavauzelle, 1899)
La Maisonfort, Marquis de, *Mémoires d'un agent royaliste sous la Révolution, l'Empire et la Restauration* (Paris: Mercure de France, 1998)
Lapierre, Antoine, *Campagne des émigrés en Argonne en 1792* (Sedan: Librairie Genin, 1911)
La Rochefoucauld, François de, *Souvenirs du 10 août et de l'Armée de Bourbon* (Paris: Calmann-Lévy, 1929)
La Rocheterie, Maxime de, *Marie-Antoinette et l'émigration d'après documents inédits* (Paris: Charles Douniol et cie., 1875)
Lecomte, M., 'Le Régiment Royal-Liégeois au service du Roi de France (1787–1792)', *le Carnet de La Sabretache*, 1938 and 1939 (Nos 388 and 389, 12 articles)
Lefranc, Jacques-François, *Conjuration contre la religion Catholique et les souverains, dont le projet conçu en France doit s'exécuter dans l'univers entire* (Paris: Lepetit, 1792)
Lefranc, Jacques-François, *Le Voile levé pour les curieux ou le Secret de la Révolution révélé à l'aide de la franc-maçonnerie* (Paris: Lepetit et Guillemard, 1792)
Le Pottier, Serge, *Duportail ou le Génie de Georges Washington* (Paris: Economica, 2011)
Le Roi, Joseph-Adrien, *Récit des journées des 5 et 6 octobre 1789 à Versailles* (Versailles: E. Aubert, 1867)
Louis XVIII, *Relation d'un voyage à Bruxelles et à Coblentz (1791)* (Paris: Baudouin Frères, 1823)
Louis-Philippe, *Mémoires* (Paris: Editions Librairie Plon, 1973)
Maeght, Xavier, 'Un Journal d'émigré en 1792', *Revue du Nord*, vol.XLIX, no.93, pp.307–326
Maignette, Félix, 'Les émigrés français aux Pays-Bas (1789-1794)' *Mémoires de l'Académie royale de Belgique – Classe des Lettres et des Sciences morales et politiques* (Bruxelles: Hayez, Imprimeur des Académies, 1908)
Maleyssie, Antoine de Tardieu de, *Mémoires d'un officier aux gardes françaises (1789–1793)* (Paris: Librairie Plon, 1897)
Marcillac, Pierre-Louis-Auguste de Crusy de Marcillac, *Mémoires de l'émigration (1791–1800)* (Paris: Librairie de Firmin-Didot et Cie., 1897)
Marcillac, Pierre-Louis-Auguste de Crusy de, *Souvenirs de l'émigration ou Mémoires du Marquis de Marcillac* (Paris: Baudouin Frères, 1825)
Marsangy, Louis Bonneville de (ed.), *Journal d'un volontaire de 1791* (Paris: Perrin et cie., 1888)
Masson, Frédéric, *Autour de Sainte-Hélène*, 2e série, (Paris: Société d'Editions Littéraires et Artistiques, 1909)
Mautort, Louis-François de Paule Tillette de, *Mémoires du chevalier de Mautort, capitaine au régiment d'Austrasie, chevalier de l'ordre royal et militaire de Saint-Louis (1752–1802)* (Paris: Librairie Plon, 1895)
Mavidal, M.J., and Laurent, M.E., *Archives parlementaires françaises de 1787 à 1860* (Paris: Société d'Imprimerie et Librairie administrative et de chemin de fer, 1884)

Mège, Francisque, 'Notes biographiques sur les députés de Basse-Auvergne – Le marquis de La Queuille', *Mémoires de l'Académie des Arts, Belles Lettres et Sciences*, vol.X, pp.81–124

Mirabeau, Gabriel-Honoré de Riquetti Comte de, *Aux Bataves sur le stathoudérat* (London/Paris: Anon., 1788)

Money, James, *Histoire de la campagne faite en 1792 par les Armees Françaises* (London: Harlow, 1794)

Money, James, *The History of the Campaign of 1792, between the Armies of France under Generals Dumourier, Valence, &c. and the Allies under the Duke of Brunswick; with an account of what passed in the Thuilleries on the 10th of August* (London: Harlow, 1794)

Monsieur et le Comte d'Artois, *Lettre de Monsieur, & de M. le Comte d'Artois, au Roi leur Frere, avec la Déclaration signée a Pilnitz, le 27 août 1791, par l'Empereur & le Roi de Prusse* (Worms: Kranzbühler, 1791)

Montlosier, François Dominique de Reynaud Comte de, *Souvenirs d'un émigré (1791–1798)* (Paris: Hachette, 1951)

Muret, Théodore César, *Histoire de l'Armée de Condé* (Paris: Bureau de la Mode, 1844)

Nichols, Alistair, *'The Soldiers are Dressed in Red' The Quiberon Expedition of 1795 and the Counter-Revolution in Brittany* (Warwick: Helion, 2022)

Nichols, Alistair, 'La levée des regiments à la cocarde blanche au service britanniques (1794–1795)', *Les Carnets de la Sabretache Carnet Spécial 2021 L'émigration militaire 1791–1815* (Bry-sur-Marne: Sabretache, 2021), pp.36–44

Nieüil, Marquise de Perry de, *Mémoires du Marquis de Toustain 1790–1823* (Paris: Plon, 1933)

Pernot, A. (ed.), *Mémoire sur l'arrestation du duc d'Enghien* (Dôle: Typographie L. Bernin, 1891)

Pinasseau, Jean, *L'Émigration Militaire: Campagne de 1792* (Paris: Éditions A. et J. Picard et Cie., 1957)

Pingaud, Léonce, 'La Franche-Comté en 1815', *Académie des sciences, belles lettres et arts de Besançon: Procès-verbaux et mémoires*, 1893, pp.82–109

Lamase, Paul et Martial de Pradel de, *Nouvelles notes intimes d'un émigré (Le chevalier de Pradel de Lamase, officier à l'armée de Condé)* (Paris: Emile-Paul Frères, 1920)

Rance, Karine, 'Le rassemblement de Coblence: le mythe fondateur', *Mythologies urbaines, les villes entre histoire et imaginaire* (Rennes: Presses universitaires de France, 2004), pp.185–203

Robinet, Jean-Baptiste, *Dictionnaire universel des sciences, morale, économique, politique et diplomatique ou Bibliothèque de l'homme-d'état et du citoyen* (London: Libraires associés, 1779)

Robinet, Marthe and Chave, Isabelle, *Fichier de la garde constitutionelle de Louis XVI (1791–1792)* (Pierrefitte-sur-Seine: Archives nationales, 2016)

Rochambeau, Jean-Baptiste Donatien de Vimeur, Comte de, *Mémoires militaires, historiques et politiques de Rochambeau* (Paris: Chez Fain, 1809)

Romain, Félix de, *Souvenirs d'un officier royaliste* (Paris: Egron, 1824)

Romillon et al, *Mémoire que présentent les Officers du régiment du Port-au-Prince...* (Cap-Français: L'Imprimerie Royale, 1791)

Ruault, Nicolas, *Gazette d'un parisien sous la Révolution* (Paris: Edition du club France Loisirs, Perrin, 1976)

Rudé, George, *Revolutionary Europe 1783–1815* (Glasgow: Fontana/Collins, 1964)

Saint-Maurice Cabany, M.E., *Le Nécrologie Universel du XIXe Siècle* (Paris: Le Nécrologie Universel du XIXe Siècle, 1845)

Saint-Cyr, Arnaud de Gouvion, 'Les gravures de l'état-major de la Légion de Mirabeau (1792)', *Carnets de la Sabretache, Carnet spécial 2021* (Editions Epopées, 2021), pp.8–20

Schoelcher, Victor, *Vie de Toussaint-Louverture* (Paris: P. Ollendorff, 1889)

Scott, Samuel F., *From Yorktown to Valmy: The Transformation of the French Army in an Age of Revolution* (Niwor: University Press of Colorado, 1998)

Sémallé, Jean-René-Pierre de, *Souvenirs du comte de Sémallé, page de Louis XVI* (Paris: Alphonse Picard et fils, 1898)

Sérent, Armand Sigismond Comte de, 'Discussion sur l'arrestation de M. de Bussy, lors de la séance du 26 octobre 1790', *Archives Parlementaires de la Révolution Français*, 1885, no.20, pp.45–46

Servien, Henri, *Petite histoire des guerres de Vendée* (Niort: Editions de Chiré, 1983)

Sinclair, John Gordon, *Colonel Sinclair's Letters to his Enemies* (London: author, 1796)

Susane, Louis, *Histoire de l'ancienne infanterie française* (Paris: Librairie militaire, maritime et polytechnique, 1853)

Sommervogel, Père, *Une correspondance pendant l'émigration 1792-1797* (Paris: Charles Douniol, Libraire-éditeur, 1867)

Ternaux, Mortimer, *Le peuple aux Tuileries. Le 20 juin 1792* (Pari: Lévy-Frères, Imprimeurs-éditeurs, 1864)

Trochon de Lorrieère, René, 'Deux Laonnois au service de l'Angleterre: Jean Frédéric et Pierre Frédéric Wolf 1794–1815', *Fédérations des Sociétés d'Histoire et d'Archéologie de l'Aisne Mémoires*, Tome II, 1955, pp.62–72

Valynseele, Joseph, *Les enfants naturels de Louis XV, étude critique, biographie, descendance et nombreux documents inédits* (Paris: Centre d'Etudes et de Recherches historiques, 1953)

Vaudreuil, Jospeh-Hyacinthe-François de Paule de Rigaud comte de, *Correspondance intime du comte d Vaudreuil et du comte d'Artois pendant l'émigration (1789–1815)* (Paris: Librairie Plon, 1889)

Verneuil, Raoul Quarré de, *L'armée en France depuis Charles VII jusqu'à la Révolution* (Paris: Dumaine, 1880)

Vidal, Gaston (ed.), *Mémoires historiques (1781-1815) du chevalier de Forton, officier de Marine* (Montpellier: Éditions de l'Entente bibliophile, 1961)

Vitrolles, Eugène-François-Auguste-Arnaud Baron de, *Souvenirs autobiographiques d'un émigré* (Paris: Emile-Paul Frères, 1924)

Werber, Karl Ferdinand, *Naissance de la noblesse* (Paris: Librairie Fayard, 1998)

Whitney, Frank, *Jean Ternant and the Age of Revolutions: A Soldier and Diplomat (1751–1833) in the American, French, Dutch and Belgian Uprisings* (Jefferson: Mc Farland &Company, Inc., 2015)

Witt, Pierre de, 'Les Protestants hollandais en France en 1787', *Bulletin historique et littéraire (Société de l'histoire du protestantisme français)*, vol.34, no.12, 15 décembre 1885, pp.569–578

Internet Sources

Roland (famille), Archives cantonales vaudoises, <http://www.davel.vd.ch/qfpdavel/0/D4681.pdf >, accessed 1 June 2015

Jean des Cilleuls, 'Le service de santé des forces armées de l'émigration et particulièrement de l'armée de Condé (1791-1801)' presented to the Société française d'Histoire de la Médecine, 29 March 1969, pp.89–105, <https://www.biusante.parisdescartes.fr/sfhm/hsm/HSMx1971x005x002_3_4/HSMx1971x005x002_3_4x0089.pdf>, accessed 25 August 2024

From Reason to Revolution – Warfare 1721-1815

http://www.helion.co.uk/series/from-reason-to-revolution-1721-1815.php

The 'From Reason to Revolution' series covers the period of military history 1721–1815, an era in which fortress-based strategy and linear battles gave way to the nation-in-arms and the beginnings of total war.

This era saw the evolution and growth of light troops of all arms, and of increasingly flexible command systems to cope with the growing armies fielded by nations able to mobilise far greater proportions of their manpower than ever before. Many of these developments were fired by the great political upheavals of the era, with revolutions in America and France bringing about social change which in turn fed back into the military sphere as whole nations readied themselves for war. Only in the closing years of the period, as the reactionary powers began to regain the upper hand, did a military synthesis of the best of the old and the new become possible.

The series examines the military and naval history of the period in a greater degree of detail than has hitherto been attempted, and has a very wide brief, with the intention of covering all aspects from the battles, campaigns, logistics, and tactics, to the personalities, armies, uniforms, and equipment.

Submissions

The publishers would be pleased to receive submissions for this series. Please email reasontorevolution@helion.co.uk, or write to Helion & Company Limited, Unit 8 Amherst Business Centre, Budbrooke Road, Warwick, CV34 5WE

You may also be interested in:

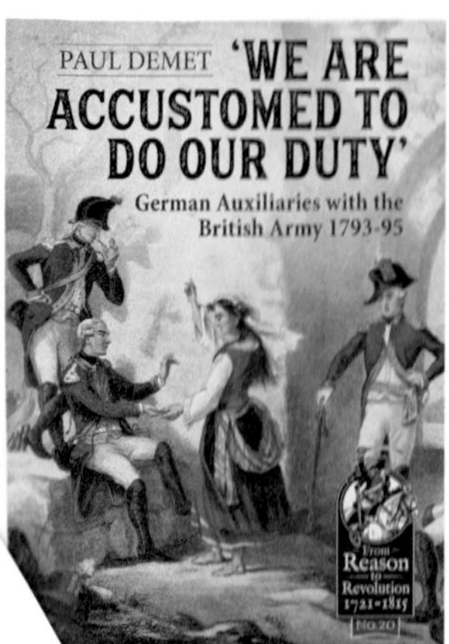

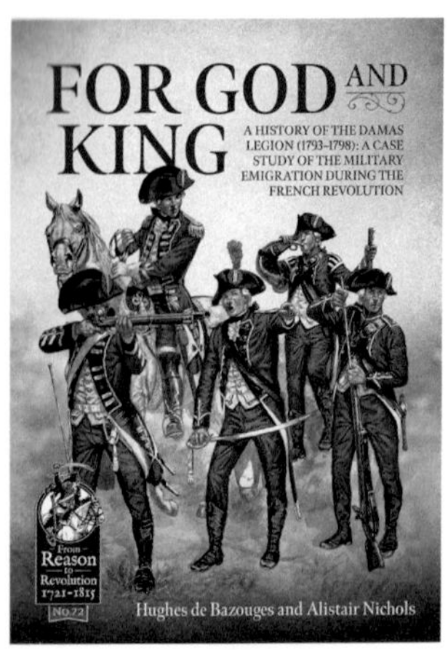

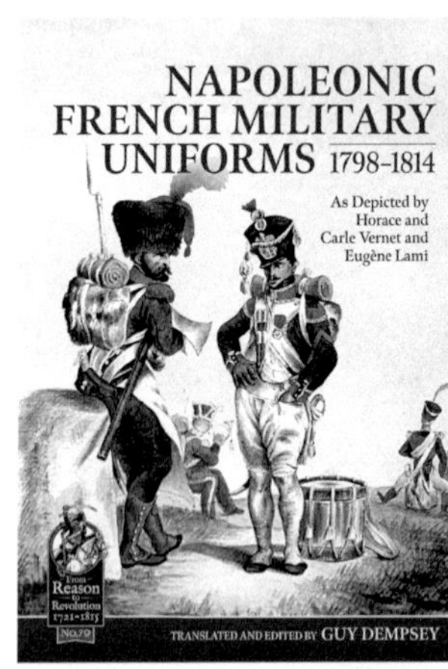

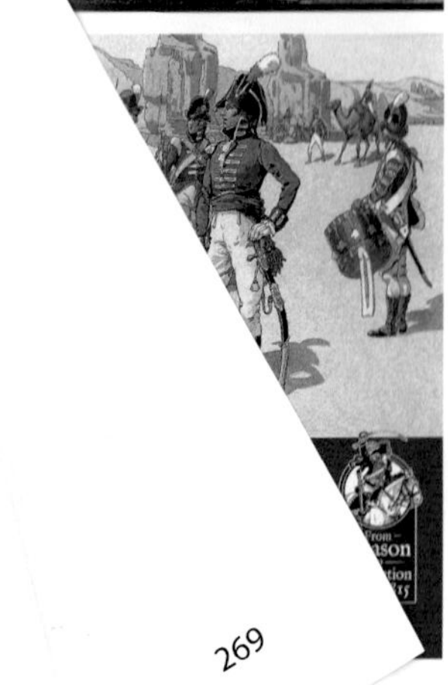

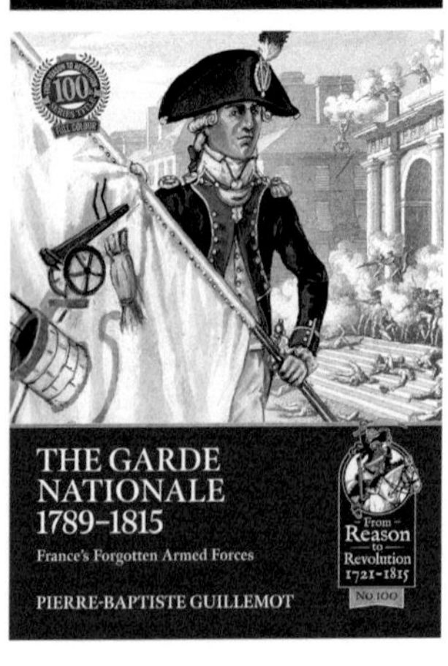

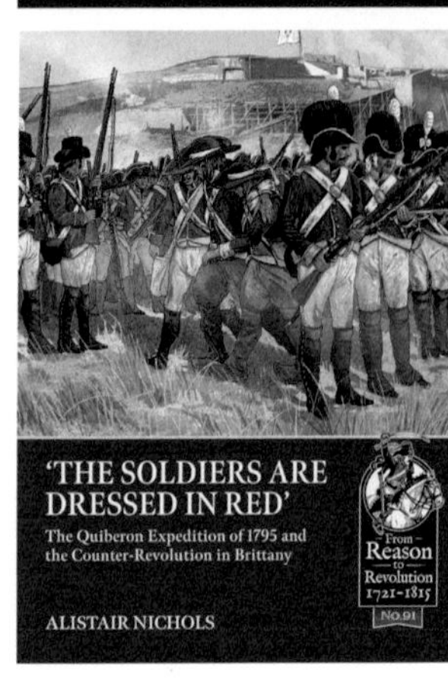